Inter-Christian Philosophical Dialogues

Inter-Christian Philosophical Dialogues offers a unique approach to the philosophical exploration of Christianity. Five leading Christian philosophers of religion are brought together to engage in a spirited dialogue, debating and discussing the merits and demerits of the diverse ideas, doctrines and practices found in the Christian tradition. Participants in this dialogue represent and defend the following traditions or movements within Christianity:

- 'Naturalist' Christian theism
- Ecological Christianity
- Catholic Christianity
- (Reformed) Protestantism
- Orthodox Christianity.

This set of volumes uncovers the rich and diverse cognitive and experiential dimensions of religious belief and practice, pushing the field of philosophy of religion in bold new directions.

Graham Oppy is Professor of Philosophy at Monash University, Australia.

N. N. Trakakis is Senior Lecturer in Philosophy at the Australian Catholic University, Australia.

Inter-Christian Philosophical Dialogues
Volume Editors: Graham Oppy and N. N. Trakakis

This set of volumes provides a unique approach to the philosophy of religion – a dialogical conversation embracing a wide range of religious faiths and spiritualities, both western and eastern, in all their multifarious diversity and concrete manifestations. Each volume stages a highly interactive, genuinely comparative and thoroughly cross-cultural dialogue involving leading scholars and philosophers of religion. Each scholar, as a representative of a particular faith tradition, is invited to consider how they think the divine; how they believe they are related to it; and how divinity figures in their lived experience. These dialogues not only traverse the traditional terrain of Judeo-Christianity but also explore an array of religions from across the world, from Islam, Buddhism and Hinduism to traditions which are rarely (if ever) studied in contemporary philosophy of religion, such as Daoism, Shinto, Confucianism and Native American spirituality. In bringing these groups together in meaningful and productive interaction, this set of volumes uncovers the rich and diverse cognitive and experiential dimensions of religious belief and practice.

Available:

Interreligious Philosophical Dialogues: volume 1

Interreligious Philosophical Dialogues: volume 2

Interreligious Philosophical Dialogues: volume 3

Inter-Christian Philosophical Dialogues: volume 4

Inter-Christian Philosophical Dialogues
Volume 4

Edited by Graham Oppy
and N. N. Trakakis

LONDON AND NEW YORK

First published 2018
by Routledge
2 Park Square, Milton Park, Abingdon, Oxon OX14 4RN

and by Routledge
711 Third Avenue, New York, NY 10017

Routledge is an imprint of the Taylor & Francis Group, an informa business

© 2018 selection and editorial matter, Graham Oppy and
N. N. Trakakis; individual chapters, the contributors

The right of Graham Oppy and N. N. Trakakis to be identified as
the authors of the editorial material, and of the authors for their
individual chapters, has been asserted in accordance with sections 77
and 78 of the Copyright, Designs and Patents Act 1988.

All rights reserved. No part of this book may be reprinted or
reproduced or utilised in any form or by any electronic, mechanical,
or other means, now known or hereafter invented, including
photocopying and recording, or in any information storage or
retrieval system, without permission in writing from the publishers.

Trademark notice: Product or corporate names may be trademarks
or registered trademarks, and are used only for identification and
explanation without intent to infringe.

British Library Cataloguing-in-Publication Data
A catalogue record for this book is available from the British Library

Library of Congress Cataloging-in-Publication Data
Names: Oppy, Graham, 1960– editor. | Trakakis, Nick, editor.
Title: Inter-Christian philosophical dialogues / edited by
    Graham Oppy and N.N. Trakakis.
Description: New York : Routledge, 2017. | "Volume 4." |
    Volumes 1–3 are entitled: Interreligious philosophical dialogues
    and cataloged separately from this title. | Includes bibliographical
    references and index.
Identifiers: LCCN 2017010105 | ISBN 9781138900097 (hardback) |
    ISBN 9781315111032 (ebook)
Subjects: LCSH: Christianity. | Theology. | Philosophical theology.
Classification: LCC BR96 .I58 2017 | DDC 230/.04—dc23
LC record available at https://lccn.loc.gov/2017010105

ISBN: 978-1-138-90009-7 (hbk)
ISBN: 978-1-315-11103-2 (ebk)
ISBN: 978-1-138-23718-6 (4 volume set)

Typeset in Sabon
by Apex CoVantage, LLC

Contents

Notes on contributors	vii
Introduction	ix
Position Statements	1
1 A 'naturalist' Christian theism JOHN BISHOP	3
2 Ecological Christianity HEATHER EATON	25
3 Catholic Christianity KEVIN HART	48
4 (Reformed) Protestantism MICHAEL C. REA	67
5 Orthodox Christianity N. N. TRAKAKIS	89
First Responses	111
6 John Bishop	113
7 Heather Eaton	130
8 Kevin Hart	148

vi *Contents*

9 Michael C. Rea   163

10 N. N. Trakakis   178

Second Responses   195

11 John Bishop   197

12 Heather Eaton   213

13 Kevin Hart   232

14 Michael C. Rea   245

15 N. N. Trakakis   257

Index   274

Notes on contributors

John Bishop is Professor of Philosophy at the University of Auckland, New Zealand. He is the author of *Natural Agency: An Essay on the Causal Theory of Action* (1989) and *Believing by Faith: An Essay in the Epistemology and Ethics of Religious Belief* (2007), as well as many journal articles and book chapters in the areas of philosophy of religion and philosophy of action.

Heather Eaton is Professor in Conflict Studies at Saint Paul University, Ottawa, Canada. Her research covers interreligious responses to ecological issues and the ecological and religious dimensions of peace and conflict, as well as gender, animal rights and nonviolence. She has authored *Introducing Ecofeminist Theologies* (2005), and has edited (with Lois Ann Lorentzen) *Ecofeminism and Globalization: Exploring Culture, Context, and Religion* (2003) and (with Sigurd Bergmann) *Ecological Awareness: Exploring Religion, Ethics and Aesthetics* (2011).

Kevin Hart is Edwin B. Kyle Professor of Christian Studies at the University of Virginia, as well as Eric D'Arcy Professor of Philosophy at the Australian Catholic University. He works mainly in the field of philosophy of religion, especially with reference to phenomenology, and largely in the area where philosophy of religion shades into Christian theology. He is the author of several books, including *The Trespass of the Sign: Deconstruction, Theology, and Philosophy* (1989); and he recently edited *Clandestine Encounters: Philosophy in the Narratives of Maurice Blanchot* (2010) and *Jean-Luc Marion: The Essential Writings* (2013). Professor Hart is also a distinguished poet, his most recent collection being *Morning Knowledge* (2011).

Michael C. Rea is Professor of Philosophy and Co-Director of the Centre for Philosophy of Religion, University of Notre Dame. He specializes in metaphysics and philosophy of religion, and his publications include *World Without Design: The Ontological Consequences of Naturalism* (2002), and as editor (with Oliver Crisp) *Analytic Theology: New Essays in Theological Method* (2009) and (with Kelly James Clark) *Reason,* viii *Notes on contributors*

Metaphysics, and Mind: New Essays on the Philosophy of Alvin Plantinga (2012).

N.N. Trakakis is Senior Lecturer in Philosophy at the Australian Catholic University. He has authored *The God Beyond Belief: In Defence of William Rowe's Evidential Argument from Evil* (2007) and *The End of Philosophy of Religion* (2008). He has also co-edited, with Graham Oppy, the five-volume *History of Western Philosophy of Religion* (2009) and the two-volume *History of Philosophy in Australia and New Zealand* (2014).

Introduction

Religious believers of a certain conservative bent, whether they be simple followers of the faith, or leaders of a religious community, or scholars and theologians, have a distinct tendency to downplay or dismiss the value of discussion and dialogue with individuals and groups of alternative religious faiths (or no faith at all). Even when dialogue is entered into by such believers, it is rarely with the express purpose of seeking to place their own assumptions, beliefs and principles under scrutiny, to have them seriously challenged and even possibly overthrown. Rather, there is either a proselytizing mission of converting the other to one's own faith tradition, or – and this is perhaps more common nowadays within 'ecumenical' circles – only a desire of seeking a better understanding of the other's beliefs and practices, where this might be underwritten by a broader practical or political goal, such as joining together to promote common goods, the public interest or the welfare of the whole, or alternatively to combat common enemies including acts of terrorism, natural disasters, illness or disease, gender and racial inequality, and so on. There is little doubt that centuries-old barriers of misunderstanding, prejudice and animosity between religious communities can be and are being broken down through genuinely open and frank dialogue and also solidarity 'on the ground' in cooperative grassroots projects. But is this as far as we can go? On the 'theoretical' front, is there nothing more that can be achieved from interreligious dialogue than a better (more accurate and more sympathetic) understanding of the history, teachings and practices of the various religions of the world? Is the only model for such dialogue the famous Augustinian–Anselmian precept of 'faith seeking understanding' (*fides quaerens intellectum*), where the faith itself is for all intents and purposes hermetically sealed from challenge or disruption? Indeed, for some hardliners, such as Wittgensteinian fideists and John Milbank's school of Radical Orthodoxy, even the project of seeking understanding is viewed as futile or problematic, since religious language-games are incommensurable (or, at least, have limited commensurability) and so can only be understood, appreciated and evaluated 'from within'. This, as Milbank has proclaimed, spells 'the end of dialogue'.[1]

x *Introduction*

Philosophers, however, tend to take a very different route, one inspired by the 'gadfly of Athens', Socrates. This provocative approach to philosophical problems, known as the *elenchus* (literally, 'examining', 'testing'), had Socrates subjecting his fellow Athenians to a prolonged process of questioning that inevitably infuriated many of them, in large part because it showed up their complacent ignorance and dogmatism. Following Socrates' lead, philosophers often adopt a dialogical model in their inquiries that places everything up for debate, including one's own highly cherished beliefs, whether they be religious or not. This is not necessarily an advocacy of complete skepticism (though even this cannot be excluded from the beginning, and may even function as a starting point in the manner of Descartes' meditations); nor is it a vain attempt to philosophize absent any cultural, historical or epistemic horizons. Rather, it is a methodology aimed at overcoming unwarranted biases and blind spots in one's thinking with the hope of arriving at a position that is closer to the truth. Various pressures in contemporary academia, under the influence of the neoliberal ideals of efficiency and productivity, are placing the dialogical model of inquiry at risk. But a delightful (some would say 'quaint') account of what this model looks like in practice is provided by Alvin Plantinga in a festschrift to his one-time colleague at Wayne State University in the late 1950s and early 60s, Hector-Neri Castañeda. Plantinga reminisces:

> In those days the Wayne philosophy department – Nakhnikian, Castañeda, and Gettier the first year, then the next year Robert Sleigh and I, and then a bit later Richard Cartwright and Keith Lehrer – was less a philosophy department than a loosely organized but extremely intense discussion society. We discussed philosophy constantly, occasionally taking a bit of time to teach our classes. These discussions were a sort of moveable feast; they would typically begin at 9:00 A.M. or so in the ancient house that served as our headquarters and office. At about ten o'clock the discussion would drift over to the coffee shop across the street, where it consumed an endless quantity of napkins in lieu of a blackboard. Here it would remain until about lunch time, when it moved back to someone's office. Of course people drifted in and out of the discussions; after all, there were classes to teach.[2]

This vigorous exchange of ideas, at its best, is not an attempt to defeat one's opponent, to 'score points' as in a debating contest and come out victorious. Although this adversarial approach is notoriously common in philosophical and religious discussions, our goal in these volumes has been to create space for discursive exchanges marked by a charitable and cooperative search for understanding and truth.[3] This implies a conception of interreligious dialogue as a form of *conversation*, a talking-with rather than a talking-to, being prepared to listen to the other, to study deeply their texts and traditions, perhaps even imaginatively empathizing with

Introduction xi

them, walking as far as possible in their shoes in the manner envisioned by phenomenological and hermeneutic approaches to religion. These are approaches which emphasize the importance of description, understanding and interpretation, at least as a first step in coming to terms with or making sense of what is presented by the other. This need not entail a philosophical quietism that, as Wittgenstein advocated, "leaves everything as it is." Explanation, evaluation and judgement, as indicated earlier, are fundamental to the academic and especially the philosophical study of religion. But judgement cannot be immediate or uninformed, otherwise difference and otherness are dissolved or reduced to our terms of reference rather than respected and appreciated in their irreducible particularity. This indeed was Milbank's fear: that dialogue merely masks the hegemonic aspirations of western liberal secularism. Ironically, however, Milbank's substitution of philosophical dialogue with theological contestation reinforces these arbitrary and violent hegemonic and homogenizing tendencies, this time in the name of a premodern Christian worldview that refuses to consider other religious faiths (and secularism) in any other way except through a Christian lens.

The encounters and exchanges in these volumes across multiple religious and philosophical boundaries will hopefully motivate readers to rethink not only the nature of religion and interreligious dialogue but also of philosophy itself and in particular the subdiscipline of the philosophy of religion. After all, the dialogues staged herein are intended as *philosophical* conversations, influenced if not governed by the kind of critical and rational inquiry into the nature of the world and our place in it that is characteristic of the principal texts and figures of the philosophical canon. The American pragmatist philosopher William James, who has had an enduring influence in philosophy of religion, expressed well the distinctive character of philosophical inquiry in the first of a series of lectures he delivered at Oxford in 1908 (subsequently published as *A Pluralistic Universe*):

> [T]here are two pieces, "zwei stücke", as Kant would have said, in every philosophy – the final outlook, belief, or attitude to which it brings us, and the reasonings by which that attitude is reached and mediated. A philosophy, as James Ferrier used to tell us, must indeed be true, but that is the least of its requirements. One may be true without being a philosopher, true by guesswork or by revelation. What distinguishes a philosopher's truth is that it is *reasoned*. Argument, not supposition, must have put it in his possession. Common men find themselves inheriting their beliefs, they know not how. They jump into them with both feet, and stand there. Philosophers must do more; they must first get reason's license for them; and to the professional philosophic mind the operation of procuring the license is usually a thing of much more pith and moment than any particular beliefs to which the license may give the rights of access.[4]

xii *Introduction*

Truth is not the only or even the chief concern of the philosopher. Equally important is the path traversed on the way to truth, and the way of philosophy – as James states – is reason: "argument, not supposition". This is what sets philosophy apart from other fields and practices, such as theology and religious faiths which do not hesitate to bypass reason and ground their creeds or systems in, say, revelation, sacred scriptures or the pronouncements of a magisterium. While not seeking to exclude confessional commitments, the dialogues in these volumes are chiefly conducted in the philosophical spirit of 'reasoned' discussion, broadly defined so as to consist in (at least at the best of times) a dynamic process of historically informed explication and rigorous rational evaluation of entire religious worldviews and ways of life.

One of the intended effects of these dialogical exchanges is to reorient and renew the philosophy of religion in a fundamental way. The field has traditionally concerned itself almost exclusively with conceptions of God and divinity that have emerged or been abstracted from the Judeo-Christian tradition. This narrow concern with western theistic religions has become narrower still in contemporary philosophy of religion, where very little time is devoted to the embodied experiences and practices of believers. Religion is primarily a form of life centred around participation in corporate worship, liturgical practices and other forms of shared spiritual disciplines. Contemporary philosophy of religion, rather than treating religion in these dynamic terms as a lived experience, tends to 'thin' religious faith down to a cognitive phenomenon, and so attention is diverted to, say, the epistemological status of theistic belief (e.g., Is belief in God rational?) or analyses of the propositional content of specific beliefs (e.g., the goodness of God, God's eternity). While these discussions are significant and legitimate, there is also much to gain from a shift away from narrow preoccupations with generic and highly abstract forms of theism to a philosophical study of *religions* in all their multifarious diversity. This, however, demands a significant broadening of the parameters of the discipline so as to include discussion of a range of 'models of divinity', including comparatively non-standard theistic conceptions of God as well as non-theistic conceptions drawn from eastern, African and Indigenous traditions. Further still, philosophers of religion will need to break away from their habit of restricting themselves to the doctrinal deposit of religious traditions and instead attend also to the various material and symbolic practices of these traditions, including their liturgies and rituals, music and iconography, and myths and poetry. Indeed, models of divinity do not arise *in vacuo* but emerge from philosophical and religious traditions that have a long and complex history which includes both 'cognitive' elements (e.g., scriptures and creeds) and practical and affective aspects (e.g., sacraments and iconography). Both of these dimensions, especially the relatively neglected material and experiential aspects of religious traditions, have to be taken into account as indispensable sources in understanding how a particular religion has arrived at its unique view of the world.

This series of dialogues therefore aims to take the field of philosophy of religion in a bold new direction. To this end, the traditional scope of inquiry is *widened* – by moving the focus away from the theistic religions of the West to non-theistic and non-western religious traditions – and the domain of concern is *particularized* – by taking seriously (both as an object of study and as a source for reflection and insight) the concrete details of specific religious traditions, from their beliefs and scriptures to their rituals, ceremonies and artistic practices. Such a cross-cultural and holistic approach may help to recover the diversity and richness of religion, thus challenging long-standing western theistic biases in the philosophy of religion and perhaps instigating something of a renaissance in the field.

* * *

In order to broaden the parameters of the philosophical investigation of religion in the foregoing ways, we invited to the discussion table a wide range of philosophers, theologians and religious scholars, each (in some sense) representing a particular religious tradition or a theoretical perspective on religion and divinity. The goal was to be global enough to capture mainstream as well as neglected though significant religious perspectives.

The participants in the dialogue were divided into four groups, with a separate volume dedicated to each:

Group 1

- Bede Benjamin Bidlack (Saint Anselm College, USA): Daoism.
- Jerome Gellman (Ben-Gurion University, Israel): Traditional Judaism.
- Freya Mathews (La Trobe University, Australia): Panpsychism.
- Trichur S. Rukmani (Concordia University, Canada): Non-theistic Hinduism.
- Charles Taliaferro (St. Olaf College, USA): Classical, Christian theism.

Group 2

- Imran Aijaz (University of Michigan-Dearborn, USA): Sunni Islam.
- Sanford L. Drob (Fielding Graduate University, USA): Mystical (Kabbalistic) Judaism.
- Lisa Isherwood (University of Winchester, UK): Radical incarnational Christianity.
- Koji Suga (Kokugakuin University, Japan): Shinto.

Group 3

- Chung-yi Cheng (The Chinese University of Hong Kong): Confucianism.
- Mahinda Deegalle (Bath Spa University, UK): Theravada Buddhism.
- Thurman 'Lee' Hester, Jr. (University of Science and Arts of Oklahoma, USA): Native American spirituality.
- Mark Manolopoulos (Monash University, Australia): Radical-secular Christianity.

xiv *Introduction*

Group 4

- John Bishop (University of Auckland, New Zealand): Naturalistic Christianity.
- Heather Eaton (Saint Paul University, Canada): Ecological Christianity.
- Kevin Hart (University of Virginia, USA): Roman Catholicism.
- Michael C. Rea (University of Notre Dame, USA): (Reformed) Protestantism.
- N. N. Trakakis (Australian Catholic University, Australia): Orthodox Christianity.

As will be noticed, the first three clusters are engaged in *multi-faith* dialogues, while the last group undertakes an *intra-faith* dialogue amongst those affiliated, whether loosely or more determinately, with the Christian community. It is worth pointing out here that the initial list of participants was much wider, but – and this is one of the pitfalls of large and ambitious projects such as this – a number of them withdrew during the course of the conversations. The dialogues were therefore originally more representative of the diversity of the world's religious traditions than this list might suggest, and this also explains some important omissions. In particular, we initially had secured representatives from the following religious traditions who eventually withdrew (in all cases inexplicably, without providing any reason, but simply falling off the radar): (group 1) Zoroastrianism; (group 2) African religions, theistic Hinduism; (group 3) Shiite Islam, Sikhism. There were many other groups we would have liked to include in the dialogues – for example, at least one of the schools of Mahayana Buddhism, Sufism and the Australian Aboriginal tradition – but we were obviously limited in how many we could allow to take part, and in some instances it was not possible to secure philosophically adept members of certain religious traditions who were available to speak on their behalf. In any case, these dialogues are merely a first, though positive, step: there is no reason why the experiment cannot be replicated with different mixes of religions.[5]

A word might also be in order about the organizing framework or rationale behind the selection of religions within each of the first three clusters. One of our primary goals was to showcase the diversity and difference that exists within the category of 'religion'. We therefore sought to include an extensive array of faith traditions from across the world, covering not only the world's greatest faiths (in terms of numbers and influence), but also some lesser known, smaller and Indigenous traditions. Clearly, the major world religions have a more pronounced philosophical heritage than some of the smaller or native traditions, but this does not mean that the latter are without philosophical underpinnings; and, moreover, it is not only the cognitive dimensions of religion but the cognitive in connection with the experiential (embodied, affective, practiced, etc.) dimensions that these dialogues are intended to explore. Also, although the groupings within the first three clusters might appear somewhat arbitrary, we were motivated by the desire to provide a unique opportunity for a thoroughly philosophical inter-faith dialogue that would not ordinarily take place between diverse groups of religions. The inevitable risk here is that participants, so far removed historically and culturally from one another, may talk past each other rather than engage in meaningful and productive dialogue. It has not of course been possible to completely remove this risk, although it is hoped that it has been minimized by the skill and willingness of participants to enter imaginatively and empathetically into worldviews very different from their own.

A question might also be raised about the framing of these dialogues in terms of specific *religions*, or individual 'believers' as exponents and representatives of specific religions. This penchant for strict and neat categorization might seem misplaced in a postmodern world where identities and boundaries are unstable and permeable. But there was no wish to deny the fluidity of identities in the modern religious marketplace, and indeed criticism of the notion of fixed, self-contained and homogenous religious traditions is a recurring theme in the dialogues of these volumes, which highlight the complicated and circuitous ways by which these traditions have evolved and continue to evolve. And it is not only traditions and institutions that undergo change and occasionally radical reformation but also individuals belonging to and formed by these traditions and institutions. It was not, of course, the aim of these dialogues to convert or deconvert anyone, but changes and transformations in ways of thinking were not ruled out and were even encouraged and expected, and in one case at least the dialogues served as a prompt for a thorough reappraisal that has resulted in the very renunciation of all religious commitment.[6] But even if other participants did not choose to go that far, they have all displayed a commendable ability to look beyond their religious affiliation for inspiration and answers. It is in this vein that some have also sought to express and live out indeterminate or multiple forms of religious belonging, as with Bede Bidlack (in volume 1), who identifies as both a Daoist and a Christian and draws parallels with other recent religious thinkers such as Paul Knitter, author of *Without Buddha I Could Not Be a Christian* (2009).

Turning now to the way in which the dialogues proceeded, the interactions ran over a five-year period (2011–2015) and began with each participant writing a 'Position Statement' (of around 10,000 words) outlining the major contours of the religious tradition they are representing and their involvement in that tradition. Participants were provided with editorial guidelines on how to approach their Position Statements, and this included the following list of questions that we asked each participant to address:

- What are your core (i.e., fundamental or most important) religious beliefs? ('Religious' is here to be understood quite broadly, so as to encompass views about God or the divine, the self or soul, the nature of xvi *Introduction*

ultimate reality, the purpose of existence, liberation or redemption, the afterlife, etc.)

- What reasons, if any, do you have for these religious beliefs?
- How do you see the relation between your religious beliefs and reason (or rationality)? In line with this, what is your understanding of rationality? And what role is played by reason (as well as philosophy and science) in informing your religious beliefs and commitments?
- How are your religious beliefs related to your views about the meaning and ultimate purpose of life?
- How are your core religious beliefs related to your ethics, your politics and your everyday life?
- How are your religious beliefs related to your views about other religions, as well as those who do not follow any religion (e.g., secular atheists)?
- How important, if at all, is it to share your religious beliefs with others (to persuade or convince others, or to evangelize)? Do you consider yourself an inclusivist, an exclusivist, or a pluralist?

A similar set of questions was given to the Christian contributors of volume 4, with the addition of Christian-specific questions, such as:

- What is your understanding of such central Christian doctrines as the Trinity, the Incarnation, the Atonement and the resurrection of the dead?
- How would you go about supporting or defending your acceptance of Christianity?
- What are your views regarding the historicity of the New Testament account of Jesus, including his purported miracles and resurrection?
- What is your understanding of the afterlife? Do you accept the traditional Christian teaching of the resurrection of the body? In line with this, how do you view the nature of the human person? For example, do you accept some form of dualism, where the human person consists of a body and a soul?

Once all Position Statements were received, they were circulated to other members of the relevant cluster. Each member of the cluster was then asked to provide a First Response (of around 7,000 words) addressing the other statements within the group. The editors directed respondents to ask for clarifications, wherever necessary; to discuss points of similarity and dissimilarity in (e.g.) conceptions of divinity, the role of reason in religion and views regarding other religious faiths; and to dispute or challenge the ideas and arguments put forward by their interlocutors, thus facilitating a robust and dynamic exchange.

The initial plan was to have all participants at this stage gather in Melbourne, Australia, for a conference where the dialogue would continue in

Introduction xvii

person. Financial constraints, however, did not allow for this, and so the dialogues were undertaken entirely in electronic format.

In the next and last stage, participants were invited to write a Second Response (again, of around 7,000 words) in reply to the First Responses, that is, to the critiques made of their Position Statement. All contributions were then collected and edited for publication.

* * *

There are a number of people we would like to thank for helping to bring these volumes to fruition. First and foremost, we are enormously grateful to the dialogue participants themselves, for their patience with a protracted undertaking such as this and for the diligence, respect and charity they exhibited in their contributions.

Secondly, we thank the publishers: Tristan Palmer at Acumen, who initially took on the project and helped mould it into its current shape; the staff at Routledge/Taylor & Francis (including Laura Briskman and Sarah Gore), to whom the project was later transferred; and Katherine Wetzel for overseeing the production process.

Thirdly, we are grateful for the financial support provided by the Australian Research Council through its Discovery Project scheme ('Models of Divinity', DP1093541); for funds provided by the Australian Catholic University as part of a broader project on 'Transcendence within Immanence' (Ref. No. 2013000569); and for two smaller grants provided by the William Angliss Charitable Trust.

Fourthly, we wish to acknowledge those who helped with the preparation of the final manuscripts. Our editorial assistants, Mark Manolopoulos and Tom Cho, took on many of the formatting, copyediting and proofreading duties. Indeed, without Tom's consummate professionalism, the end-product would not have been anywhere near as polished. Karen Gillen again loaned us her expert indexing skills. We are also grateful to Jim Pavlidis for the artwork on the covers.

Apart from these collective debts, Graham Oppy acknowledges ongoing support from friends and family, including, in particular, Camille, Gilbert, Calvin and Alfie. Graham would also like to record his immeasurable indebtedness to Nick Trakakis for his enormous contribution to yet another improbable collaborative venture.

Notes

1 See John Milbank, "The End of Dialogue," in Gavin D'Costa (ed.), *Christian Uniqueness Reconsidered: The Myth of a Pluralist Theology of Religions* (Maryknoll, NY: Orbis Books, 1990), pp. 174–91.
2 Alvin Plantinga, "Hector Castañeda: A Personal Statement," in James E. Tomberlin (ed.), *Agent, Language, and the Structure of the World: Essays Presented to*

xviii *Introduction*

Hector-Neri Castañeda, With His Replies (Indianapolis, IN: Hackett Publishing Company, 1983), p. 8.

3 We should stress that this was *our* goal, as editors of this series. To what extent this goal has been internalized or even accepted by the participants in their contributions to these volumes, is another matter.

4 William James, *A Pluralistic Universe* (Cambridge, MA: Harvard University Press, 1977 [originally published 1909]), pp. 11–12; emphasis in original. James Ferrier (1808–1864) was a Scottish idealist philosopher who taught at the University of St Andrews, and is best known for his *Institutes of Metaphysic* (1854). The passage in Ferrier's *Institutes* to which James is referring is reproduced in the editorial notes to *A Pluralistic Universe* (p. 167).

5 It would also be interesting to allow secular, non-religious perspectives into the mix, and we initially considered doing so by giving Graham Oppy a seat at the dialogue table. But that, as they say, is another project for another time.

6 We will leave it to readers to try to determine who this fortunate, or perhaps unfortunate (depending on one's perspective), fellow is.

Position Statements

1 A 'naturalist' Christian theism

John Bishop

A Christian philosopher's 'position'

Philosophers sometimes ask each other: what is your 'position' on some philosophical issue – the compatibility of free will and determinism, perhaps, or the status of moral claims, or the possibility of knowledge of an 'external' world? A satisfactory answer expresses a particular view and the reasons for holding it, ideally situating the chosen position in the conceptual space of available alternatives and explaining its (alleged) advantages over other options. Yet with some issues (think of the question whether skepticism can be refuted, for example), some philosophers who have given the issue much thought are conscious that they do not 'have a position' on it and may indeed regard their holding back as a virtue. That option is presumably not available, however, to philosophers who, like myself, are confessed Christian believers – not, anyway, with respect to those issues on which being a Christian is usually assumed *just to amount to* holding a certain more-or-less definite position. In particular, a Christian believer who is also a philosopher may be expected to 'have a position' on the divine. This chapter is an attempt to provide my own 'position statement' – to articulate how I think about the divine and my own relation to it, and how that relation to the divine figures in my life.

Yet although I accept that a Christian who is a philosopher must 'have a position', I want to sound a note of caution about the *elusiveness* of that position. Philosophers often find – under questioning, and on reflection – that what they say in the attempt to express 'their position' is *not*, or not wholly, their position but needs further qualification and recasting. And that experience may be iterated, potentially without limit. This is especially the case with so vital an issue as one's religious view of the world. The Christian stance I hold is something I am always continuing to reach for and can never wholly grasp through a transparently comprehensible and finally adequate set of propositions.

Belief 'in' and belief 'that'

Having continually to put off the ambition to possess a finally adequate *statement* of belief would be a problem if Christian commitment just amounted to accepting in practice the truth of such a statement. But it doesn't. Christian

4   John Bishop

belief is not primarily a matter of endorsing the truth of certain propositions. It is first and foremost a matter of believing *in* God. We say "Credo *in* unum Deum . . .", thereby expressing a practical commitment – and a practical commitment of an 'all-framing' kind that constitutes the foundation of an entire way of living.

Yet Christian faith does essentially involve beliefs 'that'. There must be commitment to the truth of claims about how the world is – in particular, to the claim that God is to be trusted in an 'ultimate' and 'centred' way, to use terms from Paul Tillich (1957). Christian commitment does entail existentially vital claims about reality, then; but there is a good deal of open-ended contestability about what these claims are and how to understand them.

The contestability of Christian truth-claims and the epistemology of revelation

Christians differ over whether that uncertainty and open-endedness is a good thing. At their baptism, Christians promise to believe all the articles of the Christian faith as formulated in the historic creeds. That cannot mean that they promise to find them true. One can promise to believe that *p* only in the sense of promising to *accept* that *p* is true – to take it to be true that *p* in one's practical reasoning. Many Christians do interpret the baptismal promise in that way. Other Christians, however, (and I include myself amongst them) place acceptance of the truth of the creeds at one remove, by interpreting the baptismal promise as a promise to trust that the received tradition (in creeds and scriptures) conveys divine revelation. That promise they then see as entailing an undertaking to participate in the continuing process of understanding what is revealed.

Revelation is at the heart of Christian belief. God is known only through his self-revelation. Differing assumptions about the epistemology of revelation yield differing conclusions about the nature and status of Christian knowledge of God. I believe that the revelation of God to humanity is essentially limited, fallible and developmental – not through any lack in God but as inherent in the limitedness of the recipients of revelation. On this view the revelation of the divine is necessarily an evolutionary process: humanity does indeed experience the divine, but its understanding of God's nature and will undergoes continuing change and development, never reaching a point from which no more development is possible. Theological epistemology thus shares the same overall fallibilist developmental profile as 'secular' scientific epistemology.[1]

There is, admittedly, a tendency to 'pin down' what is revealed and pronounce anathemas against any who would add to or change authorized scriptures or creeds. Those who think as I do, however, regard that tendency as betraying false consciousness about the historicity of all formulations of 'the revealed truth' and a hubristic refusal to be genuinely open to the divine. The received creeds and canonical scriptures, notoriously, emerged from a ferment of controversy and were settled through all-too-human exercises of political power. That does not disqualify them as revelatory – indeed, the evolutionist view I am sketching holds that *the only vehicles of revelation to historical beings there could possibly be* will inevitably have these kinds of limitations. What does get disqualified, though, is any understanding of what is revealed as *both* final *and* settled as to its true meaning beyond any legitimate contestability.

Philosophical issues: the 'justifiability' question and the 'content' question

It may be then – as Christians claim – that there is full and final revelation of the divine in Christ: my evolutionist view asserts only that, if so, there is then a process of evolutionary understanding (which continues today) of *what it is* that is revealed in Christ and how what is revealed counts existentially as Good News. Furthermore, I see that process as continuing, under divine providence, the process of understanding the revealed divine nature and will that characterizes the whole history of the Abrahamic faith (Christianity is unintelligible apart from its Hebrew roots). And I grant that "the Spirit blows where it wills": the process of understanding what is revealed in Christ may belong to an altogether wider context that admits revelatory events and progress beyond Christianity and beyond the Abrahamic traditions, and even in philosophies not usually regarded as 'religious'. (Scientific knowledge, of course, may be understood theologically as *general* revelation, as contrasted with the *special* revelation with which my present remarks are concerned. It is important, I think, that whatever is understood as specially revealed coheres with what is generally, scientifically, 'revealed'.)

I see myself, then, as standing in a tradition in which a specific history is understood as revealing the divine, and the task of understanding the content of revelation evolves under divine providence over many generations. Since that evolving process requires challenge and conflict and critical engagement across disagreements, the philosopher will feel at home in it. Indeed, the evolutionist perspective entails that believers (some of them, at least) have a responsibility to engage in reflective and critical philosophical activity. Philosophy thus serves theological commitment – though it is philosophy also, of course, that raises the question whether any theological commitment can be justified in the first place. How are one's commitments as a Christian and as a philosopher related, then? My view is that critical philosophical values are values which authentic Christian commitment may understand itself, on its own terms, as seeking to honour. Christian faith may thus preserve its religious ultimacy while nevertheless being open to full philosophical critique.[2]

In the closing section of this chapter (see "The justifiability of Christian commitment") I will say something about the 'justifiability' of Christian faith. Until then I will assume that Christian commitment is justifiable so as to concentrate on what I think I am taking to be true in committing myself to trust God. It is the answer people give to that 'content' question which

6 *John Bishop*

illuminates the existential significance of their Christian belief. I will 'narrow' my focus – though it is only superficially a narrowing – to a discussion of my understanding of the divine, as formed through a dialectic which I will outline. As I have emphasized, though my position is held tentatively, I regard myself as keeping firmly to my promise to believe the received Christian faith.[3]

Understanding the nature of divinity: a dominant view and its critique

What is it, then, to believe that God exists and is worthy of ultimate trust? We Christians are not alone, of course, in holding such a belief: we hold it in common with all 'theistic' believers. And the first step required to explain the content of this belief reveals a wider commonality – namely, with all religious stances that take the universe ('all that is') to constitute a certain kind of *unity*. On some views, the universe's supposed unity is *itself* identified as divine, but theism differentiates itself from that pantheistic identification by holding that the kind of unity the universe possesses is *the unity of a creation*. God is then identified as *the Creator*, the ultimate cause of the existence of the universe and the principle of its unity.

Classical theism – its perceived religious inadequacy

Classical theism emphasizes this distinctness of God the Creator from the creation and from any item within it. God is not temporal, not subject to change or to any kind of 'undergoing' ('he' is immutable and impassible). God is not contingent, not dependent on anything else for his existence. God is not something of a kind or species, for which its existence as an instantiation of its kind may be distinguished from the essence of what it is to be of that kind. This follows from God's 'simplicity': there is no complexity or 'composition' in God, not even the pervasive 'composition' of essence and existence.

Constructing a positive metaphysics out of these classical attributes of God is problematic, however. Such a construction makes the Creator into a supernatural *entity* that is simple and necessary, somehow 'existing' outside of time and change. But the notion of *an existent* that is absolutely simple and necessary is of doubtful coherence: divinity so conceived may well be open to an 'ontological disproof' (see Findlay 1955). In any case, a simple, immutable, impassible being does not fit the God who speaks and acts decisively in human history. The *thus-constructed* 'God of classical theism', then, seems patently *religiously* inadequate with respect to the lived Abrahamic faiths.

Personal omniGod theism

The temptation, now, is to adjust this supposedly 'classical' account of the divine in an attempt to bring it into line with the God of scripture and lived religious experience. God must indeed be Creator, distinct from and other

A 'naturalist' Christian theism 7

than his creation and therefore 'supernatural' in relation to the created natural order. But (on this adjusted view) God is a supernatural *person* and has the complexity required for the cognitive and conative capacities essential to personhood – that baffling divine simplicity is jettisoned. God does retain, however, the 'omni-' properties: his agency is all-powerful (he is omnipotent), his knowledge all-encompassing (he is omniscient) and his goodness supreme (he is omnibenevolent). And the necessity of God's existence is retained: if there is such a person as God, he is a denizen of every logically possible world.

In my view, however, this adjustment rescues us from the frying pan of a problematic, positively construed, classical theistic metaphysics only to land us in the fire of 'personal omniGod theism' – the understanding of God as "an all-powerful, all-knowing, wholly good person (a person without a body) who has created us and our world" (Plantinga 2000: 3). The suggestion that this understanding of God makes things worse may be startling, since personal omniGod theism is the prevailing understanding of the divine amongst philosophers of religion in the English-speaking 'analytical' tradition. Nevertheless, there are grounds for thinking that this understanding is inadequate – and primarily *religious* grounds at that.

The religious critique of conceptions of God

The religious critique of personal omniGod theism arises in the following way. As I said at the outset, Christians believe *in* God: they practically commit themselves to trust, worship and obey God. Accordingly, the concept of God is the concept of that which plays a certain role ('the God-role'), for which it is essential that God *be worthy of* the special kind of trust, worship and obedience that constitute the commitment of faith. In Tillich's terms, the authentic object of faith must be worthy of a believer's "ultimate concern" in so far as "totally surrendering" to it "promises total fulfillment even if all other claims have to be subjected to it or rejected in its name" (1957: 1). Correspondingly, an adequate conception of who or what God is – of what it is that actually fills the God-role – must be a conception of something worthy of this special kind of practical commitment.

It may thus always be questioned whether a given particular object of faith-commitment, of ultimate concern, is *in fact* worthy of that concern. It is all too possible for a "false ultimate" (again, a term of Tillich's) to be trusted for the fulfillment of human existence, with disastrous, demonic, results – as was apparent, for example, in the history of the Nazi absolutizing of the German nation and the master race. Candidate objects of theistic faith, then, need to be scrutinized to ensure they are not false ultimates. But this scrutiny is not imposed on religious tradition and experience, as it were from some independent higher ethical ground: rather, it is inherently required at the core of theistic consciousness. The dynamic of the Abrahamic faith is the passionate desire to submit only to the true God. Its first

8 *John Bishop*

imperative, therefore, is to avoid the horror of idolatry – of giving to something unworthy the commitment proper only to the true God.

Christians relate to God personally; yet God need not be understood as 'a' person

Any attempt, then, to specify what fills the God-role is open to religious scrutiny lest an unworthy, idolatrous, object be smuggled into the believer's consciousness. Could the personal omniGod be such an unworthy object? In my view, a Christian may reasonably think so. That view may at first seem preposterous. Thinking of God in personal terms is basic to Christian spirituality: Jesus himself related to God as Father, as do we whenever we pray the prayer Jesus taught us. What would be idolatrous would be to think of God too much as a person *like us*, but that is surely avoided by understanding the divine Person as bearing the omni-properties, which confer unique supremacy and thereby, surely, block idolatrous anthropomorphism. But I distinguish between what is essential to the believer's spiritual *psychology* and what is essential to the believer's *understanding*. Relating to God person-to-person is psychologically healthy and even unavoidable, but it does not follow that God is to be understood as 'a' person, however unique and supreme.

Even though God, understood as a person, is supreme, unique and supernatural, he will still be a person amongst persons, an entity among entities. As David Burrell observes, "to picture God as an additional being over against or parallel to the universe itself will be to treat God similarly to objects within the universe, related to the universe itself as objects within the world are related to each other" (1998: 72). I agree with Burrell that an understanding that treats God thus is inadequate. Everyone accepts that it is a bad error to take God to be an item within the universe. But the underlying mistake is not avoided by taking Him to be a supernatural Item in addition to the universe (even when we are careful to add the capital!): God is not 'an item' *at all*, not 'a' being, not 'an' entity. They have said well who have said that 'God is nothing' (= 'no thing'), or (Tillich again) that only an atheist can say that God exists (as an entity amongst entities).

But aren't these claims altogether too clever? One may suspect that a pure zeal for God's absolute otherness here overreaches itself! If God is not an entity, does it not follow that God is a non-entity? How will theists who take God to be real distinguish their position from atheism if God is not an entity? A possible answer suggests itself: there must be other ways of being real that do not amount to the way of being real that belongs to *existing entities*, and God's way of being supremely real must be such another way.

God as being itself, or 'the ground' of being

But how could God's ontological primacy amount to one way of being *amongst others*? The only 'thing' that could arguably be truly primary – one may think – is Being Itself (and some philosophers do suppose this to be the classical conception of the divine). But the theology of Being (with a capital 'b') faces a dilemma in understanding how God can be creator: either Being is an abstract universal, or it is the concrete reality of all that is. If the former, then, for God to be Creator, abstract universals must have the power to realize their instantiations, a conclusion that clashes with strong intuitions about causation. But if God is the concrete reality of all that is, then a pantheistic identification of Creator and creation seems unavoidable. Perhaps, then, God is not Being, but rather *the Ground* of our Being (as Tillich maintains), but then it needs to be explained how such a 'ground' can be real without counting, however exaltedly, as a being among beings.

The God-role: trust in God is salvific, transformative

What would be so bad, though, about having God as a being among beings – given that God is, as personal omniGod theism maintains, a unique and supreme entity who is the source of all other entities? Unless more can be said, rejecting as idolatrous the conception of God as a supernatural entity 'amongst entities' looks like ontological fetishism, or even a metaphysician's idolatry (setting the bar for ontological primacy so high that nothing real can meet it, thereby – it might be alleged – conveniently rationalizing one's selfish resistance to the real God). But more *can* be said, since the God-role is not confined to sheer ontological supremacy. It also belongs to the God-role that God may be trusted for 'ultimate fulfillment': that is, for human life – individually, collectively, and even cosmically – to realize its full potential and become what it 'is meant to be'. Christianity understands ultimate fulfillment as *salvation* and holds that salvation requires God-wrought individual transformation from sinful self-centredness into God-centredness, characterized by the theological virtues of faith, hope and love.

Can the personal omniGod fit the God-role? An ethical assessment, and the argument from evil

Personal omniGod theists, of course, take it that a personal omniGod fits this salvific aspect of the God-role. But how may God's grace overcome self-centredness in believers whose conception of the object of their worship is the apotheosis of the controlling ego (which an omnipotent superagent must surely be)? If you are worshiping an idealization of your sinful self, how can you escape idolatry? This provocative challenge illustrates how the claim that the supernatural supreme personal agent is an idol depends not solely on metaphysical judgements about what makes for supreme ontological greatness but also *on ethical judgements about what makes for perfect goodness.*

Ethical judgements are also to the fore in questioning whether, given the existence of horrific evils in his creation, the Creator could possibly be a person who is both perfectly good and totally in control. There is, I believe,

10 *John Bishop*

a successful version of the argument from evil against the existence of a personal omniGod – granted, anyway, certain plausible ethical norms for assessing the moral perfection of persons (a 'normatively relativized logical argument from evil'). A person who first causes and sustains horrific suffering and then – as sophisticated theodicies maintain of God – brings the participants in horrors into eternal relationship with himself could not *overall* have the most perfectly loving kind of relationship with them. The wonder of God's overcoming suffering and evil sits uneasily with his ultimate productive responsibility for it and may plausibly be judged inconsistent with God's being a perfectly morally good person.[4]

To this it might be replied that, though God is a person, his unique status as creator entails that his perfect goodness need not conform to perfect goodness according to human standards. But Locke was right, I think, in holding that our modern concept of a person is a forensic concept. One cannot, therefore, carve off from perfect personal goodness the need for excellence in exercising moral responsibility – and then we may make Mill's point that we can attach no meaning to possessing this excellence if it does not count as such according to our own best theory. Personal omniGod theists, therefore, have to maintain that God is perfectly good *as a morally responsible personal agent in relationship with other personal agents*. Yet to maintain that God has that sort of perfect goodness is problematic when God has absolute all-controlling power over all else. It is difficult to see how God could be in perfect relationship with sufferers even though he may have – to us unknown – good reasons for allowing their suffering and even though he ultimately compensates for and redeems their suffering. Perhaps, too, the provocative challenge made earlier may be pressed home: if God is the idealization of the controlling ego, then Christianity's self-transformative ethic *entails* that such a God does not realize the supreme ethical ideal.

Personal omniGod theism as inconsistent with Trinitarianism

A further objection to understanding divine goodness as the perfect goodness *of an individual person* is that doing so is directly contradicted by the central Christian doctrine of the nature of God, namely the doctrine of the Trinity. God is not 'a' person, but 'three persons in one God'. The worshipful goodness of the divine, then, is the perfect goodness of three-persons-in-one-God, which implies that divine goodness is *social*, *communal* and *relational* goodness. The unity of the divine is a unity in diversity, a unity of relationship amongst persons, and the name for the perfection of this dynamic unity is Love. Scripture affirms that "God is love, and whoever remains in love remains in God, and God in him" (1 John 4:16, New Jerusalem Bible). The doctrine of the Trinity, I believe, entails that this assertion is not merely hyperbole for God's being supremely loving (though Scripture speaks in those terms also). Rather, what is intended

A 'naturalist' Christian theism   11

is an actual identification of the divine with what the Greek fathers called the *perichoretic* relationship of the three persons (a lovely word, '*perichoresis*', meaning 'going round giving space to another'). The puzzling fact that a good many Trinitarian Christian philosophers favour the personal omniGod conception may perhaps be explained by the widespread 'modalism' in western theological thinking, which takes the 'three persons' to be different modes or guises of the 'one substance' – on their theory that one substance is a personal substance.

Seeking alternatives to personal omniGod theism

How may the divine be understood, then, if the personal omniGod is rejected? Is a return to classical theism advisable? I believe that the classical attributes of the divine – atemporality, immutability, impassibility, necessity and simplicity – are to be understood apophatically, as expressing our grasp of what God is not. It is a bad mistake to construe them as conveying positive, kataphatic, knowledge of the divine nature.[5] Indeed, as I have stated it, that is the mistake that occasions the 'adjustment' that yields personal omniGod theism – and, if my critique is correct – lands us with an idol. Once divine impassibility and simplicity are taken purely apophatically, however, they no longer generate a metaphysical clash with what is presupposed by God's being the One who brings salvation. Yet an urgent question remains as to what God could *positively* be if he acts in creation and in history, while at the same time *not* being any kind of existent item (not even – as I will henceforth assume – that uniquely supreme existent item, the supernatural personal omniGod).

Pure apophaticism not enough

This question may seem urgent, but perhaps the urge to settle it should be resisted. The Creed of St Athanasius affirms: "The Father incomprehensible, the Son incomprehensible, and the Holy Ghost incomprehensible", and yet "there are not three incomprehensibles . . . but one incomprehensible" (*Book of Common Prayer*). Indeed, God's nature is not comprehensible: but I take this to mean, not that it is unintelligible or ineffable, but only that God's nature cannot be *fully* grasped (evidently, the Athanasian Creed expects us *to understand* that the divine incomprehensibility is one!). God's being un-pin-down-able is, of course, well respected by apophatic theology: but can it be good enough, especially for *fides quaerens intellectum*, to rest content with a purely negative account of the divine? A purely negative account faces the atheist's challenge: if God is not temporal, not changeable, not an entity amongst entities, and so on, what's to stop the inference that God is, simply, not? A stand-alone apophatic theology, in other words, lacks the resources to distinguish from atheism the positive content of theistic faith-commitment.

12   *John Bishop*

Tradition-mediated positive conceptions of the divine

A positive account of the divine nature is therefore needed – though it can aspire only to making God intelligible, not to making him fully comprehensible. In fact, positive understandings of God abound – understandings which we may call *tradition-mediated*. For Christians, God is the one who called Abram and made him Abraham, the father of many nations, the one who brought the Israelites out of slavery in Egypt, who spake through the prophets, and who was incarnate in Jesus the Christ for our salvation and whose Spirit enlivens the Church, the Body of Christ. God is the one whose children we have been made in our baptism and for whose coming 'Kingdom' of righteousness and peace we hope and pray, while already here and now, in our true 're-born' selves, being active participants in and, by God's grace, contributors to it. All these claims make God positively intelligible from within the 'form of life' of Christian believers. And all these understandings richly meet the requirement of intelligibility combined with mystery, the ineliminable lack of full comprehensibility. By contrast, *philosophical* positive understandings of the divine nature are *theories about who or what it is* that we understand, through the mediation of the tradition, to have acted, spoken and wonderfully related himself to us. Personal omniGod theism is just such a theory – though, as I have argued, a flawed one.

The importance of philosophical theories of the divine for evolving theological understanding

One cautious option would be to retreat from philosophical theories of the divine altogether, combining affirmation of the positive tradition-mediated understandings of God with a pure theoretical apophaticism. After all, there is clearly a risk that anything that might attract us as an 'improvement' on an allegedly flawed theory of the divine will turn out to be equally idolatrously inadequate.

It would be a mistake, however, to dismiss as hubristic the desire to provide a philosophical theory of the divine nature. An important reason for this relates to the evolutionist perspective outlined earlier: it is a matter of *developing* judgement which tradition-mediated characterizations of God to affirm as authentically revelatory of the divine. God is the one who brought the Israelites out of slavery into the land of promise . . . but in ways that included championing their subjugation and even extermination of other nations. Consider, for example, what happened to Jericho (Book of Joshua, Chapter 6). Acts of violent conquest were experienced as happening under God's providential grace in the Hebrew heritage which we Christians need to honour as the context of our own faith. So our understanding of divine providence must somehow allow that – to continue the Jericho example – the enforcing "of the curse of destruction on everyone in the city: men and women, young and old, including the

A 'naturalist' Christian theism   13

oxen, the sheep and the donkeys, slaughtering them all" (Joshua 6:21) did indeed occur within the working out of God's purposes. But Christians need not – indeed, should not – identify God as One who destroys some peoples that others may flourish. Christians see in their heritage *an evolution* of understanding of the nature of God, an ethical progression in theological consciousness that inevitably involves challenges to established ways and conflict with religious authority. Consider, for an example of an ethically more advanced understanding, Peter's address in the house of Cornelius: "I now really understand that God has no favourites, but that anybody of any nationality who fears him and does what is right is acceptable to him" (Acts 10:34–35). The One who has no favourites cannot be one who destroys some for the sake of others.

If the revelation of God's nature and will is a matter of continuing evolution, it cannot then be hubristic for those who receive the revelation to theorize about the One who is revealed. Indeed, I think it is necessary at least for some of the faithful to engage in such theorizing for the sake of the whole community of faith. If aspects of the inherited tradition are to be modified or set aside in the light of what are judged more central disclosures – for example, patriarchal restrictions, in the light of there being in Christ neither male nor female (Galatians 3:28) – then there must be some justification for such shifts, and such justifications can have weight only in the context of overall theorizing about the nature and will of the God who reveals himself. But theological theorizers must guard against an error of which authority-claiming religious institutions are especially susceptible – namely, confusing the One who is revealed with any human theory, even our current best theory, of who that One is. To theorize is not hubristic; to take one's theorizing as completing the revelation is.

A naturalist, euteleological, conception of the divine

In positive theorizing about the nature of the divine, is it possible to do better than personal omniGod theism? Perhaps. Let me outline my own current, tentative, proposal for a positive alternative to personal omniGod theism.

For Christian theism, God is the Creator, that is, the ultimate cause of all that is. But God is also the ultimate end, purpose or goal of all that is. At Revelation 22:13, God is represented as saying: *ego to Alpha kai to Omega, ho protos kai ho eschatos, he arche kai to telos* ("I am the Alpha and the Omega, the first and the last, the beginning and the end"). Now, my proposal is that God's being the ultimate *telos* ('end', 'purpose') of the universe *is the very same thing* as God's being the ultimate cause of the universe. If that is so, the universe can be a creation and have God as its Creator, *even though it has no producer*, not even a supernatural personal agent. If the universe is a creation, then there must be an explanation of its existence – an explanation in terms of a creator. But, according to this proposal, there *is* such an explanation – what I call a *euteleological* explanation: the universe

14   *John Bishop*

exists because it has a point, an end, a purpose – a purpose which is actually realized and which is perfectly and supremely good.[6]

How can such a teleological explanation of the universe's existence be 'an explanation in terms of a creator'? Standardly, teleological explanations are reducible to causal explanations. An explanation of the universe as existing for the sake of an ultimate end (the supreme good) therefore looks as if it must be an intentional explanation of the universe *as produced by an agent whose intention it is to achieve the supreme good*. That reduction, of course, requires us to postulate such an agent and so lands us in personal omniGod theism. But, mindful of the fact that any explanation of the existence of the universe will inevitably have unique features, we may, I suggest, take the theological explanation of the universe to be (uniquely) *an irreducible* teleological explanation. If that is so, no *productive* agent need be postulated. Yet, in a suitably broad sense, the actuality of the universe will (on this proposal) have an efficient cause, because it will be explicable in terms of its actually realized ultimate and supremely good *telos*. Its *telos* will be its cause; its Omega will be its Alpha.[7]

This proposal offers a 'naturalist' understanding of the divine – but just in the sense that it is *anti-supernaturalist*: it rejects the ontological realm separate from and prior to the natural universe that is required for personal omniGod theism. There is no implication, however, that the divine is graspable through natural scientific inquiry: any viable theism will reject such 'natural scientism'. Nevertheless, the euteleological proposal does insist that there is but one unified concrete reality and divine reality can belong nowhere else. This proposal may seem to buy naturalism at the price of concluding, scandalously, that, in the order of productive causality, the Creator is dependent on his own creatures. But scandal of just this kind is entrenched in Christian tradition, in the endorsement of Mary's title as *theotokos* (God-bearer) at the Council at Ephesus in 431, so it may not, after all, be perverse to persist with a euteleological conception of the divine.

God as realized telos and the nature of the supreme good

Many Christians will disagree with my denial that God is the cause of the universe in the sense of being its supernatural producer. But I expect all Christians to agree in holding the belief basic to the euteleological proposal, namely, that the universe is a creation that has and achieves a good purpose. What do we Christians take this purpose to be? As the divine purpose, it must be the greatest conceivable purpose there could be – the supreme good (which Aristotle shows to be also the most final end – an end to be sought for its own sake, but which could not be sought for the sake of any further end). Furthermore, no purpose could be the divine purpose without actually being fulfilled – the supreme good is realized and actual. But now, I ask, how is God related to the supreme good? God can hardly be an agent who *seeks* the supreme good and has to do something (create a universe) in order to achieve it, for then God would be lacking, and so would not be 'that than which a greater cannot be conceived', a key formal feature of the God-role as captured in Anselm's famous formula. No, somehow God must 'already possess' the supreme good. How that is so may be understood by appeal to the doctrine of the Trinity. On a 'social' interpretation of the Trinity, the divine *is* the perichoretic love that unites the divine Persons. Living in this kind of perfectly loving inter-personal relationship is the supreme good. The divine *is* perfectly loving relationship of this kind, not merely *qua* ideal but *as actually realized*.

That last qualification is important. My proposed identification of the divine with the love that is the supreme good, the *telos* of the universe, might at first seem to reduce divinity to the ethical, which would definitely be a mistake. The divine must be *ontically* as well as ethically supreme. But the proposal is not to identify the divine with an ethical ideal. The euteleological explanation of existence is an explanation in terms of the *realized* supreme good. It does not say that the universe, or, indeed, anything within it, exists because it would be (supremely) good that it should. Rather it says that what explains why everything that exists does exist and counts as created is that it belongs to a unified order whose *telos* is the supreme good *that is actually fully realized*. (Yes, this does imply that the reason why animal predation, unrelieved 'natural' suffering, violent deliberate destruction, institutional oppression and many other created ills exist is that the supreme good may be realized – a conclusion which generates *a* problem of evil, but with contours significantly different from the problem generated by personal omniGod theism. I return to this point later.)

How (not) to identify the divine on the euteleological view

Am I saying, though, that the divine is to be identified with loving interpersonal relationships within the universe – maybe with the sum total of them? Well, yes and no! On the one hand, the answer seems to be 'yes' because, if the divine is the realized supreme good, it must surely consist in instantiations of a certain kind of thing (on the given account, of genuinely loving relationship). That this is a theme in Christian thinking is evident from the verse quoted earlier from the First Epistle of John, echoed in the Maundy Thursday antiphon: *Ubi caritas et amor deus ibi est* ("where there is charity and love, there God is"). This theme may also be supported by a reflection on the Lord's Prayer. We say, "Our Father which art in Heaven."[8] But where is 'Heaven'? The fourth petition of the prayer gives the clue: "Thy will be done on Earth, as it *is* in Heaven." Heaven is therefore the place where the divine will is done: that is 'where' our Father is. It is thus a fundamental principle that God is where God's will is done. (And, though *the metaphor* of a personal agent is obviously engaged by talk of God's 'will', on my non-personal view of the divine, God's will is not a power of choosing what to intend. God's 'will' is unchanging, its content well expressed in Jesus' new

16 John Bishop

commandment, that we love one another as he has loved us. But an essentially unchanging will is a will only in an analogous sense, with significant elements of disanalogy to the will of a finite agent.)

On the other hand, identifying the divine with truly loving interactions and relationships seems a false move because it implies that the reality of the divine is simply one, relatively rare, aspect of the universe. And, if it was a fair objection to personal omniGod theism that it makes God 'an entity among entities', the same charge must surely be an equally fair objection to my 'God is Love' theory.

The principle of Incarnation and the inexhaustibility of what is incarnated

How can it be true then that, where there is love, there is God? There could be no objection to the claim that actual instances of love are *manifestations* of the divine. Manifestations of the divine will be particular items in the created world, but that does not reduce *the divine itself* to any such items. There is, of course, a sense in which *every* particular entity, aspect or feature of the existing universe may be described as a manifestation of the divine: every existent is a creature of the divine and so manifests or expresses its creator. But this sense is much attenuated relative to the sense in which instances of agapeistic love manifest the divine. Actual genuinely loving relations *fully* manifest the nature and character of the divine – and they *are* 'entities among entities', shining jewels realizing the *telos* for the sake of which all that is exists. The principle that there are, within the natural universe, manifestations of the divine which are *full* manifestations, holding nothing of the essential divine character back, is a core principle of Christianity – the principle of Incarnation.

A Christian understanding of the exemplification of the divine, then, is importantly different from a Platonist understanding of the exemplification of an ideal, for which exemplifications mirror the ideal with always some degree of imperfection. The exemplification of the divine in Christ lacks nothing of the divine nature. In response to Philip's request, "Lord, show us the Father and then we shall be satisfied," Jesus replies, "Anyone who has seen me has seen the Father . . . I am in the Father and the Father is in me" (see John 14:8–11). Now, indeed, the *incarnate* divine *is* an aspect of reality, an entity among entities. But it does not follow that *the divine* is an entity among entities, since the incarnate divine *does not exhaust the divine*, though it is absolutely necessary to it – as is made clear by the fact that the Christ, the Incarnate Word, is the Second Person of a Trinity of Persons.

On this 'God is Love' theory – as indeed orthodox teaching has it – no one of the Persons exhausts the divine. But this relational account of the divine does imply that each Person of the Trinity is God in a derivative sense, namely, that each equally has the property of being essential to the interpersonal perichoretic relationship that is God in the primary sense. So the divinity of Christ, on this account, is only derivatively the divinity of the person Jesus: what it is primarily is *the loving relationality* into which Jesus consistently and steadfastly enters, even while tortured to death by combined political and religious authority. But those exemplary loving relations, manifesting the divine perfectly as they do, do not exhaust the divine. 'God' is not a synonym for 'loving as Jesus did', even though when we experience Christ-like love we have indeed 'seen the Father' in the sense that we are now fully acquainted with the true character of divinity.

What 'more' is there, then? Infinitely, inexhaustibly more! The divine love is a power for good than which there could conceivably be no greater, and the victory of this power – its undefeatable realization of the supreme good – is that for the sake of which all that is exists. In Christ we know both the character of this power and that it is victorious – supremely in Christ reigning on the Cross, as vindicated in his resurrection and ascension, yet ever open to consummation in his 'coming again'. What is divine is not just actual Christ-like relationships, but *the full cosmic meaning* of such loving relationship.

Ethics as requiring orientation to the world as fit for seeking the good

To explain my last remark further, let me connect my euteleological alternative to personal omniGod theism more explicitly with Christian ethics – with Christianity as an answer to the question, 'How should we live?'

What do we need for a satisfactory answer to this fundamental ethical question? First and most obviously, a complete ethical theory will specify ethical ideals. It will answer the question what it is to live well, by giving an account of right action, good character and right relationship (different theories here place their focus variously). Notice, however, that specifying ideals will not by itself answer the question how we should live: one has to say further that to live well is to believe or at least accept that these are indeed the correct ideals and to carry them out in practice (and, arguably also, to do so *because* you accept them as the ideals – or, at least, not for some purely extraneous reason).

But then we may ask: What has to be presupposed if the carrying out of the ideals is to be a real, practical, possibility for human agents? Answering this question is the second – and not so obvious – main task for an ethical theory, and it is here that connections between ethical theory and religion become most salient. A specific ethical theory needs to say how things have to be if its account of the ethical ideals captures the right way *for us* to live – rather than amounting to a fantastic pipe dream, a set of ideals that no actual human individual or community has any hope of meeting. Practical commitment to a particular ethical theory will then be commitment, not only to its ideals, but to the world's *being the way it must be* if those ideals are to be, so to speak, *accessible* to us. Those who live well in accordance with the right ideals, then, must also have the right overall cognitive orientation to

18   John Bishop

the world: they will need to take the world to be the way it must be if living by those ideals is to be a real possibility for finite human agents.

How the world may be fit for seeking Christian ideals of the good

There is room for considerable dispute about what is required for ethical ideals to be accessible in the sense here implied. As far as Christianity is concerned, I think the position is this. First, the Christian ethical ideal may be summed up readily enough: to live well is to live lovingly. Getting the measure of what the loving of neighbour as oneself concretely means is not so readily achieved. Indeed, learning how to love takes generations, and we have a long way to go, especially in understanding how social and political institutions can truly embody agapeistic love. On the question of accessibility, Christianity holds that the Christian ethical ideal is accessible to us only if (i) there are grounds for holding that persisting in love is always profoundly worthwhile, even in adverse circumstances when so doing looks contrary to our interest and, furthermore, for hoping that those who love (even to the extent of laying down their lives for others) are ultimately vindicated; and (ii) our natural tendency to self-centredness and control-freakiness (the root of the sin that separates us from living the ethical ideal) may be overcome by a grace from outside ourselves to which we need only be open. Christianity further holds that these conditions *are* met: our sinful selfishness *can* be overcome, and there *are* grounds for persisting hopefully in the life of love, even in times of severe trial.

Kant famously held that meeting these conditions requires a supreme agent good enough to intend and powerful enough to ensure that all and only those morally deserving of happiness ultimately receive it. He thereby reinstated, as a 'postulate of practical reason', the personal omniGod whose existence he thought it beyond the limits of pure reason to establish. Kant also thought it necessary to postulate personal immortality to allow scope for final justice, which so obviously does not get done within mortal history. Though Christians must believe that the world meets the ethical ideal's accessibility conditions, they need not, I think, agree with Kant about how those conditions are met. Indeed, if my critique of personal omniGod theism is correct, an alternative account must be found of how the reality of the divine secures the point of commitment to the ethic of love and the transformative possibility of living out that commitment. It is thus a test of the euteleological alternative whether it provides what is required for accessibility of the Christian ethical ideal.

The unlimited power of love within creation . . .

To pass that test, a naturalist euteleological account of the divine must make a strong claim about real, salvific and transformative, divine agency in the world. What can that agency be, if it is not directed by a supernatural

A 'naturalist' Christian theism   19

controlling providence? My stance is that it can only be the 'agency' of love itself, understood as a power that *emerges* from individual loving actions in relationship. The idea of 'supra-individual' or 'transpersonal' agency seems at least conceptually available, given the coherence of the notion of group action.[9] The idea of corporate agency emerging from and through the actions of suitably related individual agents provides an analogical base for understanding what is meant by the emergence of divine agency within the world, though divine agency will be vastly more powerful – in a dimension of power 'for the good' that cuts across our usual assessment of power as the controlling capacity to bend to one's purpose.

This strong claim about the power of love in the world will seem outrageous from any ordinary (let alone scientific) perspective. But Christianity has ever stressed the foolishness of its proclamation that the Crucified One, defeated and dying, yet reigns supreme in the power of the Resurrection that, without limit, overcomes sin and death. On my naturalist understanding, the Resurrection is not effected by external supernatural agency but by the altogether more amazing *inherent* effect of absolute steadfastness in living lovingly. Jesus is not restored to the *status quo ante* but raised 'to the right hand of the Father'. This transforms his existence as a historical individual into eternal relationship with God (from which also he had come, his goal also being his source). That transformation is a feature of the natural order, expressed in the continued incarnation of the divine love through the Holy Spirit ('another Comforter'). The Church which is Christ's Body is the continuing historical incarnation, and its members are nurtured by Christ, as a mother her child, with the very substance of his own life. I accept the Gospel 'resurrection appearances' as straightforwardly factual and caused by the power of Christ's love but am most influenced by the story of the Emmaus Road, which expresses and reinforces the Church's experience of Christ being really present in the breaking of bread and encounters with others. The first disciples had the appearances, which were transient: now that the Spirit has come, we have something more solid – the Eucharist and its essentially related experience of being Christ to one another, serving and being served in his love.

. . . and its significance for an individual life

To be a Christian is to be baptized – made a member of Christ, the child of God, and an inheritor of the Kingdom of Heaven. Baptism is rebirth in the Spirit, transforming human self-centredness into true humanity, measured by the full stature of Christ. The true human really is capable of living in accordance with the ideal of love (and so incarnating the divine), and, in consequence, coming to share the resurrection life of God's eternity. Christianity does affirm Christ's uniqueness – God's 'only begotten son' – but it is a uniqueness that turns out to be inclusive without limit! The pattern set by Christ has its purpose in its being potentially repeated by all humanity: *theosis*, divinization, is the human

20 *John Bishop*

ideal. The transformation involved in 'becoming', or entering into, the divine is shown in Christ, and it involves laying down one's life that one may gain it. A naturalist view, obviously, eschews personal immortality in a supernatural realm. Immortality as an endless continuation of finite human personal existence would anyway be tedious and falls far short of the transformation beyond individual personhood that the divine love effects. Yet I do affirm Jesus' own simple argument: the God of Abraham, Isaac and Jacob is not the God of the dead but the God of the living.

Christian life, then, is the simple commitment to being transformed through openness to love: the cognitive correlate of that commitment is a view of the world as profoundly hospitable to and aimed at fulfillment through such transformation. Such a world must be marvellous indeed, but it needs no supernatural agent to produce it nor to sustain and control its course.

The justifiability of Christian commitment

What view do I take of the justifiability of Christian commitment? First, I think that this question is fundamentally a *moral* one, since what is being asked about is a *practical* commitment influencing a believer's whole way of life. (Its existential pervasiveness is what makes this commitment a *religious* one: it centres the believer's life, 'binding together' its elements into a unified whole: 'religion' comes from '*religere*', which means 'to bind together'.) As I have argued, however, though the Christian's commitment is to an ethical ideal, it is also a commitment to the world's being fit for hopefully and steadfastly seeking that ideal. So the question arises whether it is *epistemically* justifiable to take it as true that (to abbreviate my euteleological proposal) sin and death are indeed overcome by the power of love that is both goal and source of all that is. We are, I think, morally entitled to commit to a religious view of the world such as this only if we are epistemically entitled to its truth. (Examples may be given where moral considerations justify practical acceptance of truth-claims independently of one's epistemic situation. The case of religious commitment may not be assimilated to these, however. The 'all-framing' truth-claims of religious faith need to be brought within the scope of epistemic concern: one cannot rest easily with the thought that one may be founding one's whole life on a lie.)

The Christian worldview is so totalizing, however, that the epistemic worth of holding it could not, as a matter of principle, be secured by appeal to independent, external, supporting evidence. Some might take the hard line that this precludes epistemic entitlement to Christian belief, or to any similarly all-framing worldview – though that hard line threatens to undermine itself when taken by an atheist/naturalist, the truth of whose worldview lies similarly beyond non-circular evidential support. An alternative is simply to observe that foundational Christian beliefs are in fact accepted (by Christians) as basic and give rise to their own well-established 'evidential practice', in a manner analogous to our 'perceptual evidential practice' that

A 'naturalist' Christian theism 21

allows epistemic entitlement to (undefeated) perceptual beliefs without any further inferential support. The analogy, as such, is fair – and may be supported by reflecting that worthwhile 'externalist' epistemic status arising from a belief's having appropriate causes (rather than being inferred from other held beliefs) might belong to basic Christian beliefs. Nevertheless, the two cases are not to be assimilated, if only for the reason that *it is an option* whether one commits to the truth of Christian basic beliefs in a sense in which, within the bounds of sanity, it is not an option whether to commit to the truth of perceptually basic beliefs.

A theory of permissible faith-ventures . . . and a pluralist implication

In fact, then, people do opt to commit to religious (and similar all-framing) worldviews, not on the basis of independent evidence supporting their truth but because of their upbringing within the relevant tradition, or because (as converts) they find a given worldview admirable and inspiring, or because they find or expect benefit in so doing. I maintain that they *can* be perfectly entitled to make such a 'doxastic venture' (taking to be true in practice a belief they recognize not to be supported by adequate independent evidence). The question is, though, under what conditions? Not all 'leaps of faith' are virtuous, even if they happen to latch onto the truth. Purely epistemic evaluation of a doxastic venture only takes you so far. Venturing *contrary to* the weight of your total available evidence is epistemically wrong. But venturing *beyond* what can in principle be rationally evidentially established is not always right – even though it may arguably involve no epistemic fault (beyond the fault you find in any such venture if you take the hard 'evidentialist' line I mentioned earlier). Where epistemic evaluation gives out, moral evaluation may yet apply – and the overall judgement of justifiability is here, as I have argued, anyway a moral one. A religious doxastic venture is permissible, I claim, if what motivates the venture is not morally flawed (thus ruling out wishful thinking, for example) and, as well, the worldview concerned depicts a morally good way for the world to be.[10]

Applying these criteria to my own case, I judge that faith-commitment to Christian belief on my naturalist euteleological understanding is morally justifiable. Arguably, there is some circularity arising from the moral assumptions I make in judging that the world's being fit for steadfast and hopeful pursuit of the good is itself a good way for the world to be (this may be a theologically loaded judgement: maybe an opponent would maintain that what makes steadfast and hopeful pursuit of the good itself admirable is precisely that it is *not* understood as grounded as an apt response to how things are). An opponent might also maintain that the amount and nature of the evil that exists in the world counts as strong evidence against the euteleological claim that existence is ultimately for the sake of the good. And I agree that, absent the appeal to revelation, that claim is fair. But 'dysteleological'

22   *John Bishop*

evil *does not contradict* the content of Christian revelation – not anyway on the account of that content that I have proposed. This, I believe, is an important point of contrast with the account of revelatory content given by personal omniGod theism.

Finally, I recognize that this way of justifying my own religious venture leaves it open that commitment to different and contrary all-framing world-views (religious and atheist/naturalist) may equally well be permissible. I welcome that pluralist implication. Given the facts of religious diversity, if any religious commitments are morally and epistemically permissible, then many (though not all) are. That *prima facie* judgement is confirmed on the 'modest fideist' account of the justifiability of faith-commitments that I favour.

Inclusivism without relativism

Having to allow a plurality of equally justifiable, but different and in some respects mutually contrary, religious commitments has important consequences for someone who, like myself, stands firmly within a particular religious tra-dition. Those consequences, however, emphatically do not include – as is sometimes suggested – accepting relativism with respect to religious truth. Important Christian truth-claims are, of course, rejected from other religious (and secular) all-framing perspectives that I, if I am to apply my own criteria consistently, must accept as commitments that carry for others the same kind of entitlement that I have to my own Christian commitment. From my perspective, others are entitled to be wrong! But that does not make me, in any interesting sense, an exclusivist (again, contrary to what is sometimes suggested).

I am not an exclusivist because, in the first place, I recognize the entitlement of others to hold commitments in significant respects contrary to mine, and I respect their stance as one that I might hold or have held myself (the modal-ity of this 'might' is subtle and worth a lengthier explication than I can here attempt). Loving others as myself, then, as I have promised to strive to do, I love them as committed to their stance in qualitatively the same way that I am to mine – and that generates in me a profound respect for religions not my own.

In the second place, when I bring the fact of the diversity of ethically and epistemically justifiable all-framing worldviews (religious and non-religious) into the scope of my own, Christian worldview, I recognize that this fact must cohere with my understanding of the divine purpose. I believe that this diversity comes under divine providence: God delights in the breadth of reli-gious disagreement as essential to the process of continuing evolution in the understanding of his self-revelation to humanity. And so I repudiate those aspects of my own tradition which are properly called 'exclusivist', which assume that God abhors the diversity, favouring and saving only those who adhere to a specific religious orthodoxy.

Nevertheless, it does follow from an understanding of religious diversity as ultimately in accordance with the divine will that, however much the many permissible religious worldviews differ, there must be a common core

A *'naturalist' Christian theism*   23

expressed variously in each. The evolving understanding of the positive cognitive content of each of these religious worldviews may be expected to show signs of convergence on such a common core. But the ineliminable mystery, or 'incomprehensibility' (beyond *full* comprehension), of the existentially significant reality to which all these worldviews are profoundly valuable human responses ensures that the diversity will persist throughout history. There will be no 'grand merger' into one commonly shared religion for all humanity. Yet, at a higher-order, we can – and must, for our very survival, perhaps – achieve a common respectful and loving tolerance of these ineliminable differences in religious and non-religious worldviews, and the overcoming of perspectives – religious and ideological – that resist that tolerance.

Notes

1 For a helpful recent discussion of the epistemology of revelation, see King (2008).
2 I defend this view in my essay on "Philosophy and Religious Commitment," in Bubbio and Quadrio (2011: 26–52).
3 I undertook this baptismal promise for myself at my confirmation on 8 October 1961.
4 See Bishop and Perszyk (2011) for a fuller articulation and defence of this version of the argument from evil.
5 I am greatly indebted to Thomas Harvey for convincing me – when technically I was his teacher in a graduate class in Auckland in 2009 – that the core classical divine attributes must be treated apophatically.
6 I have previously made the proposal that the universe has a euteleological explanation in collaborative work with Ken Perszyk. In Bishop and Perszyk (2014), we explore the associated understanding of the divine, placing particular emphasis on the question of how such an understanding can accommodate divine action, both in creation and in history.
7 I am indebted, again, to Thomas Harvey for the reminder that Aquinas' Aristotelian notion of an efficient cause is broader than our usual contemporary notion of efficient causality, which requires an efficient cause to be an ontologically (and typically temporally) prior producer of its effect (see Harvey's unpublished essay, "Divine Action and Divine Simplicity").
8 I prefer this traditional wording because its use of 'which' as the relative pronoun rather than the explicitly personal 'who' fits my view that it is a mistake, even while we are addressing him so intimately personally, to think that our Father actually is 'a' person.
9 For discussions of group action, see, for example, Copp (1979), De George (1983) and May (1987).
10 I articulate and defend this theory of permissible faith-ventures in Bishop (2007).

References

Bishop, J. 2007. *Believing by Faith: An Essay in the Epistemology and Ethics of Religious Belief.* Oxford: Clarendon Press.
Bishop, J. and K. Perszyk. 2011. "The Normatively Relativised Logical Argument from Evil." *International Journal for Philosophy of Religion* 70: 109–126.
Bishop, J. and Perszyk, K. 2014. "Divine Action beyond the Personal OmniGod." *Oxford Studies in Philosophy of Religion* 5: 1–21.

24 *John Bishop*

Bubbio P. and P. Quadrio (eds.). 2011. *The Relationship of Philosophy to Religion Today*. Newcastle-upon-Tyne, UK: Cambridge Scholars Publishing.

Burrell, D. 1998. "The Attributes of God: (a) Simpleness." In *Philosophy of Religion: A Guide to the Subject*, edited by B. Davies, 70–74. London: Cassell.

Copp, D. 1979. "Collective Actions and Secondary Actions." *American Philosophical Quarterly* 16: 177–186.

De George, R. T. 1983. "Social Reality and Social Relations." *Review of Metaphysics* 37: 3–20.

Findlay, J. 1955. "Can God's Existence Be Disproved?" In *New Essays in Philosophical Theology*, edited by A. Flew and A. MacIntyre, 47–56. London: SCM Press.

King, R. 2008. *Obstacles to Divine Revelation: God and the Reorientation of Human Reason*. London: Continuum.

May, L. 1987. *The Morality of Groups: Collective Responsibility, Group-based Harm, and Corporate Rights*. Notre Dame, IN: University of Notre Dame Press.

Plantinga, A. 2000. *Warranted Christian Belief*. Oxford: Oxford University Press.

Tillich, P. 1957. *The Dynamics of Faith*. New York: HarperCollins.

2 Ecological Christianity

Heather Eaton

Preamble: presuppositions

I studied Christian theology in depth (predominantly Catholic perspectives), and in particular feminist, liberation and ecological theologies and ethics. My positions have changed considerably over time. I maintain that there is no objective or truthful vantage point in the past or present. There is no 'religion' or Christianity outside of the myriad historical forms and the experiences and interpretations of adherents. The variations are limitless. Whatever theological enterprise is undertaken, it is in response to a particular rather than a universal question, in spite of comprehensive declarations. Further, all theology is autobiographical (Frederick Buechner, this volume): likely religious reflection of any kind.

My starting point for reflection on these questions is a loose composite of the following. *From the social sciences:* (i) justice, political and liberation movements, theories of social change; (ii) feminist concerns and gender analysis: patriarchy, misogyny, women's movements; (iii) ecological issues analyzed through economics, globalization, equity and justice. *From the study of religions:* (i) the development of 'religion' from the Upper Paleolithic (Neolithic revolution), axial age views and present pluralities; (ii) the plethora of historical and contemporary religions, and their distinctions in forms, worldviews, beliefs, images (Gods, Goddesses, spirits), context; (iii) most religions that ever were are no longer; specific religions are transitory, whereas religious sensibilities, quests or impulses are not; (iv) contemporary theories of religion and pluralist religious paradigms; (v) religious anthropologies: imagination/consciousness/experiences/spirituality; (vi) circumspection about theological and worldview assumptions; (vii) epistemology: more interest in *how* we know rather than *what*; (viii) postmodern epistemologies: humans construct reality; knowledge is mediated, socially constructed, and replete with bias and partial understanding; (ix) gender and ecological critiques, revisions and challenges to Christian theologies; (x) ecological issues and the challenges to the plurality of religions. *From the sciences:* (i) time: 13.7 billion years, space, and the expanding, complexifying universe; (ii) Earth sciences: history and evolutionary processes of 4.6 billion years; (iii) processes, dynamics,

26 Heather Eaton

emergent complexity, self-organizing systems; (iv) periods of extinction and regeneration of life pathways and forms; (v) study of the development and mechanisms of symbolic consciousness; (vi) ecological crisis: planetary systems (air, water, climate, biomass), diminished evolutionary pathways, species extinctions, toxins and pollutants. *My preoccupations:* religious responses to the planetary and regional ecological crises, gender autonomy, peace and theories of religion.

I see myself at the margins of the Christian tradition. The questions of this chapter [i.e., the questions posed by the editors] represent classical, somewhat dated, language to me. At times I will explain my response in light of traditional interpretations. The first section is longer than the others, as I delve into the quest for an adequate theory of religion, which underlies all the questions and responses.

How do you understand the nature of God (or divinity)?

To speak of God is to speak of how humans imagine and desire a plethora of matters under an umbrella term 'God' or other similar imagery. Regardless of the sources or claims of authority – scriptures, traditions and ecclesial bodies – discussing anything about God is to first locate the activity within the human imagination and the dynamics of symbolic consciousness. We can believe, speculate, ruminate and contemplate images, or enter alternative states of consciousness, but we cannot know the nature of God, or have any certainty about the existence of a divine entity. This is not an apophatic leaning. It is that humans invent Gods, Goddesses, energies and spirits, and for myriad reasons and purposes. That humans envision God(s) or divinity is irrefutable. This does not negate or reduce the validity of the activity, or suggest there is no divine referent outside of human imaginings.

"To what question is this the answer?" (Bernard Lonergan)

The topic of the nature of God follows diverse forms of reasoning: morality, truth, beauty, cosmology or nature. It is broached through distinct and detailed arguments: reason, evidence, will, submission, belief, and so on. There are numerous disciplines in the conversation now: cognitive sciences and embodiment, empathy and attachment theories, to name a few. Given this, my *modus operandi* is that I am not inclined towards speculative or highly abstract theology. I reject beliefs, concepts, doctrines or 'eternal truths' on the basis of tradition, authority, unverifiable revelations or non-evidentiary arguments.

My primary considerations are thus evidential and reasonable, not magical, supernatural or esoteric. More so than morality, I seek a coherent framework able to address the origins, emergence, histories and presence of 'religions'. I desire an epistemologically comprehensive view, one that includes a cosmological horizon and is capable of including phenomenological and scientific evidence. Cross-disciplinary dialogues, transversal rationality or bridge theories are beneficial. I also seek a view that grapples with the human impulse to experience and articulate something as sacred or divine, without confining it to culture, custom, social or moral systems, or psychological dynamics or attachment theories.

The realm and complexities of human experiences (not revelation, tradition, biblical texts, etc.) are my starting point. God-language is symbolic imagery and comes from and speaks to experiences. Likely, for some people, God-language is a formality, habit, tradition or culture, and in effect has little potency. For others, God-language comes from intense experiences entwined with emotions, intuitions, cognition, insights, dreams or imagination. It is then symbolized, represented and energized with divine imagery. For myself, the image of God, while potent, carries unwanted baggage. I will first assume that God-language, at its most intense, represents experiences that can only be articulated with ultimate language such as 'God' or 'divinity'.

A theory of religion

I will take a circuitous route in responding, as my thinking involves many inquiries and uncertainties. An adequate response to the question requires an operative theory of religion – a consistent theme here. For now, and assuming a functioning image of God or divinity, to probe in depth 'How does one understand the nature of God?' requires many disciplines: anthropology, psychology, sociology, cultural studies, and so on. Each of these disciplines offers a distinct theory (or theories) of religion. They share the observation that 'religion' and what we believe about God reflect such things as personality structures, cultural ethos and traditions. God-language is situated in symbolic representations of the world – worldviews – which organize societies and have a range of influences upon individual and social lives. Cognitive science and neuroscience are recent partners in this conversation, offering more new insights. I will not focus on these aspects, although I stress their importance for a comprehensive response.

Theology, in my view, is notoriously poor at presenting a robust theory of religion, regardless of the in-house premises (evil, morality, grace, redemption, ontology, teleology, aesthetics and the less convincing ones based on tradition, authority and revelation). The internal, self-referencing scaffolds are crumbling, to some extent. My current formulation is cobbled together from natural sciences, consciousness studies, symbolic imagination and the uneven field of 'religious experiences'. I will condense together parts that may have intellectual traction for a tentative theory of religion.

Symbolic consciousness

According to some (David Lewis-Williams, John Dixon, Gaston Bachelard), religious consciousness can be understood as a way of mediating and

28 Heather Eaton

managing the subtle dimensions of consciousness including dreams, intuitions, external and internal immensities, and the expansiveness of human symbolic representations, including representations of divinity.[1] Such depictions are nested in larger representations of the world, the latter being an activity innate to *homo sapiens*. It seems indisputable that humans require worldviews, social imaginaries or a coherent image of 'the world'.

Within the evolution and development of the hominid species emerged the capacity to navigate the world symbolically. The human brain evolved so as to enable us to engage with each other and the natural world through symbols (Deacon 1997). This capacity for symbolic interaction is a shared virtual reality or an intersubjective world – that is, a web of symbolic communications by which we indicate and experience parts of reality in indirect yet shared ways. Attachment and embodiment theories are further developing explanations as to how humans acquire a communally intelligible world (Sheets-Johnstone 2008: 194).

The formation of a consciousness that could function symbolically and sustain the capacity to manoeuver and coordinate images, thoughts, emotions, intuitions and insights was acquired over millennia. Experiences become layered with emotions, images, somatic sensations and movement, and memories. They are then interpreted, symbolized and re-experienced within an enlarged horizon of meaning. This symbolic, metaphoric and imaginative mode of being is the *modus operandi* of humans. A symbolic consciousness is the way humans process and navigate the world. It is not through or with symbols or images that we think and comprehend; it is within symbols, including religious symbols, that we do so. Humans are incapable of existing outside of symbolic renderings of the world. Thus, humans are best understood as a symbolic species.

Four aspects of symbolic consciousness are relevant to understanding the dynamics of religion. The first is that symbols participate with other symbols, and we interconnect symbols to make a systematic representation of the world. This postulates cohesion, provides an orientation and offers a capacity to navigate the whole of life as experienced. Further, these symbolically linked activities are nestled within worldviews or social imaginaries of the 'whole world'. Second, these worldviews are contextual, making religio-cultural diversities comprehensible. The symbol and its psychic power are undecipherable outside of the context and are not readily translatable or transferable. Thus, the power of religious symbols or God-language is impossible to perceive outside of both the context and the related experiences. 'God' or 'divinity' is a rich, perhaps the most rich, symbol. It will always be part of an interconnected symbolic system embedded in a larger worldview, enigmatic to outsiders. To be evocative, symbols must be invested with emotion and cognition, and they vary in complexity and purpose. Although the dynamics of symbolic functioning can be dissected into aspects involving the external realities of culture, religion and context and the internal realities of emotion, cognition, ideation and identity formation, this provides a superficial, even false, understanding. These facets are interrelated in ever-moving exchanges within a sea of influences.

Third, the use of tools, which predates 'religion', required the capacity to imagine and indicates a nascent form of symbolic consciousness. When a rock becomes a tool, it becomes more than it is. There is a surplus of meaning. In symbolic processes, something becomes other than or greater than it is. These 'symbolized' experiences are self-amplifying loops that increase the intensity and power of related experiences, which in turn can strengthen the symbol. This process of amplification was reinforced with the capacity to act with conscious purpose, wherein the self has a purpose and becomes 'more'. The elasticity of consciousness – that we experience more than we are, and our consciousness can transcend its own boundaries – is a critical component of divine imagery. We 'become more' within the intensity of divine symbols.

Symbolic vocabulary, imagery and depictions have changed, but the various mechanisms of symbolic consciousness – including symbols, gestures, signs, metaphors, rituals, imagination, abstractions and representations – remain the navigation apparatus of *homo sapiens*. An illustration may help. Earth symbolization is the earliest and most consistent religious symbolism across time and traditions. Earth activities impress upon human consciousness, often evoking intense affect – terror, joy, awe, inspiration, sadness, calm, love – which require representation. We are not only 'responding' to these realities. These are dynamics experienced within ourselves in rapport with the dynamics of the place. For example, experiences of caves or forests are described in terms of intimacy, intensity, envelopment or interiority. I find Gaston Bachelard's (1964) account of "*the immensity of the forest*" illuminates this well.[2] Bachelard understood that the immensity felt *in the forest* and perceived as *of the forest* is an immensity experienced *within our self-consciousness*. It is an *intimate immensity*, felt as an expansion of being. When encountered as such, the forest is deemed sacred by virtue of its immensity and otherness, which we perceive intimately within ourselves. We describe these experiences as mysterious, divine, sacred or eternal, as losing oneself and going deeper into a limitless world. Bachelard used the term 'the *material imagination*'.

I see possibilities here for a theory of religion and religious language that has explanatory power. It does not reveal the content of specific religious language but does indicate the power and potency of such language. This helps explain the multiple significance of God-language, as well as its lack of meaning. It also corroborates that there are no *a priori* reasons as to why religious claims, beliefs or doctrines are correct (Kirkpatrick 2005: 354). The categories of 'true' and 'false' are inapplicable. Religious symbols are active, alive or dynamic, or they are dying or dead.

God

From my own sensitivities and studies, there is a 'lure of the sacred'. There is something within the intensity of humans, as a species, that draws our attention to dimensions of reality beyond our direct knowing. There are depths to reality that the human mind or heart cannot know with clarity but are there nonetheless. Their presence presses on human consciousness. While religions have many aspects and functions, one is to make sense of the limits of human knowing, as well as time, space, interiority, beauty, goodness and suffering. We respond with images that are codified into beliefs, enmeshed with values, imbued with emotions and embedded into our identity. All these are active within talk of God. I would add 'truth', except that humans are too hasty to make truth-claims, and too certain once they are made.

I estimate that certain imagery is appealing for autobiographical reasons. For example, the query of a sacred aspect to reality has always preoccupied me, in spite of abandoning a feeble church relationship before age 12. Briefly, four aspects of my life have propelled this quest and shaped preferences and values prior to academic studies: early fascination with stars, sky, Earth and life; familiar suffering; endless hours on the shores of Lake Huron, Canada, where I lived; and seven years in L'Arche communities with Jean Vanier during my twenties.[3] These facets moulded a strong desire for intelligibility and coherence, inclusive of profound sensitivities towards and appreciation of the natural world and the cosmological realm, and for an understanding of suffering and a thirst for justice. It seemed evident to me that we live in a '*divine milieu*' (Teilhard de Chardin). I cannot prove this, but I would stake my life on it.

I am not attracted to any claims about God that assume certainty, for several reasons. One, there is no certainty. Two, the plethora of Christian images of God are collectively incoherent. They are a jumbled assortment: present, absent; static, dynamic; loving, punitive; accepting, judgemental, forgiving; omnipotent, omniscient; patriarchal, misogynist; law-maker, law-breaker; father, friend, lover; elsewhere, everywhere; and so on. Images are used to support innumerable values, political views, peace, war, wealth, change or stasis, etc. The current western climate encourages images that are immanent, embedded, creative and supportive for some, and for others it is quite different. Three, I agree with Mary Daly: if God is male, then the male is God (Daly 1985: 19). Whatever images we operate within structure our inner and outer lives, regardless of their foundations. Four, I am offended by all the God-talk and Christian teachings that denigrate this world, that claim human origins and destiny are 'elsewhere' and presume a better and future life 'somewhere else' uniting humans and God. As such, the Christian tradition, overall, functions as an inoculation against 'this life' – to varying degrees. Classical fall-redemption theology is not persuasive to me. I remain unconvinced about both the fall and the redemption aspects. Hegemonic Christian God-language and teachings are rooted in anthropocentrism and attitudes of human superiority and supremacy to the degree I consider it to be a colossal sin of arrogance and error. Five, I am intellectually suspicious and apophatic.

Ecological Christianity   31

I am attracted to particular images: Elijah did not find God in the earthquake, hurricane or fire but in the quiet breeze of the evening (1 Kings 19:12); Pseudo Dionysius' *"God is the hidden darkness of a brilliant silence."* Langdon Gilkey suggests that the best we can do is to intuit traces of the divine. Joan Chittister says that we should be wary of anyone who knows a lot about God. Yet, whatever divinity is, if we fix our gaze there, it orients us, changes the reference points from self-interest to something larger than ourselves. We become 'situated' in greater horizons, aligned with some other *élan vital* (Bergson) or a zest for life within yet beyond our own existence.

I am more drawn to imagery of God that deals with origins and history than with morality and evil, although not decisively. God-language is to be intelligible and commensurate with current knowledge. It has to be about the breadth and depths of reality. Thus it must take into account the 13.7 billion-year cosmogenesis, in a universe of over 100 billion galaxies and full of dark matter. It must be intelligible in the face of 4.6 billion years of Earth dynamics, of processes of evolution that mostly did not include, or design for, humans. It must accept that humanity emerged from Earth processes as a self-conscious component of Earth and a member of an Earth community in a living biosphere. 'All this reality', when contemplated, expands consciousness, cultivates interiority, situates and enhances a sense of self, develops humility and gratitude and evokes reverence. These are religious responses to the intimate immensities within which we live.

Finally, something must account for all this creativity, ingenuity, intelligence, complexity and dazzling magnificence – that is not from or about us. Most customary God-language is unable to incorporate these dimensions or is inadequate and flaccid. *Divine milieu* comes the closest. Intelligent design theories of God are not persuasive, as they are replete with undefended theological presuppositions, anthropocentrism and a dubious teleology. Also, that 'all this reality' is by chance, random or meaningless is a *non sequitur*. I may be wrong.

I share with those who conceive of (or perceive) divinity or sacredness as embedded, within and immanent. God is a verb rather than a noun. We are enveloped by and within the divine milieu. We have sensitivities to 'spirituality', to a depth dimension, to something akin to divinity, because it is there. I am a classical panentheist – the divine is present and beyond, at least beyond our knowing. Thus, for myself, divinity is both a perception and an act of the imagination.

Christianity is ill-equipped to deal with my concerns: contemporary cosmology, evolution, the multiplicity of religions, and the ecological crisis. The commitment to salvation from Earth to another life elsewhere is an obstacle to the religious sensitivities I value. I find it difficult to draw much from the tradition or from customary God-language. I think that evolution and symbolic consciousness offer substantial aspects towards a theory of religion, but to date few theologians are involved.

32   *Heather Eaton*

What is your understanding of such central Christian doctrines as the Trinity, the Incarnation, the atonement, and the resurrection of the dead?

Given my position that religious language is experiential, symbolic, imaginative and a response of human consciousness rather than an injected revelation into human history, I will bypass most of the histories of beliefs and interpretations of these doctrines.

The Trinity

The doctrine of the Trinity has a long history, with multiple interpretations. What people actually suppose the Trinity to be varies beyond recognition. I am not convinced that the Trinity is a functioning doctrine any more. It is not alive in the religious imagination of most Christians I encounter, except as an insensible, at times rigid, belief. Nothing in their life experiences relates to this image of God as one and three persons, or to the East-West discussions about 'procession' (as in the *filioque*, the procession of the Son from the Father and the Holy Spirit). The doctrine of the Trinity rarely illuminates something vital about life, in personal, social or larger horizons of meaning. People/theologians 'believe' in it (for different reasons) and may know the historical variations. Yet belief does not generate a living symbol. Belief as such is a type of Gnosticism: a form of religiosity the tradition has opposed. The Trinity has no authentic religious meaning in a Gnostic form, from my standpoint.

The only version of the Trinity that makes sense to me is, alas, my own, and I am fairly sure that it falls outside the traditional boundaries. I consider the Trinity to be an extraordinary constellation of images that are experientially meaningful. The three parts, taken separately and as a unity, are images containing packages of meaning. What it means to me has little or no bearing on what it means for others.

The image of God, in this instance, refers to an immanent and transcendent 'activity'. The language of creator, creativity and sustainer also resides within this imagery. The experiences to which this refers are multiple: origin stories (religious, scientific), creativity and stability, assurances as to the validity and nobility of life and that a mature response to life involves humility, gratitude and reverence. God, as imaged within the Trinity, serves as a constant reminder that we do not know much about the breadth and depth of reality and that we are confronted with and yet enveloped by mystery. This symbol of God enhances awareness that there are realities and reference points outside of and beyond ourselves and that an expansive horizon is a worthy focal point. Last, such an image of God functions to dampen certainties and encourage radical openness.

The image of Jesus offers a different set of insights. I find high Christologies problematic for a dozen different reasons. A few are these: the obstacles

Ecological Christianity   33

in interreligious activities; feminist theologies; Christian imperialism; other-worldly emphasis; and the limitations of fall-redemption theologies. Thus I opt for low Christologies and a historical Jesus. As such, Jesus, in the Trinity, serves as one image of the values and virtues of a human person. The maleness of Jesus is overlooked in favour of what can be known of his ethics. Jesus as a non-conformist and as an educated, ethical and cultural critic is important. Jesus exemplifies one who broke various laws for a greater justice, to reduce suffering out of compassion or to expose religious idolatry. Jesus, insofar as anyone knows, was a God-centred, prayerful human. The invitation to give one's life for the betterment of the whole is a weighty ethical position – extremely challenging and worthy of consideration. Various feminists have contributed to this symbolic rendering of Jesus and refer to him in terms of an ethical or spiritual teacher, a prophet, a human exemplar, a person embodying the biblical themes of liberation or justice, a Christian archetype or a way of Christoform living. This is not the conventional image of *Jesus as saviour*, and it is not situated within a fall-redemption theological worldview. It is loosely biblically based, with an emphasis on what is known of the person Jesus and his historical activities. There are other such teachers in human history.

From another angle, Jesus in the Trinity functions to instill two meanings to 'incarnation'. Again, from a low Christology and symbolic stance, Jesus as an (not the) image of God gives traction to human rights and the validity and worthiness of human life. On a larger scale, the emphasis can be put less on Jesus the human and more on the concept of incarnation. What is incarnated is religiously important. This view can be expanded to include the Earth community, so that all forms of life are a mode of divine presence. The symbol of Jesus does not have to be limited to humanity – it can be emphasized as incarnation writ large. All matter and life are divine incarnations (Teilhard de Chardin and Thomas Berry). This understanding is found within other religious and spiritual traditions.

While the latter interpretation of incarnation is reasonable, I do not develop it as there are more effective ways to envisage a divine significance to the Earth. Others connect incarnation with the resurgence in the concept of creation and orient this towards ecological concerns. For both, the central problem is that many Christian doctrines are rooted in or tied to commitments to an afterlife. I do not share these commitments.

I have used the interpretation of Jesus as a divine incarnation to remind Christians with otherworldly aspirations that what happens in this material world is of religious significance. Such an interpretation can also stretch the imagination and religious horizon and raise the possibility that we do not need to be saved from Earth life. What I oppose are customary theological positions, efficiently formulated on a bumper sticker: the iconic image of the Earth from space with the phrase 'Jesus: don't leave Earth without him'.

The spirit within the Trinity functions, for me, as an image of creativity, change, surprise and wisdom. It reminds me that nothing is closed, including 'revelation', and including the canon. It counters fatalism, predestination or predetermined consequences. The image of the spirit as dynamic, vital, creative and unpredictable translates into a stance of radical openness as a requisite for a spiritually attentive life. Once again, this cautions against certainties and eternal truths.

Earlier in my life I pondered that the role of the spirit within the doctrine of the Trinity signified that evil and injustice could not be the finality of a situation. There are always life-giving activities beneath appearances, even in the most dire circumstances. Life will emerge from death, not triumphant, but significant. Now I consider that there are only potentially life-giving options. Injustice, evil and destruction can prevail. After extensive work on gender injustices and the ostensibly intractable nature of the oppression of women, I am ambivalent about the inevitability of life-giving possibilities. In-depth study of ecological ruin, humanity's inability to react, and the accumulating knowledge that the Cenozoic era of 65 million years is coming to an end due to anthropogenic causes increase the plausibility of the view that destruction can be the last word. Some forms of life, drastically diminished, will find a way, but the pathways of rejuvenation and evolutionary possibilities are being devastated.

However, I do deliberate that the image of the spirit within the Trinity also indicates that situations can change: nothing is determined. There are options and possibilities outside of our realms. This image is very powerful as it means that there are no fixed interpretations, no fixed eternal truths, no sacred/secular divide, and everything is of religious significance. Thus Earth sciences, the theories of emergent complexity and adaptation, of cosmology and quantum dynamics are all pertinent to a religious worldview. For myself, these are now primary religious references and supersede the Bible and the tradition as sources. Interpreted as I do, this symbol requires attentiveness to the present, which in turn requires a vulnerability, lack of certainty, wakefulness and listening to all aspects of life.

Finally, the Trinity, as a whole, functions as an image of relationality, interdependence and community. Nothing is isolated, discrete and extraneous. This Trinitarian image educates the moral imagination in important ways for a sustainable future. The Trinity, taken separately and together, functions as a Christian life-teaching, meaning one cannot be a Christian adherent unless one takes seriously all three realms and their interconnection.

That the Trinity is symbolized as persons is likely due to the fact that this is the most intimate and vital image operative in human psyches. It could be imaged in other manners. Although Jesus is difficult to image other than as a person, the symbols of God and spirit incorporate many other symbols. Thus the Trinity could have more symbolic capacity than it usually does.

However, as mentioned, I do not see the Trinity functioning with much personal or cultural power, in spite of its established and liturgical durability. It could be expanded and enlivened in the manner described earlier. However, changing the content of religious symbols is not a linear process. It does not occur readily or with precision and requires a community.

Ecological Christianity 35

The Incarnation

Most cultures have notions of incarnation: spirits, traits, Gods/Goddesses, divine attributes, destructive or constructive forces or energies, etc. How they function depends on the culture and context. I assume that incarnations serve diverse purposes – for example, to explain and deal with various existential challenges, to specify moral limits, to provide social boundaries, to ritualize undesirable sentiments, sensations or actions, etc.

The Christian interpretations of the incarnation are of Jesus, and what this means for humanity has varied over its history. Today, at one end of the spectrum, the incarnation is the high Christology of Jesus as Christ, saviour and redeemer, one sent by God, perhaps pre-existing, and who will return. The questions that intrigue me are about how a symbol of incarnation functions. Its veracity, on its own, is not relevant or possible to answer.

High Christologies often lead to the customary concepts and activities of Christian imperialism, which form an exclusive inter-religious paradigm. The maleness of Jesus as God incarnate continues to be used to justify male clergy, authority and leadership. It can mean that to be Christian is to maintain a church/world divide and be focused on collecting converts to the belief-system. It can mean that the ecological crisis is irrelevant to the ultimate afterlife realms. Such certainty closes the mind to other investigations. In a more subtle form, because salvation has occurred, truth has been revealed and eternal rewards await, there is not a strong impetus to address the severe injustices and the systemic and complex problems of the world.

Although it is difficult to define with precision and clarity, Christianity is an aggressive religion, and not simply due to the declarations of ultimate truth. All religions make universal, teleological claims. What is evident is that within the Christian worldview operates an image that the world is not acceptable as it is. The doctrines of the fall, albeit diverse, share an understanding that humanity, the world and 'all of creation' are not as God intended due to various inadvertent failings: fallen angels, original or other sin, misused freedom, human disobedience, wilful ignorance. Anthropologically, humanity is construed with varying degrees and modes of sinfulness. As a result, there is death, and the divine is absent, obscure or imperceptible.

Salvation, in the form of God incarnated through Jesus, offers a way to be saved from this corrupt creation, sinfulness, mortality and the failings of one's body. Humans will be saved to another dimension – redeemed, healed and (re)united with God in an afterlife. It is important to grasp that life and existence are interpreted to be inadequate or flawed and thus unacceptable. The incarnation is the symbol of that repair.

The inadequacy of the world can lead to anticipating the afterlife, or aggressive actions to bring salvation to the world in this interim time. It is an impetus to change the world, with divergent forms of action. It can compel missionaries to convert peoples and cultures to Christianity. Or, it compels some to redress injustices. Many liberation theologies operate with a high Christology but with a view that redemption is a historical possibility and required project – even a precursor to afterlife possibilities measured in terms of incarnated justice, not converts. Although abbreviated here, these high Christological incarnational formulations are prevalent across most Christian theologies, past and present.

At the other end of the spectrum, there is no 'incarnation'. Jesus is a symbolic salvific figure, prophet and paradigm; unique but not exclusive, one among many who call the human community to authenticity. He models a Christian way of life. Given that humans require worldviews, this is an option. This position conveys a positive anthropology. There is no need for salvation as such, as there was no fall. However, there are vulnerabilities, limits, unjust suffering, systemic oppressions, greed, unrestricted desires and other problems that require transformation. Emphasis is given to the ethics of Jesus. This proposal leaves room for interreligious exchanges, supports liberation theologies, disputes otherworldly afterlife theologies, defies hierarchy and confronts christofascism. This is a different scaffold for Christian theology, one that is more attractive to pluralists, like me.

The atonement

Atonement is a human capacity to re-order and restore an injustice, imbalance or transgression. There are multiple forms of atonement in every society, and even among mammals such as primates, wolves, dogs, elephants, etc. It is a need, often ritualized, in social animals, and likely has evolutionary usefulness. Atonement is a very powerful deed. One person and one significant act can become symbols of reparation for whole communities, healing wounds and rifts from previous eras and situations. The process of atonement and its accompanying symbols and rituals engage and transform human depths and can alter seemingly intractable situations or peoples.

In the traditional Christian worldview, the actual sin requiring atonement is not clear to me. Original sin, fallen nature or other comprehensive notions of sin do not make sense. The relationship between Jesus, the historical person, and this universal sin is not cohesive. That Jesus was executed for his beliefs and actions is difficult to link to a meaningful notion of atonement. Atonement, in Christian contexts, is virtually always rooted in a high Christology in a fallen and sinful world needing salvation. Jesus' death is the atonement, as some guarantor of salvation. To me, this is a highly abstracted worldview that is obsolete. And these theologized versions of Christic atonement do not illuminate the actual existential realities where atonement should or does occur.

The impulse for a moral system is endemic to humans. All communities create moral codes, but the content is highly variable. They differentiate among intentions, acts, degrees of moral trespassing, culpability and reparation. What constitutes morality is relative, not absolute. Thus it is not evident that trespassing society's moral boundaries and the Christian notion of sin have much in common. However, I would say there is 'sin': various forms of moral transgressions in individuals, in actions and within social systems. These require atonement and redress. The belief that atonement is possible, that people can feel remorse and be forgiven for unspeakable crimes is enormously important, especially when restoration or reparation is impossible. These versions of sin and atonement make sense to me. But in the face of anthropogenic species extinction and ecological sin, even these ideas are ineffectual.

The resurrection of the dead

This theological doctrine is speculative, consisting of beliefs without evidence of any kind. Perhaps it reflects the desire to live forever, the fear of death and the difficulty of severed relationships given that the barrier between life and death is absolute. I cannot fathom an intelligible world where humans exist and reunite after death. It seems like magical, wishful thinking. It may be correct, but I am more than skeptical. It defies all other processes of the universe and the natural world. (The topic of the afterlife is discussed further later in this paper.)

What are your views regarding the historicity of the New Testament account of Jesus, including his purported miracles and resurrection?

The New Testament is not a historical record. It is a theological document, although some historical facts can be gleaned from it. Historical accuracies are contested. I proceed with caution in terms of historical precision. I have no doubt that Jesus lived, was born in Bethlehem and died in Jerusalem, was a reformer of Judaism, had followers from distinct streams of Judaism and was executed under Roman law. This information is in other documents. It is likely he had respectful relations with some women, which were uncustomary. It is probable he was informed about aspects of Judaism and was an itinerant teacher and preacher, as were many others. He must have contested several authorities with his teachings and behaviours, enough to be executed.

As I understand the cultural ethos at the time of Jesus, to talk of miracles was not uncommon, similar to faith healings, speaking in tongues and other such activities. If the question refers to miracles as supernatural or that which breaks with natural processes, then I am disinclined to believe in miracles. While many of life's mysteries are not decipherable, there is not a supernatural stratum or miraculous or magical activity interspersed with existing complex processes. It is evident that humans have a propensity to expand and enhance, to amplify and symbolize events or people in order to emphasize their impact or give them deeper significance. Magical thinking is common, but it signifies interpretative processes, not external actualities.

38   *Heather Eaton*

The resurrection is a very powerful symbol. Whatever Jesus meant to his followers, be that through his person and/or his teachings, it did not die at his death. The impact was too great to subside and be forgotten. I can imagine that the amplification of meaning around Jesus' life and death fortified the symbolic power. The resurrection is not literal. Yet the intense influence of Jesus' life must have been factual, as his symbolic power increased after his death. It was an *intimate immensity* within the followers that became contagious to those who never met him.

What is your understanding of the afterlife?

We all need an intelligent conversation about the resurrection, the afterlife and eternity. As I see it, the evidence is scant. There are myriad beliefs: that life is resurrected, reincarnated, (re)absorbed into a greater Self, returned to a Great Mystery or Spirit, returned to Mother Earth, and so on. These beliefs signify many things. The perception that life does not end with death is persistent within the human psyche. The most likely explanation is that the imperative to live overpowers an awareness of death. It is a genetic, biological and instinctual imperative: a cellular and species life force. Perhaps it is a recognition that everything – atoms, molecules, biomass – is reprocessed and is important to something else. Perhaps it is the fact that we arose from, are embedded in and surrounded by an immense project of life. Or, seemingly banal, if one is alive, one is not dead: we have no knowledge about death, and we cannot imagine *not being*. Other explanations are that the embodied empathetic disposition and evolutionary attachment capabilities were inscribed into our neural circuitry long before the symbolized theories of an afterlife. The afterlife symbology may be a logical extension of our evolutionary dynamics. Thus an end to life and the loss of loved ones genuinely feels contrary to 'how it should be'.

Death is not 'embraced' by any species, although some animals seem to resign themselves to dying – they stop eating or moving, or leave the group. Elephants recognize dying and death. They grieve it, especially for those who are cherished: mothers, offspring, siblings and friends. The loss of close relationships through death is mourned in many species. Humans, as a symbolic species, have countless rituals, symbols and meanings surrounding death.

Although each religious worldview has some perception that life does not end with death, the Christian tradition has built a fortress here. The fortress of salvation ideology combined with afterlife beliefs are a barricade to rethinking the resurrection and the wishful thinking of an afterlife where we are somehow reunited and preserved for eternity. Christianity has a particular resistance to and denial of death. I think that this is because Christianity has developed an extreme opposition to, even refusal of, the conditions of life as given: vulnerability, finitude and mortality. This rejection of life's limits has created distortions throughout theological assertions. The beliefs surrounding the afterlife are interlaced with those of salvation, which are connected to the 'nature of creation'. Throughout Christian history, in one way or another, the phenomenological order (or just humanity) is fallen, corrupt, sinful, imperfect or incomplete. Death is the result. Humans must be saved, redeemed or restored from death. Christianity promises eternal life. Such an afterlife is given only to humans, due to Christianity's strong anthropocentrism. Although some now talk of creation also being redeemed, I have no idea what that means.

From my viewpoint, the conditions of life are not sinful, but the refusal is. I agree with Ivone Gebara that the primal sin is negating the non-negotiable existential circumstances of life. The consequences are escapist spiritualties, otherworldly ideations. The result is a *fall* into domination – of land, animals and peoples (see Ruether 2000: 105). For Gebara, our salvation is found in returning to our embodied selves, away from escapism and domination, and embracing with joy and sorrow the genuine limitations, richness and struggles of life in community and solidarity with all life.

We have the privilege of conscious life for an instant, in a dynamic universe. And we die. Given what we know about the universe and the Earth, how can we still be convinced of our ultimate importance in the scheme of things? We are simply not the reference point for the amplitude of reality. I think that beliefs about the resurrection, eternity and the afterlife need to be abandoned. Apart from their epistemological frailty and verification limits, we need to (re)turn to creation, humanity and nature. This would sharpen our appreciation for existence as given – ours and that of the entire Earth community, *the divine milieu*. It could heighten our awareness of an indwelling divine or sacred presence, one in which we live and have our being. Perhaps that would be enough salvation for a lifetime.

Do you accept the traditional Christian teaching of the resurrection of the body?

No, for all the reasons mentioned, I do not. I also do not accept a body-soul separation. Here is the conventional teaching, from the *Pocket Catholic Catechism*:

> We not only believe that the human soul is immortal, but that the human body is destined to rise immortal from the grave. Unlike our souls, which as spiritual substances are naturally immortal, our bodies are mortal by nature. They were not created subject to death, according to God's original plan for mankind [*sic*]. But the sin of our first parents deprived them and their descendants of the gift of bodily immortality. All of us must die because we are all sinners. One of the great benefits of Christianity to human wisdom is its clear teaching about both spiritual and bodily immortality.

How is it "clear"? This makes no sense to me – not any part of it. Not even as a spiritual intuition. It comes from an archaic Greek anthropology

40 *Heather Eaton*

and worldview that are obsolete and are now absurd, groundless beliefs. I may be wrong. If I am, and there is a resurrection of the body, I would prefer my more youthful body. It would follow that for those who die very young, very old, or frail, sick or injured, special bodily adjustments must be made.

How do you view the nature of the human person? For example, do you accept some form of dualism, where the human person consists of a body and a soul?

The nature of the human person is a rather large and vague question. One's response will depend on one's starting point, from which anthropology and from what discipline one begins: for example, mind/body studies, cognitive research, evolutionary psychology or consciousness research. In general, I consider that the question about dualisms of body and soul represent an outdated anthropology.

My starting point is the human animal in an evolutionary schema. We need to understand ourselves as emergent from and in continuity with the biosphere. We are also integrated into its processes: we require oxygen and are thus dependent on photosynthesis; we require water, and are thus reliant on a sophisticated hydrological cycle; our food depends on multiple life networks, etc. Over 50 per cent of our DNA is shared with all life forms, and 98 per cent with bonobos, our closest kin. As a species, most fundamentally, we are a social animal, mammalian and a relatively recent form of primate. Our differentiation from other primates does not reside in language, tool-making, mating for life, intricate social systems, rituals, or consciousness and self-consciousness. Even our claim to being the only animal with a moral compass is unfounded, as many animals have developed refined moral codes (Bekoff and Pierce 2009).

What differentiates *homo sapiens* is the form of consciousness; its elasticity and its limitless and potent symbol-making capacities. While other species navigate by sight, smell, sound and other sensory faculties; can swim, fly or run with speed; and can use claws, teeth, strength or poisons when needed, we are comparatively feeble in these capabilities. We navigate the world and defend ourselves within worldviews. We use a huge range of cues that never function in isolation: physical signals, facial expressions, gestures and vocal tones interpreted through cognition, emotion and intuition. Outside of our awareness, there are acute but relatively unconscious activities that combine movement, sound, action, sensations and moods with wind, rain, clouds and colour, and blend them into interpretive schemas that combine thoughts, emotions, memories and images that can mean purpose, destiny, safety, meaninglessness, etc.

Humans use interpretative networks. Some offer theories of multiple intelligence, while others suggest that humans are like a Swiss army knife with specialized intelligences or 'blades', including linguistic, musical, logico-mathematical, spatial, bodily-kinesthetic and personal intelligence, for reflecting on the self, and another for reflecting on others. The mind is not a general-purpose tool – it has specialized modules to solve different kinds of problems and is always a blend of thought, emotion, images, intuitions, memories and other more subtle functions. These cognition theories are receiving considerable attention. Another line of research, equally prolific, is that of embodied intelligibility schemas, which are dismantling any mind/body dualisms. In fact, there are no mind/body or body/soul dualisms that are consistent with contemporary anthropologies. The working hypotheses are holistic, postulating differentiated and interrelated facets that never function independently, except in the ways we conceive of them.

The language of 'soul', or the more recent version of 'spirit', reflect both a dualism and a worldview that I do not share. The intuition of interest is that the uniqueness, complexity and intensity of each person are startling, even astonishing. As a species, we can bond deeply between persons such that our lives are intertwined and amplified, and the loss is at times insufferable. While all this may have evolutionary significance, I think the distinctive nature of each human is of ultimate significance . . . to us. We want ourselves, our person, to continue on and cannot bear that we might be a fleeting presence. It would be a heartless universe, which is unacceptable. So we image some body/soul dichotomy that solves this existential angst and relate it to the previously mentioned theories of a resurrection and an afterlife.

How would you go about supporting or defending your acceptance of Christianity?

To whom? The arguments I would rally to my cause would depend on the audience. If I were defending my views to Christians, I would begin by developing a theory of religion such that it is evident that Christianity is one religion among many. I would describe how symbols function within human consciousness and become systematized in social imaginaries or worldviews. Because symbols amplify experiences, the power of religions and their ability to harness psychic energy are defensible. These are connected to the need to manage multiple layers of exterior and interior existential pressures and insights.

I would defend my tentativeness around the ultimate truths of Christianity by emphasizing the fact that many religions no longer exist and that the content of particular religions in the larger scheme of human societies is both fluid and temporary. I would discuss hermeneutics and social constructions of worldviews and show that historically there is no such actuality as 'Christianity'. There are countless forms, interpretations, contradictions and inconsistencies. I would further defend my caution around hegemonic interpretations due to the limits I see within the Christian tradition's overall ethos and anthropocentrism. I would suggest that Christianity has insights, teachings and wisdom that are valuable, but not indispensible, for the contemporary challenges we face. They are one set of symbolic responses to the existential challenges, demands and angst of human life.

42   *Heather Eaton*

I would suggest that given the 13.7 billion-year cosmogenesis and the 100 billion other galaxies, it is simply not reasonable to claim that Christianity is the main reference point for all this reality. I would defend my absolute conviction that religious sensibilities – at their most profound – are responding to a depth dimension active in the phenomenological order.

If I were defending these views to scientists, I would bring in more evolutionary science and cognitive and anthropological studies about religion. I may open a cautious conversation on religious experiences. If my case for Christianity were before ecological activists, who are often allergic to religion, I would likely discuss spirituality and social movements from various religious traditions. These are conversations I actually have where my overall goal is the validity of 'religious experiences' prior to discussing Christianity.

I am not certain of my acceptance of Christianity, or even what acceptance means. I have learned and do learn from the tradition and seek to expand my interpretive horizons with respect to the concerns and questions I have. But I do not feel compelled to stay inside the periphery, wherever that is. Further, I don't think notions to do with the 'acceptance' or 'rejection' of a particular religion are viable in a postmodern world swirling with images and amalgamations of worldviews. I am also convinced religions are unstable in the current global situation and are epistemologically challenged beyond their current modes of interpretation. Their self-understanding does not correspond to contemporary challenges. Christianity and other world religions originated and matured within worldviews that are outdated. They are not prepared to accommodate the radical pluralities that exist today. It is difficult for Christianity in its hegemonic forms to absorb contemporary insights or meet current cultural and ecological needs.

I appreciate the words of Rabbi Schachter: "Many religious structures have become ossified remnants of another time. All traditional systems – Moses, Jesus, Mohammed, and Buddha – were embedded in the social and economic systems in which they arose. Their reality maps are obsolete" (quoted in Barasch 2000). I am also attentive to Karl Jasper's notion of an 'axial age' and the prospect that we are entering a second axial age (see Berry 1988 and Cousins 1999). The magnitude of the ecological crisis is unprecedented in human history and is challenging the interpretative frameworks of religions beyond their capacities. Berry makes a provocative statement that has captivated my attention for years: "any effective response to these issues requires a religious context. . . . We cannot do without the traditional religions, but they cannot presently do what needs to be done. We need a new type of religious orientation" (Berry 1988: 87). Many affirm, as do I, that a new horizon or context of interpretation is entering into human awareness. It includes a genuine multi-religious understanding requiring a vigorous theory of religion. It entails that what is known about planetary processes and evolution be taken seriously (Eaton 2007). For Berry, this also means a new religious dimension at a cosmic level. Further, I am more interested in religious responses to the ecological crisis, precisely because I experience the natural world and all it entails as a *divine milieu*. I will draw from many wells to do this. Revitalizing a sense of the Earth as sacred is more important than defending Christianity.

How do you see the relation between your Christian faith and reason (or rationality)? In line with this, what is your understanding of rationality? And what role is played by reason (as well as philosophy and science) in informing your religious beliefs and commitments?

The whole thrust of my work is about seeking an intelligible and robust theory of religion that affirms religious sensibilities and the human quest for and sensitivities toward a sacred or divine dimension to reality as we encounter it. It must be reasonable and rational, commensurate with the best knowledge of the phenomenological realm. To engage reason and rationality means that one does not rely on magic, miracles, supernatural interventions from undetectable dimensions, revelations that cannot be verified, esoteric knowledge or ultimate truths from religious texts that have great insights and wisdom but operate within now untenable worldviews. Tradition, authority, habit and longevity are also not necessarily 'reasonable'.

Religious insights, knowledge, teachings or revelations are *always* in extremely symbolized forms, with layers of interpretations and meanings. It is the failure to understand the nature of religious knowledge that accelerates the slide into fundamentalisms, among other factors (resistance to modernity, overwhelming pluralities, social violence, poverty, ecological stress, etc.).

Perpetuating symbols that no longer function in the religious imagination – in order to preserve traditions – is also stifling Christianity. (I am speaking mainly about the more authoritarian traditions: Reform, Roman Catholic, Orthodox, Evangelical, Pentecostal.) Christianity is often presented as either true or false. But the theological theories of the nature of these truths are exceedingly impoverished – or never get outside of academia. One is a believer or not. Belief in what is nonsensical, not reasonable or rational is often a sign of lunacy . . . in other circles. It is rational to be a religious person, but not using the conventional explanations. Overall, I do not think Christianity is presented as reasonable.

From a different angle, those who give primacy to the affective rather than the intellectual/cognitive dimension of material experience and imagination intrigue me. As Gaston Bachelard wrote, humans live in a material realm, and engage the world by valorizing it:

> It is not *knowledge* of the real which makes us passionately love it. It is rather *feeling* which is the primary and fundamental value. One starts by loving nature without knowing it, by seeing it well. . . . Then, one seeks it in detail because one loves it on the whole, without knowing why.
>
> (Bachelard, cited in Kaplan 1972: 4, emphases in original)

44 Heather Eaton

The emphasis on the sentiments dovetails with aspects of the work of the American pragmatist, C.S. Peirce. He wrote about three developments of the mind: the rational, the progressive and the instinctual mind. The rational is the most recent in evolutionary development, hence the most immature. The conclusion is that the instinctive impulses, sentiments, dreaming, imagination and memory – the community of passions – are the more mature. The rational mind requires this community of passions for optimal functioning (Halton 2007: 45–6).

Faith, as I see it, is not opposed to reason. Faith does not begin at the limits of reason and is not confined to the realm of 'just believe'. It is not content. Faith is an existential stance towards existence. Is life absurd, meaningless, incongruous and empty? Or is life a privilege, a thrill, a gift to be responded to with gratitude and reverence? Although challenging to defend, the latter is a faith stance – faith that the project of the universe, of Earth, evolution, life and our lives is worthy and good. We are surrounded by intimate immensities that evoke reverence and continually remind us that we are not the main reference point. This is faith. Suffering, injustice, poverty and diminished existence all hamper – but oddly do not make impossible – a faith response. Faith is reasonable, to me.

Although reason and rationality are essential, they are insufficient. The primary mode of knowing in western societies is analytic. Analysis exposes patterns, systems, causes and effects and unmasks power dynamics. But it cannot open the door to profound insights. Awe is a different way of knowing – a dimension of religious awareness. Abraham Heschel remarks: "Awe is a sense for the transcendence, for the reference everywhere to mystery beyond all things. It enables us to perceive in the world intimations of the divine. . . . What we cannot comprehend by analysis, we become aware of in awe" (1983: 3). Wonder and awe cannot be analyzed, only experienced. Again, Heschel is eloquent: "To become aware of the ineffable is to part company with words"; and "We can never sneer at the stars, mock the dawn or scoff at the totality of being. Sublime grandeur evokes unhesitating, unflinching awe. Away from the immense, cloistered in our own concepts, we may scorn and revile everything. But standing between earth and sky, we are silenced by the sight" (p. 2).

What is the relation between your church or religious affiliation and your work as a philosopher?

I have been an academic theologian and engaged intellectual for twenty years, and previously worked or studied in explicitly Christian contexts for fifteen years: thirty-five years in total. I am now in a Conflict Studies Department, with a focus on gender, ecology, religion/spirituality and peace. I have virtually abandoned the institutional church and what is proffered as 'the tradition'. I have a tenuous relationship with a particular church and have been a regular member of a house church of about twenty-five people for twelve years. The interchanges between Christianity and the spiritual journey I have undertaken are significant, ongoing and intense and are both personal and professional.

How does your commitment to Christianity inform your ethics, your politics and your everyday life?

A very abridged description would include Christian teachings about social ethics and a preferential option for the poor and the necessity of ritual, mourning, celebration and hope. The importance of authentic relationships of mutual respect is a Christian value, although obviously not exclusively. Feminist theological analyses and critiques are indispensible, as are certain exchanges between religion and science. Our family lives a relatively simple lifestyle for an affluent culture, and we try to be aware of consumption, local food and the costs of our activities to the global south and the Earth. Integrating ideas and practices of left-leaning Christianity influences much of this. I also learn from other traditions, such as Buddhist practices and teachings about cultivating interiority, educating desires, the tricks of the ego, mindfulness and the nature of illusions. Professionally, I work within an international community of academics and activists at the growing inter-section of religion, ecology, peace and gender equity. Some are Christian identified; many are friends.

How important, if at all, is it to share your religious beliefs with others (to persuade or convince others, or to evangelize)?

I have never been interested in evangelizing, at least not in the customary sense. As a professor of theology, I was constantly sharing my beliefs, positions, interpretations and education. Most of that was about persuading others to open their mind, embrace uncertainty, explore new ideas and be less rigid. Often this was successful. Yet I eventually left theology. It is simply too narrow, rigid, ecclesial-fixated and riddled with subtle and increasingly blatant fundamentalist religiosity. I may be wrong, but it seems to me that most contemporary facets of Christianity – traditions, adherents, institutions, churches, academics – are not motivated by what is shaping the world or diminishing the Earth. Many are reluctant to incorporate new insights from a plethora of sources, particularly the sciences. The perceptiveness within religions, the vigour of religious experiences and the power of religious sensibilities and symbols to transform problematic situations animate some, but overall few, Christians. The universe and the Earth as starting points for considering religion are peripheral. For me these are central.

Do you consider yourself an inclusivist, an exclusivist, or a pluralist?

A pluralist.

46 *Heather Eaton*

Notes

1 This understanding of symbolic consciousness comes from several sources: biological anthropologist Terrence Deacon (1997); theologian John W. Dixon (1996), who studied the Neolithic symbolic dimension of religious consciousness; theologian Wentzel van Huyssteen (2004); and anthropologists David Lewis-Williams (2002), Stanley I. Greenspan and Stuart G. Shanker (2004), and John E. Pfeiffer (1982).
2 Bachelard's stellar book describes in depth how humans interact with spaces via the imagination, symbolic consciousness and interiority.
3 L'Arche communities are intentional Christian communities living together with people with intellectual disabilities and mental health issues, with a view that everyone has beauty, ultimate importance and can contribute. They are found in forty countries. See Vanier (2012).

References

Bachelard, G. 1964. *The Poetics of Space*, translated by M. Jolas. Boston: Beacon Press.
Barasch, M. I. 2000. "Two for the Road: Religion's Path Ahead." State of the World Forum. http://www.simulconference.com/clients/sowf/dispatches/dispatch23.html.
Bekoff, M. and J. Pierce. 2009. *Wild Justice: The Moral Lives of Animals*. Chicago: University of Chicago Press.
Berry, T. 1988. *Dream of the Earth*. San Francisco: Sierra Club Books.
Cousins, E. 1999. "The Convergence of Cultures and Religions in Light of the Evolution of Consciousness." *Zygon: Journal of Religion and Science* 34: 209–219.
Daly, M. 1985. *Beyond God the Father: Toward a Philosophy of Women's Liberation*. With an original reintroduction by the author. Boston: Beacon.
Deacon, T. 1997. *The Symbolic Species: The Co-Evolution of Language and the Brain*. New York: W. W. Norton.
Dixon, J. 1996. *Images of Truth: Religion and the Art of Seeing*. Atlanta: Scholars Press.
Eaton, H. 2007. "The Revolution of Evolution." *Worldviews: Environment, Culture, Religion* 11: 6–31.
Greenspan, S. and S. Shanker. 2004. *The First Idea: How Symbols, Language, and Intelligence Evolved from Our Primate Ancestors to Modern Humans*. Cambridge, MA: de Capo Press.
Halton, E. 2007. "Eden Inverted: On the Wild Self and the Contraction of Consciousness." *The Trumpeter* 23: 45–77.
Heschel, A. J. 1983. *I Asked for Wonder: A Spiritual Anthology*, edited by S. H. Dresner. New York: Crossroad.
Kaplan, E. 1972. "Gaston Bachelard's Philosophy of Imagination: An Introduction." *Philosophy and Phenomenological Research* 33: 1–24.
Kirkpatrick, L. A. 2005. *Attachment, Evolution, and the Psychology of Religion*. New York: The Guilford Press.
Lewis-Williams, D. 2002. *The Mind in the Cave: Consciousness and the Origins of Art*. New York: Thames and Hudson.

Pfeiffer, J. 1982. *The Creative Explosion: An Inquiry into the Origins of Art and Religion*. New York: Harper & Row.

Ruether, R. R. 2000. "Ecofeminism: The Challenge to Theology." In *Christianity and Ecology: Seeking the Well-being of Earth and Humans*, edited by D. T. Hessel and R. Radford Ruether, 97–112. Cambridge, MA: Harvard University Press.

Sheets-Johnstone, M. 2008. *The Roots of Morality*. University Park: The Pennsylvania State Press.

van Huyssteen, W. 2004. *Alone in the World? Science and Theology on Human Uniqueness*. Grand Rapids: Wm. B. Eerdmans Publishing.

Vanier, J. 2012. *The Heart of L'Arche: A Spirituality for Everyday*. Toronto: Novalis.

3 Catholic Christianity

Kevin Hart

Christian theology properly begins by considering the confession that Jesus is the Christ. A great deal follows from this starting point. Affirmatively, it means that Jesus is held to be the one who receives the revelation of God, and indeed over time is taken to be that revelation itself. The event of Christian revelation takes place within Judaism, is to be interpreted within the sphere of its relations with YHWH, and involves a readjustment of its traditional understandings of 'Messiah'. Negatively, it marks a break with other choices of starting points in the *ordo theologiæ*, though only as starting points and not necessarily as themes to be elaborated later in a systematic theology. Set aside, among other possibilities, are attempts to begin by arguing for the existence of God (Aquinas), by reflecting on the interconnection of the knowledge of God and ourselves (Calvin), by discerning a feeling of absolute dependence on God (Schleiermacher), by unfolding the self-consciousness of God (Hegel), by an appeal to 'ultimate concern' (Tillich), or by affirming God in his triune revelation (Barth). Of course, Christian theology must be able to tell a coherent narrative of God's involvement with created beings from eternity to eternity, but it cannot begin with creation since that would presume a doctrine of God worked out without reference to Jesus as the one who receives the revelation of God. Rather, Christian theology's starting point is the relationship with the God of Jesus, and this claim is not merely a bow to the authority of historical criticism but is rooted in regarding Jesus as the datum of revelation who is also, as the Church came to see in the years before and after Nicaea I (325), the genitive of revelation. Christian theology therefore requires a phenomenology of the Christ before anything else; it needs both to examine how Jesus becomes meaningful for us as the Christ, first and foremost through our reading of scripture, and to see how Jesus himself does a peculiar form of phenomenology, how he brings the kingdom of God to the very horizon of appearing in his words and acts.

Several things immediately call for clarification. The first is the nature and scope of phenomenality, one of the dramas of modern philosophy, which I give in a highly condensed form. Kant begins the action by limiting phenomenality to the realm of synthetic *a priori* judgements and by prizing phenomena that are low in phenomenality: numbers, for example.

Catholic Christianity   49

In his quest to pass from theoretical formations to living intentions, Husserl detaches phenomenality from judgements of the understanding and reattaches it to intuition, regarding it as shared between transcendental consciousness and phenomenon and maintaining a sense of 'phenomenon' as limited by presence to consciousness (see Husserl 1997: 218, Husserl 1983: §24). For the phenomenon is what appears in intentional experience. Heidegger extends phenomenality so that it is coextensive with the field of being. For him, Husserl is mistaken to adopt a Cartesian account of consciousness, even if it is refined by way of a doctrine of intentionality; and so he eliminates transcendental consciousness in favour of disclosedness (*Erschlossenheit*) to Dasein. Since being for Heidegger is finite (and, as he later claims, at home in language), the infinite God becomes a matter of faith, not thought (see Lacoste in Kearney and O'Leary 2009: 365–366; for Heidegger's claim about language and being, see Heidegger 1998: 239). Theology is the unfolding of the logic of faith, which holds God to be pregiven, and phenomenology needs to restrict itself to the study of Christian life (see Heidegger 2004). Marion follows Heidegger in fully crediting the phenomenon with phenomenality, though he finds the latter in givenness rather than being. That which must come before any grasping of an appearing is of course prior to being (see Marion 1998: 51). This insight allows him to consider revelation from the side of philosophy with a vigour that has not been witnessed since Schelling's *Spätphilosophie*; it is, he argues, saturation to the second degree. In revelation there is an excess of intuition with respect to all the categories of the understanding. The integrity of the intentional horizon is compromised with respect to quantity, quality and relation, while the transcendental ego is suspended with respect to modality. And yet in electing givenness as the site of phenomenality Marion distances the latter from the intentional experience that ἐποχή makes available. For what gives itself does so before it shows itself. Accordingly, the phenomenon gives itself before it appears in experience. I shall return to this oddity in due course.

Revelation for Marion upsets the Kantian categories while remaining within their limits. He can document the *reception* of revelation in the mode of counter-experience – as unexpected, dazzling, absolute, exceeding any gaze – but not the *giving* of revelation, including the granting of it to Jesus (see Marion 2002: §21–§24). The self-revelation of God must be reckoned a special mode of manifestation, one that cannot be prompted by way of ἐποχή and reduction but that is given only by the God who himself does not appear (John 6:46). Already, modern philosophy is being used to interpret the New Testament, for 'self-revelation' is a modern notion that reached its first maturity in Hegel and was adopted and adapted by Barth in the interests of a reformed dogmatic theology. 'Self-revelation' can also be understood phenomenologically, and I shall propose later a dialectical movement that I take to be central to Christianity that has nothing to do with Hegel. For now, though, it needs to be said that for a Christian the self-revelation of God in Jesus Christ cannot be a matter of eidetic possibility

50   *Kevin Hart*

but must be claimed as an actuality. An actuality can overflow horizons; a possibility cannot saturate anything, and the most that a modification of the Kantian understanding, even one as robust as Marion's, can yield is revelation as an eidetic possibility. Phenomenology, for Marion, is philosophical, yet a philosophy with bad intent towards some of those who precede him, since his account of givenness seeks to blunt the critiques of revelation by Kant and Fichte by agreeing to sequester actuality to faith and to affirm possibility, which is certainly allowable within philosophy (see Kant 1960; Fichte 1978). It also has a place within the study of religion. When a Christian attends to Hinduism or Islam as a faith requiring existential decisions, he or she speaks of eidetic possibilities but does not do so when personally responding to Christ, except of course when engaging in imaginative variation in order to discern something about the Christ (king, messiah, priest, prophet, and so on) or his teaching.

We may say, then, that as a matter of principle phenomenality must be granted unlimited extension so as not to exclude anything that gives itself, in whatever way, from whatever 'region of being', to intentional experience and how to value what is given depends on the degree of intuitive fullness that it yields. We may speak theologically, and not only philosophically, of the phenomenality of revelation only if we accept that it belongs to revelation. Marion insists that this revelation is merely received; yet even though it may well surprise a listener, what Jesus says is surely constituted, made present to the understanding and of course interpreted on many levels, including pre-interpretation. Like other phenomena, revelation will have meaning (*Sinn*) and ways in which it is given (*Gegebenheitweise*). It may occur in various manners, in signs as well as in perceptions, and be subject to all sorts of syntheses, active and passive (both primary and secondary). It is to be weighed by the degree of *Evidenz* that it supplies, and for Christians this general revelation is restricted to the first-century witnesses whose testimony that Jesus is the Christ remains central to the faith. Special revelations, such as given to those we moderns call 'mystics', or, more traditionally, the deep understandings of those granted the grace of passive contemplation, might also supply *Evidenz* (yet, as we know, with some *beatas* these may be no more than delusions or deceits) (see, e.g., Imirizaldu 1977). Most Christians, however, make an act of faith on the basis of testimony that has become concrete in the context of a community and a tradition and not just on a possibility that comes into view. In other words, phenomenological theology must draw on genetic and generative issues as well as those that come from static intentional analysis.

The second clarification required is what 'Jesus' means for a phenomenological theology. Certainly one needs the wealth of material supplied by modern historical criticism partly for purposes of clearing away pious constructions and partly to determine the realm of discursive possibilities for a rabbi of the first century. The historical Jesus, however, is an abstraction that comes into focus only through the lens of modern historical research, and

Catholic Christianity   51

this research is entirely unable to deal with the question of *Evidenz* required by faith. No amount of testimony about the resurrection of Jesus could ever satisfy a historical critic that it was a historical event, the crucial one for Christian faith. The historical critic, writing as a historian, limits phenomenality to the realm of the empirical.[1] We cannot expect to find a neutral narrative of Jesus and must confine our sense of him to the last two or three years of his life when he was teaching in the rural villages of the Holy Land. All that we have about him is selected and interpreted; and less important than whether the testimony comes from a canonical gospel, or from Q, L, or M, among other early texts, including Paul's letters (1 Thessalonians, in particular), is the sense of finding a relation with God through Jesus. So when I speak of Jesus I am thinking first and foremost of the testified Jesus in the Gospels and not the one who is the richly theorized subject of the Nicene Creed. The Creed was written for various reasons, some political and others doctrinal (if one can draw a neat line between them), and its Christological part is a firm rejection of the philosophical Arianism of Eunomius; it is not intended to be the basis of a systematic theology. The Creed is preoccupied with how Jesus was conceived, suffered, died, was resurrected and ascended into heaven. Yet a phenomenological theology is primarily concerned with something that the Creed leaves out, that Jesus lived and taught and that his words and acts disclosed the meaning of God's kingly rule to those with whom he came into contact.

The third clarification turns on whether a phenomenology of the Christ subtly transforms Jesus into a twentieth-century philosopher and so becomes subject to the criticisms that Albert Schweitzer (1998) directed to the liberal *Leben-Jesu-Forschung*. In answer we must distinguish between phenomenology as a way of seeing and as a particular philosophical position clarified and ramified by Husserl and his successors: the structure of an intentional act, the delineation of formal and material ontologies, the elaboration of *Befindlichkeit*, and so on. Only the former is at issue here, a phenomenology *avant la lettre*, and one that differs significantly in important ways from the styles of philosophizing we recognize in *Ideas* I, *Being and Time*, *Being Given*, and elsewhere. It differs chiefly, as I shall argue, by not being practiced as philosophy, though it can be identified today by using the vocabulary and procedures of phenomenology. No story is told without ἐποχή and reduction, however partial; religious persons perform a conversion of the gaze, look for manifestations of the holy, seek the divine wherever it can be found concretely and claim that truths become evident over time, though not as fully as logical, mathematical or even straightforward perceptual truths. Of course, we must take care to see Jesus as a historical figure, a rabbi of the first century, and not to discount the eschatological dimensions of his religious vision or to diminish his strong sense of the election of Israel. We begin with the synoptic Jesus "who, as man, is our road to God," as Aquinas puts it.[2] Also, Jesus is not to be made to subscribe, even covertly, to philosophical positions that were determined by far later generations.

52   Kevin Hart

Yet the phenomenological basis of what he does can be brought out more completely: he helps people see what is essential in being in relation with God. Phenomenology is sometimes an extension of an earlier and partial phenomenology. In the case of the ἐποχή and reduction as practiced by Jesus, we meet a quite different practice of disclosure, in some respects, from those developed in the twentieth century. To draw it out to its fullest extent, clarifying it as one does so, is to produce a phenomenological theology.

* * *

Phenomena give themselves in different ways, with varying modes of clarity and degrees of intuitive fullness; they offer themselves to us by way of a formal or material *a priori*; they become evident to a greater or lesser extent, depending on whether the presentation of a phenomenon corresponds to the intentional aim of the person and the nature of the intentional rapport. This aim can be perceptual, imaginative, recollective, anticipatory, schematizing, wishful, hopeful and so forth, and it takes place from one or another bodily perspective. For Husserl, perception allows a phenomenon to present itself to consciousness (*Gegenwärtigung*), while anticipating, imagining and the rest allow presentification (*Vergegenwärtigung*). A phenomenological theology would begin with Jesus as phenomenon, given to us in scripture, with a determinate material core, as seen, heard, questioned, believed in and rejected; and detailed attention would have to be given to his relations with his followers and critics, his styles of teaching, his understanding of the Sabbath, his prohibition of oaths, his sense of purity laws, his exorcisms, healings, miracles and inevitably his suffering, death, resurrection and ascension. It would also distinguish Jesus from prophets who were roused to action by a call from YHWH but who did not receive the revelation considered definitive for Christianity. Since this examination would rely on what others have said about Jesus, it would be a hetero-phenomenology, and, for the modern reader of scripture, would begin from a baseline of empty intentions. No one receives the historical Jesus with intuitive fullness. The important question is how one receives the testified Jesus who is believed to be the living Christ.

In addition, and more importantly, phenomenological theology would attend to Jesus as phenomenologist, that is, to how he receives phenomena. As already indicated, in the New Testament God is not regarded as a phenomenon: the one Jesus calls 'Father' does not appear. What comes to the horizon of appearing is the kingly rule of the Father, what Jesus calls the βασιλεία – I use the Greek word from now on in order to preserve the strangeness of what it means – though even here one must be wary of calling it a 'manifestation', pure and simple. For the βασιλεία is both here and to come (Luke 17:21, Matthew 25:34), external and internal (Luke 17:20–21, Thomas 3), and one aspect of this being still to come is Jesus' eschatology: only the Father can bring on the βασιλεία in its fullness at the time he chooses. We might say that it is revealed and re-veiled, never fully present to consciousness. It needs to be acknowledged that the βασιλεία is not wholly original with Jesus, for it is mentioned in the Targum Jonathan to the Prophets (Isaiah 52:7, for example), though it becomes elaborated and vivid only with Jesus. The central issue is how Jesus makes 'God', that most abstract of abstract nouns, name a concrete reality in his parables, sayings and acts by telling us or showing us what the kingly rule of God looks like. Consider what happens in the parable of the father and his two sons (Luke 15:11–32). As soon as Jesus says, "There was a man who had two sons", he has performed ἐποχή: he and his listeners bracket the world of work, of contingencies and worries, for a few minutes so as to step back to hear a story that will tell them something essential about life and, in particular, their relations with God. This is not merely a mental act of putting aside an attitude that we have to the world; it is a loosening of Jesus' hearers from captivation by the world, to the world and in the world that can be extended, in the parable, to a way of overcoming that captivity (see Fink 1995: 42). In hearing or reading the parable we seize concretely what it is to be a father. Concretion, for Husserl, is not the finding of an instance of an abstraction but rather the drawing out of a definite situation in which an abstraction – here 'fatherhood' – has solid, pointed meaning here and now (see Husserl 1973: §93).

'Concretion' comes from the Latin *concrescere*, 'to grow together', which has the sense of coalescing in order to form something enduring. When we hear the parable of the father and his two sons we begin to see how God comes to us in the ordinariness and trouble of our lives; we recognize that God is best approached relationally, in the metaphor of 'father', and that fatherhood is understood in terms of compassion: not an exercise of legal authority but a graciousness and even vulnerability. For the person who shows compassion exposes himself or herself to a loss of face in the eyes of the world. God too can be rebuffed. We can begin to see how a family can grow together by turning to the father for forgiveness, as the younger son does, and we wonder what will happen if the older son does not also turn to him. Certainly we are not told everything about the family, and we have no clear sense of what will happen on the following day: we see a scene of forgiveness, and glimpse the older son's justified anger, but we do not see if or how justice will play into the family's life (see Hart 2017). The parable reaches into silence; we feel its look upon us. It stimulates us to think about how to live with God as our father, and part of that invitation to think is to ponder that God is at once like a father and unlike any father we have known, which is something to which I shall return.

Biblical scholars do not usually regard the story of the father and his two sons as a parable of the βασιλεία, and yet it shows that God's rule is like that of a compassionate father rather than that of an imperious king. We can be in relation with God as children with a loving parent. On realizing this, God is no longer an abstraction, a deity regarded as "distant, difficult", but we draw close to him in faith.[3] This faith is not a pallid mode of knowledge

54   Kevin Hart

but a firm sense of trust that we are present to God, a trust that is warranted by God's raising of Jesus as the firstborn from the dead. We do not have experience of God as proposed by Schleiermacher ('feeling of absolute dependence') or a direct intuition of the deity as advocated by Hamann and Jacobi, or even the 'transcendental experience' of God affirmed by Rahner (1978: 31–35) We do not have any experience at all, except as intentional rapport with the noema given to us ('βασιλεία'). Nor do we have knowledge of God, as Hegel thinks can be achieved. Instead, God has become thinkable; we know better now what it means to say 'God', that it means 'God-for-us', and to orient one's entire life around his kingly rule. We do not have a metaphysical description of God's properties, we have no idea of the divine essence, but we are able to turn towards God and receive him in the ways in which he gives himself, that is, in the βασιλεία: here and to come, within and without.

Note also that we have not understood God outside all perspective, as some philosophers might wish to do, but he has become thinkable for us from one particular vantage point, the story of a father and his two sons, each wayward in his own manner. God has become thinkable for us not as an extraordinary item in reality or even the ground of reality but as given in and through a story of the βασιλεία. Other parables and attention to other acts and words of Jesus will give further angles on the βασιλεία, though nothing that is testified in the Gospels or the letters of the New Testament will present the one Jesus calls 'Father' as he is. To call God 'Father' is to know him by way of a relation, not as a being or an essence. So the Father reveals himself only through the coming of the βασιλεία, the dynamic breaking into the world of his kingly rule. And Jesus teaches us to respond by saying "Thy kingdom come" [ἐλθέτω ἡ βασιλεία σου] (Luke 11:2). The βασιλεία works a peculiar logic of 'already – not yet'; it calls for a conversion of the gaze for the here and now and a phenomenology of anticipation for what is to come.

It remains entirely possible for someone to hear a parable and not find that God is thinkable. Such a person may not accept the authority of Jesus, or may doubt that the story comes from Jesus, or may be looking for God to give himself more clearly, more fully or in some other way: through the proofs of natural theology, for example. Concretion does not supply *Evidenz* by itself; it only enables one to think God concretely and to venture into the presence of God by living one's life in the manner disclosed by the parables of the kingdom and by imitating Jesus. Of course, even the firm believer engages in doxic modification with respect to revelation; one wants more certainty or further grounds for certainty, and the shadows of daily life can sometimes fall across us and hide God. So one may seek assistance from the proofs in natural theology in order to understand better what 'God' means, and indeed to have an appropriate awe of him (*primum movens, efficientem primam, aliquid quod est per se necessarium, aliquid quod est causa esse et honitatis, aliquis intelligens a quo omnes res naturales ordinatur ad finem*), and to do so in the spirit that ultimately reason and revelation are one.[4] God may reveal himself to some extent in the elegance of a mathematical theorem, though Christianity sees this as supplementary *Evidenz* that needs to be grounded in antecedent belief in the revelation of God's kingly rule in and through Jesus. Or, equally, the beauty of the theorem might attune one to the Christian revelation, though it can never substitute for it. And one may read the works of the mystics to be buoyed up by those who have received special graces or the gift of passive contemplation and been led to a fuller life with God. Yet Christianity is finally not a matter of bringing God to the presence of human consciousness but rather of allowing oneself to come into the presence of God, the two modes of 'presence' being quite different, one a matter of presence to consciousness, cashed out (if one can) as knowledge, and the other a matter of ἀγάπη. If taken alone, as a relentless hunger for proof or experience of God, the quest to make God present leads to pride or conceptual idolatry, while the trust that we are present to God is the very meaning of 'faith' (*fides qua*).

In Christianity, then, God does not usually give himself directly but rather in and through the βασιλεία; and the preaching of the βασιλεία, along with acts and words that also point to it, is done first and best by Jesus of Nazareth. There are exceptions to the general rule: the baptism of Jesus (Matthew 3:13–17) and Saul on the road to Damascus (Acts 9: 1–31), for instance, and of course these have different statuses. No example, however, and certainly neither of those just cited, changes the fact that Jesus is the datum of divine revelation, and when we accept his authority, his closeness to the Father, and understand that intimacy theologically in terms of unity (and finally, in the mode of high theory, as consubstantiality), we see that he is also the genitive of revelation. Such is the deep truth that Origen saw when he called Jesus the 'αὐτοβασιλεία', the kingdom in person.[5] And such is the basis for the Christological theses formulated at Nicaea I. Before we pass from the dative to the genitive of revelation, however, we need to clarify some further aspects of what has been suggested. In what sense is a parable a revelation of God, even God as given solely in the βασιλεία?

It will be noticed that a parable has a double structure of revelation. On the one hand, the parable we have been considering reveals that God is *like* a father; and on the other hand, it reveals that God is *unlike* any father we have known. Mostly we attend to the former, which of course is the concretion that makes God thinkable, and yet the parable also indicates to us that God not only embodies fatherhood in an eminent manner – his compassion and mercy are endless – but also is beyond all known fatherhood. What is revealed is also partly hidden: God the Father does not give himself to us as he is but only through Jesus and only in relational terms. A parable calls forth apophasis; it sets us on the path to approach God in the darkness of unknowing, which, I underline, presumes the acceptance that we cannot make God present to ourselves though we can take ourselves to be present to God. The Christian life is devoted to an endless dialectic of this *like* and *unlike*, of the friendship to which God calls us and the divine transcendence

56   *Kevin Hart*

that humbles us. We are established in the revelation of the Father in the βασιλεία, and, at the same time, kneel before the God whose very holiness requires him to re-veil himself before a sinful mortal. The Christian hope is that if we live according to the revelation we shall behold God as he is. Only in heaven is one not burned by divine glory. Saul was blinded when the risen Christ admonished him (Acts 9: 9).

Jesus performs ἐποχή and reduction in his parables; the 'world' is put out of play for the time of the story and perhaps for a little while longer, and we are led back to a state that is anterior to it, namely the Father's kingly rule. It appears, if only for a moment or two, and in doing so it breaks our sense of what is normal and concordant and exposes us to what is abnormal and discordant yet nonetheless offering the possibility of a more optimal relation with God (for more on the generative phenomenology sketched here, see Steinbock 1995: esp. Part 2). The world is pre-given, Husserl teaches, yet the βασιλεία is given to us as an uprooting of the captivation that this world holds over us. It takes many years of Christian life, for some almost the whole of it, before the βασιλεία does not seem alien, a joyful yet grievous interruption to life as it insists on being lived in the natural attitude: the *conatus essendi*. Only Jesus performs this reduction in his parables and implicitly in all that is testified of him. We cannot do it, no matter how hard we try, though we may tell ourselves and other people 'secular parables', as Barth names them, and so try to find analogues for the kingdom within the limits of human imagination (1961: 114–122). In the basilaic reduction, as I shall call it, we are led back to a prefatory state: not transcendental consciousness but something that is at once inside and outside ourselves, here and still to come – the βασιλεία. It is *Gegenwärtigung* and *Vergegenwärtigung* both at once.

We are brought to the βασιλεία not by intentional analysis but by the counter-intentionality in which the parable confronts us; it stirs us to look and see something that we cannot see by our own efforts. So there is no first move in which we suspend the natural attitude and, by passing to transcendental consciousness, constitute God – make him present – as he appears on our intentional horizons. We cannot consider the Father as an eidetic essence that we can revolve and inspect at our leisure. To be sure, once we have been led back from 'world' to βασιλεία we may engage in phenomenological exercises to do with many things that Christianity presents to us, including reading scripture and responding to sacred places and practices. If we have taken an interest in Jesus beforehand, that interest will be redoubled, and of course we may perform reductions on what is testified of Jesus and do so to our spiritual benefit. We may see, if we relax our intentional rapport with the Jesus we often receive through Church and culture, that we have inherited too much theological or cultural construction and may need to return to scriptural testimony. As Otto Weber would say, we seek the exemplary Jesus Christ, not the Jesus Christ who is a moral exemplar (see Moltmann-Wendel 1997: 24).

Another way of approaching this thought is by way of what I shall call the supernatural attitude. It is akin to the natural attitude, and it also needs to be suspended in phenomenological theology. In the supernatural attitude we think of Christianity as so many theses taught by the Church (and therefore authoritative): virgin birth, resurrection, second coming, and so on. We think of the uncreated world as parallel to the created world and (paradoxically) as another 'world' rather than as 'kingdom'. We have limited pre-thetic experience of the βασιλεία when we hear a parable – we see one or two facets of how God wishes to be in relation with us – and we may well pass from this intentional experience to form one or more theses about the βασιλεία. For example, we may think of it within the natural attitude as a moral commonwealth (Ritschl) or as a theo-political state that will be formed in some future present, as some American evangelicals and Russian Orthodox believe. Or we might think of it within the supernatural attitude, as a heavenly community of the Trinity, angels and the blessed, including Mary as the first of the blessed. The truths of these theses can be weighed by theologians and by ecclesial authorities. For the ordinary Christian, though, what is important is to be led back from the world to the βασιλεία, figured as how to live in such a way that is pleasing to God.

The βασιλεία cannot be captured neatly by way of theological theses, for it eludes concepts, being at once within us and outside us, here and to come; it never becomes fully present in our terms – moral, political or even religious – and it never can be used as a set of clearly defined norms that can guide us in each and every event that we shall experience in life. The relationships in which we are embedded in and through Christ are shifting, challenging, sometimes insuperably difficult; and we often lack the concretion that we need. Jesus tells us what 'neighbour' means with all possible imaginative specificity in the parable of the Good Samaritan (Luke 10: 25–37), but we must largely work out for ourselves what 'friend', 'citizen', 'husband' and 'teacher' mean with the same density of specific gravity. In short, the Christian must learn first to say the βασιλεία, to grasp where he or she has been led back to, and be open to unsay it as well: to rethink it, re-imagine it and to inhabit it differently than before. The βασιλεία is the way to God the Father through Jesus, whom we come to see as the Son; and if it 'contains' the Father – as a relation, not as an item – then it cannot be formulated as a mundane statement or set of statements. The divine life, transcendent and always creative, resists being netted, even by the Church.

Doubtless it will be objected that the parables that give God to be thought could well be stories that Jesus made up for pedagogic use, just as other rabbinic *meshalim*, and that they are not vehicles of divine revelation. After all, concretion is to be found in secular poems and stories and novels, as well as in scripture. It needs to be kept in mind, though, that the concretion of 'God' is ensconced in narratives of testimony that pivot on the resurrection of Jesus from the dead. We do not have access to any *Evidenz* of the resurrection except through the Gospels and Paul. To be sure, a Christian can grow in holiness by living the sacramental life, by daily prayer and acts of charity, and while all of this makes Christian faith

58   *Kevin Hart*

concrete it does not supply compelling *Evidenz* of God or God's revelation in and through Jesus. A sacramental life, twinned with contemplative prayer, may attune us to God, but these things do not and cannot nudge God to appear in an audition, a vision, an intellectual structure or anything of the sort. The Christian relies at heart on biblical testimony and supplements it as needed. Christian life, as I am proposing it, turns on Jesus' reduction from 'world' to βασιλεία. All that we rely on as grounds of life – work, family, political order, our children as our future – are bracketed; what seems to make up life for us, to be a rich totality, is suspended, and we are led back to something that lays claim on us before these things take hold. The basilaic reduction reveals that a mode of passivity is primary, that is, being taken outside oneself as the centre of activity and being receptive to God's kingly rule. The other things I have mentioned may be good in themselves, but they are shown not to be good as grounds of life; they are active, sometimes violent – think of the Roman *imperium mundi*, and think too of the 'principalities and powers' that are hard at work today (Stringfellow) – and we need to be situated in another order, one that Jesus says is sanctioned by God and that 'contains' the divine.

There is a rhythm disclosed in the basilaic reduction that can be explicated by way of two Greek words associated with Paul: κένωσις and ἐπέκτασις. A parable such as that of the father and his two sons jogs us to convert our gaze, to recognize that we are asked to live in the βασιλεία and to help bring it on by our acts in the world and our prayer, and in order to do so we must contract ourselves, our desires and our deeds; we must give up the security we anxiously search for in the world about us. This is the moment of κένωσις: not a retreat into ourselves but a step back into an anterior claim on us that is made by God and revealed by Jesus. This κένωσις can be refused, for God wishes it to be accepted freely. Yet if it is accepted – taken as a cross, as the Gospel frankly warns (Luke 9: 23) – then we are invited to experience another moment: ἐπέκτασις. We are given many opportunities to stretch ourselves into the βασιλεία, not in order to experience God, as though he were a phenomenon, but rather to experience life under divine rule, which is compassionate and fatherly. This expansion into the βασιλεία is social and temporal; it is here, partly, and to come, partly; it is ethics and eschatology, each written on one side of a piece of paper whose ends are taped together and given a half-twist; and if it offers consolations from time to time, it offers frustrations and pain more often. The basilaic reduction that Jesus performs does not happen once for all; we are returned to κένωσις, led back to the very margin of the world, stripped of relying on anything mundane, and once again released into community and hope by way of ἐπέκτασις. The rhythm of Christian life is constant, κένωσις and ἐπέκτασις, but seldom regular, and our hope of eternal life is that it shall be ἐπέκτασις without κένωσις.

* * *

The model of divinity I am proposing is perhaps unusual in that it does not begin with God but with the revelation of the Father to Jesus. The model answers solely to Christianity and does not seek a point beyond it from which to secure a sense of God outside his revelation. Certainly it does not seek a God whose nature or will, once determined, explains the world or the course of history. Appeals to a transcendent reality do not explain experience and indeed can account for it in skewed ways ("I get sick because I am sinful"); yet the lived experience of what Jesus teaches contains principles or structures that can orient one's life to a transcendent God. Not that philosophical questioning and construction have no parts to play in theology. They do, but neither of them can establish the ground of a living, historical faith. The model may well be called 'phenomenological theology', although it would be more accurate to say that this expression names only the base of the model. A systematic theology must reach back to creation and forward to the eschaton from the midpoint of salvation history, which is given in the life, death and resurrection of Jesus. A certain amount of construction is needed. Also, the doctrine of God will finally involve metaphysics, even if the triune nature of God is regarded as a development of the phenomenon of the Christ (see Hart 2012). Such is the work required of a systematic theology in addition to what is sketched here: a doctrine of the triune God, an understanding of creation and creativity, an account of being human with God and an exploration of the end of all things. None of this can be discussed here.

What we have seen so far is that God is radically irreducible to human consciousness but that Jesus performs a reduction from world to βασιλεία that leads us back to the life that his Father wishes us to live. Phenomenological theology, as I propose it, would therefore run in quite the opposite direction to that of most classical phenomenology. Husserl tells us that we cannot bring God to consciousness because his mode of transcendence exceeds all intentional rapports (Husserl 1983: 134). He is correct in his reasoning but misses the opportunity to see that *we* are reduced, not *God*. This approach would also run a different path from others that deviate from Husserl's, such as Michel Henry's non-intentional phenomenology, including that portion of it that has a bearing on Christianity (see Henry 2000, 2002, 2003). Only to the extent that the βασιλεία is within us could it be thought by way of enstatic phenomenality that is at once God's and mine, and further distinctions would need to be drawn before the claim can be made in a sound and clear way.

The model I advocate is concerned with Christianity, not religion, although, when sufficiently developed, it would include a theology of religions. Indeed, such a theology is implied in the very opening of the prayer that Jesus taught us to say about the coming of the βασιλεία: "Our Father" [Πάτερ ἡμῶν]. By what right could we restrict the scope of 'Our' or, in a more violent gesture, seek to limit the divine fatherhood? Religion has no such right, and if it claims it then it becomes demonic. (I shall return to the

60   *Kevin Hart*

theology of religions a little later.) In phenomenology we are dealing genetically with Christianity, uncovering its sediments, and recognizing that while its claims are absolutely binding on believers they are not thereby necessarily universal. The Christian is concerned with understanding his or her home – in the *habitus* of belief, in Church, in parish life – and is therefore engaged with generative phenomenology, whether knowingly or unknowingly. The Jew or the Buddhist, for example, can be seen by Christians to live in the βασιλεία as a Jew or a Buddhist (and not as an 'anonymous Christian'; see Rahner 1979: 52–59). There is no path to God other than the βασιλεία, but it is spoken of in other ways in other faiths: I have already mentioned the Targum Jonathan to the Prophets, and I shall add the *Lotos sutra*, thinking in particular of the story of the son who left his father. But this is to veer into difficult territory, far from the "mooring of starting out" (Ashbery 1970: 19), and I leave it for another occasion.

Phenomenological theology differs too from the fledgling phenomenology of God that one discerns in Husserl. There is no quest to find transcendencies in immanent consciousness or to speculate about an absolute monad (see Husserl 1983, 2006: 177–178). To be sure, the Husserlian conversion of the gaze draws from and resituates Christian discourse on θεωρία; but to my mind contemplative prayer is properly not a gaze that rises simply from the visible world to the invisible God, as one finds so beautifully presented by the Victorines, especially Richard, but rather one that begins in the βασιλεία and seeks to find repose on the assurance of God's kingly rule, here and to come, rather than on his being. There is a conversion of the gaze, but it involves recognition of an antecedent claim made upon us by God, not a purification of how we see so that we can mentally encompass him: the temptation of all temptations. To be sure, the Victorine language has roots in the New Testament, especially in Paul (Romans 1:20, Colossians 1:15–16, 1 Timothy 1:17) and Hebrews 11:27, though the model of contemplative prayer at issue is more complicated than their guiding idea of a movement from the visible to the invisible: the βασιλεία appears as invisible in people's hearts and minds, on the one hand, and the king is himself invisible, on the other. The passage from kingdom to king is apophatic, a quest that finally suspends 'king' with all its earthly associations, as we enter into the darkness of divine love.

Also, phenomenological theology differs from the evangelical theology that seeks to find the βασιλεία in the parable; instead, the parable is a special sort of literary prompt to see the βασιλεία (see Jüngel 1983: 294). The parable does not give us the βασιλεία as an object of experience; for it is not given in perception but is constituted by Jesus in the intentional synthesis that is a parable. I see the βασιλεία in hearing Jesus; it is intelligible, an intentional correlate of an act; but whether there *is* such a thing is a risk, one that I must engage by trying to live the life one calls Christian. The eidetic possibility of the βασιλεία can be imaginatively revolved before one decides to live it out or to keep on living as before. The experience of the essence

Catholic Christianity 61

is subjective – it turns on a human subject engaging with what the parable reveals – yet it is also inter-subjective, for the structure of the βασιλεία can be read, as it were, on the noematic structure of the phenomenon. In Reinarch's terms, the *a priori* at issue here is not epistemological (as it is with Kant) but ontological and subsists in the 'state of affairs' that is given in the parable (see Reinarch 1969). With all that said, it should nonetheless be clear that phenomenological theology begins with attention to a literary form, the parable. It is the study of metaphor and narrative that grounds Christian theology, not metaphysics or philosophy, or even phenomenology as a school within philosophy.

One consequence of this approach is that the account of the self, in the context of Christian theology, does not seek to determine the essence of 'being human' in the individual. Whereas modern philosophy attempts to find the animating centre of human being in the reason, the will, consciousness, the unconscious, a structure of responsibility, a genetic string or somewhere else, Christianity affirms that "the central of our being" is in God and not in our selves (Stevens 1997: 329). As Augustine says at the start of the *Confessions*, "You stir man to take pleasure in praising you, because you have made us for yourself, and our heart is restless until it rests in you" [*tu excitas ut laudare te delectet, quia fecisti nos ad te et inquietum est cor nostrum donec requiscat in te*] (1991: 1). Despite the vigour of this view, Augustine has frequently been quietly suborned to the modern quest for the essence of human being as within ourselves, as though he is simply a forerunner of Descartes. After all, it is often thought and said, Augustine insists "Return within yourself" [*in teipsum redi*] in *De vera religione* (1953: 262). And so he does. Yet in this early work he is marking a need to hear the call of God and is not urging a retreat to subjectivism. The theology of disclosure also prizes a conversion of the gaze, but it seeks the truth outside us as well as within us.

Jesus' parables offer pre-thetic experience of the βασιλεία; we begin to see what it might mean to live as God wishes us to do, and if we seek to bring on the βασιλεία by following Jesus we also have pre-thetic experience of Christianity. We do not have direct experience of the Father, only experience of living under his kingly and fatherly rule when we see it indicated by Jesus. We take ourselves to be present to him ('redeemed', as we say in church) and do not presume to make him present to us. We should be aware that it is possible to mistake the βασιλεία as it is with any phenomenon (to the extent it *is* one). I may see an act or perform one myself and think that it helps to bring on the βασιλεία, only to discover that the actor has acted from crude self-interest. Here, as with anything, we must follow Husserl's advice and always look more than once, which includes looking within (1978: §59). The βασιλεία is within and without; with strict spiritual direction we might be able to tell if we are truly conforming ourselves to the Gospel or deceiving ourselves, but it is endlessly harder to know about others. It should not be an interest in any case, for only God can tell what brings on the βασιλεία,

62   Kevin Hart

and we discern it, if we do, in intentional life and not in ordinary experience. It is enough to shuttle back and forth from the one to the other. Such is 'Christian experience'.

The βασιλεία does not remain a theme of the New Testament, not even in Paul, although it is central to Jesus' teaching. And even in disclosing the βασιλεία what Jesus reveals is limited. The rest of Christian doctrine is largely left unsaid: nothing is said precisely, for instance, about the crystallization of the Church in and through the Holy Spirit or the Trinitarian nature of the deity – for such things one must look for the proto-Catholic stratum of scripture after the fact – and the claim that Jesus is one with the Father, and what this unity means, must be worked out in passing from the pre-thetic to the thetic. This passage takes place over a complex history in the first, generative centuries of the faith and culminates in Gregory of Nyssa's redefinition of 'divinity' as that which is marked by infinity rather than by unbegottenness, a trait that is restricted to the Father (1999: 297). Of this passage phenomenological theology can say little, except to say that it turns on imaginative variation. One might think that there is also nothing that can be said of Jesus' resurrection. Certainly there is no proof that can be offered of it, and even if it were established strongly by one means or another it would not compel us to regard Jesus Christ as God Incarnate. God could raise from the dead a holy man or an incarnate angel, as the Arians believed. Yet something can be said in a phenomenological key of what the resurrection means for thinking of God's kingly rule.

* * *

Christianity comes to think of Jesus as the genitive as well as the dative of revelation because of the testimony that he was raised from the dead. In the Creed the βασιλεία is mentioned only after the ascension of Jesus into heaven, and of course the Fathers of Nicaea I in their crafting of the Creed were not interested in Jesus' life and preaching, only the Christological theses about his conception, death, resurrection and relationship with the Father: same substance, similar substance or different substance. We gain phenomenological insight into Christianity when we begin with the preaching of the βασιλεία. What we see is that the affirmation of God's kingly rule is invariably in conflict with worldly rule, whether it come from the centre of political life in Rome or from the centre of religious life in Jerusalem. When Jesus tells the Pharisees, "Render therefore unto Caesar the things that are Caesar's, and to God the things that are God's" (Matthew 22:21) and, later, when he tells Pilate, "My kingdom is not of this world" ['Η βασιλεία ἡ ἐμὴ οὐκ ἔστιν ἐκ τοῦ κόσμου τούτου] (John 18:36), he indicates that one can participate in the βασιλεία while also being in the world as a political and social order. Christianity is not concerned to reject 'the world'; it dismisses it only as the ground of life. Yet the conversion of the gaze, the perception of the βασιλεία's prior claim upon us, is inevitably a challenge to political

Catholic Christianity 63

and social structures. Simeon saw clearly that Jesus was to be "a sign which shall be spoken against" (Luke 2:34). It may well be historically that the cleansing of the Temple was a trigger, perhaps the main one, for bringing about the execution of Jesus (see, e.g., Saunders 1985: 301–302). Yet even if one excludes misunderstandings about Jesus' preaching among some of his followers, the aristocratic priests of Jerusalem and the Roman civil authorities, it seems clear that early Christian self-understanding was that preaching the βασιλεία leads to the cross, which is a curse as well as a hideously cruel death (Deuteronomy 21:23).

The central moment of the Christian faith is the resurrection of Jesus not only because this is an astonishing event, an interruption of world history, but also because it tells us something about the βασιλεία. In raising Jesus from the dead, the Father both confirms his kingly power (as distinct from his authority) and restores Jesus' preaching to the fullness of life. The body of Jesus hung on the cross, and so did the body of the βασιλεία; it was, in effect, mocked as so many poetic stories defeated by imperial and religious powers. The disciples scattered when Jesus was arrested. Yet the resurrection brings both the body of Jesus and the body of the βασιλεία to new life; indeed, the resurrection is the Father's vindication of the βασιλεία as the right way of being in relation with him. It is not one philosophy among others – Cynic, Epicurean, Platonic, or whatever – and not even a philosophy in the first place. It is a manifestation of how to live in a way that is pleasing to God, one that is affirmed above and beyond what is offered by the Essenes, the Pharisees, the Sadducees, the Scribes, the Herodians and the Zealots. That it comes to us by way of the humility of metaphor and narrative rather than from the grandeur of metaphysics is a facet of the divine condescension. To clarify the βασιλεία using a philosophical vocabulary associated with Husserl and his successors is a task for the theologian. In doing so, of course, we realize that it can never be reduced to anything we can master – it is here yet also to come, in the hands of the Father – and once again we are, to a degree, passive with respect to it, open to what it asks of us and free to reject it.

For Jesus, the preaching of the βασιλεία leads to the cross, and the resurrection overcomes the cross and affirms his preaching. This is the central dialectic of Christianity – one that redeems the βασιλεία as truth and not as the subject of so many lyrical stories – and for Jesus it ends, for resurrection is being raised to eternal life with the Father and the Spirit. For Christians, it is different; we live until eternity in a ceaseless melody of kingdom-cross-resurrection that is played in minor keys. Our attempts to bring on the βασιλεία upset the powers of the world in small ways but ways that can be sufficiently painful: one can be marginalized, reproached, mocked. That God restores us through prayer and sacrament is our share in the resurrection here and now; and the βασιλεία is uplifted in the sacraments. The Christian dialectic plays itself out, as we have seen, by way of κένωσις and ἐπέκτασις, and we can think of the dialectic as a rhythm of ἐπέκτασις, κένωσις and ἐπέκτασις. Jesus' parables, along with his other words and acts, perform

64 *Kevin Hart*

ἐποχή and we are led back to the claim that the βασιλεία makes on us. We hold the βασιλεία in intentional experience for a moment; and we may well inquire about the phenomenality of what comes to the horizon of appearing. As we have seen, the βασιλεία does not simply or fully show itself; it is here yet to come, and its coming is in the gift of the Father. So its phenomenality cannot be said to abide at the level of givenness, for it is not given before it is shown.

The Father gives himself only in and through the βασιλεία; so if we inquire after the phenomenality of God we shall have to say that it consists in the revelation of the βασιλεία: a revealing and a re-veiling. Yet if the revelation is finally Christ himself, if the Church is right to say that Christ is not simply the vehicle of communicating God's revelation but is the content of that revelation as well, "the image of the invisible God" (Colossians 1:15) – the exemplary life that is pleasing to God – then we may say that Christ is the phenomenality of God. So the phenomenality of God, as Christianity understands things, is apparently divided, βασιλεία and Christ, though only *apparently* since the two are one. Neither is given before it shows itself. Neither is fully given in the first place, and both give themselves on their own terms and not in response to a gaze. Christianity reflects on the early experiences people had of Jesus and the testimonies to which they give rise, and this reflection ends in a number of theses assembled in the Nicene Creed, the Apostles' Creed and all the other Creeds. Yet these dogmas come after the fact, after pre-thetic experience of the βασιλεία and Jesus Christ, and are not naïvely posited (on dogmatic claims made after reduction, see Fink 1995: 111). This situation is valuable for ecumenicalism, for we may speak within Christianity of Christ as the phenomenality of God while also speaking, without any diminution of the faith, to members of other religions of the βασιλεία as the phenomenality of God. A Muslim or a Jew, say, may participate in the βασιλεία here and now and live a life that is pleasing to God. They too may enjoy pre-thetic experience of God. No religion, including Christianity, is at heart a series of theses about the supernatural world and its relations with the natural world. The theses of the Nicene Creed are binding on mainstream Christians, but being brought to the anterior claim to serve God in and through the βασιλεία is primary in the faith.

Notes

1 Clearly, it is possible for a historical critic also to be a believer. John P. Meier, for example, is a Catholic priest and the author of *A Marginal Jew: Rethinking the Historical Jesus* (4 vols., 1991–2009).
2 Aquinas, *Summa theologiæ*, 1 a. q. 2 prologue.
3 Geoffrey Hill writes, "God / Is distant, difficult. Things happen" in his poem "Ovid in the Third Reich" (1985: 61).
4 See Aquinas, *Summa theologiæ*, 1a, art. 3 *responsio*.
5 See Origen, *Commentarium in Evangelium Matthaei*, 14.7.10.

References

Ashbery, J. 1970. "Soonest Mended." In *The Double Dream of Spring*, 17–19. New York: E. P. Dutton & Company.

Augustine. 1953. "Of True Religion." In *Earlier Writings*, edited and translated by J. H. S. Burleigh, 218–283. London: SCM Press.

Augustine. 1991. *Confessions*, translated by H. Chadwick. Oxford: Oxford University Press.

Barth, K. 1961. *Church Dogmatics*, vol. 4, edited by G. W. Bromiley and T. F. Torrance, translated by G. W. Bromiley. Edinburgh: T & T Clark.

Fichte, J. G. 1978. *Attempt at a Critique of All Revelation*, translated by G. Green. Cambridge: Cambridge University Press.

Fink, E. 1995. *Sixth Cartesian Meditation: The Idea of a Transcendental Theory of Method*, translated by R. Bruzina. Bloomington: Indiana University Press.

Gregory of Nyssa. 1999. "Against Eunomius." In *Nicene and Post-Nicene Fathers*, 5: *Gregory of Nyssa: Dogmatic Treatises, Etc.*, edited by P. Schaff and H. Wace, 33–248. Peabody: Hendrickson Publishers.

Hart, K. 2012. "Trinitarian Theology: Notes towards a Supreme Phenomenology." In *Rethinking Trinitarian Theology: Disputed Questions and Contemporary Issues in Trinitarian Theology*, edited by G. Maspero and R. Wozniak, 308–327. London: T & T Clark.

Hart, K. 2017. "The Manifestation of the Father: On Luke 15:11–32." In *Phenomenologies of Scripture*, edited by A. Wells, 88–113. New York: Fordham University Press.

Heidegger, M. 1998. "Letter on 'Humanism'." In *Pathmarks*, edited by W. McNeill and translated by F. A. Capuzzi, 239–276. Cambridge: Cambridge University Press.

Heidegger, M. 2004. *The Phenomenology of Religious Life*, translated by M. Fritsch and J. A. Gosetti-Ferencei. Bloomington: Indiana University Press.

Henry, M. 2000. *Incarnation: Une philosophie de la chair*. Paris: Éditions de Seuil.

Henry, M. 2002. *Paroles du Christ*. Paris: Éditions de Seuil.

Henry, M. 2003. *I am the Truth: Toward a Philosophy of Christianity*, translated by S. Emanuel. Stanford: Stanford University Press.

Hill, G. 1985. *Collected Poems*. Harmondsworth: Penguin.

Husserl, E. 1973. *Experience and Judgment: Investigations in a Genealogy of Logic*, revised and edited by L. Landgrebe, translated by J. S. Churchill and K. Ameriks. Evanston: Northwestern University Press.

Husserl, E. 1978. *Formal and Transcendental Logic*, translated by D. Cairns. The Hague: Martinus Nijhoff.

Husserl, E. 1983. *Ideas* I, translated by F. Kersten. Dordrecht: Kluwer.

Husserl, E. 1997. "The Amsterdam Lectures." In *Psychological and Transcendental Phenomenology and the Confrontation with Heidegger (1927–1931)*, edited and translated by T. Sheehan and R. E. Palmer, 199–253. Dordrecht: Kluwer.

Husserl, E. 2006. *The Basic Problems of Phenomenology: From the Lectures, Winter Semester, 1910–1911*, translated by I. Farin and J. G. Hart. Dordrecht: Springer.

Imirizaldu, J. 1977. *Monjas y beatas embaucadores*. Madrid: Editora Nacional.

Jüngel, E. 1983. *God as the Mystery of the World: On the Foundation of the Theology of the Crucified One in the Dispute between Theism and Atheism*, translated by D. L. Guder. Grand Rapids: Wm. B. Eerdmans Publishing.

Kant, I. 1960. *Religion within the Limits of Reason Alone*, translated by T. M. Greene and H. H. Hudson. New York: Harper and Row.

66   *Kevin Hart*

Kearney, R. and J. S. O'Leary (eds.). 2009. *Heidegger et la question de Dieu*. Paris: Presses Universitaires de France.

Marion, J.-L. 1998. *Reduction and Givenness: Investigations of Husserl, Heidegger, and Phenomenology*, translated by T. A. Carlson. Evanston: Northwestern University Press.

Marion, J.-L. 2002. *Being Given: Toward a Phenomenology of Givenness*, translated by J. L. Kosky. Stanford: Stanford University Press.

Meier, J. P. 1991–2009. *A Marginal Jew: Rethinking the Historical Jesus*, 4 vols. New York: Doubleday.

Moltmann-Wendel, E. 1997. *Autobiography*, translated by J. Bowden. London: SCM Press.

Rahner, K. 1978. *Foundations of Christian Faith: An Introduction to the Idea of Christianity*, translated by W. V. Dych. New York: Seabury Press.

Rahner, K. 1979. "Anonymous and Explicit Faith." In *Theological Investigations, vol. 16: Experience of the Spirit: Source of Theology*, 52–59, translated by D. Morland. New York: Crossroad.

Reinarch, A. 1969. "'Concerning Phenomenology', translated by D. Willard." *The Personalist* 50: 194–221.

Saunders, E. P. 1985. *Jesus and Judaism*. Philadelphia: Fortress Press.

Schweitzer, A. 1998. *The Quest of the Historical Jesus: A Critical Study of Its Progress from Reimarus to Wrede*. Baltimore: Johns Hopkins University Press.

Steinbock, A. J. 1995. *Home and Beyond: Generative Phenomenology after Husserl*. Evanston: Northwestern University Press.

Stevens, W. 1997. "Notes toward a Supreme Fiction." In *Collected Poetry and Prose*, edited by F. Kermode and J. Richardson, 329–352. New York: The Library of America.

4 (Reformed) Protestantism[†]

Michael C. Rea

Many of the most well-known Protestant systematic theologies, particularly in the Reformed tradition, display (more or less) a common thematic division.[1] There are prolegomena: questions about the nature of theology, the relationship between faith and reason, and (sometimes treated separately) the attributes of scripture and its role in faith and practice. There is the doctrine of God: divine attributes, God's relationship to creation, etc. There is the doctrine of humanity: the nature and post-mortem survival of human persons, and the human condition, including the Fall and human sinfulness. There are parts devoted to the person and work of Christ: most especially, the Incarnation and atonement. There is discussion of questions in practical theology: the organization and function of the church, morality and politics. Other matters get discussed along the way as well. Most of these topics are ones which we contributors to this volume have been asked to address in our Position Statements. So I take my assignment to be, in effect, the production of a miniature sketch of a partial systematic theology. Even in miniature, this is a monumental task for a mere chapter, and a daunting one for someone whose formal training lies outside of theology. The remarks that follow represent my best effort to articulate such views on these topics as I currently hold – albeit briefly and incompletely. I hope that the views hang together in a reasonably systematic way; but, as this is but a first effort at accomplishing a task of this sort, I wish to emphasize the programmatic nature of what I shall be saying.

Since I am writing specifically as a representative of Protestantism (in all of its wide diversity),[2] it seems fitting for me to structure my chapter in accord with the thematic divisions just described. I begin with prolegomena, focusing primarily on faith and reason, and doctrines about scripture. The next three sections are devoted, respectively, to the doctrine of God, the doctrine of humanity (in which I include doctrines about the person and work of Christ) and practical theology.[3]

Prolegomena

In this section I shall focus on the relationship between faith and reason and on what I take to be the proper role of rational intuition, science and scripture in the development of one's theological views. In the first part I try to

68   *Michael C. Rea*

explain two things: my views on the nature of faith and my understanding of the relationship between faith and evidence. In the second part I turn briefly to the interplay of reason, science and scripture in theological theorizing.

Faith and reason

The term 'faith' refers sometimes to an attitude taken toward a proposition and sometimes to an attitude taken toward a person. Charlie Brown might have faith *that* Lucy will not pull the football away when he attempts to kick it, or he might have faith *in* Lucy herself. Both sorts of faith might be evaluated as rational or irrational; and both sorts might be supported or undermined by the deliverances of reason, which I shall take generally to be beliefs with propositional content. Here I shall focus mainly on propositional faith – specifically, on the sort involved in *believing something on faith* or *taking something as an article of faith*. Insofar as I talk about *rationality*, it shall be epistemic rather than (say) practical rationality that I have in mind.

A useful starting point is Richard Dawkins' cavalier characterization of faith as "belief that isn't based on evidence" (2012: 564). It is easy to see why one who holds this view about faith might also say (as Dawkins does) that faith is "one of the world's great evils" (2012: 564). Religious faith is a core motivator for much of the morally significant behaviour of those who have it, and it is, in general, both bad and dangerous to allow wholly ungrounded convictions to exert such strong and pervasive influence. But, *contra* Dawkins, having religious faith need not involve this sort of recklessness. For purposes of serious discussion about the nature of faith, Dawkins' characterization is obviously inadequate. But it is instructive to consider why.

I doubt whether many of us would be inclined to call just any ungrounded conviction an instance of faith. The superstitious view that one ought not to open an umbrella indoors is surely a belief not based on evidence. But no one would consider it an article of faith. Likewise, insane beliefs – for example, someone's belief, due to serious mental illness, that her head is made of glass – are not sensibly said to be 'taken on faith'. More interesting, however, is the idea implicit in Dawkins' statement that *having evidence* for a view precludes one from believing it on faith.

Consider again Charlie Brown and Lucy. Suppose Charlie Brown learns that Lucy has completed a year of intense therapy aimed at curing her malicious football-yanking tendencies. Lucy and her therapist both assure Charlie Brown that today she will not pull away the football when he tries to kick it. She passes a lie detector test. She offers her most prized possession as surety. Charlie Brown now has a *lot* of evidence for the proposition that Lucy does not now intend to pull away the football. But, given their past history, it will still take *faith* for Charlie Brown to believe this.

Still, saying that a view is taken on faith does imply that there is something lacking in one's evidence. It implies that one's belief is underdetermined by the evidence – other viable alternatives are compatible with the evidence.

(Reformed) Protestantism   69

This does not mean that faith is present everywhere we find underdetermination. Even our best scientific theories are underdetermined by the data, but it is hardly a matter of faith to believe that the earth revolves around the sun.

The difference lies in the degree to which the relevant alternatives are viable. It does not take faith to believe that the earth revolves around the sun because the 'viable' alternatives are nothing more than coherent propositions that do not fall afoul of known empirical data. Charlie Brown, on the other hand, faces more than a mere coherent alternative. There is a long history of elaborate deception and betrayal; the lie detector test and proffered assurances could be more of the same. In other words, despite the fact that there is much evidence in support of the proposition that Lucy does not intend to pull away the football, there is genuine and weighty counterevidence as well. As I see it, believing on faith is (roughly) believing in the face of genuine and weighty counterevidence, where counterevidence is taken to include not only evidence that contradicts one's belief, but also evidence that one lacks warrant for it (e.g., because the evidence in favour is too weak or derived from an unreliable source).[4]

How weighty? Can we be more precise? I think so. I don't imagine that there is *no evidence whatsoever* against the heliocentric model of our solar system. But for most of us nowadays, disbelieving that model on the basis of whatever evidence might speak to the contrary would manifest serious epistemic malfunction. Specifically, it would manifest malfunction in one's ability to understand, appreciate, properly weigh, and form beliefs in accord with evidence that one knowingly possesses. (Importantly, it would *not* manifest malfunction in one's ability to gather relevant evidence; nor would it manifest the sort of malfunction that I take to be involved in cases of self-deception, which is a matter of hiding evidence from oneself.) By contrast, Charlie Brown would not manifest such serious malfunction if he were to refrain from believing that it is safe to trust Lucy not to pull away the football. Indeed, even if it is *more rational* for Charlie Brown to trust Lucy, and even if the preponderance of evidence *justifies* or *warrants* the belief that it is safe to trust her, his refusing to believe that it is safe (or, for that matter, his positively believing that it is unsafe) still would not manifest the sort of serious epistemic malfunction just described. Likewise with other paradigm instances of propositional faith.

I propose, then, the following somewhat fuller (but still only partial) characterization of *believing on faith*. A person believes a proposition p on faith only if the following three conditions are met. First, the evidence for p of which she is aware is compatible with not-p. Second, believing p for whatever reason she in fact believes it does not in and of itself manifest serious cognitive malfunction or mental illness. Third, she is aware of counterevidence such that, if she were to refrain on the basis of that evidence from believing p, she would not be manifesting serious malfunction in her ability to understand, appreciate, properly weigh, and form beliefs in accord with evidence that she knowingly possesses.

70   *Michael C. Rea*

One advantage of this characterization is that it is consistent with the commonsense view that faith comes in degrees. Another advantage is that it is consistent with the view that faith is sometimes rational and sometimes not and may or may not count as knowledge, depending on the strength of the relevant counterevidence.

A third advantage – at any rate, *I'd* call it an advantage – is that it allows for cases in which it is irrational *not* to have faith. (Such might be the case if one lacked faith in God as a result of fear or self-deception.[5]) Indeed, it is even consistent with the possibility that failure to believe something that one takes on faith would involve noetic malfunction. It could involve malfunction in one's ability to appreciate, understand, weigh and form beliefs in accord with evidence, so long as the malfunction is not *serious*. Or it could involve serious malfunction of other kinds – for example, a breakdown in one's inbuilt faculty for directly perceiving the presence of God.[6]

Fourth, my characterization allows that believing on faith is consistent with a general policy of trying to form one's beliefs in accord with reason. The latter, I take it, is a policy of trying to believe *only what we are rationally permitted to believe* and, if beliefs come in degrees, to believe those things just to the degree to which we are permitted to believe them. This is obviously compatible with sometimes (sanely) believing what we are not rationally *required* to believe, which is roughly what I have identified as the necessary condition for taking something on faith.

So reason and religious faith are not, as such, fundamentally at odds with one another. Still, I do not mean to suggest that the acquisition of religious faith is just a special case of ordinary reasoning. The Christian tradition has typically emphasized that (Christian) faith is a gift from God that comes by way of divine grace. My characterization is consistent with this view. Thus, even if having Christian faith is consistent with a general policy of trying to believe *in accord* with reason, it does not follow that reason alone might lead someone to full-blown Christian faith.

Let me close this section by saying a few words in response to the question (posed by the editors of this volume) of how I might defend my theological beliefs. I think that the best that one can hope to do by way of defending *any* belief is to examine such evidence as one takes oneself to have and then try to present the publicly available evidence and describe the private evidence. Presenting publicly available evidence generally means displaying forensic evidence or giving an argument whose premises are supported by something like rational intuition, sensory experience, testimony or scientific theory. Describing private evidence means describing things like memories or personal experiences that, unlike ordinary sensory experiences, cannot be produced in others by telling them where to look, listen, smell, taste or touch. I think that all of these sorts of evidence can be marshalled in support of Christian belief.

As Alvin Plantinga (2003) and William Alston (1991) have argued (in different ways), warrant for some distinctively Christian beliefs can come from religious experiences[7] – for example, putative experiences of divine love

(Reformed) Protestantism 71

washing over you, of God speaking to you through the scriptures, etc. As Richard Swinburne has argued (2003), for those who take claims like *there is a God* and *if there is a God, God would likely reveal Godself by way of something like an incarnation* to be reasonably probable, historical evidence for the resurrection of Jesus should lead one to assign high probability to the claim that Jesus rose from the dead; and this, in turn, should lead one to assign high probability to the truth of other things that one reasonably takes Jesus to have said. For those who find their premises intuitive, traditional arguments for the existence of God (the ontological argument, the cosmological argument and the design argument) also lend support to certain Christian doctrines. There is, furthermore, a vast body of testimony (about religious experiences, expert assessments of the coherence or viability of various theological propositions, answers to prayer, intuitions in support of this or that premise in an argument for the truth of some Christian doctrine, and so on) to which many of us have access as well. Finally, there is the 'experience' of having all of this sort of evidence seem to hang together and make sense of one's world – the experience, in other words, of having a large body of different kinds of evidence seem to provide cumulative support for an overall worldview, some details of which are central and thus taken to be highly likely to be true and other details of which are perhaps less central and more tentatively held (cf. Holley 2010).

I take myself to have evidence of all of these sorts, some of which is communicable and some of which is not. Defending my faith, then, is just a matter of trying to communicate what is communicable and (when I am 'defending' it to myself) attending closely to what is not. I take it that *everyone* is in this position with respect to their basic worldview. Some of the evidence supporting it is communicable, some is not. So this is not a strange feature of Christianity or other religious faiths. Rather, it is true of every worldview, atheistic ones included. The differences in worldview among intellectual peers who are not suffering from self-deception and other such hard-to-detect failures of rationality are, I think, just to be explained in part by differences in our incommunicable evidence and also by differences in how we weigh various aspects of the vast body of communicable evidence that we have at our disposal. For this reason, it seems that at least some of the tenets of every worldview must be taken on faith.

Sources for theology

One of the major distinctives of Protestantism is the '*sola scriptura*' slogan, which has implications for how theology is to be done both individually and corporately. As I understand it, the slogan expresses at least three attributes that the Reformers held to be true of scripture: *authority*, *clarity* and *sufficiency*.

Concerning the authority of scripture, I take the traditional position to be that scripture is what we might call *foundationally authoritative* – that is,

72   Michael C. Rea

more authoritative than any other source of information or advice – within the domain of all topics about which it aims to teach us something.[8] (For convenience, let us refer to the topics in question together as *matters of faith and practice*.[9]) The claim that scripture is *clear* and *sufficient* amounts, roughly, to the claim that all doctrines and prescriptions necessary for salvation can easily be derived from scripture by persons concerned about the salvation of their souls without the help of the Church or Church tradition.[10] Together, these claims about authority, clarity and sufficiency provide what I take to be the core idea underlying the *sola scriptura* slogan.

I affirm *sola scriptura* as I have just glossed it. In what follows, I would like to highlight just three points in connection with it that pertain specifically to the question of how scripture, reason and tradition ought to interact in our theologizing.

First: The doctrine carries no substantive interpretive commitments. It is consistent with the most wooden literalist approach to biblical texts; it is also consistent with rampant allegorical interpretations and all manner of others. To this extent, it permits a great deal of theological diversity. Its import is simply to provide a loose but significant constraint on the development of theology. *Sola scriptura* implies that when we do theology, what we ultimately say must be consistent with our best judgement about what the text of scripture teaches. Proponents of *sola scriptura* cannot sensibly think "scripture teaches X, but it is more reasonable for me to believe not-X"; but they are free to use any and all tools at their disposal to determine for themselves what exactly it is that scripture teaches.

Second: I take the doctrine to be plausible only on the assumption that scripture asserts and advises only what God, as divine author, asserts and advises. Absent that assumption, it assigns far too much authority to scripture *alone*. Surely if the assumption were false there would be no reason to regard scripture as a greater authority in the domain of faith and practice than *every other* human experience or testimonial report. For those who make the assumption, however, it is no light matter to pronounce either on what scripture teaches or on what topics fall within the domain of 'matters of faith and practice'. For the doctrine implies that once we have reached a settled judgement about what the text of scripture teaches, we have in the content of that teaching reasons for belief and action that are at least as authoritative as reasons from any other source.

Third: A consequence of my first two points is that proponents of *sola scriptura* have good reason to make careful and judicious use of all available tools for determining what the text of scripture might be saying. These tools include science, moral and other rational intuitions, the techniques of historical biblical criticism and literary analysis, and so on. Moreover, the assumption that scripture has a divine author licenses a particular way of using these tools. We know in general that it is perfectly legitimate to interpret texts in light of what we reasonably believe about their authors. Historians of philosophy, for example, often allow their interpretations of

(Reformed) Protestantism 73

great thinkers to be constrained by assumptions about the sorts of errors to which these thinkers may or may not be susceptible. If interpretation X implies that Aristotle was not very bright or well-informed with respect to the science of his day, that by itself is a reason not to favour interpretation X. So likewise, it seems, with a divinely authored text. If our best science tells us that the sun, moon and stars existed long before terrestrial plant life, that fact by itself constitutes good reason – as good as the science itself – to believe that a divine author would not teach anything to the contrary. If moral intuition tells us that slavery is wrong, or that conquering armies should not seek to annihilate their enemies, or that men and women are equally suited for positions of ecclesial authority, these facts by themselves constitute good reason – as good as the intuitions involved – to believe that a divine author would not teach anything to the contrary. And these considerations will appropriately guide our interpretation of the relevant texts.

Of course, the reasons just mentioned can be defeated. It is possible, for example, to acquire evidence that scripture really does contradict some of our moral views or some of our scientific views. But the only condition under which *sola scriptura* would bind someone to revise her intuitions or scientific beliefs in light of scripture (instead of revising her understanding of scripture in light of her intuitions or scientific beliefs) would be one in which her reasons for believing that scripture teaches something contrary to reason are evidentially stronger than the intuitions themselves.

God

The following passage from the Belgic Confession, one of the doctrinal standards of the Christian Reformed Church, fairly accurately captures my understanding of the essential attributes of God:

> Article 1: We all believe in our hearts and confess with our mouths that there is a single and simple spiritual being, whom we call God – eternal, incomprehensible, invisible, unchangeable, infinite, almighty; completely wise, just, and good, and the overflowing source of all good.
> (Christian Reformed Church 1988: 78)

Fairly accurately; but not perfectly. For example, the attributes of incomprehensibility, simplicity, unchangeability, and infinity are so difficult to understand that ascribing them to God is apt to mislead without extended comment (which I shall not provide here). I think that the attributions express truths; but I do not, for example, think that divine simplicity implies that there are no distinctions to be made within the Godhead or that incomprehensibility implies that God cannot be understood or talked about except via analogy or metaphor, or that divine unchangeability implies that it is false to say that God *became* incarnate, etc. More importantly, the quoted passage leaves out some attributions that I would want to include (most

74   *Michael C. Rea*

of which the Confession itself includes, at least implicitly, elsewhere in its text). For example, I would say that God is necessarily existent, essentially triune and omniscient; God is loving and merciful and capable of sorrow and anger; God is a perfect person,[11] and the creator and sustainer of the concrete contingent universe. None of these additional attributes, however, are mentioned in the quoted passage.

For some of these attributions, there is clear scriptural warrant. For others, however, there is not. What, then, justifies their presence in standard confessions, creeds and other formal statements of Christian belief? A traditional but controversial answer is that the attributions not clearly derivable from other parts of scripture can nonetheless be derived from the scriptural claim that God is perfect. This answer has methodological implications that deserve further comment. I shall discuss those in the first part of this section. In the second part, I shall focus on *triunity*, the attribute that is at once the most distinctive to Christian theology and the most puzzling.

Perfection

In accord with many others in the Christian tradition, I think that our grasp of perfection can serve as a reliable guide to discovering and understanding other divine attributes. It is not an infallible guide, for there is no good reason to think that any of us has a perfect grasp of it. But I take it that, to the extent that we have warrant for the claim that a perfect being would have some property p, we also have warrant for the claim that God has p.

If this is right, then the claim that God is a perfect being is on somewhat different footing from claims like 'God is a father' or 'Christ is a redeemer'. The difference is that 'God is a perfect being' is to be understood strictly and literally, so as to license the following inference pattern for all substitution instances of F that render (1) true:

1   Perfect beings are F.
2   Therefore, God is F.

The same is not true of 'God is a father' or 'Christ is a redeemer', for there are generalizations true of fathers and redeemers that are not true of God or Christ. Here are two obvious ones: fathers are male; redeemers deliver captives from their captors. Even if it turns out to be true that God is in some sense male or that Christ literally delivers us from a captor, I do not think that we can validly infer these claims from the two generalizations. To put the point another way, then: *Perfect being theology*, the project of developing a theory about what God is like by consulting our intuitions about perfection, is a more promising endeavour than (say) *cosmic father theology* or *redeemer theology* or *creator theology*.

Our grasp of *perfection* also serves as a defeasible guide to interpreting scripture. Sticking with one of our same examples: Scripture tells us that

God is our heavenly father; now we face an interpretive choice. Must we make inferences that imply that God is male? To say 'yes' is to treat *being a father* with the methodological import that I assign to *being perfect*. To say (as some might wish to) 'no – and, indeed, we should actively resist such inferences because a perfect being would entirely transcend gender' is to allow our intuitions about perfection to serve as our interpretive guide.

Note, too, that in saying all of this I presuppose that at least some of our concepts apply univocally to God and express truths about what God is in his very nature. If that presupposition were false, then one could not validly infer that *God is F* from the claim that *God is perfect and perfect beings are F*. This is, of course, strongly at odds with the views that motivate apophatic and so-called 'therapeutic' approaches to theology.[12]

Triunity

According to the doctrine of the trinity, there is exactly one God, but three divine persons – Father, Son and Holy Spirit. A bit more precisely, the doctrine includes each of the following claims:[13]

T1 There is exactly one God, the Father almighty.
T2 Father, Son and Holy Spirit are not identical.
T3 Father, Son and Holy Spirit are consubstantial.

To say that two things are consubstantial is to say that they share a common nature – that is, they are members of exactly the same kind. Saying that two or more divine beings are consubstantial, then, implies that they are *identical with respect to their divinity* – they are not divine in different ways, neither is more or less divine than the other, and if one is a God then the other is a God too.[14]

It would be quite an understatement to say that this is a puzzling doctrine. At first glance (and, many would say, even after a much closer look) it appears to be incoherent. There are various ways of trying to demonstrate the incoherence. The one I prefer proceeds as follows: Suppose T1 is true. Then the Father is a God. But, given what I have just said about consubstantiality, T2 and T3 say that the Son and the Spirit are *distinct from the Father* (and from one another) but *exactly the same kind of thing* as the Father. So if the Father is a God, then the Son is a God, the Spirit is a God, and each is distinct from the other two. But then it follows that there are *three* Gods, contrary to T1. So the doctrine is incoherent.

Resolving the contradiction means giving up a premise or saying that one of the inferences is invalid. I have written at length elsewhere both about what *not* to say in response to this problem (if one cares about creedal orthodoxy), and about the solution I myself favour.[15] Here I shall simply cut to the chase and recap my own solution, which will also serve to explicate

76   *Michael C. Rea*

the attribute of triunity. In short, the solution is to reject the inference from T4 to T5:

T4   The Father is a God, the Son is a God and the Spirit is a God; and each is distinct from the other two.
T5   Therefore: There are three Gods.

The challenge is to explain how this can sensibly be done.

The model I favour begins with the Aristotelian idea that every material object is a compound of *matter* and *form*. The form might be thought of as a complex organizational property – not a mere shape, but something much richer. For Aristotle, the form of a thing is its *nature*. Thus, on this sort of view, St Peter would be a compound of some matter and the form *humanity*; St Paul would be a compound of the same form but different matter. Sharing the same form is what it means for Peter and Paul to be consubstantial.

Now imagine a case in which some matter has two forms. Suppose, for example, that *being a statue* and *being a pillar* are forms; and suppose an artistic building contractor fashions a lump of marble that exemplifies both. The contractor has made a statue. She has also made a pillar. Furthermore, the two compounds are genuinely distinct: for example, the pillar could survive erosion that would obliterate the statue. But surely we don't want to say that two material objects – a statue and a pillar – occupy exactly the same place at the same time. What then might we say about this situation?

What Aristotle would have said is that the statue and the pillar are the *same material object* but not the *same thing* or even the same *compound*. This sounds odd. How can *two things* or *two compounds* count as *one material object*? Answer: All there is to being a material object is being some matter that exemplifies at least one form. So we count one material object wherever we find some matter that exemplifies at least one form. To say that the statue and the pillar are *the same material object*, then, is to say no more or less than that the two things share all of the same matter in common.

If this view is correct, then the following will be true: The statue is a material object, the pillar is a material object, the statue is distinct from the pillar but each is the same material object as the other; so exactly one material object (not two) fills the region occupied by the statue.

Now let us return to the trinity. God is not material, of course; but we might still suppose that each divine person has constituents that play the same *roles* that matter and form play in material objects.[16] If we do, then we can say about the divine persons something like what we said about the statue and the pillar. Suppose that the divine nature plays the role of matter in the divine persons; and suppose that three separate properties (let's just label them 'F', 'S' and 'H') play the role of form. Then we can say that all there is to being 'a God' is being a compound of the (one and only) divine nature and some person-making property (like 'F'). Furthermore, to say that Father, Son and Spirit are the *same God* is just to say that Father, Son and

(Reformed) Protestantism 77

Spirit share the same 'matter' – that is, the same divine nature. Father, Son and Spirit are, on this view, genuinely distinct *compounds* and genuinely distinct *persons*; but, precisely by virtue of sharing the same divine nature, they count as one and the same God.[17]

If all of this is right, then (as in the statue/pillar example) we can say the following about the divine persons: The Father is a God, the Son is a God and the Holy Spirit is a God, but each is the same God as the others; so, since there are no other Gods, there is exactly one God. The inference from T4 to T5 is therefore blocked. Furthermore, we can say without qualification that God is a person, because on any way of resolving the ambiguity of 'God', 'God is a person' comes out true. We can even say unqualifiedly that *God is triune*, so long as we understand triunity as the attribute (possessed by each divine person) of sharing one's 'matter' with exactly two other divine persons.

Humanity and the human condition

We come now to doctrines concerning human nature and the human condition. On the subject of human nature, I shall focus on three questions: What are we? What is our *telos*? And what is the chief obstacle to human flourishing? This last question marks a natural transition to the subject of the human condition, under which heading I plan mainly to focus on Christian teaching about God's plan for rectifying the human condition – that is, the doctrines of incarnation and atonement.

Human nature

What are we? According to the Christian scriptures and the most well-known creeds and confessions of the major strands of Christianity, we are rational creatures created in the image of God; we are moral agents who are subject to praise and blame for at least some of our acts; and we are capable of being resurrected (that is, restored to bodily life) after the death of our physical bodies and of living forever in the presence of God. These claims, all of which I accept, seem to me to constitute the core of Christian teaching about what we are.

The *imago dei* doctrine provides a defeasible guide to further ways of fleshing out our views about human nature. Importantly, however, neither that doctrine nor anything else in Christianity pushes us toward the view that we are ultimately destined to live as *disembodied* beings. Contrary to what seems to be the prevailing view in the popular imagination, the Christian concept of the afterlife is not one that involves life as a ghost or disembodied soul. Instead, the hope expressed in the scriptures and the creeds is for bodily resurrection and physical life in God's new creation.

Similarly, I do not think that the *imago dei* doctrine, Christian doctrines about the afterlife or anything else central to Christianity clearly commits one to a position on the question that most contemporary philosophers of

78   *Michael C. Rea*

religion would take us to be asking with the words, 'What are we?' – namely, the question of whether we are immaterial souls, soul-body composites, wholly material beings or something else. In the places where talk of souls shows up explicitly in scripture or conciliar pronouncements, it is generally easy to construe such talk neutrally or perhaps metaphorically as pertaining to *minds* and thus to refrain from reading into the text a commitment to immaterial (human) souls.

As it happens, I lean strongly toward the view that human beings have immaterial souls and either *are* the souls they have or are somehow composites of body and soul. The main reason for this is that I am already committed to believing in at least one immaterial mind – the mind of God – and the hypothesis that all minds are immaterial seems to me to be simpler and no less plausible than the hypothesis that some minds are material and some are immaterial. I acknowledge the impressive array of facts about how mental phenomena correlate with and depend upon neurological and other physical phenomena. I acknowledge, too, that these facts provide very good reason to accept materialism for those whose philosophical and theological commitments do not push in the other direction. But I do not think that dualism is *refuted* by the evidence we have from science. So, for the reason just given, I lean toward the view that persons have immaterial souls. But I do not think that much of import hangs on this belief.

This section on human nature is also a natural place to comment on human freedom and its relationship to divine providence. Are we free? If so, are we free in a way that precludes divine foreknowledge or divine predestination? I mention these questions only to set them aside. Scripture affirms, and so I believe on faith, that we are morally responsible, that God is sovereign and knows our future, that those who will live eternally in the presence of God have been somehow "chosen before the foundation of the world" for this destiny and that the very faith by which we are saved comes to believers by divine grace as a free gift from God (cf. Ephesians 1 and 2). But how all of this interacts with human freedom is, to my mind, a complete mystery. Furthermore, I take it to be not so much a mystery peculiar to Christianity (as, say, the precise nature of the atonement might be) but one that arises out of the simple fact that freedom itself is ill-understood, and perhaps intractably so.

What is our *telos*? The Westminster Shorter Catechism asks, "What is the chief end of Man?" and gives the answer: "To glorify God and enjoy him forever." This captures the heart of Christian teaching about the human *telos*. It implies that we cannot flourish outside of a relationship with God, that the purpose for which we are created is wholly oriented toward God, that we are capable of living forever and that our purpose includes eternal *enjoyment* of God.

But Christianity also teaches that human beings are not capable on their own of coming anywhere close to realizing their *telos*. They need divine help, owing to a further (contingent) fact about human nature. In short, human nature has become corrupted. This corruption is supposed to be something we are born with, a result somehow of the first human sin, and a condition that makes it very likely – most would say *inevitable* – that we fall into further sin. These claims constitute the main part of the doctrine of original sin.[18] The other part, more controversial, is the doctrine of original guilt, which implies that the corruption of our nature is sufficient, even in the absence of voluntary sin in our earthly lives, to preclude us ultimately from eternal life with God.[19]

Both parts of this doctrine are puzzling; both parts are theologically important. Why should the first human sin (assuming there was such a thing) result in *universal* corruption? Why should corruption present in us *from birth* pose an obstacle to our relationship with God *even in the absence of voluntary sin* on our part? There are no easy answers to these questions.[20] But neither is it easy simply to abandon the doctrine. Original sin (taken to include original guilt) is supposed to explain two facts about the human condition. First, sin is universal. Everyone is disposed to sin, and everyone who lives long enough to commit voluntary sin does so. Second, everyone needs salvation. The supposition that there was a *first sin* that damaged human nature explains the universality of sin without implying that God created us in a damaged condition or that it is sheer coincidence that we are all damaged. The supposition that it is *human nature* that got damaged, and damaged in such a way as to separate us from God, explains why *absolutely everyone* needs salvation.

I think that the two facts just mentioned can be accepted independently of the doctrine of original sin, simply on the strength of the scriptural evidence that supports them. I also think that the doctrine itself can be reasonably accepted as an article of faith, even in the absence of answers to the challenging questions mentioned earlier. Still, it would be nice to have at least some idea of how the first sin might have resulted in the consequences that the doctrine affirms.[21] I do not have a full theory to offer, but I can take some initial steps in that direction.

Suppose that it is part of the human design plan for us to exist in a kind of emotional and psychological union with God (analogous to but deeper even than the sort of union that takes place between close friends or spouses). Under 'normal' circumstances, we would experience this union in rudimentary form from the first moment of our existence as psychological beings, and it would grow stronger and deeper throughout our lives. Furthermore, it is absolutely necessary for proper moral and psychological development. Being apart from this relationship is like being at the bottom of the sea without a pressurized suit: we become damaged, distorted and subject to further moral and psychological deterioration for as long as we are without it. Suppose that the first human person(s) came into the world already united with God in the requisite way but that one consequence of the first sin was that God partially withdrew God's presence from creation, so that the union for which we were designed was no longer readily available – it could be had only dimly in this life and only with special divine help and as a result of actively seeking God.

80 *Michael C. Rea*

This is a story according to which the first sin does indeed result in universal corruption. Although there is clearly a sense in which human nature remains the same after the withdrawal of God's presence, there is also clearly a sense in which it does not. Being human after the Fall is a fundamentally different thing from being human prior to the Fall. Post-Fall human beings find themselves in a world lacking something they desperately need in order to achieve their *telos*, and they are corrupted and moving toward further ruin from the first moment of life. On the supposition that living in a world bereft of the divine presence results in damage so utterly devastating as to pervade our entire psyche, it is even appropriate to say (with Calvin) that one result of the Fall is the *total depravity* of the human race.

The story just given explains the universality of sin. Sin is universal because humans can avoid sin only by being fully in the presence of God, and the first sin resulted in the partial withdrawal of God's presence. It also provides the resources to explain why God's plan of salvation is relevant to everyone. Standard Christian soteriology maintains that the work of Christ makes us fit for God's presence and contributes to our sanctification. We might suppose, then, that even infants who die without voluntarily sinning require (as a result of their being conceived and born in the conditions just described) divine help to become fit for the presence of God, without which help they would remain damaged in their afterlife and would experience precisely the sort of moral deterioration and ruin that characterize natural human life.

The human condition

The human condition, then, is fundamentally a condition of sin and misery. The idea is not that we are constantly *committing* sin and *feeling* miserable, never experiencing pleasure, never displaying virtues, always displaying vices, and so on. Rather, the idea is this: First, our lives are characterized by sin, in that we are unable without divine assistance to order our desires in the right way, and doing the right thing involves moral struggle against strong and pervasive self-oriented inclinations. Second, this situation is one in which we are 'objectively miserable', not happy in the Aristotelian sense, failing to flourish, and subject as a result to feeling miserable far more often than we should expect in a world created by a loving God.

The Christian gospel, however – the *good news* – is that this tale of sin and misery is not the whole story about the human condition. The rest of the story is that, despite our sin and despite how things may look, God still loves us, desires union with us and wants us to flourish and has therefore intervened dramatically in human history in order to save us from our condition. The essential details of this propitious intervention, *sans* explanatory comments, are as follows. The second person of the trinity became human and lived among us as the man, Jesus of Nazareth. He lived a perfectly sinless life and fulfilled the human *telos*, showing us in the process both what God the Father is like and what human beings were meant to be like. During his life on earth, he worked miracles – healing the sick, walking on water, feeding his followers, raising the dead and much else besides. At the end he suffered unjust persecution, torture and death at the hands of his contemporaries, after which he rose bodily from the dead and ascended into heaven. All of this, but perhaps especially his suffering, death and resurrection, somehow delivers us from the power of sin and death and contributes to reconciling the whole world to God. Moreover, after Jesus' ascension, the Holy Spirit came to dwell within individual believers and to help them realize the sort of union with God that they were intended to have.

I believe this story, as I have told it, in its entirety; and I believe that the miracles reported therein literally occurred. I believe all of this in part because I take the New Testament authors to be reliable reporters of the events in Jesus' life. But, of course, there is much in the story that merits extended discussion.

First, how shall we understand the claim that the second person of the trinity became human? As with the doctrine of the trinity, the Christian tradition does not offer a full-blown theory of the incarnation but simply imposes boundaries on our theorizing. Whatever else we say about the incarnation, a fully orthodox theory (i.e., one that respects the pronouncements of the ecumenical creeds) must at least say this: In becoming human, the second person of the trinity retained his divine nature, so that the incarnate Christ is *one person* with *two natures* rather than (say) one person with a single hybrid nature or two persons in one body, each with his own nature; and, whatever else it involved, taking on human nature at least meant coming to have a rational soul, or mind, and a physical human body and having two wills, human and divine.

From this basic core, the doctrine may be fleshed out in various ways. Often the fleshing out is done in response to puzzles that highlight tensions between Jesus' manifest humanity and his alleged divinity. For example, the Bible says that Jesus grew in wisdom. It also says that he was tempted to sin. But a divine being would always know and take the wisest course of action and so could not *grow* in wisdom; and, being perfectly good, a divine being would never want to do sinful things and so could hardly be tempted to do so.

Since orthodoxy already requires positing something *like* two minds in the incarnate Christ, my own response to these puzzles is to flesh out the doctrine along the lines of Thomas Morris' 'two-minds' view (Morris 1986). On this view, the divine mind of Christ displays all of the perfections that we expect of divinity, but the human mind of Christ suffers some of the deficiencies that afflict humanity and that Jesus himself manifests. Admittedly, positing two minds suggests that we are also positing two *persons*, contrary to orthodoxy. But we can resist this suggestion by maintaining that the divine mind functions in the psychology of Jesus in the way that a 'subconscious' mind is supposed to function according to certain (probably false) theories about human psychology.[22] According to such theories, one's first-person

82   *Michael C. Rea*

perspective, self-awareness and conscious life are associated with one's conscious mind; but a lot of further mental content, including beliefs, desires and even acts of will, resides in and occasionally wells up from the subconscious. So likewise, we might suppose, with the two minds of Christ. The subconscious divine mind can provide access to all of the knowledge, power, moral strength and so on that a divine being is supposed to possess. But it can leave the human mind ignorant of certain facts and allow it to experience temptation or weakness. Since there is only one first-person perspective in Jesus on this model, there is no danger of its committing us to the claim that there are two persons in the incarnate Christ; but there is still quite obviously room for saying that Christ has a human soul (in addition to the divine mind) and a human will (in addition to the divine will).

Second, what shall we say about how the suffering, death and resurrection of Jesus contribute to rectifying the human condition? Our condition, again, is one of sin and misery, brought on by a primordial change in the relationship between God and creation. Whereas God's presence in the world and to human beings was once vivid and readily available, now it is hidden and available only with difficulty. But scripture tells us that the work of Christ has changed all of this for the better. As a result of Christ's work, God's presence and assistance are now more readily available. We who embrace Christ's work on our behalf are no longer at odds with God in any deep way; we therefore have access to the divine help we need in order to avoid sin and reach our *telos*. Although we cannot fully achieve our *telos* in this life, we are assured that our lives will continue after our physical death and that we will in the afterlife be able to reach it. The New Testament employs a variety of terms (in addition to *salvation*) to describe what the work of Jesus accomplished on our behalf: for example, *justification*, *redemption* or *ransom*, *reconciliation* with God, *deliverance* from sin, *re-creation* or *rebirth*, the offering of an *atoning* sacrifice, *abundant life* and *eternal life*. But, I take it, the very simple message is that somehow, through Christ, the human condition has been rectified so that we are now able ultimately to glorify God and enjoy God forever.

But how exactly does it all work? Which of the aforementioned terms are to be taken literally, and which are mere metaphors? Different decisions on these matters push one in radically different theoretical directions. Taking the *justification* and *atoning sacrifice* language quite literally and treating *ransom* language as more metaphorical, for example, tends to push theologians in the direction of a penal-substitutionary model: Jesus' death on the cross was a sacrifice to God the Father, wherein Jesus bore in his body and soul exactly the penalty that we ourselves deserved in order to satisfy the wrath of God. Taking the redemption and ransom language more literally, on the other hand, pushes in the direction of a *Christus victor* model, in which concerns about *justification* are (at least) de-emphasized and Jesus' death is seen as a literal *transaction* of some sort which delivers us from genuine bondage to the Devil, or to the power of sin, or to some other kind of evil other-worldly force.

The view that the legal/penal imagery deserves pride of place, and that the *justification* of sinners is first and foremost what was accomplished by Christ's atoning sacrifice on the cross, has sometimes been referred to as the 'Protestant Orthodoxy' (cf. Aulén 1931). I do not deny this view. But, at this stage in my thinking about the matter, neither can I defend it. For it is not clear to me that there is sufficient scriptural data for elevating *any* of these images over the others for theory-building purposes. Furthermore, it seems that one available theoretical option is to say simply this: The main soteriological message of the New Testament is that the work of Christ accomplished, in some sense, *all* of these things for us. It made us justified in the eyes of God; it delivered us from the power of sin, evil and death and resulted in their utter defeat and humiliation; and it brought us new life, eternal and abundant, and made us into new creations. But as to how and why and in exactly what sense all of these things happened, perhaps we cannot say without offering a model that ultimately lapses into metaphor, leaves out important truths or otherwise misleads.

Life and practice

As the previous section makes clear, I think that we human beings come into the world morally and spiritually damaged, and I think that we tend to go on to damage and be damaged by one another in ways that produce all manner of corruption and psychological dysfunction. Much of this I take to be readily evident to any competent observer of humanity, regardless of religious commitments. But I have to admit that the fundamental truth of this teaching is nowhere more evident to me than within my own life and soul. When I look within, the Christian story about the human condition rings deeply true; and the Christian story about how we might be saved from this condition comes as powerfully good news. The good news, in turn, is, to the extent that it can rationally be believed, a story to orient one's life around – a story that one ought to struggle hard to understand, to communicate (respectfully, lovingly) to others and to model one's behaviour around. As I have indicated throughout this chapter, I do believe the story; and after many years of hard and critical thinking about it and many years of learning from others wiser and smarter than me who have also thought hard and critically about it, I remain convinced that the story can be and is rationally believed by a great many people. All of this has implications for my views about morality, politics and my professional life.

In morality, my views about the human condition lead me to a deep skepticism about the prospects for successful ethical theory-building. Profoundly corrupt people ought not to have high hopes for reaching the full and unvarnished truth about morality and the good life. I am not a moral anti-realist,

84   *Michael C. Rea*

and I do think that we have a lot of moral knowledge. Scripture is one source of such knowledge; but there are also plenty of obvious, objective facts about what is obligatory, non-obligatory, permissible or impermissible. It is quite obvious, for example, that, in the course of a routine trip to the supermarket, it would be absolutely wrong to go on a shooting spree, to set up a tryst with a married friend, to steal a car, and so on. But basic moral knowledge is one thing; moral theory-building and reasoning about 'hard cases' are wholly another.

Plato's Socrates sometimes conveys the impression that one cannot be truly virtuous without being in possession of a philosophical theory about the nature of virtue, or goodness. From a Christian point of view, however, living well (morally and otherwise) does not depend so much on philosophical understanding as on life in the Church. Scripture enjoins us to cultivate the "fruits of the spirit" – love, peace, patience, and so on – and to be "transformed by the renewing of our minds", which is largely supposed to be a matter of learning to love God and neighbour in a way that emulates Christ. There is no indication that *theorizing* about these things will help us much in our efforts to accomplish them. Rather, we are enjoined to accomplish these things by having regular fellowship with other believers, confessing our sins to one another and praying for one another, diligently studying scripture together and submitting ourselves to one another in various ways – partly in order to cultivate humility and treat one another kindly but also for the sake of receiving help in the Christian life. The liturgies of the Church, the sacraments and the Church calendar, and the spiritual disciplines are all likewise directed toward the end of helping individual believers to take their place in a body that is working corporately in an effort to manifest Christ and to bring healing and the good news of the gospel to a broken world. Moral theory is, at best, a secondary or tertiary aid.

In addition to capturing something important about the relation between Christian faith and the moral life, this last idea of working corporately to manifest Christ and bring healing to a broken world seems also to capture something important about the relation between Christian faith and politics. But from the fact that Christians as such ought to be involved *somehow* in this sort of corporate work, not much seems to follow about exactly what form that involvement ought to take. (Much can be derived from a developed eschatology; and differences in views on that topic help to explain dramatic differences in the political involvement of various Christian groups. But my own eschatological views are undeveloped and wholly tentative at best.)

What should I as a Christian think about (say) public policies pertaining to abortion, or climate change, or factory farming, or industrial pollution, or the welfare system? How can I, together with the rest of the Church, respond to these concerns in a way that "manifests Christ and brings healing to a broken world"? The fact that we are called to love our neighbours means, I think, that we must *care* about such questions and try to reach answers in a timely manner to the ones that are most salient in our circumstances.

(Reformed) Protestantism 85

Otherwise we will likely fail to manifest appropriate concern for our neighbours. But *how* one answers these questions will depend not only on truths of the Christian faith but also on one's assessments of relevant empirical data and authoritative testimony, negotiable philosophical presuppositions and independent value judgements and value prioritizations, all of which might vary among equally intelligent, mature, and reasonable Christians. Thus, I doubt that we can reliably reach general principles that tell us how Christians as such ought to think about and respond to the political issues we face. So my political views and involvement tend to bear only loose and indirect connections with the particulars of my faith.

Lastly, the relationship between my faith and my professional life: I said earlier that I think that the basic doctrines of Christianity constitute something that one ought to orient one's life around, communicate to others, struggle to understand, and so on. I suspect that this thought gives the primary reason why I became a professional philosopher. Although I have plenty of research interests outside of the philosophy of religion, the impetus to take up a profession where I could spend a lot of time thinking and teaching about the topics on which I've written and taught is primarily just the idea that doing so constitutes the best way for *me* (given my particular skills and interests) to orient my life around my faith, to struggle to understand it, to communicate it to others, and the like.

There is another way, too, in which my faith and my professional life interact. One of the most important job skills of an analytic philosopher is strongly correlated with whatever skill is involved in successfully rationalizing bad behaviour, deceiving oneself, putting a positive spin on bad circumstances, and so on. Also, there are certain modes of behaviour – ways of being ambitious, or arrogant, or disrespectful to others, for example – that seem much easier to fall into in professions (like philosophy) where reputation and having one's own reputation elevated over the reputations of people with whom one works is often correlated with promotions, job security, pay raises, and the like. To this extent, I find that being a philosopher (or being an academic generally) poses certain obstacles, or challenges, to my own moral and spiritual development as a Christian. Accordingly, I see a variety of ways in which being a Christian can or should enable one to achieve a degree of critical distance from certain kinds of widespread but dysfunctional norms and values in the profession. This is, of course, not to say that being a Christian is the only way of achieving such distance; but it is, or should be, *a* way of doing so.

Notes

† For helpful comments on an earlier draft of this essay, I am very grateful to Michael Bergmann, Jeff Brower, Oliver Crisp, Thomas McCall, Cristian Mihut, Sam Newlands, Alvin Plantinga, Christina Brinks Rea, and Jeff Snapper.

1 There are notable exceptions. I am painting with a broad brush.

2 I do not claim that my theological views are *paradigmatically* Protestant (if views can be that), nor even that they are paradigmatically Reformed. I am simply the chosen, even if not elected, delegate from the Reformed Protestant camp; but my assignment is to report my own views rather than the party line.

3 In laying out these views, I draw on other things I have written – especially Rea (2007), (2009a), (2009b), Murray and Rea (2008) and (2015). Those sources contain not only further development of the views laid out in here but also references to other works that expand along lines discussed here.

4 I do not here intend to take a position either on whether faith might attach to other attitudes – acceptance, for example – or on whether certain uses of 'faith' (e.g., 'I have faith that . . .') imply a pro-attitude toward the object of faith. Thanks to Dan Howard-Snyder and Robert Audi for conversations that led to this clarification.

5 As sometimes seems to happen; cf. Nagel (1997: 130–131).

6 On the idea that we have such a faculty, see Plantinga (2003: 148, 170–177).

7 In accord with Rea (2002: 68), I shall characterize religious experience as "an apparent direct awareness of either (a) the existence, character, or behaviour of a divine mind, or (b) the fact that one of one's own mental states or a testimonial report communicated by others has been divinely inspired."

8 For discussion of what it means to say that one source is 'more authoritative' than another and for fuller discussion of what it means to say that scripture is authoritative, see Rea (2016).

9 It is a matter of interpretive dispute – and hardly a trivial one! – exactly what topics fall within this domain.

10 My gloss closely follows Bavinck (2003: 477, 488); cf. Berkhof (1996: 167–168). Note that the clarity doctrine does not imply that it is easy to see *that* anything in particular is necessary for salvation – as if adherents of other religions are simply failing to understand scripture if they doubt (say) that faith in Christ is necessary for their own salvation.

11 The Christian tradition maintains that God exists in or as *three* persons, but it also resoundingly affirms that God is personal and that God is perfect as a personal being. Not every way of understanding the trinity can comfortably accommodate the unqualified claim that God is *a* person; but (as we shall see) mine can.

12 Cf. Hector (2011) for discussion.

13 This is not the only way of formulating the doctrine. But I choose this formulation because it is faithful to the creeds, suffices as well as others to raise the problem I wish to discuss and emphasizes one central tenet of the doctrine – T3 – that is all too often omitted in the contemporary literature. On the importance of T3, see Rea (2009a) or, at length, Ayres (2004).

14 For purposes here I treat 'God' as a kind term rather than a name, obviously in keeping with its use in T1.

15 See esp. Brower and Rea (2005) and Rea (2009a).

16 In fact, I think some of the most important theologians who hammered out the Niceno-Constantinopolitan formulation of the doctrine of the trinity *did* think of God in this way. Cf. Rea (2009a) for discussion and references.

17 Why do Peter and Paul not count as two persons but *one human being*? Because, unlike the divine nature, human nature does not play the role of matter.

18 Or 'ancestral sin' in Eastern Christianity; but my characterization more closely follows western lines of thought.

19 In the confessions of the Reformed tradition, the doctrine of original guilt is normally taken to include the claim that we are *guilty* for the corruption of our nature or that God *blames* us for it. It is also commonly said that God is *angry*

with us for it. I do not reject these statements outright, but I think that they are apt to mislead; and I think that the 'divine wrath' claims are particularly unfortunate in this regard. Since I cannot possibly hope to do them justice in the short space allotted here, I simply set them aside.

20 But see Rea (2007) for extended discussion of alternatives.

21 We might also ask how belief in a 'first sin' or a 'historical Adam' could be reconciled with evolutionary theory. This is a matter of interesting and active controversy right now, and several proposals strike me as promising; but I shall not pursue this issue further here.

22 The falsity of these theories does not matter. What matters for the model is just the *possibility* that two minds may be related in this way in one person.

References

Alston, W. 1991. *Perceiving God*. Ithaca, NY: Cornell University Press.

Aulén, G. 1931. *Christus Victor: An Historical Study of the Three Main Types of the Idea of the Atonement*, translated by A. G. Hebert. London: Society for Promoting Christian Knowledge.

Ayres, L. 2004. *Nicaea and Its Legacy*. New York: Oxford University Press.

Bavinck, H. 2003. *Reformed Dogmatics, vol. 1: Prolegomena*, edited by J. Bolt, translated by J. Vriend. Grand Rapids: Baker Academic.

Berkhof, L. 1996. *Introductory Volume to Systematic Theology*. Originally published as a single volume in 1932. In L. Berkhof, *Systematic Theology*. New combined edition. Grand Rapids: Wm. B. Eerdmans Publishing.

Brower, J. and M. Rea. 2005. "Material Constitution and the Trinity." *Faith and Philosophy* 22: 487–505.

Christian Reformed Church. 1988. *Ecumenical Creeds and Reformed Confessions*. Grand Rapids: CRC Publications.

Dawkins, R. 2012. "Is Science a Religion?" In *Philosophy of Religion: An Anthology*, edited by L. Pojman and M. Rea, 6th ed., 564–568. Boston, MA: Wadsworth.

Hector, K. 2011. *Theology without Metaphysics: God, Language, and the Spirit of Recognition*. Cambridge: Cambridge University Press.

Holley, D. 2010. "Treating God's Existence as an Explanatory Hypothesis." *American Philosophical Quarterly* 47: 377–388.

Morris, T. 1986. *The Logic of God Incarnate*. Ithaca, NY: Cornell University Press.

Murray, M. and M. Rea. 2008. *Introduction to the Philosophy of Religion*. Cambridge: Cambridge University Press.

Murray, M. and M. Rea. 2015. "Philosophy and Christian Theology." In *The Stanford Encyclopedia of Philosophy*, Winter 2015 ed., edited by E. N. Zalta. https://plato.stanford.edu/archives/win2015/entries/christiantheology-philosophy/.

Nagel, T. 1997. *The Last Word*. New York: Oxford University Press.

Plantinga, A. 2003. *Warranted Christian Belief*. New York: Oxford University Press.

Rea, M. 2002. *World without Design: The Ontological Consequences of Naturalism*. Oxford: Clarendon Press.

Rea, M. 2007. "The Metaphysics of Original Sin." In *Persons: Human and Divine*, edited by P. van Inwagen and D. Zimmerman, 319–356. New York: Oxford University Press.

88 *Michael C. Rea*

Rea, M. 2009a. "The Trinity." In *The Oxford Handbook of Philosophical Theology*, edited by T. P. Flint and M. C. Rea, 403–429. Oxford: Oxford University Press.

Rea, M. (ed.). 2009b. *Oxford Readings in Philosophical Theology*, 2 vols. Oxford: Oxford University Press.

Rea, M. 2016. "Authority and Truth." In *The Enduring Authority of the Christian Scriptures*, edited by D. A. Carson, 872–898. Grand Rapids: Wm. B. Eerdmans Publishing.

Swinburne, R. 2003. *The Resurrection of God Incarnate*. Oxford: Oxford University Press.

5   Orthodox Christianity

N. N. Trakakis

I was baptized and brought up in the Orthodox tradition of Christianity, and despite many a wrong turn off the beaten track, it is this tradition that I continue to follow as an authentic and faithful, although also difficult and challenging, expression of Christianity.[1] As for many others who have come to know Orthodoxy for the first time (as converts) or as if for the first time (after a period of neglect or rejection), it was a little but remarkable book by Bishop Kallistos Ware – entitled *The Orthodox Way*, first published in 1979 – which initiated me to the life and wonders of the Orthodox Church in a way that I found captivating as well as convincing. Since then, after many re-readings, I have come to dispute or disagree with some of the positions and emphases of the book, but it remains a lucid and powerful introduction to the Orthodox tradition. In what follows, therefore, I will take as my starting point the first four chapter headings of Ware's book in order to delineate the distinctive Orthodox way of thinking about the divine or God. But, to begin with, it might be helpful to say something about (what are held to be) the authoritative sources in the Orthodox tradition, as this in many respects is what sets the Orthodox apart from other churches and denominations in Christendom.

Sources and authorities

It was only after the first millennium that the three major divisions of contemporary Christianity – Roman Catholicism, Protestantism, and Orthodoxy – came into existence. This common ancestry inevitably means that there is much in faith and in practice that remains common across the three major Christian traditions. However, the unfortunate divisions also mean that various disagreements have appeared within the Christian community, and from the Orthodox view at least many of these disagreements stem in part from differences over the way in which specific authorities and sources are understood and evaluated. This is particularly the case with Scripture, Tradition, and the Church. So, let's briefly look at the Orthodox perspective on each in turn.

Scripture

The Scriptures – both Old and New Testaments – are regarded by the Orthodox as "the supreme expression of God's revelation to man" (Ware 1964: 207): in terms at least of the written revelation of God to humanity, there is no greater authority than the Bible, which is therefore held up as 'the Word of God' (thus making God the primary author of Scripture). In this respect, there is no difference between the Orthodox and all other major branches of Christianity, even though there may be some dispute as to the precise content, or canon, of the books of the Bible. Therefore, to arrive at a proper understanding of God, the first and most important point of reference is the Bible.

But the Bible, in the Orthodox view, is not something separate and distinct from the Church. The New Testament canon was established by the Church during the first four centuries (even though some dispute persisted afterwards), and this indicates something of profound theological significance: *it is only in and through the Church that the Scriptures can be interpreted authoritatively*. As Ware (1964: 207) puts it, the Bible "must not be regarded as something set up *over* the Church, but as something that lives and is understood *within* the Church" (emphases in original). Individual interpretation of Scripture is of course permitted (witness, for example, the influential biblical commentaries of John Chrysostom and Gregory Nazianzus), but ultimate authority rests with the broader Christian community, the Church. Individual or personal readings of Scripture can go wrong or mislead in innumerable ways, and for this reason the Orthodox turn to the guidance of the Church when something in Scripture is unclear or in dispute. But this is not to say that the Church has ever had a uniform way of reading Scripture: in fact, exegetical methods have always been many, as the famous rivalry between the Alexandrian (allegorical, symbolic) and Antiochene (historical, literal) hermeneutical schools in the early church testifies. This may explain why the Orthodox can accommodate (within bounds, of course) the methods of modern biblical criticism in a way that those who adhere to fundamentalist readings of the biblical texts cannot.

Tradition

For the Orthodox, 'Tradition' is the primary source of our knowledge and understanding of God. Such a statement is easily open to misunderstanding, especially given the negative connotations the word 'Tradition' carries today (in a world obsessed with novelty and change). Indeed, the liturgy and even the theology of the Orthodox Church often strike outsiders as 'conservative', 'archaic' and 'pre-modern' and therefore 'traditional' in the worst sense. But when the Orthodox speak of 'Tradition', they have something very different in mind. 'Holy Tradition', in the Orthodox Church, does not simply or even primarily refer to some long-established or inherited way of thinking or acting which has been passed down from one generation to another. Uncorrupted historical continuity with the earliest Christian

Orthodox Christianity 91

community may reflect one aspect or dimension of Tradition, but certainly not its most important, or inner, sense.

The difficulty in capturing the Orthodox conception of Tradition is indicated by its broad inclusivity: Tradition is not a separate source of revelation in addition to Scripture but rather encompasses the entirety of revelation – both the Scriptures and the 'lens' through which the Scriptures are read, where this includes the Creeds of the Councils and the writings of the Fathers (hence the emphasis on patristic theology in Orthodoxy), but also the worship of the Church and its iconography and architecture.[2] It is important to note that although these have come to form part of Tradition, they are not all placed on the same level: the writings of Gregory Nazianzus, no matter how erudite and eloquent, will never have the standing of, say, the Gospel of John. Indeed, not everything handed down from the past – no matter how highly regarded or ingrained it may be within the church community – is regarded part of 'Tradition'.

But rather than seeing Tradition 'horizontally', in terms of the texts and practices that have been transmitted over the centuries, a more profound understanding of Tradition may be given 'vertically' as "the unique mode according to which this transmission is received in the Holy Spirit". The quote is from Lossky (1974: 154), who explains this notion of Tradition as follows:

> It [Tradition] does not impose on human consciousness formal guarantees of the truths of faith, but gives access to the discovery of their inner evidence. It is not the content of Revelation, but the light that reveals it; it is not the word, but the living breath which makes the words heard at the same time as the silence from which it came; it is not the Truth, but a communication of the Spirit of Truth, outside which the Truth cannot be received.
>
> (1974: 151–152)

On one level, then, Tradition refers to the content of revelation which has been given in the body of Christ, the Church. But on another level it refers to the way in which revelation is received, lived out and understood in the Church. In either case, however, it is the Holy Spirit who is at work, inspiring the revealed content and guiding its proper reception. Lossky therefore defines Tradition as "the life of the Holy Spirit in the Church" (1974: 152). Part of the point of this reference to the activity of the Spirit is to highlight that Tradition, far from being something static and a valorization of the past (e.g., Byzantinism), is rather the dynamic movement of God in history, and especially the continuing activity of the Holy Spirit in the Church and our experience and appropriation of this in the present. Kallistos Ware brings out this dynamic and life-giving character of Tradition very well:

> Tradition is not simply a protective, conservative principle, but primarily a principle of growth and regeneration. It is not a form of sound

92 *N. N. Trakakis*

words or a 'deposit of doctrine', but a 'style of living'; it is not a mechanical acceptance of men's statements in the past, but a living experience of God's actions in the present. Holy Tradition is not merely a collection of texts and documents, the record of what others have said before us; it signifies rather a direct and personal meeting on our part, here and now, with Christ in the Holy Spirit.

(Ware 1970: 134)

Church

The Church, as the ongoing living community of God's people, is in some sense the foundation for Scripture and Tradition. Although Scripture, Tradition and Church are viewed within Orthodoxy as "a comprehensive unity" (Stylianopoulos 2008: 21), this mutual or harmonious interdependence between them should not belie the foundational reality of the Church: Scripture and Tradition are received, preserved and interpreted through the experience of the faithful which helps form the Church. But this doesn't mean that the Church 'controls', in a kind of unilateral way, the meaning and message of Scripture and Tradition. As Stylianopoulos puts it with regard to Scripture (and similar things could be said about Tradition): "The Church does not possess the Bible in such a way that it can do whatever it pleases with it, for example through virtual neglect or excessive allegorisation. . . . The Bible as the supreme record of revelation is the indisputable norm of the Church's faith and practice. The scriptures thereby bear God's authority and challenge the Church, making it accountable to the revealed will of God" (2008: 25). Church, Scripture and Tradition are therefore accountable to one another, but it is only through the Church – and primarily through the liturgical or sacramental life of the Church – that Scripture and Tradition find their ultimate meaning and purpose.

If that be the case, then what understanding or 'model' of God does the Orthodox Church provide through its Scriptures and Tradition?

God as mystery (epistemology)

> The Divinity is both infinite and incomprehensible, and this alone is comprehensible about Him – His very infinity and incomprehensibility.
>
> – St John of Damascus (*c.* 675–*c.* 749)[3]

Perhaps the dominant model or motif of God in the Orthodox tradition is that with which Kallistos Ware begins *The Orthodox Way*: God as Mystery. Ware explicates this by way of the notion of two 'poles' or dimensions in the divine reality. On the one hand, there is the radical alterity or otherness of God: "God is 'the wholly Other', invisible, inconceivable, radically transcendent, beyond all words, beyond all understanding" (Ware 1995: 11). On

Orthodox Christianity   93

the other hand, God is also a personal reality that is immanent in the world and intimately related to each of us: "This God of mystery is at the same time uniquely close to us, filling all things, present everywhere around us and within us" (Ware 1995: 12). Ware quotes from the fourteenth-century Orthodox theologian Nicholas Cabasilas, who beautifully expresses the nearness of God in his *The Life in Christ* when describing God as:

> more affectionate than any friend,
> more just than any ruler,
> more loving than any father,
> more a part of us than our own limbs,
> more necessary to us than our own heart.
>   (quoted in Ware 1995: 12)

In short, as Ware puts it, "God is both further from us, and nearer to us, than anything else" (Ware 1995: 12).

This understanding of God has come to be expressed in Orthodox theology in terms of the 'essence/energies distinction', an idea popularized by another fourteenth-century Orthodox theologian, Gregory Palamas, but which has had a long history in the Christian East, going as far back at least as the Cappadocian Fathers in the fourth century. One element of this distinction relates to 'the divine essence' (*ousia*) – that is to say, "God as he is known to himself, as distinct from how he is manifested" (Bradshaw 2008: 234). What the Orthodox have wanted to say is that God, in his essential nature, is totally inaccessible to human nature. And this, furthermore, is something intrinsic to human nature and not something that could be remedied by, for example, an encounter with or vision of God in the afterlife. But even though God is unknowable and unapproachable in essence, we can come to know and experience God insofar as we can participate in his 'energies' (*energiai*). Roughly put, the divine energies are the operations and actions of God in the world, or (as Bradshaw [2004: 273] describes them) "acts of self-manifestation" which disclose God's power and presence in creation. It is this divine presence that the hesychasts on Mount Athos famously claimed to have beheld in contemplative prayer as uncreated light, the same light that transfigured Christ on Mount Tabor. The divine energies, therefore, signify everything that God has revealed of himself in the economy of salvation, including such attributes or names as goodness, power, wisdom and love. But these operations or energies are not to be understood as created entities or beings, or reified intermediaries standing between God and creation, or emanations proceeding from the divine essence. The divine energies are not separate or distinct from God: they do not exist apart from God as though they were created by him. Rather, the energies are God himself, or more precisely God himself in his action and revelation to the world.

Whether we wish to emphasize the otherness (essence) of God or his nearness (energies), the conception of God as 'mystery' cuts across this distinction.

94   N. N. Trakakis

Although something at least can be said or known about God in light of our participation in God's energies, this does not at all reduce or remove the mystery of the divinity. No definition of God is possible, and no concepts (no matter how precisely analyzed and clarified) can allow us to achieve comprehension (in the sense of an exhaustive understanding) of God. It is in this spirit that Evagrius of Pontus warned against what might be called 'conceptual idolatry' when he commented that "God cannot be grasped by the mind. If he could be grasped, he would not be God" (quoted in Ware 1995: 11) – a comment repeated almost verbatim by Evagrius' illustrious contemporary Augustine, when he said: "*Si comprehendis, non est Deus.*"[4]

It is this emphasis on the mystery of God that gives Orthodox theology a strongly apophatic character.[5] In apophatic (or negative) theology, God is viewed as radically transcendent and incomprehensible, as the 'holy other' (the *mysterium tremendum et fascinans*) who is therefore also 'wholly other' (*tout autre*). In other words, God will always lie beyond the reach of our comprehension (i.e., our conceptual mastery), and so whatever positive statements we make about God (e.g., the various perfections we ascribe to him: 'God is omnipotent, omniscient, etc.') will always fall short in some way. For this reason it is thought that we can better (or more accurately) say what God *is not* than say anything about what he *is*, and so what we deny about God is more ultimate or truer than what we affirm about him. One can trace elements of this apophaticism back to Scripture (e.g., "No one has ever seen God," John 1:18; cf. Exodus 33:20, 1 Timothy 6:16), but it was only in later centuries that apophatic thought received a fuller and more detailed treatment. This was especially the case during the trinitarian battles fought by the Cappadocians against their contemporaries Eunomius and Aetius, who claimed that the human intellect can come to know the essence of God in a precise and complete way (and this by simply coming to understand that God's essence consists in 'unbegottenness', *agennesia*).[6]

In response to such claims, the Cappadocians highlighted the absolute incomprehensibility of God's nature. For example, Gregory of Nyssa states in *Contra Eunomium* (II 67–170) that we cannot fully know God, and he justifies this by arguing that finite human reason cannot comprehend the infinite God: "human nature has not the capacity in it to understand precisely the being of God" (*Contra Eunomium* II 67) – and the justification for this is given in terms of the ontological distance or difference (*diastema*) between the infinite creator and the finite creation. Similarly, in Part II of his *Life of Moses*, Gregory offers Moses' ascent of Mount Sinai in the Book of Exodus (chs. 32–33) as an allegorical image of *apophasis* (as do many other patristic writers). For Gregory, the ascent of Moses is an allegory of our own eternal progression toward the Divine. But this is a movement from 'light' into 'darkness', where our understanding of God is increasingly deepened and perfected, moving from the familiar (e.g., standardly accepted assumptions and conceptions) to the unknown, to the point where (for Gregory, at least) any analogy or representation of God whatever is regarded as idolatry.

Orthodox Christianity 95

This is not to say that the passage is one from the light of knowledge to the darkness of ignorance. Rather, it is a journey to a more profound kind of knowledge, signalled by the phrase the 'darkness of unknowing', where we are blinded by the divine excess and come to see (in Socratic fashion) how little we truly know and understand (Ware 1995: 14). But, for Gregory and the Orthodox tradition more broadly, this journey involves the whole person, the body as well as the mind, and so the apophatic ascent demands not simply an intellectual operation (e.g., refining or discarding concepts) but also the *katharsis* or purification of all of one's being (through such practices as meditation, prayer and silence). *Apophasis*, in other words, must be an *ascesis*. (For further elaboration of this idea, see Ellsworth 2002.)

But as in Wittgenstein's *Tractatus*, the conclusion of the mystical ascent is silence, and this is as it should be when it comes to our talk of God, 'theology'. The Ecumenical Patriarch Bartholomew recently put it this way:

> The most appropriate method of theology is the way of silence before the awesome divine mystery that can never be fully grasped or described. . . . The final word, then, of theology is silence; its essence lies in the absence of words. For if it is difficult, as Saint Gregory the Theologian claims, to conceive God, it is impossible to define God. Theology is best not said; it is most authentic when it is expressed in silence.
>
> (2008: 50–51)[7]

Although silence might be the last word, it need not be the first word. This is because the otherness of God does not erase all speech but in fact allows us (frees us, or even forces us) to speak of God in a multitude of ways (or tropes), though always aware that whatever we say will inevitably fail to delimit the divine mystery. Denys Turner makes this point well when he writes: "God is beyond our comprehension not because we cannot say anything about God, but because we are compelled to say too much," and to illustrate his point he quotes Dionysius' dictum that "There is no kind of thing which God is, *and there is no kind of thing which God is not*" (2004: 144).[8] "That is why," Turner concludes, "we cannot comprehend God: the 'darkness' of God is the simple excess of light" (p. 145). Negative theology, therefore, does not merely complement but also makes possible the practice of positive or kataphatic theology: the way of negation does not forbid but opens up and widens the space for the way of affirmation. This is even indicated, as Ware (1995: 15) observes, by the very word 'mystery', which "signifies not only hiddenness but disclosure": we shut our eyes and mouth, and a new world opens up before us.

Given the foregoing conception of the divine, as a mystery that cannot be comprehended by any finite intellect, what kind of epistemology of religious belief should be adopted? In particular, how, on the Orthodox view, is knowledge of God to be understood? Aristotle Papanikolaou, summarizing the views of Vladimir Lossky, writes: "In the end, true knowledge of God is

96 N. N. Trakakis

not propositional or conceptual; it is mystical knowledge that goes beyond reason without denying it, and is given in the experience of God – in *theosis*" (2008: 234). I will return to the notion of 'theosis' later, but for now it may be noticed how the emphasis placed on 'the mystical' in statements such as this does not amount to a form of fideism or irrationalism. As the quote makes clear, reason is not rejected; it is only surpassed in recognition of its limitations.[9] Does this mean, however, that the Orthodox theologian cannot endorse natural theology – the project of attempting to prove the existence of God through philosophical argumentation – as at least useful, if not also necessary, for coming to the knowledge of God? My own view of the matter (which I think is in keeping with Lossky's view as presented earlier) is roughly analogous to the position of Reformed epistemologists: one can be rationally justified (or 'warranted', in Plantinga's sense) in believing in God even if one does not have any (propositional) evidence or proof in support of one's belief in God. Nevertheless, such evidence or proof can be immensely helpful in many ways – for example, in helping to move an agnostic into the theistic camp, or in helping to strengthen the beliefs of someone who is already a theist, or even helping to give the theologian a better understanding of the concept of God (which is what, according to some, primarily motivated Aquinas' 'five ways'). And so, even if natural theology is not necessary, it can certainly be a valuable undertaking – and perhaps the Orthodox would do well not to be dismissive of it.[10]

God as Trinity (ontology)

> No sooner do I conceive of the One than I am illumined by the splendour of the Three; no sooner do I distinguish them than I am carried back to the One. When I think of any One of the Three I think of him as the whole, and my eyes are filled, and the greater part of what I am thinking escapes me.
> – St Gregory Nazianzus (*c.* 330–*c.* 389)[11]

In unison with the broader Christian community, the Orthodox uphold the trinitarian conception of God, according to which God is a trinity of three persons: Father, Son, and Holy Spirit. Lying at the heart of Christian faith is the paradox that God is one and God is three – "a cross for human ways of thought," as Lossky once put it (quoted in Ware 1995: 28). The first element of this paradox is indebted to the radical monotheism proclaimed by Israel long ago: "Hear, O Israel, the Lord is our God, the Lord is One" (Deuteronomy 6:4).[12] God is thus conceived as a single reality: a single 'substance' or 'essence' (*ousia*), or 'nature' (*physis*), a single 'what'. Despite their unbiblical provenance, these terms found their way into the conciliar formulations of the early church as a way of combatting mistaken or heretical views of God. In response, for example, to the Arian view that Christ did not have a divine nature or substance, that Christ was a creature (albeit a superior or exalted creature) and hence had a beginning ("there was once when the Son was not", to quote the famous Arian slogan), the Council of Nicaea stated in 325: "We believe in . . . one Lord Jesus Christ, the Son of God, begotten from the Father, only-begotten, that is, from the *ousia* of the Father, God from God, light from light, true God from true God, begotten not made, of one substance (*homoousion*) with the Father, through whom all things were made." The divine persons, then, are 'consubstantial': each is God since all share the same essence or substance.[13]

But although God is one, God is also three. On the level of 'who' (or, even better, of 'how'), God is three 'persons' (*proposa*) or 'hypostases' (a difficult word to translate, but which can be rendered as something like 'subsisting entities'). Importantly, each divine person is fully God, and each is distinct from the others in some respect: the Father is unbegotten, while the Son is begotten by the Father, and the Holy Spirit proceeds from the Father. However, the doctrine of God as Trinity is not to be construed as a form of 'tritheism' (belief in three gods), nor is it a version of 'modalism' (or Sabellianism), where the three persons are merely varying modes or manifestations of an underlying singular deity. It is tempting, from the point of view of logic or common sense, to adopt either tritheism or modalism in explicating the Trinity, but classical trinitarian faith cannot be purchased so cheaply – hence the 'cross' (as Lossky stated) and the apophatic dimension of theology mentioned earlier, though this does not necessarily amount to the acceptance of contradiction or incoherence.

At least part of the difficulty in coming to grips with the notion of God as Trinity is generated by the language of 'person'. John Zizioulas (2006), in particular, has emphasized that the Cappadocian understanding of the persons of the Trinity is far removed from the ways in which we ordinarily think of a 'human person' – for example, as a separate, individual centre of consciousness bearing a unique bundle of natural and moral properties (e.g., gender, skin colour, benevolence). To conceive of the Trinity in this way, Zizioulas states, "would be an anthropomorphic monstrosity, unworthy of the name of God" (2006: 171). On the Cappadocian view, by contrast, the divine persons "are distinguished only by their relations of ontological origination" (2006: 173). This is why the Cappadocians do not refer to each divine person as ἄτομον (roughly 'individual', and intended as a non-relational term), but as τρόπος ὑπάρξεως ('mode of existence') and σχέσις ('relation'). Gregory Nazianzus, for example, states: "The Father is a name neither of *ousia* [substance] nor of *energeia* [activity], but of *schesis* [relationship]."[14] This underscores the centrality of relation in thinking about the divine being, and when the nature of God is conceived in such terms the result is a conception of God as *dynamic movement*: God as Trinity consists in interpersonal and perichoretic communion. In line with this conception of the divine persons, true and authentic human personhood is something we are called to *attain*, or at least strive towards. We begin, in our tragically fallen state, as isolated and self-centred individuals, but our highest vocation is to become 'authentic' persons,

98   N. N. Trakakis

mirroring the mutual indwelling of love amongst the three divine persons. As Ware writes: "Egocentricity is the death of true personhood. Each becomes a real person only through entering into relation with other persons, through living for them and in them" (1995: 28).[15]

Zizioulas (1985, 2006) further argues that the personal or relational understanding of God as Trinity effected nothing less than an ontological revolution in Greek philosophy. The key figures here, once again, were the Cappadocians, but it was Athanasius' teachings against the Arians and more fundamentally the eucharistic experience of the early ecclesial community which prepared the way. To highlight the momentous nature of this change, one could follow Zizioulas in setting it against the prevailing Greek philosophical ways of thinking about such concepts as 'substance' (*ousia*) and 'person' (*prosopon*). Take, for example, Aristotle's understanding of 'substance': although he has no uniform account of the term, at least one important way in which he develops the notion is in terms of the concrete individual thing which could exist in itself or on its own (a thing-in-itself). On this view, a substance has an independent existence, as opposed to the parasitic or derivative mode of existence had by qualities and relations (Aristotle offers an individual man or a horse as examples of substance in this sense). One such relational category was considered to be the *prosopon* (literally 'face', referring to the mask worn by actors in theatre, and translated in Latin as *persona* to mean the 'role' one assumes in society), which was thought in the ancient Greco-Roman world to lack ontological content or depth, whereas *hypostasis* (literally 'that which stands under', and so translated in Latin as *substantia*) designated a concrete and particular (or unique) reality.

Athanasius, however, radically transformed these categories. By placing the eucharistic experience of communion at the centre of his reflection on God and God's relation to the world, Athanasius developed an ontology that is communal, personal and relational. Specifically, Athanasius held that the Son is of 'the same essence' (*homoousios*) as the Father, thus rejecting Arius' view that the Son is a created, finite being whose glory is infinitely transcended by that of the Father. But in holding that the Son shares the same substance as the Father, Athanasius was in effect claiming that "substance possesses almost by definition a relational character" (Zizioulas 1985: 84). In other words, Athanasius was claiming that God's very being or substance is communal and relational. This raises the category of 'communion' (*koinonia*) from the level of will and action to that of substance, so as to make communion – or, more precisely, persons in communion – the primary or ultimate ontological category.[16] Such a "Christianization of Hellenism" was, according to Zizioulas (1985: 86), Athanasius' principal contribution to theology, and one that would fundamentally alter Greek ontology and cosmology. For this made it possible for the Cappadocian Fathers to differentiate the concept of *hypostasis* from that of *ousia*, identifying instead *hypostasis* with *prosopon* – with the result that "*to be* and *to be in relation* becomes identical" (Zizioulas

1985: 88).[17] Thus, the characteristics of personhood (e.g., relationality, freedom, otherness, uniqueness, communion) are no longer viewed as accidents but are taken to be of the essence of being: 'Being as Communion' (as Zizioulas entitles his most famous work). That is to say, God as Trinity discloses the most basic character of reality to be communion in love. As Zizioulas asks rhetorically: "If God's being is by nature relational, and if it can be signified by the word 'substance', can we not then conclude almost inevitably that, given the ultimate character of God's being for all ontology, substance, inasmuch as it signifies the ultimate character of being, can be conceived only as communion?" (1985: 84).[18]

God as creator (cosmology and anthropology)

> All creatures are balanced upon the creative word of God, as if upon a bridge of diamond; above them is the abyss of the divine infinitude, below them that of their own nothingness.
> – Metropolitan Philaret of Moscow (1782–1867)[19]

The Orthodox have traditionally placed great significance on the doctrine of *creatio ex nihilo*. To accept this doctrine is to accept, first of all, that the world has a creator and that it has not always existed (as Aristotle, for example, held). But to say that God created the world 'out of nothing' is also to say that God has ontological primacy in the sense that the ultimate source for everything is God and nothing else has the same level of ultimacy, whether it be pre-existent matter (as Plato held) or a competing primeval principle (as in Manicheanism).[20] As a corollary, the world created by God is an altogether new and essentially different reality: it is not identical with God (thus avoiding pantheism), nor is it a diffusion or emanation from him (in the way in which all that exists in the universe emanates from the One in Plotinus' system). Rather, the world is the product of the divine creative word and will, but not the divine essence, thus forming an ontological gap (or *diastema*, to make use of Gregory of Nyssa's notion again) between the uncreated Creator and the contingent creation, a gap that no created being can ever bridge.

But the *ex nihilo* doctrine is also intended to emphasize the element of divine choice and freedom, so that the existence of the world is seen as the result of God's free will and not the product of either necessitation or chance. This can be spelt out more fully by deferring to the picture, outlined earlier, of God as a trinity of interpersonal communion in love. For if it is in the nature of love to share and relate with others, then it is not surprising that God as trinitarian love would freely choose to create in a way that would extend the circle of love within the divine persons so as to embrace human persons and the natural world at large. This kind of 'ecstatic' movement, where God goes out of himself to create things different from him, has been characterized (by Pseudo-Dionysius) as a divine 'eros' – in which case,

100   N. N. Trakakis

as Ware notes, creation *ex nihilo* is better described as creation *ex amore* (Ware 1995: 44–45, 2010: 123–124).

Although the pinnacle of God's creation is man, Orthodox cosmology is more accurately viewed as 'theocentric' than 'anthropocentric' (Theokritoff 2008: 70–71). This is especially due to the influence of Maximus the Confessor, who "remains to this day the single most important figure in Orthodox cosmological thought" (Theokritoff 2008: 66). For Maximus, the human being and the cosmos are mutually reflecting images. He therefore describes the human being as a 'microcosm' – literally, a 'little universe' – in the sense that the human being (and only the human being) exists at the same time in all levels of created reality.[21] Our body (*soma*), for example, moves within the material or sensible realm, while our 'spirit' (*pneuma*: a faculty of spiritual perception, unique to man, which enables him to know and love God[22]) participates in the spiritual world with the angels.[23] By virtue of being a microcosm, the human being is also for Maximus a 'mediator', someone who forms a 'natural bond' (*physikos syndesmos*) between the disparate elements of the created world. As such a mediator, man's calling is not simply an individual mystical union with God; rather, he is called to draw the whole created (dis)order into harmony with itself and into union with God, thus healing the divisions within the human person and the cosmos (Thunberg 1995, Louth 1996: 63–77).[24] This cosmic vision, which has become a distinctive feature of Orthodox cosmology, has far-reaching ecological implications for our times.[25]

The human capacity for connection and communion is founded in the creation of human beings "in the image and likeness" of God (Genesis 1:26). The 'image of God in man' has been variously interpreted by the Fathers, but at least one helpful way of understanding this idea is in terms of the relational ontology outlined earlier with reference to the Trinity. On this view, to be in the image and likeness of God is to be persons-in-relation, in the manner of the persons of the Trinity. Kallistos Ware explicates this notion of the human person as an image or 'icon' of the Trinity particularly well:

> The being of God is relational: so also is our being as human persons. Without the concept of communion it is not possible to speak about the being of God: so also without the concept of communion it is not possible to speak about human being. God is self-giving, sharing, response: such also is the human person. God is coinherence, *perichoresis*: so also are we humans. God expresses himself from all eternity in a relationship of I-and-thou: so also within time does the human person. The divine image in which we as humans are created is not possessed by any one of us in isolation, but comes to its fulfillment only in the "between" of love, in the "and" that joins the "I" to the "thou". To be a person after the image of God the Trinity is therefore to be a person-in-relationship.
>
> (2010: 126)

Orthodox Christianity 101

A consequence of this view is that human beings are not autonomous and self-sufficient but are truly human only insofar as they exist in relation, and above all in relationship with God. In other words, humans are made for fellowship with God, for as Augustine put it at the beginning of his *Confessions*, "You made us for yourself and our hearts find no peace until they rest in you" (I.1). This notion found expression in the Greek patristic tradition in terms of the idea of 'participation in God' (*metousia theou*), where such participation is conceived as essential to human being.

The Fall, however, marred or corrupted the image of God in us and hence our very humanity. But unlike western traditions of Christianity influenced by Augustine, which took the consequence of the rebellion of Adam and Eve to be the transmission of sin and guilt to each future member of the human species, in the Greek and Byzantine patristic tradition the primary consequences of the Fall were not sin and guilt but (physical and spiritual) death: Adam's descendants are not necessarily guilty, though they all inherit the disfigured (but not totally depraved) human nature that resulted from Adam's fall, a nature that is now subject to physical death and illness, and divided and alienated from God, the natural world and even from itself.[26] But, it needs to be stressed, this is an unnatural condition for humanity: it is contrary to human nature to be cut off from God, which is what (physical) mortality and (moral and spiritual) corruption bring in their wake.[27]

God as man (christology and soteriology)

> Ineffably the infinite limits itself, while the finite is expanded to the measure of the infinite.
>
> – St Maximus the Confessor (*c*.580–662)[28]

If the Fall is the problem, the Incarnation is the solution. Both original and personal sin introduced a further and more pernicious gap between God and man, one founded this time on will rather than on differences in nature. However, man through his own efforts could not bridge this divide ('self-help' is useless here), and so God took the initiative: "Since man could not come to God, God has come to man, identifying himself with man in the most direct way" (Ware 1995: 68). This is the doctrine of the Incarnation: the Second Person of the Trinity (the Son) became incarnate as a human being (Jesus of Nazareth). "The Word became flesh and dwelt among us" (John 1:14). The belief that God became human in the person of Jesus is perhaps what most clearly distinguishes Christians from non-Christians. Other religions do not think of Jesus in this way (even Hindus who accept Jesus as a divine incarnation do not see his incarnation as unique), and they do not ascribe to their own founders (if they have any) the same authority or status: Muslims, for example, view Muhammad as completely human and in no sense divine (he is not regarded as a saviour or redeemer, and he

102 N.N. *Trakakis*

is not worshiped).[29] But the doctrine of the Incarnation also distinguishes orthodox (or traditional) Christians from liberal, revisionist Christians who think of Jesus as merely a great moral teacher, prophet or reformer, but not as God in the flesh.

The Incarnation reinforces the 'ecstatic' nature of God alluded to earlier. The love of God knows no limits, and so God goes out of himself, abandoning and emptying himself (*kenosis*) by identifying completely with his creation and becoming human. For some Fathers, in fact, this is not merely a remedial or restorative act, something that God did simply in response to man's Fall into sin, but should rather be seen as an act of love that would have happened even if man had not fallen.[30] Be that as it may, the Incarnation is understood in the patristic, conciliar and liturgical tradition of Orthodoxy as revealing at least the following central christological insights:

1   Jesus Christ is fully God.
2   Jesus Christ is fully human.
3   Jesus Christ is not two persons, but one.
4   It is because Jesus Christ is 'God-Man' (*Theanthropos*) that he can save us.

The Fathers, following the apostolic witness, considered Jesus to be the long-awaited Messiah (the term 'Christ' being a Greek translation of the Hebrew word 'Messiah' or anointed one) and the incarnate Son of God who provided for the redemption of humankind by his death and was himself resurrected from the dead. This is expressed, in part, by the affirmation in (1) that Christ is completely God, not half-god and half-man, and not merely a superior creature who received the title 'God' in a moral sense and by participation (as the Arians held). Rather, the Fathers spoke of the 'consubstantiality' of Christ with God the Father ("light from light, true God from true God") to emphasize the absolute equality of the Son with the Father.

But as indicated by (2), Christ also has a completely human nature, enabling us to speak of a 'double consubstantiality' in Christ. Christ is fully God because he is of the same essence as the Father, and Christ *qua* God can be described as the second person of the Trinity and the 'only-begotten' Son of the Father. But Christ is also fully human because he shares our nature as human beings, and Christ *qua* man can be described as a first-century Jew who was born in Bethlehem and raised in Nazareth. The fourth Ecumenical Council (held in Chalcedon in 451) put this by saying that there are in Jesus Christ *two natures*, one divine and the other human. According to the Definition (or Creed) of Chalcedon, Christ is to be "recognized in two natures, without confusion (*asynchytos*), without change (*atreptos*), without division (*adiairetos*), and without separation (*achoristos*)." This was in response to the Monophysite view that Christ has only one nature – a divine nature – even though he has taken on an earthly and human body with its cycle of birth, life and death (though, as is becoming increasingly clear, much of the Monophysite dispute resulted from conflicting interpretations over the meaning of 'nature'[31]).

The Council of Chalcedon also taught, in line with (3), that although Christ has two natures, he is *one person* – a single and undivided person, not two persons coexisting in the same body. After describing the two natures with the four negative (or 'apophatic') adverbs quoted earlier, the council's Definition goes to on say: "the distinction in natures is in no way annulled by the union, but rather the characteristics of each nature are preserved and come together to form one person and subsistence (*hypostasis*), not as parted or separated into two persons, but one and the same Son and Only-begotten God the Word, Lord Jesus Christ". This has come to be known as the doctrine of the *hypostatic union*, the union of the two natures in the one person of Christ – a union which, as the Definition makes clear, does not abolish the distinction of natures but rather preserves in full their characteristic properties. Lying in the background here is Nestorius (*c*. 381–*c*. 451), a bishop of Constantinople who preferred the term *synapheia* (conjunction) to the word *henosis* (unity) to express the relationship between the two natures in Christ, as he wished to avoid any suggestion that the union resulted in a mixture or confusion of natures. But a mere 'contact' or a loose 'conjunction' between the two natures was not sufficient for the Chalcedonians, who insisted on complete (and hence 'hypostatic') union and identification.

The reason for this insistence is brought out in (4), the belief that it is because Jesus Christ is 'God-Man' that he can save us. The underlying principle may be put in terms of Gregory Nazianzus' oft-repeated statement: "The unassumed is the unhealed."[32] In other words, Christ can heal and restore our fallen and broken humanity only by 'assuming' it as his own, by taking it entirely into himself, by becoming exactly what we are. This means that, in order to save us, Christ must not merely become embodied (take on some body or other) or assume some immunized, sanitized or quarantined humanity, but must assume *fallen* human nature, our nature as it is now, a humanity under the penalty of the corruption of physical and spiritual death.[33] And this is precisely what Christ did, freely accepting not only the physical consequences of the Fall (e.g., hunger, thirst, even bodily death) but also its moral and spiritual disfigurements (e.g., alienation, sorrow, temptation). "For we do not have a high priest who is unable to empathize with our weaknesses, but we have one who has been tempted in every way, just as we are – yet he did not sin" (Hebrews 4:15). But if the unassumed is the unhealed, then God must become fully human in order to save us – the Apollinarian view that Christ took on a human body but not a human intellect (or rational human soul) is therefore rejected, as is the Nestorian view that the divine and the human in Christ were conjoined but not united. God must go all the way down, he must hit 'rock-bottom' as it were, before we can start getting up. "God's descent makes possible man's ascent" (Ware 1995: 74).

This structure of divine condescension and human ascension found expression in the patristic tradition by means of the so-called 'exchange formula':

"God became man so that man might become God," to quote Athanasius' version of it.[34] The ontological distance between God and humanity (inherent in the shape of things, but exacerbated by the Fall) is overcome by God's stooping down to humanity (the Incarnation) and humanity's rising up to God – and this human ascent the Orthodox dare to call *theosis*, 'deification'. The intrinsic human vocation is to be "partakers of the divine nature" (2 Peter 1:4), to become by grace (and by means of a synergy or cooperation of divine grace and human freedom) what God is by nature.

However, *theosis* does not mean being transformed into a god in a literal, ontological sense. We do not, in the process of deification, cease to be human beings and become consubstantial with God. Athanasius explains that "we are sons, but not as the Son; and gods but not as he is",[35] and later writers clarified this by way of the essence/energies distinction so that deification is described as participation in the divine energies, as opposed to a unity with or absorption into the divine essence. By the same token, *theosis* is not the elevation of humans into 'super-humans' but (in line with the anthropology sketched earlier) the restoration of our authentic and full humanity, where to be fully human is to be in communion with God, to be partakers of the divine life. *Theosis*, therefore, does not diminish or destroy humanity but is the very fulfillment of the human being.[36] Indeed, in Maximus' cosmic perspective, deification is not only the *telos* of human nature but of the whole created order. On this view, the deification of man is achieved not in isolation from the rest of creation but together with it, and it is only via Christ, the God-Man, that the creation can be united from within with its Creator.[37]

No doubt, much more could be said about the Orthodox conception of God. For one thing, and continuing with the method of following the chapter headings in Ware's *The Orthodox Way*, something could have been added about 'God as Spirit' (especially the eucharistic ecclesiology developed by Zizioulas and its connections with the relational conception of human and divine being), 'God as Prayer' (particularly the integral link between the ascetic life and theological reflection, as expressed by Evagrius: "If you are a theologian, then you will pray; and if pray truly, then you are a theologian"[38]), and 'God as Eternity' (where God's relation to history is reconceived along the lines of an inaugurated or realized eschatology). These are all distinctive and indeed fascinating elements of the Orthodox understanding of God, but they could not be pursued here. Also, I have not delved into the reasons why I continue to follow the Orthodox Way, or even simply the 'Way' (as Christianity was originally called), particularly in the light of the various historical and philosophical objections that have been mounted against it, from criticisms of the reliability of the Gospel accounts of Jesus to philosophical objections against the intelligibility of the doctrines of the Incarnation and Trinity. In the end, I suspect, we must fall back on the authority of the Church, and above all the witness of its holy Fathers and Mothers who found in Christ "the Way, the Truth and the Life" (John 14:6).

Notes

1 I regard the qualifier 'Eastern' when speaking of Orthodox Christianity as not only unnecessary but also misleading. As Lossky (1991: 16–17) stated, "The Orthodox Church, though commonly referred to as *Eastern*, considers herself none the less the universal Church; and this is true in the sense that she is not limited by any particular type of culture, by the legacy of any one civilization (Hellenistic or otherwise), or by strictly eastern cultural forms."

   Further, although I set out here in the spirit of the wider project to state what I believe about God, I remove as far as possible the first-person perspective (in the manner of a personal confession or creed) and instead seek to provide the Orthodox perspective on God. This is deliberate, since in the Orthodox view it is not individual judgements that count but the beliefs and practices of the Church as a whole over the centuries. This is why in the Orthodox tradition icons and hymns are not signed, as they are not viewed as expressions of an individual (as a modern painting, song or poem would be), but as the creation of a community.

2 See also Florovsky (1972: esp. ch. 5) on the early patristic view of Tradition as a 'hermeneutical principle' for helping the faithful achieve a correct understanding of Scripture.

3 John of Damascus, *Exposition of the Orthodox Faith* I, 4; quoted in Sweeney (1961: 99–100).

4 Sermon 52, 16; *PL* 38: 360. The full passage reads: "So what are we to say, brothers, about God? For if you have fully grasped what you want to say, it isn't God. If you have been able to comprehend it, you have comprehended something else instead of God. If you think you have been able to comprehend, your thoughts have deceived you" (translation by Edmund Hill, in Augustine 1991: 57). Cf. Gregory of Nyssa: "God's name is not known; it is wondered at" (*Commentary on the Song of Songs*, quoted in Ware 1995: 14).

5 Indeed, for Lossky it is apophaticism (of a certain sort, which he seeks to delineate in his work) which "constitutes the fundamental characteristic of the whole theological tradition of the Eastern Church" (1991: 26). The first chapter in Lossky (1991) provides an excellent introduction to the apophatic dimension of patristic theology.

6 Apophatic theology was developed further still in the short but highly influential work *The Mystical Theology*, attributed to Dionysius the Areopagite and dating perhaps from the late fifth century.

7 The reference to Gregory of Nazianzus is from his *Oration* 28.4 (or Second Theological Oration), which has been translated (by Lionel Wickham) as "To know God is hard, to describe him impossible, as a pagan philosopher taught," the philosopher in question being Plato in his *Timaeus* 28c (Gregory of Nazianzus 2002: 39). Pseudo-Dionysius likewise opens his *Mystical Theology* with the image of a peak at the top of which lie "the mysteries of God's Word . . . simple, absolute and unchangeable in the brilliant darkness of a hidden silence" (1987: 135). Also, at the end of *The Celestial Hierarchy*, he speaks of his concern "to honor in respectful silence the hidden things which are beyond me" (p. 191). Silence in the patristic tradition, however, is not a mere negative phenomenon (the absence of speech), but is rather "an attitude of mind that signifies knowledge as communion at its deepest and most intense" (Chryssavgis 1998: 76).

8 Emphasis in original. The quote from Dionysius is taken from *Divine Names* 817D.

9 The emphasis on 'the mystical' is also liable to lead to the mistaken confluence of Orthodox theology with 'mysticism', as this has come to be understood and practiced in some quarters of the contemporary West. But as John Meyendorff explains, "in Byzantium 'mystical' knowledge does not imply emotional indi-

106 *N. N. Trakakis*

vidualism, but quite the opposite: continuous communion with the Spirit who dwells in the whole Church" (1979: 14). Similarly, Lossky rejects mystical individualism as "alien to the spirituality of the Eastern Church" (1991: 21), even though he draws a close connection between theology and mysticism in the opening pages of his *The Mystical Theology of the Eastern Church* (1991: 7–9).

10 Kallistos Ware writes: "God . . . is the One whom we love, our personal friend. We do not need to prove the existence of a personal friend. . . . If we believe in God, it is because we know him directly in our own experience, not because of logical proofs" (Ware 1995: 18). Ware therefore eschews "logical demonstrations of the divine reality," but he allows for what he calls 'pointers' – "facts which cry out for an explanation but which remain inexplicable unless we commit ourselves to belief in a personal God" (1995: 18–19). He goes on to provide three such pointers, none of which (he is careful to emphasize) amounts to a logical proof: (i) the existence of the world, especially the goodness, beauty and order found in the world; (ii) the human person, especially our conscience and sense of duty, and our thirst for what is infinite; and (iii) interpersonal relationships, especially "sudden moments of discovery when we have seen disclosed the deepest being and truth of another" (1995: 21). What Ware here calls 'pointers' may rightly be considered 'arguments for the existence of God', provided that arguments of this sort are not held up to unrealistic standards such as universal acceptance amongst all rational persons before they can count as 'successful' or 'convincing'.

11 Gregory Nazianzus, *Oration* 40.41.

12 This, of course, is the *Shema* (Hebrew 'hear'): the fundamental, monotheistic statement of Judaism, traditionally recited twice daily in prayer. The belief that there is 'only one God' does not sound startling now, but it certainly was in the ancient world, where there were many gods and goddesses.

13 This is not to say that God's unity or oneness is founded upon the consubstantiality of the three persons, so that God is one *because* the three persons share the same essence. Such a view would run counter to the doctrine of the 'monarchy of the Father', according to which God the Father is the source (ἀρχή) and cause (αἰτία) of the Trinity, not the divine essence in general. On this view, the unity of the Trinity is grounded solely in the person of the Father: in generating the Son and the Spirit, the Father fully conveys his Divinity to them, causing them to possess the same divine nature, so that all three together are one God. However, there is some dispute (even amongst Orthodox theologians) as to whether the doctrine of the monarchy of the Father is at all theologically defensible or even patristically sound.

A further controversial issue I will not touch upon here is the *filioque*, the belief that the Holy Spirit proceeds from both the Father and the Son, a view traditionally rejected by the Orthodox and endorsed by the Roman Catholic Church. For a comprehensive historical account of the *filioque* controversy, see Siecienski (2010).

14 Gregory Nazianzus, *Oration* 29.16. This is not to say that for Gregory (or for Zizioulas, for that matter) the divine persons are *nothing but* relations. Communal relation is the means by which we distinguish the persons, but it does not constitute their identity as persons. In other words, relations do not define the persons but only manifest them. On this matter, see Ware (2010: 117–118) and Zizioulas (2010: 148).

15 See also Zizioulas (1985: 50–65), where a distinction is drawn between the 'hypostasis of biological existence' (a form of personhood we all have by nature) and the 'hypostasis of ecclesial or eucharistic existence' (the kind of personhood we are enjoined to realize). On the notion of personhood in contemporary Orthodox theology, see Papanikolaou (2008).

Orthodox Christianity   107

16 I add the qualifier 'persons in communion' to indicate that what has ontological primacy in this scheme is *the particular* (specifically, the person), not *the general* (e.g., communion, being, nature).

17 Zizioulas emphasizes the great significance of this Cappadocian innovation: "The Cappadocian Fathers gave to the world the most precious concept it possesses: *the concept of the person, as an ontological concept in the ultimate sense*" (2006: 166; emphasis in original).

18 An excellent recent collection of essays (including contributions from Ware and Zizioulas) exploring the relationality of being (of the divine being as well as creaturely being) is to be found in Polkinghorne (2010).

19 Quoted in Lossky (1991: 92).

20 See, for example, Athanasius, *The Incarnation of the Word of God*, §28: "Because there is Mind behind the universe, it did not originate itself; because God is infinite, not finite, it was not made from pre-existent matter, but out of nothing and out of absolute and utter non-existence God brought it into being through the Word."

21 Maximus sees the whole of reality as consisting of successive divisions, the most fundamental division being that between uncreated reality (consisting only of God) and created reality. The latter is divided into the 'intelligible universe' and the 'sensible universe', with the intelligible universe subdivided further into the celestial realm (consisting of angels) and the terrestrial realm (consisting of humans). The sensible realm is divided between living beings and non-living or lifeless beings; living beings are divided into those that are sentient and those that are not sentient; and, finally, those that are sentient are divided into those that are not rational (animals) and those that are rational (human beings). As this indicates, human beings occupy both the intelligible and the sensible worlds.

22 This is sometimes rendered as *nous* or 'spiritual intellect', though as Louth points out, the word *nous* in Greek has a very different meaning from the English word 'intellect':

> Whereas 'intellect' can refer simply to the human ability to argue and calculate (as in the notion of an IQ), *nous* is the means by which the soul "aspires to a knowledge that is a direct contact, a 'feeling' (*sentiment*), a touching, something seen. It aspires to a union where there is total fusion, the interpenetration of two living beings."
>
> (2003: 358, quoting A.-J. Festugière)

23 Apart from the physical body and the spirit, the patristic tradition also postulates a soul (*psyche*) in man: this is the principle of life that animates the body, and in man (but not in other animals) it is the locus of mental and emotional faculties, including the ability to engage in reasoning. See Harrison (2008: 82–84) and Ware (1995: 47–49).

24 Zizioulas (2000) speaks of man as 'priest of creation', offering the world back to God in thanksgiving and thus bringing it into communion with God. This sacramental or eucharistic approach again traces back to Maximus, especially his notion of 'cosmic liturgy'. See Theokritoff (2008: 73–74, 2009: ch. 6).

25 The current Ecumenical Patriarch, Bartholomew, has become well known for recovering the ecological dimension in Orthodox theology – see Bartholomew (2008: 89–119; 2009). See also Theokritoff (2009).

26 See Meyendorff (1979: 143–146) and Daniélou (2001: 11). Interestingly, for Maximus the Confessor, the Fall occurred *at the very moment of creation*: Adam lapsed "at the instant he was created" (*Quasteiones ad Thalassium* 61, and *Ambigua* 42).

108　N. N. Trakakis

In *The Incarnation of the Word of God*, Athanasius presents the consequences of the Fall in the following striking terms: "As they [human beings] had at the beginning come into being out of non-existence, so were they now on the way to returning, through corruption, to non-existence again" (§4). What is striking about this is that non-existence, and not a lower level or sinful mode of existence, is taken to be the consequence of the Fall. This is because, for Athanasius, sin or evil involves a turning away from God (from the God who is the source of life and life itself), and so the sinner is someone who moves toward nothingness. All this makes complete sense against the background of a relational ontology: if to be fully human is to be in relation with God and others, then in rejecting God, one is annihilating one's own being – which is why Athanasius later speaks of post-lapsarian humanity as 'dehumanized', as having lost its rationality (§13).

27 This, of course, raises the notorious 'problem of evil': If God is perfectly good, and if he creates everything "exceedingly good" (Genesis 1:31), then why is there evil (and so much of it) in the world? The best strategy, in my view, is not to attempt to answer the question directly (by, e.g., constructing a theodicy), but to question some of the presuppositions and principles that give rise to the question in the first place (see Trakakis 2008). For the development of this line of thought by a contemporary Orthodox theologian, see Hart (2005).

28 Maximus the Confessor, Letter 21.

29 Admittedly, the divinization of human beings has occurred in some other religions – for example, in Roman emperor cults and in those Mahayana traditions of Buddhism where the Buddha has qualities that are very much like those ascribed to God.

30 Defenders of this view include St Athanasius (at least according to Unger 1946), St Maximus the Confessor, and the sixth-century Syrian bishop St Isaac of Nineveh.

31 As Peter Bouteneff (2008: 100–101) points out, the Chalcedonians were employing 'nature' in a generic sense to mean "a set of defining characteristics or qualities, specifically the sum total of characteristics that make something what it is" (2008: 101), while the Monophysites were thinking of 'nature' in a concrete sense to refer to a specific hypostasis (or a concrete person).

32 Letter 101, to Cledonius the Presbyter; in Gregory of Nazianzus (2002: 158). Cf. Origen: "The whole man would not have been saved, unless he [God the Son] had taken upon himself the whole man" (*Dialogue with Heracleides*, quoted in Ware 1995: 85).

33 See Athanasius, *On the Incarnation* §8, and Lossky (1991: 142).

34 Athanasius, *On the Incarnation* §54.

35 Athanasius, *Orations against the Arians* 3.20.

36 As Gregory of Nyssa states, "The life that bears a likeness to the divine is completely in accord with human nature" (*Homily I on Ecclesiastes*; quoted in Bouteneff 2008: 104). For an excellent and comprehensive study of *theosis*, see Russell (2004).

37 On this broader conception of deification, as encompassing the created order as a whole, see Louth (2007: 34–36).

38 Evagrius Ponticus, *Chapters on Prayer* 60.

References

Augustine. 1991. *Sermons III (51–94) on the New Testament*, edited by J. E. Rotelle. Brooklyn, NY: New City Press.

Bartholomew, Ecumenical Patriarch of Constantinople. 2008. *Encountering the Mystery: Understanding Orthodox Christianity Today*. New York: Doubleday.

Orthodox Christianity 109

Bartholomew, Ecumenical Patriarch of Constantinople. 2009. *Cosmic Grace, Humble Prayer: The Ecological Vision of the Green Patriarch Bartholomew*, edited by J. Chryssavgis. Grand Rapids: Wm. B. Eerdmans Publishing.

Bouteneff, P. 2008. "Christ and Salvation." In *The Cambridge Companion to Orthodox Christian Theology*, edited by M. B. Cunningham and E. Theokritoff, 93–106. Cambridge: Cambridge University Press.

Bradshaw, D. 2004. *Aristotle East and West: Metaphysics and the Division of Christendom*. Cambridge: Cambridge University Press.

Bradshaw, D. 2008. "Augustine the Metaphysician." In *Orthodox Readings of Augustine*, edited by A. Papanikolaou and G. E. Demacopoulos, 227–251. Crestwood, NY: St Vladimir's Seminary Press.

Chryssavgis, J. 1998. *The Way of the Fathers: Exploring the Patristic Mind*, 2nd ed. Minneapolis: Light & Life Publishing.

Daniélou, J. 2001. "Introduction." In *From Glory to Glory: Texts from Gregory of Nyssa's Mystical Writings*, edited and translated by H. Musurillo, 3–78. Crestwood, NY: St Vladimir's Seminary Press.

Ellsworth, J. 2002. "Apophasis and Askêsis: Contemporary Philosophy and Mystical Theology." In *Rethinking Philosophy of Religion: Approaches from Continental Philosophy*, 212–227. New York: Fordham University Press.

Florovsky, G. 1972. *Bible, Church, Tradition: An Eastern Orthodox View. Volume One in the Collected Works of Georges Florovsky*. Belmont, MA: Nordland Publishing Co.

Gregory of Nazianzus. 2002. *On God and Christ: The Five Theological Orations and Two Letters to Cledonius*, translated by. F. Williams and L. Wickham. Crestwood, NY: St Vladimir's Seminary Press.

Harrison, N. V. 2008. "The Human Person as Image and Likeness of God." In *The Cambridge Companion to Orthodox Christian Theology*, edited by M. B. Cunningham and E. Theokritoff, 78–92. Cambridge: Cambridge University Press.

Hart, D. B. 2005. *The Doors of the Sea: Where Was God in the Tsunami?* Grand Rapids: Wm. B. Eerdmans Publishing.

Lossky, V. 1974. *In the Image and Likeness of God*. Crestwood, NY: St Vladimir's Seminary Press.

Lossky, V. 1991. *The Mystical Theology of the Eastern Church*. Cambridge: James Clarke & Company.

Louth, A. 1996. *Maximus the Confessor*. London: Routledge.

Louth, A. 2003. "The Theology of the *Philokalia*." In *Abba: The Tradition of Orthodoxy in the West: Festschrift for Bishop Kallistos (Ware) of Diokleia*, edited by J. Behr, A. Louth, and D. Conomos, 351–361. Crestwood, NY: St Vladimir's Seminary Press.

Louth, A. 2007. "The Place of *Theosis* in Orthodox Theology." In *Partakers of Divine Nature: The History and Development of Deification in the Christian Traditions*, edited by M. J. Christensen and J. A. Wittung, 32–44. Grand Rapids: Baker Academic.

Meyendorff, J. 1979. *Byzantine Theology: Historical Trends and Doctrinal Themes*. New York: Fordham University Press.

Papanikolaou, A. 2008. "Personhood and Its Exponents in Twentieth-Century Orthodox Theology." In *The Cambridge Companion to Orthodox Christian Theology*, edited by M. B. Cunningham and E. Theokritoff, 232–245. Cambridge: Cambridge University Press.

110   *N. N. Trakakis*

Polkinghorne, J. (ed.). 2010. *The Trinity and an Entangled World: Relationality in Physical Science and Theology*. Grand Rapids: Wm. B. Eerdmans Publishing.

Pseudo-Dionysius. 1987. *The Complete Works*, translated by C. Luibheid. New York: Paulist Press.

Russell, N. 2004. *The Doctrine of Deification in the Greek Patristic Tradition*. Oxford: Oxford University Press.

Siecienski, A. E. 2010. *The Filioque: History of a Doctrinal Controversy*. Oxford: Oxford University Press.

Stylianopoulos, T. G. 2008. "Scripture and Tradition in the Church." In *The Cambridge Companion to Orthodox Christian Theology*, edited by M. B. Cunningham and E. Theokritoff, 21–34. Cambridge: Cambridge University Press.

Sweeney, L. 1961. "John Damascene and Divine Infinity." *New Scholasticism* 35: 76–106.

Theokritoff, E. 2008. "Creator and Creation." In *The Cambridge Companion to Orthodox Christian Theology*, edited by M. B. Cunningham and E. Theokritoff, 63–77. Cambridge: Cambridge University Press.

Theokritoff, E. 2009. *Living in God's Creation: Orthodox Perspectives on Ecology*. Crestwood, NY: St Vladimir's Seminary Press.

Thunberg, L. 1995. *Microcosm and Mediator: The Theological Anthropology of Maximus the Confessor*, 2nd ed. Chicago: Open Court Publishing.

Trakakis, N. 2008. "Theodicy: The Solution to the Problem of Evil, or Part of the Problem?" *Sophia: International Journal for Philosophy of Religion, Metaphysical Theology* 47: 161–191.

Turner, D. 2004. "On Denying the Right God: Aquinas on Atheism and Idolatry." *Modern Theology* 20: 141–161.

Unger, D. 1946. "A Special Aspect of Athanasian Soteriology." *Franciscan Studies* 6: part I, 30–53; part II, 171–194.

Ware, T. (Kallistos). 1964. *The Orthodox Church*. Harmondsworth: Penguin.

Ware, T. (Kallistos). 1970. "Tradition and Personal Experience in Later Byzantine Theology." *Eastern Churches Review* 3: 131–141.

Ware, T. (Kallistos). 1995. *The Orthodox Way*, rev. ed. Crestwood, NY: St Vladimir's Seminary Press (first edition published in 1979).

Ware, T. (Kallistos). 2010. "The Holy Trinity: Model for Personhood-in-Relation." In *The Trinity and an Entangled World*, edited by J. Polkinghorne, 107–129. Grand Rapids: Wm. B. Eerdmans Publishing.

Zizioulas, J. D. 1985. *Being as Communion: Studies in Personhood and the Church*. Crestwood, NY: St Vladimir's Seminary Press.

Zizioulas, J. D. 2000. "Man the Priest of Creation: A Response to the Ecological Problem." In *Living Orthodoxy in the Modern World: Orthodox Christianity and Society*, edited by A. Walker and C. Carras, 178–188. Crestwood, NY: St Vladimir's Seminary Press.

Zizioulas, J. D. 2006. *Communion and Otherness: Further Studies in Personhood and the Church*. London: T & T Clark.

Zizioulas, J. D. 2010. "Relational Ontology: Insights from Patristic Thought." In *The Trinity and an Entangled World*, edited by J. Polkinghorne, 146–156. Grand Rapids: Wm. B. Eerdmans Publishing.

First Responses

6 John Bishop

I have responded to each participant in turn, in the following order: Nick Trakakis on Orthodoxy, Kevin Hart on Catholicism (though from a contemporary phenomenological perspective), Michael Rea on Protestantism and, finally, Heather Eaton whose 'ecological' position resists any simple option of 'accepting' or 'rejecting' Christianity. I have not attempted to integrate my responses into a single discussion, even though important themes recur.

Response to Trakakis: Orthodox Christianity

Nick Trakakis brings to light an important issue about *the status* of our 'Position Statements' on Christian conceptions of divinity and related matters. Are these personal philosophical positions, or are they intended as something more, namely, our best attempts to articulate what we take to belong to the content of the faith of the Christian Church? In his first footnote, Trakakis says that he "seek[s] to provide *the* Orthodox perspective on God" (this volume: 105n1; my emphasis). He observes that "in the Orthodox view it is not individual judgements that count but the beliefs and practices of the Church as a whole over the centuries" (105n1), and he adds: "[t]his is why in the Orthodox tradition icons and hymns are not signed, as they are viewed not as expressions of an individual (as a modern painting, song or poem would be), but as the creation of a community" (this volume: 105n1). At the end of his account, Trakakis admits that he has "not delved into the reasons why [he] continue[s] to follow the Orthodox Way" and concludes by saying that "[i]n the end . . . we must fall back on the authority of the Church, and above all the witness of its holy Fathers and Mothers who found in Christ 'the Way, the Truth and the Life' (John 14:6)" (104). It seems clear, then, that Trakakis has aimed to articulate, as best he can, an understanding of divinity that belongs to the faith of the Church rather than just to his personal philosophical position or even to his own merely individual Christian faith.

The 'euteleological' conception of divinity I set out in my own position statement may seem to many to be quite unorthodox (even relative

114   *John Bishop*

to standards of orthodoxy broader than those of capital-O Orthodoxy). Yet I am prompted by Trakakis' framing of his own Position Statement to emphasize that I, too, was attempting an understanding of divinity that is Christian in the sense that it professes insight into the nature of the God in which the Church (the whole – catholic – Body of Christ) believes. Given the widespread assumption by Anglophone analytical philosophers of religion that God is a supernatural personal agent ('the personal omniGod'), the non-personal and naturalist conception of divinity I propose might well seem intended simply as my own personal best effort at making coherent philosophical sense of the idea of God. I might be construed as a philosopher who, judging the 'orthodox' understanding of God problematic, nevertheless finds metaphysical and ethical interest in a conception of divinity that he willingly recognizes as departing from the God in whom Christians believe. That is emphatically not how I see it myself, however: I see myself as keeping my baptismal promise to "believe all the articles of the Christian faith". (I set out what I take that to imply in my own Position Statement.) The historic Christian creeds express the Church's 'normalized' understanding of the cognitive content of the Christian faith, and my own proposal for understanding the conception of divinity is quite seriously intended to be an understanding of the God in which the Church believes.

That intention is not – I hope I need hardly add – the hubristic intention authoritatively to define for all the faithful the nature of their God. Bishops (by ordination, that is!) are the guardians of the faith, but the tradition they guard, though it has normalized formulations which the baptized promise to believe, is essentially a tradition in which the meaning of God's revelation, perfected in Christ, is open to evolving understandings. Trakakis' opening discussion of Scripture, Tradition and the Church as sources and authorities of the faith is fully consonant with this evolutionary perspective.[1] Scripture is authoritative, but only as interpreted in and through the Church whose tradition encompasses variety and tension and which may be defined – as Trakakis says, following Lossky – as "the life of the Holy Spirit in the Church" (91). The promise of John 16:13, that the Spirit when He comes "will guide you into all truth", is no doubt commonly regarded as already fulfilled (e.g., by the time of the First Council of Nicaea). A bolder interpretation takes the Spirit's guidance to be open-ended and continuing, with ever more light and truth capable of emerging from God's Word, and I sense that Trakakis is sympathetic to that bolder view. Quite certainly, though, he accepts that received *philosophical* understandings of the content of Orthodox faith are to be considered critically. Church and tradition do provide authoritative doctrines of the nature of God – as Creator, as incarnate, and as Trinity – but philosophical inquiry is not thereby closed off, and a plurality of competing conceptions may be proposed as characterizing God in accordance with *the* faith of the Church.[2]

I will now comment on some substantive points in Trakakis' characterization of God as understood in Orthodoxy.

First Response 115

Under the heading 'God as mystery', Trakakis introduces the distinction between God's essence and God's 'energies'. It seems to me contradictory to say both that God is "unknowable and unapproachable in essence" and also that 'the energies' by which God is known and approached "are . . . *God himself* in his action and revelation to the world" (93; my emphasis). Trakakis is surely right that "[n]o definition of God is possible, and no concepts . . . can allow us to achieve comprehension (in the sense of an exhaustive understanding) of God" (94), and he endorses Augustine's famous remark: "*Si comprehendis, non est Deus.*" But Augustine did not say "*Si intelligis, non est Deus*": God is beyond full comprehension and cannot be known *in that special sense*, but it does not follow that God cannot be known, nor even that he cannot be known in his essence, since the doctrine of Incarnation entails that true divinity is present in the finite historical order. Grasping the full dimensions of the divine love is beyond us: but in Christ, by divine grace, we come to know what that love is. The divine incomprehensibility entails that, as Trakakis says, "whatever positive statements we make about God . . . will always fall short in some way" (94). We can, however, grasp completely the truth of certain claims about what God is *not*: that is the thesis of apophaticism.[3] But apophaticism as forbidding any attempt at positive understanding of the divine nature (as it is often construed) does not follow. In fact, as Trakakis notes following Turner, negative theology actually makes positive, kataphatic, theology possible.

Trakakis has a paragraph on the epistemology of Christian belief in which he defends the view that knowledge of God "goes beyond reason without denying it" (96), which accords with the Jamesian, modestly fideist, epistemology I myself find persuasive (though Trakakis follows a widespread practice, which I avoid, of using the term 'fideism' to imply irrationalism). Trakakis seems, however, to endorse the view that knowledge of God as "mystical" is "not propositional or conceptual" – but if that is so, it is hard to see how he can then consistently conclude (as he does) that natural theology, though not necessary for faith, can be useful in supporting or engendering it. This is because natural theological arguments aim at supporting *propositional* conclusions; thus, if they are useful, it must follow that, even if knowledge of God does indeed have a non-propositional component (some kind of direct acquaintance, or participatory experience?) it must have a propositional component too. Certainly, on my own account, Christian faith involves practical commitment to a foundational 'highest-order framing' proposition about the world's being a certain way (namely, such that it is God's creation existing to realize the divine will).

Returning to ontology, Trakakis considers God as Trinity, focusing on (and endorsing) the work of John Zizioulas. A key question is how the concept of a person is used in the doctrine that God is 'three persons in one God'. The persons of the Trinity are not to be understood – Zizioulas says – as "individual centres of consciousness": that would be "an anthropomorphic monstrosity" (quoted in Trakakis, this volume: 97). Presumably they are

116   *John Bishop*

not to be conceived as individual personal agents either: the Lockean, forensic, conception of a person is not the right one. Rather, the persons of the Trinity are 'modes of existence' or 'relations'.[4] This is puzzling, though the puzzle begins to be resolved in the light of Zizioulas' account (again, I think, endorsed by Trakakis) of the "ontological revolution" wrought by Athanasius. To explain this revolution it is helpful, I think, to recognize a distinction between the *concept* of substance (or *hypostasis*, in Greek) and *conceptions* of substance/hypostasis. The concept of substance is the 'role' concept of that which is ontologically fundamental or ultimate, and conceptions of substance are conceptions of *what it is* that fills the 'substance' role by being ontologically ultimate. Now, the revolution Athanasius brought about was a shift from the Aristotelian conception of substance as independently existing individual bearers of qualities and relations to a Christian conception – born of the Church's experience of eucharistic communion – of what is ultimately real as 'communal, personal, relational'. Through this revolution, as Zizioulas says, "substance possesses almost by definition a relational character" (quoted in Trakakis, this volume: 98) . . . but, of course, the claim is *not* the (bizarre) claim that substance *under the Aristotelian conception* possesses a relational character; it is rather the claim that "persons in communion is the primary or ultimate ontological category". The category of person – *prosopon* (face, mask, role) – which is a relational category is thus identifiable as the true *hypostasis* (substance, or fundamental ontological category). So the persons of the Trinity are not individual *atoma* but *persons-in-relation* – where the hyphens indicate something ineliminable from their essence.

The idea that God, as what is most ultimately real, is dynamic interpersonal 'perichoretic' communion[5] has seemed to me for some time to represent a promising Christian alternative to the personal omniGod conception of the divine. We need the 'Athanasian revolution', as Zizioulas describes it – and it fits with the Scriptural claim that "God is Love" (1 John 4:8), which entails that divine reality is relational. There is, however, a problem in *identifying* God with the sum total of loving relationships – such a God seems 'too small' (I try to deal with this problem in my Position Statement). Here I want to raise a different problem, arising from Zizioulas' (and Trakakis') claim that the persons of the Trinity are *not* to be conceived as individual centres of consciousness and agents. The problem is straightforward: isn't it precisely *that* conception of a person that we need for the conception of God as dynamic *interpersonal* relationship? Don't we have to recognize the persons of the Trinity as persons in the Lockean sense in order to see their relationality as perfect interpersonal love? And, if participation in Trinitarian love is the fulfillment of human existence, will it not be necessary that the relata in loving relations are persons in our contemporary sense? To deal with this problem, I suspect, we will need to employ Aquinas' doctrine of analogical predication, recognizing that the personhood of the persons of the Trinity has to be conceived as analogous to human individual personhood even though its reality transcends it. Yet it is that transcendent reality

First Response 117

(conceivable to us only *via* this analogy) that is the archetype of which our personhood (which serves as the basis for the analogy) is an image – indeed the significance of the doctrine of man created in the image of God is emphasized by Trakakis as showing that authentic humanity is lived in accordance with our being persons-in-relation (see the quote from Ware, 100). I leave for another occasion any further elaboration, granting that it is a major challenge for my own euteleological conception of God to explain how it lines up with the doctrine of the Trinity.

In discussing the doctrine of *creatio ex nihilo*, Trakakis accepts the usual view that the world is *produced* by divine free will – even though, on his account, it is not the personal omniGod who is the world's supernatural producer but rather the eternally existing society of the Trinitarian persons who (collectively) produce the creation *ex amore* (and it is an interesting question how much of a difference this shift makes, if any, to the problems arising from the existence of evil in the creation). The euteleological conception rejects this view of God as *productive* efficient cause, while nevertheless retaining the doctrine of *creatio ex nihilo* through a bold identification of overall final and efficient causes. Trakakis takes *creatio ex nihilo* to entail that "the world . . . has not always existed" (99), but I think this claim is disputable, given that 'the world' must here refer to *all* God creates, which may turn out to be a 'multiverse' if contemporary cosmology is correct. If it turns out that, on our best cosmological theory, there exists from all eternity some underlying state of affairs that produces a multiplicity of spatiotemporal universes, that will need to be consistent with the theistic claim that all that exists is a divine creation (otherwise theism degenerates into a high-level falsifiable scientific hypothesis). On the euteleological conception, such a development in our knowledge would remain quite consistent with the theistic doctrine of creation, but on Trakakis' account it would not.

Finally, Trakakis considers Christology, focusing on the 'exchange formula': "God became man so that man might become God." Only because Jesus the Christ is a hypostatic union of divine and human nature in one person is it possible for him to save us. But why should this be? Maybe because "the unassumed is the unhealed", as Gregory Nazianzus taught . . . but why should *that* be? I confess that the Chalcedonian formula is the aspect of orthodox Christianity I find hardest to understand. One problem arises from the implications of the Athanasian ontological revolution: is it supposed to be Christ *the individual human person* (that particular animal, that instantiation of *homo sapiens*) who is *as such* both fully divine and fully human? But, then, what has become of the view that being divine is essentially a relational mode of being? My own inclination is to hold that what primarily incarnates the divine must be *Christ-involving relationships*, so that as an individual, the Christ is divine only in the secondary sense, that he possesses the disposition to incarnate divinity in all his relationships. And I also incline to the view that, really, God becoming man and man becoming God are, in Christ, one and the same thing.

118 *John Bishop*

Response to Hart: Catholic Christianity

One might think that Kevin Hart's chapter could as well have been entitled 'A Phenomenological Theology', since its key claim is that the core content of the Catholic – the universal Christian – faith rests on the lived experience of the near-at-hand yet still-to-come 'Kingdom of God' (the *basileia*) revealed through Jesus the Christ. What is the *basileia*? It is the condition of living in true justice, love and peace (though 'peace' here does not connote absence of conflict but rather dealing with conflict in the right way). The *basileia* is, to continue a theme from Trakakis' account of Orthodoxy, the extension into the creation (even, ultimately, into all of it) of the *perichoresis* of the Holy Trinity.

I have no doubt that Hart's emphasis on the *basileia* revealed through Christ does identify the beating heart of the Christian faith. "To call God 'Father' is to know him by way of a relation, not as a being or essence," Hart says, "[s]o the Father reveals himself only through the coming of the βασιλεία, the dynamic breaking into the world of his kingly rule" (this volume: 54). 'The supernatural attitude', which understands the Kingdom as realized in another world, should thus be rejected ("hear! hear!" say I), and metaphysical speculations about God's nature are to be shunted into the background. But why, then, do we need any reference to God at all? Is it not sufficient to characterize 'the Kingdom of God' in theologically neutral ethical (and political) terms? The suggestion that ethical characterization would be sufficient is further supported by Hart's allowing – I think wisely – that non-believers may participate in the *basileia*. If doing God's will does not require belief in God, why not cut to the chase with a purely ethical account of what constitutes what the Christian tradition has called 'doing God's will'?

I note that Hart says that his model of divinity "may well be called 'phenomenological theology', although it would be more accurate to say that this expression names only the base of the model" (59). This remark may indicate that Hart would agree that a *merely* phenomenological theology would be inadequate – perhaps in part because of the difficulty I have mentioned? In any case, I will focus the rest of my response to Hart on trying to explain why a reduction of the theological to the ethical is *not* the result of giving primacy to God-as-known-through-the-Kingdom-as-proclaimed-by-the-Christ, even though, as Hart puts it, this must form 'the base' of the model.

In the first place, any attempt at ethical characterization of what the Reign of God is like raises the epistemological issue of where we are to go to obtain such knowledge. From where do we get our most basic ethical intuitions or the skill to make nuanced ethical judgements in particular cases? How are *developments* in ethical understanding possible, as opposed to shifts in ethical fashion? The Christian view is that ethical knowledge requires divine revelation, which involves a process of evolving understanding of what has been revealed in which earlier basic intuitions may be overturned by later insight into the divine will (as, for example, in the move from sacrifice as

First Response   119

requiring the ritual burning of crops and animals to understanding it as "acting justly, loving mercy and walking humbly with your God" [Micah 6:8]). Jesus' teaching was revelatory in this way, subverting established understanding and causing offence so that, as John 6:66 records, many initial followers gave up on him. But when Jesus asks the Twelve whether they want to leave also, Simon Peter replies: "Lord, to whom shall we go? You have the words of eternal life" (John 6:68).

My point, then, is that it doesn't seem as if we could *just construct* increasingly satisfying theories of the good and the associated capacities for good practical judgement any more than we could construct increasingly satisfying scientific theories of physical nature without the 'revelation' of the world of perceptual experience. Developing ethical knowledge seems to require revelatory input, but, unlike the general revelation of perceptual experience, the revelation of the nature of the good seems to be 'special', linked to historically specific experiences mediated through living traditions. Though Christians take ethical revelation to be *in some sense* complete in Christ – in 'the coming of the *basilea*' – there need be no Christian insistence that other traditions cannot themselves mediate special revelation independently of the Christ phenomenon and its Jewish antecedents. Of course, the content of any independent special revelation will have to be consistent with what is revealed in Christ to be acceptable to Christians – but, since the potential for deepened understanding of Christian revelation is open-ended, it may happen that Christians come to understand more fully what has been revealed in Christ by attending carefully to what is understood as revealed in other religious traditions.

The second main reason why God does not become redundant when primacy is given to the essentially ethical/political coming of the *basileia* is ontological rather than epistemological. The proclamation of the Kingdom of God is not just an assertion of a set of ethical/political ideals: it is also the assertion that the world (reality) is profoundly hospitable to the realization of these ideals, notwithstanding the 'principalities and powers' that war against them. Humans really are capable of 're-birth' into a transformed existence that overcomes the limitations of self-centredness – and (I think it is important to add, as a claim accepted by faith!) this transformation is possible collectively, institutionally and ecologically. Furthermore, human fulfillment – individual and collective – is to be achieved through commitment to the ideals of the Kingdom *here and now*. We are right to pray that the 'bread of tomorrow' (the bread we will eat festively when the Kingdom comes in its fullness) may be given us *today*. This further content, going beyond the proclamation of ideals as such, irreducibly involves substantive metaphysical commitments of a theological kind. It is essential to the God-role that God is the One who redemptively, salvifically, *brings in* the Kingdom: unless that role really is filled, the ideals of the Kingdom will be no more than a pipe dream.

120 *John Bishop*

Response to Rea: (Reformed) Protestantism

Under the heading 'Prolegomena', Michael Rea considers what it is to 'believe on faith'. He seeks to reconcile broad support for the view that to believe rationally is to believe to the extent justified by one's evidence with the intuition that faith-beliefs are held beyond the support of evidence and yet may nevertheless be held reasonably. Rea sets up his discussion by describing as "obviously inadequate" Richard Dawkins' characterization of faith as "belief that isn't based on evidence", pointing out that there can be beliefs not based on evidence (that one ought not to open umbrellas indoors, for instance) that we don't classify as faith (this volume: 68). Rea agrees, nevertheless, that some kind of (shall we say?) transcending of the relevant available evidence for its truth is a *necessary* condition for a belief to be held "on faith". But what *kind* of evidence-transcendence could that be? It is not the pervasive underdetermination of empirical theoretical beliefs by the observational evidence for their truth: though such beliefs do *in a certain sense* go beyond their supporting evidence, we do not normally suppose that any act of faith is involved here. This is because, Rea suggests, there is typically no viable alternative to evidentially well-supported empirical theories such as the theory that the Earth goes round the Sun. But – and this is Rea's leading idea about the nature of faith – sometimes there *are* viable alternatives to an evidentially supported belief because there is significant counterevidence, such that someone who held the contrary belief would also be believing reasonably. Paradigm cases of propositional faith are like this, Rea thinks: believing on faith is necessarily believing "in the face of genuine and weighty counterevidence" (69).

When it comes to religious beliefs (where this connotes belief commitments to overall worldviews – including atheist/naturalist worldviews not generally labelled 'religious'), the position is not, I think, best described in the terms Rea has in mind, namely, as one where there is mixed evidence, some favouring a given religious stance and some countervailing. The position is rather one of *evidential ambiguity*: distinct and mutually incompatible worldviews make equally coherent sense of all the evidence we have. Religious faith is thus commitment to some specific overall worldview – say, that the universe is a divine creation existing for the sake of realizing the divine purpose revealed in Christ – under conditions in which there *could not in principle* be any certification on the basis of independent evidence of the truth of the foundational 'framing principles' specific to the worldview concerned.

What we need, I think, is exactly what William James attempted in his (misleadingly titled) lecture, "The Will to Believe": we need a defence of practical commitment to the truth of a foundational religious framing principle "that cannot *by its nature* be decided on intellectual [= evidential] grounds" (1956: 11; my emphasis). At the end of his discussion of faith and reason, Rea says that "[t]he differences in worldview among intellectual

First Response   121

peers . . . are . . . to be explained in part by differences in our incommunicable evidence and also by differences in how we weigh various aspects of the vast body of communicable evidence that we have at our disposal. For this reason, it seems that at least some of the tenets of every worldview must be taken on faith" (71). Here Rea expresses an idea that fits with the Jamesian view that religious faith involves commitment under evidential ambiguity, namely, the idea that the same evidence can be weighed – I'd say, more broadly, interpreted – differently by different, equally reasonable persons. Following James, I would press the point that our different interpretative dispositions *issue from* our basic commitments to the cognitive foundations of our worldviews, which have 'passional' (i.e., non-evidential) causes (typically, the fact that we are brought up in a specific cultural and religious context). Rea may see things more the other way round, however, taking it that different incommunicable experiences and differently interpreted communicable evidence constitute *evidential and justificatory* causes of our faith-commitments to our different religious worldviews.

How, exactly, does Rea see believing on faith as "consistent with a general policy of trying to form one's beliefs in accord with reason" if believing 'in accord with reason' requires believing in accordance with supporting evidence and believing on faith somehow transcends supporting evidence? He places weight on his analysis of the example of Charlie Brown believing that, at last, this time, Lucy *can* be trusted not to whip the football away as he runs up to kick it. Rea invites us to consider the case where Charlie has a great deal of evidence of Lucy's, now reformed, good intentions, and argues that, even so, "given their past history, it will still take faith for Charlie Brown to believe [that she can be trusted]" (68). If Charlie does form this belief, it will be well supported by evidence, yet it will take faith to hold it because the past history of these encounters provides "genuine and weighty counterevidence" against the truth of the claim that Lucy will finally prove trustworthy this time. The alternative belief, that Lucy still cannot be trusted, is thus "viable", which (Rea suggests) comes down to the fact that to hold it would indicate no "serious malfunction in [one's] ability to understand, appreciate, properly weigh and form beliefs in accord with evidence that [one] knowingly possesses" (69; here Rea expands on his initial characterization of believing on faith as necessarily involving belief in the face of significant countervailing evidence).

Having the policy of believing to the extent justified by one's evidence is, Rea says, "obviously compatible with sometimes (sanely) believing what we are not rationally *required* to believe, which is roughly what I have identified as the necessary condition for taking something on faith" (70; emphasis in original). But, in fact, this is not obvious. The 'evidentialist' policy is typically understood as the policy of *not* believing *beyond* what is justified by one's evidence. Thus, in cases where one's evidence does not – under the norms of the applicable intersubjective evidential practice – sufficiently support the belief that p, the evidentialist policy requires *suspending judgement* on the

122   *John Bishop*

question whether *p*, and therefore counts as irrational one's formation of the belief that *p*. Charlie Brown, then, in the case as imagined, has mixed evidence as to Lucy's trustworthiness. If (as indicated in Rea's "rough" statement of what is necessary for believing on faith) that evidence does not *require* him to believe that she will prove trustworthy, then it is hard to see how an evidentialist can avoid concluding that if he does form this belief 'on faith' he will do so irrationally. Yet, if (as suggested by the "fuller [but still only partial] characterization" Rea gives), it is the case that Charlie does weigh the mixed evidence (correctly) as supporting the belief that Lucy will be trustworthy but does so while recognizing that *had* he formed the contrary belief on the basis of the countervailing evidence that would not have been a *serious* epistemic malfunction, then Charlie's believing that Lucy can at last be trusted will be rational on evidentialist grounds but difficult to interpret as displaying faith. Where's the faith in believing in the face of "genuine and weighty counterevidence" if, in fact, that weighty evidence is *out*weighed by even more weighty evidence in support of the truth of what is believed? Had the contrary belief been formed, there would have been epistemic irrationality. But, if I understand him correctly, Rea maintains that there yet might not have been *serious* epistemic irrationality. And then (on Rea's account) the faith in holding a belief on the basis of the overall support of one's evidence comes down to one's recognition that *part* of the evidence is sufficiently countervailing for it to be true that, had one believed to the contrary on the basis of that evidence, one would have done so irrationally but without *serious* epistemic malfunction. It seems implausible, however, that believing on faith should rest on appreciating a – surely either vague or recondite? – distinction between non-serious and serious epistemic malfunction. It seems to me, then, that the Jamesian route to an account of believing on faith will prove more satisfactory.

Rea affirms the Protestant doctrine of *sola scriptura*, glossing it as implying that doctrines necessary for salvation can "easily be derived from scripture . . . without the help of the Church or Church tradition" (72). But this claim seems in tension with Rea's acknowledgment that scripture needs interpretation, with believers "free to use any and all tools at their disposal to determine for themselves exactly what it is that scripture teaches" (72). If it is agreed – as surely it ought? – that one should not rely on an interpretation that took no notice of Church tradition and was accepted independently of any interaction with other believers, then the need for interpretation of scripture entails that saving doctrine will *not* be derivable "without the help of the Church or Church tradition". I am also concerned about Rea's understanding of God as the divine author of Scripture and reject his claim that if divine authorship is false "there would be no reason to regard scripture as a greater authority in the domain of faith and practice than *every other* human experience or testimonial report" (72; emphasis in original). Scripture's books may have human authors and yet be reasonably accepted as a paramount inspired source of authoritative revelation.

The relationship between scriptural assertions and saving doctrine is anyway more complex than suggested in the picture Rea puts forward of 'easy' derivation of the latter from the former. Notoriously, scripture nowhere affirms the doctrine of the Trinity as articulated in the historic creeds, yet Protestants surely do affirm that doctrine as necessary for salvation rather than (as Rea's account seems to me to suggest they ought) reject it as inconsistent with the method of *sola scriptura*. Of course, the doctrine of the Trinity can be 'proved' by scripture, in accordance with traditionally established interpretations: and *that*, I suggest, is what is really meant by *sola scriptura* – namely, the illegitimacy of holding as necessary for salvation doctrines which are not scripturally 'provable' (a good example is the pious tradition of the Assumption of the Blessed Virgin Mary, controversially defined as part of the faith by the Pope in 1950).

Rea's conception of God is as "strictly and literally" a perfect being. I think there is an important question as to whether God's ontological perfection can possibly be the perfection of 'a' being, since a particular being, however ontologically magnificent, will be one being amongst others, and it might – I think reasonably – be thought that being as a whole has greater ontological status than that of any individual being. I will focus on Rea's account of the Trinity, a doctrine which seems in tension with the notion that God is 'a' being or 'a' person. The usual way of expressing Trinitarianism – and what's puzzling about it – is to say that the Father is God, the Son is God, the Holy Spirit is God; Father, Son and Holy Spirit are distinct Persons; yet there are not three Gods but one God. Rea's formulation is as follows:

T1 There is exactly one God, the Father almighty.
T2 Father, Son and Holy Spirit are not identical.
T3 Father, Son and Holy Spirit are consubstantial.

T1 strikes me as an oddly reductionist way of expressing the divine unity – I think because it suggests that 'God' is the name of a kind or species and that the doctrine of the divine unity is the claim that there is just one instance of this kind. T3 expresses the equal divinity of each of the Persons by saying that they are 'of one substance' (*homoousios*). The Nicene Creed affirms consubstantiality of the Son with the Father but does not affirm it of the Spirit, claiming rather that the Spirit *proceeds* from the Father (and the Son – but I leave aside the '*filioque*' controversy): so it seems to me safer in setting out what is essential to Trinitarianism simply to affirm the equal divinity of the Persons and leave it at that. Rea does, however, explain 'consubstantiality' as 'sharing a common nature' or 'being of the same kind', so that indeed it will follow, for example, that 'Peter and Paul are consubstantial' because they share the same nature or form. Again, this seems too reductionist, reducing the unique relation of Son to Father in Trinitarian theology to the mundane phenomenon of multiple instantiation of one general kind. The risibility of actually announcing that Peter and Paul are

124 *John Bishop*

consubstantial surely witnesses to the ineptness of this reduction – as too the oddity of the formulation of the doctrine of the Trinity to which this account of consubstantiality leads, namely, that "The Father is *a* God, the Son is *a* God, and the Holy Spirit is *a* God, but each is the same God as the others; so, since there are no other Gods, there is exactly one God" (77; my emphases).

Rea makes an interesting attempt to resolve the Trinitarian puzzle. His basic move seems right: he rejects the inference from the non-identity and divine equality of the three Persons to the conclusion that there are three Gods. His explanation of how that inference fails does not seem satisfactory, however. He relies on an analogy with the kind of situation where a statue and a pillar are distinct in form but constituted by the same matter. Statue and pillar are distinct, and each is a material object, and yet there are not two material objects but one material object. For this to yield an analogous understanding of how Father, Son, and Spirit can be distinct, and each equally God, yet there are not three Gods but one God, the crucial speculation is required that "the divine nature plays the role of matter in the divine persons" (76). I see no reason to accept that claim (even if it is intelligible[6]), except that doing so supports this analogical understanding of the Trinity. Yet even if we did accept this analogy, the result would surely be an unacceptably modalist account of the Trinity – with Father, Son and Spirit no more than distinct masks of the underlying divine nature somehow playing the matter-role? I am therefore inclined to favour the alternative suggested by the social doctrine of the Trinity, where the equal divinity of the Persons is understood as their equal participation in *the relationship* of the Three, and divine unity is understood as the supreme unity-in-diversity found at the heart of the eternal divine Love.

Rea next moves on to Christian understandings of human nature, its end or purpose, and what is needed for that purpose to be achieved. I am struck by the fact that he does *not* insist – as I think many Protestant analytical philosophers would – either on immaterial human minds or on libertarian human freedom. He does himself incline to believe that we have immaterial souls, on the grounds that given that the divine mind is immaterial, it is a simpler hypothesis to take immateriality to be intrinsic to minds in general. I do not share that inclination – on my view God is not literally 'a' mind, let alone an immaterial one. Indeed, I take the view that minds are *necessarily* embodied in complex arrangements of matter – and that imagining an 'immaterial' mind can amount only to imagining minds realized in some substrate quite different from the physiological one that applies to human and animal minds. It's good, though, that Rea allows materialism about (creaturely) minds as consistent with Christian understanding – and this is because he recognizes that Christian belief in the resurrection is in the resurrection *of the body*. I do, however, find problematic Rea's focus on postmortem existence in his understanding of resurrection (surely the rebirth of baptism makes new, resurrected life possible also in *this* life?), and his explication of resurrection as restorative (he says: "we are capable of being resurrected [that is, restored to bodily life]" [77]), since the example of Christ's resurrection and ascension makes abundantly clear that it involves an incomprehensibly radical transformation of existence as an individual embodied person. On the question of freedom, I agree with Rea that Christians affirm at once that we are free and responsible (within limits), yet at the same time ultimately wholly dependent on God's absolute sovereignty for our existence and everything we do, including our free and responsible acts. I agree with him that "freedom itself is ill-understood, and perhaps intractably so." I do believe, however, that there is a legitimate task for the philosopher in seeking to refute philosophical theories which maintain or imply that the kind of compatibilism essential to Christian understanding of human agency is incoherent. Such refutations may, however, be unable to dispel – or may even make a virtue of preserving – ineliminable mystery in the notion of free creaturely action.

Christians understand humanity as in need of salvation in virtue of original sin, and the plan of salvation as involving atonement through the incarnation. *Original* sin is problematic, since, on the typical analytical philosopher's understanding of God as literally a supernatural personal agent who produces the universe *ex nihilo*, anything original must be solely God's responsibility. The idea that original sin results from the first human sin, freely chosen, serves to assign responsibility for it to humanity – though God's *ultimate* responsibility for this defect in his creation still remains. We therefore get what I think is the uneasy, and, in the end, unsustainable view that God's great plan of salvation rescues us from a mess for which he is himself responsible: such a set-up is, I believe, inconsistent with God's being perfect *qua* person in relationship with created persons. Rea's attempt at explaining why the first human sin so damaged human nature as to engender a universal need for salvation gives rise to just this kind of uneasiness. On Rea's view, though humans are designed to live with God, in response to the first sin God "partially withdrew", with the result that "the union for which we were designed was no longer readily available – it could be had only dimly in this life and only with special divine help and as a result of actually seeking God" (79). But why would God make such a 'partial withdrawal'? To do so looks like a drastic overreaction, or a ploy intended to give himself scope to demonstrate how wonderfully he could save (some of) us! In my view, we can begin to understand the way we are bound in original sin and the marvellous salvation wrought for us in Christ only when we abandon any *literal* understanding of God as personal player in this drama, recognizing what is inescapably anthropomorphic about our understanding as resting on analogy only.

On the question of how our salvation is effected, Rea endorses the Chalcedonian formula of the incarnate Christ as one person with two natures, divine and human, yet he takes it that having two natures entails having two wills and two minds, even though he admits that "positing two minds suggests that we are also positing two *persons*, contrary to orthodoxy" (81;

126 John Bishop

emphasis in original). His suggested solution is to hold that Jesus' divine mind operates subconsciously; but that view, I think, is hard to reconcile with the orthodox claim that there is a 'hypostatic union' of the two natures. The personal fragmentation involved in the subconscious having the status of a separate mind is inconsistent with the full integrity intrinsic to perfection as a person. On the question of the atonement, Rea is admirably cautious and does not insist – as some Protestants and Protestant institutions do – on requiring acceptance of the doctrine of penal substitution (the innocent Jesus punished in the place of sinners) as a test of orthodoxy. The work of Christ accomplished justification, deliverance from sin, evil and death, and "brought us new life, eternal and abundant, and made us into new creations. But as to how and why and in exactly what sense all of these things happened, perhaps we cannot say without offering a model that ultimately lapses into metaphor, leaves out important truths or otherwise misleads" (83): a wise conclusion, I think, and one which fits with Rea's general point, made in his final section on Christian life and practice, that theorizing about what is involved in "learning to love God and neighbour in a way that emulates Christ" (84) is of only secondary or tertiary importance.

Finally, I was grateful for Rea's closing personal reflections on the relationship between growing in the Christian life and the academic life of a professional philosopher. Now, later in my career, I better appreciate the truth of Rea's observations about how the latter poses obstacles to the former. The question of how our *collective*, institutional lives (such as, for ourselves, our lives in universities) can become more open to transformative grace seems to me an urgent one and deserving of more attention by philosophical theologians.

Response to Eaton: Ecological Christianity

I have a lot in common with Heather Eaton. Like her, I reject a 'two worlds' interpretation of Christianity, according to which God, and, therefore, eternal life with God, belongs in a separate supernatural realm. I do not see the incarnation as the incursion of the supernatural into the natural, nor do I understand the mechanisms of salvation as enabling (for some) an everlasting continuation of individual personal existence (either bodily or as an immaterial soul) somehow transported away from the perishable (and ultimately dispensable) natural realm into the imperishable supernatural one. There is one, integrated Reality – either the whole of the spatio-temporal universe of which we are a part or an entire multiverse of such universes. God's being real does not amount to the reality of any item within or specific aspect of this Whole Reality, nor could it amount to the reality of some item outside the Whole Reality, since on this 'one world' view there can be no 'outside'. I also share with Eaton the rejection of a purely anthropocentric view of the divine purpose: on her ecological view, non-human life on Earth and 'life' (or other features of existence beyond our imagining) in other parts of the spatio-temporal universe may also be capable of participating in fulfilling the divine purpose and may thus possess the inestimable worth that accompanies this capacity. (Humanity can, of course, still 'matter to God' without being exclusively at the centre of the universe's purpose: we need not adopt a completely *an*anthropic theism, as considered by Tim Mulgan (2015), under which human existence is irrelevant to the divine purpose.)

Unlike me, however, Eaton presents herself as having moved away from what she regards as orthodox Christianity and reports that her current relations with the Church are tenuous. Has she 'come clean' in a way that, really, I ought also? Well, I am indeed a quite passionate atheist *relative to* personal omniGod theism. If I agreed with the (vast) majority of analytical philosophers of religion that personal omniGod theism, with its commitment to a separate supernatural world, is essentially implied by orthodox Christianity, then indeed I would accept that I ought to recognize myself as 'post-Christian'. But I do not agree with that majority view. And I cannot help but wonder whether Eaton may have acquiesced in that view too readily.

Although some of what she says suggests a wholly non-realist view of Christian God-language, my impression is that Eaton does remain a realist. That is, she accepts that God-language, metaphorical and 'symbolic' as it is, does refer to something vitally and pervasively important about reality. Concepts and images of the divine are, of course, constructed by us humans, but our representational constructions may nevertheless succeed, at least in part, in grasping something of the real wonder of the *milieu* in which we live. Eaton uses de Chardin's term, 'the *divine milieu*', to express this – and, obviously, a contrast is intended with the 'standard' understanding of the universe as the product of a supreme supernatural Creator. But I think it is important to make the attempt, under the banner '*fides quaerens intellectum*', to understand how we could be immersed in the divine milieu even though there is no supernatural Producer and Controller of All That Is. In my view, the euteleological conception of God as Creator *ex nihilo* that I have sketched in my own Position Statement offers a promising alternative that seems to fit with a good deal of traditional, orthodox Christian belief even though it certainly challenges the decidedly non-ecological spirituality of the quest for personal salvation that is dominant in some Christian quarters.

I agree with Eaton – herself following Ivone Gebara – that the 'are you saved?' spirituality is prone to "the primal sin" of "negating the non-negotiable existential circumstances of life" (this volume: 39). Yet I think we need to retain the elements of Christian soteriology, albeit shorn of their supernaturalist expressions. There is something that needs to be added, I think, to the noble ideal Eaton sets out, again following Gebara: "our salvation is found in returning to our embodied selves . . . and embracing with joy and sorrow the genuine limitations, richness and struggles of life in community and solidarity with all life" (39). What needs adding is the transcendent

128   *John Bishop*

power of the love revealed and vindicated in Christ, for it is this which grounds Christian hope in the midst of life's struggles. Is it possible to understand the transcendence of the power of love without falling back into 'two worlds' supernaturalism? I dare to think that this is possible – and I suspect that, in the end, Eaton agrees with me, given her own suggestion that, in following Gebara's ideal of ecologically accepting our embodied finiteness, we may "heighten our awareness of *an indwelling divine or sacred presence*, one in which we live and have our being" (39; my emphasis).

Notes

1 I would, however, question Trakakis' remark that God is "the primary author of Scripture" – a remark which, anyway, does not seem to fit with the account Trakakis gives of the Orthodox view as locating the work of the Holy Spirit in the practical life of the Church as it grapples with (at times amidst differences and disputes) the meaning and implications of divine revelation. Scripture expresses the primary authority of the Word of God, but that does not make God *the author* of scriptural writings: their authors are decidedly human. Thinking of Scripture as God's word in the sense of God's writings (written instructions, even), and construing God as in that sense the primary author of Scripture (via human mediation) is a heresy of certain Christian fundamentalisms, surely, and not a tenet of Orthodoxy.

2 The – often misunderstood – Wittgensteinian method in the philosophy of religion requires seeking to characterize the content of Christian belief from the 'insider' perspective of one who is committed to the Christian 'form of life' (which need not require actual Christian commitment). This method of specifying the subject-matter for a philosophy *of religion* ought not to be controversial, as it seems entailed by recognizing that religious concepts (such as the concept of God) do not float free but belong to a historically situated context. A philosopher might choose, if he liked, to set out a free-floating concept of God, which might prove worth discussing as a metaphysics abstracted from religious life. But the conception of the God *of Christian faith* offered by a philosopher of religion will need to meet constraints arising from lived Christianity: whether a particular conception meets those constraints – or needs to be recognized, perhaps, as 'post-Christian' – is an important question that can be answered only by first trying to settle what the essential features are of the Christian 'God-role', namely, the essential functions of belief in God in the existential and conceptual economy of Christian life.

3 The claim of Eunomius and Aetius (reported by Trakakis) that the human intellect can understand God's essence as *agennesia* (unbegottenness) looks to be properly apophatic, so presumably the Cappadocians (who opposed them) really were taking the (surely hopeless?) view that God's nature is absolutely unknowable (not merely beyond full comprehension in its positive character).

4 One might think that taking the persons of the Trinity to be 'modes of existence' commits the 'modalist' heresy – but perhaps it needn't, if the modes are not attributes of one underlying Aristotelian substance.

5 Trakakis uses the term 'perichoretic' but does not explain it. I suggest that 'perichoresis' is best translated as 'going round giving space to another'.

6 The key metaphysical role of matter is to individuate distinct instances of things of the same kind or nature. How a nature, which is inherently general, could play that role, even analogously, certainly boggles my metaphysical imagination!

References

James, W. 1956. "The Will to Believe." In *The Will to Believe and Other Essays in Popular Philosophy*, 1–31. New York: Dover.

Mulgan, T. 2015. *Purpose in the Universe: The Moral and Metaphysical Case for Ananthropocentric Purposivism*. Oxford: Oxford University Press.

7 Heather Eaton

Response to Hart: Catholic Christianity

General comments

I appreciate the nuanced and carefully presented understanding of 'the kingdom' offered by Kevin Hart. I believe that I can see the trajectory of his thought towards our becoming present to God, the conversion of our gaze and the keen interest in living in the world under compassionate divine rule. While I would use different language, I concur with this preoccupation and interpretative framework.

The structure of Hart's paper is not overly clear to me, and many of the guiding questions (presented to contributors by the editors) are not answered, at least not in an overt manner. The exclusive male language for God reveals a male bias. This is not generally acceptable, except in male-dominated and conservative Christian streams, which are commonplace, and I assume this is Hart's context.

Hart carves a path through a plethora of other thinkers and positions dealing, in general, with specific topics in phenomenological theologies. He writes that phenomenological theology is most concerned that Jesus lived and taught and that Jesus' words and acts disclosed the meaning of God's kingly rule. Is this accurate? It does not seem to reflect the breadth of phenomenological theology, considering the wide range of themes, preoccupations and topics that fall within this umbrella term.

Most of my comments concern Hart's manner of thinking rather than the content of his paper. From my stance, his reflections are autobiographical. They are personal views and interpretations, nestled within Hart's worldview, addressing a profoundly religious dimension to existence, in a highly symbolic form, embedded in Christian imagery. The language Hart uses (true of all theology, in my view) is not self-explanatory or even transparent, because the references are 'theology', 'philosophy', 'scripture', 'Jesus', 'God', etc., and the existential or experiential roots are not exposed. Theological language does not explain or describe: it illuminates experiences. Much religious language and Christian elucidation at this depth require a

First Response 131

further interpretative map or 'pin number' – which I may not possess – and so I do not claim to grasp the profundity of Hart's contribution.

Clarifications and questions

There are several *a priori* statements throughout Hart's paper that I would question. For example, Hart opens his Position Statement by saying: "Christian theology properly begins by considering the confession that Jesus is the Christ" (this volume: 48). Later, he writes: "Christian theology's starting point is the relationship with the God of Jesus" (48). Hart contends that the central moment of the Christian faith is the resurrection of Jesus. And again, Hart states that these claims are absolutely binding on Christian believers. These are bold claims. Must all Christians adhere to them? And in what manner? Does Hart's starting point act as a litmus test for 'true' Christians?

Yet Christians are not monolithic. They 'believe' in distinct content, adhere to these beliefs differently, and associate the beliefs with their lives in a further differentiated way. Starting points diverge. For some, the starting point is truth. For others it is salvation in a future world, or the possibility of redemption from sinful predispositions, or to be chosen, or a belief in social amelioration if not liberation, and so on. Many (perhaps most) people who consider themselves to be Christian have little theological understanding. They do not seek a coherent intellectual framework. Many consider they have been saved, but when asked from what, there is no clear answer. Being 'saved' can function as a protection from the uncertainties, confusion, meaninglessness, suffering and the messiness of life. Some 'believe in Jesus', and this is sufficient, but when asked 'believe in what, precisely?' their reasoning crumbles. Some have only scraps of scriptural knowledge but believe scriptures are the 'truth'. Many fervently hold beliefs close to their identities and worldviews. Others are Christian because of culture, habit or the desire to be in a supportive community. There is a plethora of additional emotional reasons as to why people are adherents to Christianity.

I am not suggesting people are duped or unintelligent. Rather, I am suggesting that from thirty-five years of experience in many Christian settings, as a chaplain, church pastor, theologian and teacher, there is little unity among Christian adherents as to what they believe. Further, there is little unity among theologians across and within Christian streams. Rosemary Radford Ruether has stated that when Catholic feminists meet Vatican theologians, it is an interreligious dialogue. Given this, who determines the nature of Christian theology, or who is Christian, and on what grounds? Who gets to speak for the 'tradition'? And which tradition? The spectrum of beliefs historically and in the present is very large. Hart himself disagrees with fundamental claims of (e.g.) Husserl, Heidegger and Kant, and his tone is that he is uttering objective truths (about God, the kingdom, Jesus, etc.). I consider these to be interpretations, or interpretations of interpretations, or complex manipulations of imagery arising from deep intuitions

132   *Heather Eaton*

and personal experiences of living symbols operating intra-psychically and within communities.

A second question concerns knowing: what is known and how? Hart holds to the centrality of scripture, and he points out that everything we can know about Jesus from scripture is selected and interpreted. He further reminds us that the historical Jesus is an abstraction and the Jesus/Christ of the Nicene Creed is richly theorized. So, where does that leave us with Jesus being the "datum of revelation"? What hermeneutics do we use, and how do we measure their veracity? In terms of adequacy? Explanatory power? Interpretative possibilities?

Further, the core of Hart's theology hinges on grasping how Jesus understood or even experienced God. How can we reliably know this? How do we bring this into our lives, given that God is "radically irreducible to human consciousness"? Hart states that we need to recognize there is an antecedent claim made upon us by God, prior to any further understanding. Later, he remarks that some of this comes in the form of apophatic understanding. In another place, Hart states that we must largely work out for ourselves the implications of Jesus' relationship with God. So, how are we to know what Hart claims to know? How does he know? He comments that one knows these things through 'faith'. When we accept the authority of Jesus, we see. If you have faith, you know. I have never found this argument compelling. There is an implicit tendency towards two epistemologies operating in Hart's essay: one natural, the other supernatural.

Hart sees Jesus as the "datum of revelation" (48). I find this to be problematic. Which aspect of the 'datum' is being used? There are many facets to the gospel accounts of the life of Jesus – historical, interpreted and imagined – and a plethora of particular teachings, only a few of which can be attributed to a historical Jesus. All of this bears dozens of interpretative possibilities. The phrase "datum of revelation" is ambiguous at best. Further, whatever 'datum' is selected is then interpreted by means of other desires and frameworks. For example, when the particular datum is Jesus' maleness, some Christian traditions use this to bar women from ordination. This specific 'datum' about Jesus has formed the basis of ordination and celibacy arguments, postulating for example the fiction of a lineage of priests from Peter to the present. All such cases have the same structure of argument: an appeal to the datum of revelation. This 'datum' has also been used to suppress other religious and spiritual traditions by claiming the superiority of this 'datum', as seen with colonizers and evangelization in its imposing forms. Others use different aspects of this 'datum', such as emphasizing the social ethics of Jesus to support liberation movements, a preferential option for the poor or the need to live in Christian communities. There is a rather large spectrum of data to choose from. Some employ this datum to enforce Christian supremacy, while others employ it to affirm religious pluralism. The difficulty is that people use the 'datum of Jesus' in contradictory ways, claiming theirs to be more revelatory, accurate, authentic, valid and truthful, and then act upon this. What is Hart using to ground his stance?

Hart also remarks that we are brought to the kingdom not by intentional analysis but by the counter-intentionality with which we are confronted: "it stirs us to look and see something that we cannot see by our own efforts" (56). We must pass from a "natural attitude to a transcendental consciousness". Further, "[t]he βασιλεία . . . eludes concepts . . . it never becomes fully present in our terms" (57). This is again highly problematic, in my view. Such an 'in the world but not of the world' theology is a staple in most Christian accounts, and yet there is no consistent meaning to be found. Hart offers an attractive interpretation of converting our gaze to see and live in the world within God's reign. Yet it is an interpretation lacking in any verification or demonstration of what it means; what is this gaze, how we are to develop it and why do Christians come to see such different realities? Perhaps such a stance could be bolstered by appealing to the lived realities Hart alludes to in relationships and community, or by developing a more robust theory of religious consciousness.

I genuinely like Hart's notion that within the Christian imagination there is a need to convert our gaze, to cultivate a mode of passivity, to give up the security we anxiously search for and to be reduced in front of the breadth and depth of God. In many places, Hart cautions against Gnosticism, pride, ego and trust in our capacities to grasp the numinous or ultimate. Yet all these thoughts or even intuitions are occurring within the realm of human knowing and consciousness, of which Hart is suspicious. The assumption is that there is a kind of 'mystical' form of knowing. The divide between natural and transcendental is, in my view, a manner of speaking, not an ontological boundary. So, of what does it speak? How does one know the difference? Furthermore, many in their Christian certitudes find the security we crave, which, within Hart's logic, renders them no longer spiritually valid. This is a conundrum to be grappled with, and Hart goes back and forth on this, making claims and then undoing them. I appreciate this.

Hart states: "God has become thinkable" (54). What does this mean? Humans 'think' about, and have conjured up, imagined, prayed to and given their lives to many gods and goddesses. Thousands of images of God have been, and perhaps still are, present in human thoughts. The assumption is that the one Hart affirms is the true one. Does this mean that all other conceptions are false? Or are they simply not included in this reflection? Hart claims that God has now become thinkable, and yet he draws from a very narrow band of images of God. He eschews the imperial images of God (as ruler, king): "God's rule is like that of a compassionate father rather than that of an imperious king" (53); but he ignores the warrior, vengeful, punitive images. Is this not the usual selective reading of scripture to suit our interests, values and desires?

134 *Heather Eaton*

Points of similarity and dissimilarity

I share with Hart a desire for an existential, lived religiosity, and I share the belief that a religious orientation requires attentiveness (I would add cultivation and interiority) and ultimately a realization that we do not and cannot produce it. We experience this as an invitation, a summons, or we are drawn towards levels of reality that are not immediately apparent. I would use the spiritual language of awakening or awareness, moving from death to life, sleep to waking, closed to open, or towards freedom.

Hart offers a rich interpretation of the parable of the father and the two sons, revealing that God is best approached relationally, understood as compassion, and indicating what draws Hart to his faith-stance and commitments. Still, others will pick a different parable to be central to 'Christianity' (e.g., woman at the well, the raising of Lazarus, various healings). Yet I share Hart's interpretation, and there are other scriptural references in both testaments to support this compassionate God, this conversion of our gaze and this invitation to see the kingdom present. But I want to point out that it is a choice, a stance, a position, or preference. Hart's version of Christianity is an interpreted one (as they all are), but masquerading as of greater truth than any other (as they usually all do).

Hart writes: "Christianity is finally not a matter of bringing God to the presence of human consciousness but rather of allowing oneself to come into the presence of God" (55). I completely agree with this religious orientation and understanding. But to substantiate this is much more difficult. This is why I believe we need a theory of religion, religious consciousness and religious experience.

Hart also writes: "when we accept his [Jesus'] authority . . . we see that he is . . . the genitive of revelation" (55). I cannot think of a phrase more often used in Christian discourse, with endless and contradictory interpretations, and which has had an impact on the world in inconsistent ways. There are countless interpretations: what does Hart mean, and how is he making this claim? The next question is: how does it function? If we examine how images function, we can trace them backwards to find out what they mean. I see this as a more fruitful endeavour than trying to determine directly what an image might mean.

The statements Hart makes appear as if they are self-sustaining and held within a system of external truths. It would be more revealing if Hart were to explain his driving questions and his attraction to these interpretations, to elucidate how these are woven into his life experiences and why he is convinced of their validity. To quote scripture and church 'fathers' to validate one's views is not convincing – it is what most theologians do, and yet they arrive at very different conclusions. It would be more revealing if Hart also wrote about the questions that haunt him, why he is deeply drawn to scripture, what is revelatory, what he has learned in living life within this worldview and why Jesus is such a compelling historical figure and/or religious symbol. It is these aspects, in my view, that define his theology.

Response to Bishop: 'Naturalist' Christian theism

Bishop offers an interesting reflection on the possibilities and limits of a logical theism with a moral foundation, or a moral orientation derived from a theistic foundation. I am not a conversation partner in such discourses; thus, my questions and challenges come from outside the parameters of such discussions.

Bishop begins his reflections with the notion of 'believing in God' as a practical commitment, the foundation of an entire way of living. He further acknowledges the contestability of theistic beliefs, but states that, "At their baptism, Christians promise to believe all articles of the Christian faith as formulated in the historic creeds" (this volume: 4). He states that this does not mean that Christians promise to find these beliefs true, but only promise to accept that they are true. I do not understand this. How could it be valid to promise to believe something if one is not certain of its truth? How do we 'accept' a received tradition in trust? What about the fact that over a lifetime we reinterpret traditions again and again? What about the interpretative dimensions of 'believing'? And furthermore, which aspect? These 'truths' have been interpreted in diverse ways, with quite dissimilar yet specific consequences.

Claims to certainty in having received divine revelation are worrisome and have specific consequences. Consider, for example, the Inquisition: the inquisitors were certain. The spiritual genocide of First Nation people in different parts of the world is another example. The turbulent relationship between Christianity and science hinges upon alleged certainties and receiving traditions in trust. Do we lean towards the Christian creationists or the evolutionists? There are also the uninspiring, often misogynist, concepts about women from several Christian traditions. Are these aberrations? Did humanity simply not understand 'what is revealed', or has our thinking 'evolved'? Did we not 'believe' the proper content?

Bishop carefully refutes absolute claims, noting many limitations within our understanding, false consciousness, historical processes, political agendas and other human frailties. And yet it seems to me that because we are within these processes, our understanding is always historical-contextual, limited and biased. Bishop places 'revelation' outside these processes: revelation must squeeze into historical processes. While I am familiar with this kind of theology, I find it epistemologically frail. How can we both be within these veiled realities and claim to know that there is full and final revelation of the divine in Christ? It seems there are several dualisms presupposed and operating in an interconnected manner: historical and ahistorical, temporal and atemporal (rather than eternal), and phenomenological and extra- (or non-) phenomenological orders of reality, together with forms of knowledge which are either ultimate or partial. Yet humans are always historical beings, creating the aforementioned categories within our minds, traditions and worldviews. Thus, the certainty that there is absolute revelation must arise from 'faith', or something in the order of a stance, a position, a belief, a claim, a conviction or a commitment. What kind of certainties are these?

136   Heather Eaton

I find this epistemological dance problematic in many ways. How can we possibly know what exists outside the phenomenological domain, as even our 'faith' and/or beliefs lie within historical processes? It is easy to claim divine revelation: millions have and do. I want to separate the wheat from the chaff so as to be very precise about what we can and cannot know, and how we know. Here philosophy could be a great asset. Constructive postmodern epistemologies can offer assistance, without forcing us to repudiate religious consciousness: they make it possible to acknowledge that we construct reality and that we also intuit reality and respond to levels of reality that are not immediately apparent.

Bishop holds that our understanding of God's nature undergoes continual change and development, an evolutionary process. I would like some clarification on what he means by 'evolutionary'. Is this a process with a teleological thrust? Does it involve progression more than development or change? Does the notion of 'evolution', which Bishop uses repeatedly, have any relationship to the evolutionary sciences and the notions of emergent complexity, adaptation or the symbiotic processes in evolution? Or is Bishop referring to a process that is never complete and is dynamic and never fully understood?

Later in his Position Statement, Bishop writes that "Christians need not – indeed, should not – identify God as One who destroys some peoples" (13). He claims there is an ethical progression in theological consciousness. Is this verifiable? On what is such a view based? Or is it that we find many images of God in scripture and within the tradition to be deplorable or unacceptable? If we refer to the integration of human rights into theological images of God, which has occurred in the latter part of the twentieth century, then are we not saying that theology is contextually bound and responds to the historical images and exigencies of its time? Or we could refer to the use of Christian just-war theory to destroy the cultural base in Afghanistan and Iraq during the 'war on terror'. What progression is Bishop speaking of? Christians identify God with their own interests. I see Bishop doing the same, even if I support his images and conclusions.

Bishop uses scripture in order to critique scripture on the topic of acceptable images of God (Acts), and then later uses scripture (Galatians, Revelations) as a form of proof-texting. One cannot use scripture in these selective ways unless one grounds one's scriptural interpretation in historical consciousness rather than in ahistorical truths.

Bishop widens the horizon of interpretation, noting that theists share a "belief that God exists and is worthy of ultimate trust" (6). I would suggest that other religions share this orientation, with multiple divine imagery, or with none (Daoism, for example). This is important because it shifts the focus from God-imagery to the dynamics of human trust in the ultimate validity (worthiness) of life and the transcendence (in one way or another) of death. Life is made or shown to be meaningful and/or sacred by us through the use of myriad imagery: the intuition, desire or need to trust life is prior to any imagery.

Bishop further contends that the various religions agree that the universe constitutes a profound and decisive unity. I would rather say that this is a claim made by humans, often from a religious orientation. I think a stronger argument in support of Bishop's view is made by studying the internal processes of humans who attend to this sense of unity rather than situating the authority for such a view within the 'religions', which only describe what humans imagine, understand or intuit.

In that respect I differ from Bishop. Religion constitutes a language about human experiences. However, I am not persuaded by the certainty asserted in specific creeds, doctrines and other religious formulations of these human processes. The experiences are perhaps universal, but the language and interpretations are not. Religious language and imagery are not transparent and are dissimilar across traditions. I am more than skeptical about specific 'revelations' that come from outside history and time or are sourced from outside any aspect of the phenomenological order. How could we ever know these 'truths'?

Bishop claims that Christians believe in God and "commit themselves to trust, worship and obey God" (7). But is that really the case? I find Christians do a whole lot of contradictory things and always have. Christians do not agree on what "trust, worship and obey" mean. Also, Christianity has been an aggressive religion, a world-changing historical force, but with ambivalent consequences.

I understand that Bishop seeks a path that takes logic seriously: God is not an item or a person; God must be supernatural but not in a simplistic manner; God must retain the omni-properties. Bishop asserts also that God is a creator and engaged with creation. He writes, for example:

> God must indeed be Creator, distinct from and other than his creation and therefore 'supernatural' in relation to the created natural order. But (on this adjusted view) God is a supernatural *person* and has the complexity required for the cognitive and conative capacities essential to personhood – that baffling divine simplicity is jettisoned. God does retain, however, the 'omni-' properties: his agency is all-powerful (he is omnipotent), his knowledge all-encompassing (he is omniscient) and his goodness supreme (he is omnibenevolent). And the necessity of God's existence is retained: if there is such a person as God, he is a denizen of every logically possible world.
>
> (6–7; emphasis in original)

How can anyone know these things? A reminder: God is also not male. Bishop thus devotes considerable discussion to the nature of God while also saying something about all that God is not. I remain skeptical about what kind of knowledge this is, about the processes of knowing and further about the formulations of such knowledge.

This type of discourse has a long, substantial and at times blustery history within Christian philosophical traditions. My question is: to what end? What

138   *Heather Eaton*

is the purpose of such a discourse? It is highly speculative and abstract, and its core concern seems to be: how should we think? (Gnosticism?) Further, it bypasses the existential difficulties and planetary ruin that are structuring the world (these being addressed, however, in the ethical dimensions of the gospel stories).

Later, Bishop dabbles with the question of 'how should we live?' and argues that moral evaluation may apply if epistemic evaluation gives out. What does this mean?

Liberation theologies (which also have a philosophical ground and cannot be reduced to 'ethics') challenge armchair theologies to address structural sin as a gospel imperative. Bishop does bring in the question about ethical judgements and how these relate to arguments about the nature of God. But he does not give any intimations about the connections and consequences between theory and action. He writes: "Those who live well in accordance with the right ideals, then, must also have the right overall cognitive orientation to the world" (17–18). He then goes on to state the conditions needed for the Christian ethical ideal to be realized, which are many and challenging. Herein lies the rub, and in my view the limits of this speculative type of philosophical theology.

For Bishop, we have a sinful nature and we require "grace from outside ourselves" (18). Sin and death are overcome. More dualisms are evident here, though they are undefended or unsubstantiated. What Bishop offers is the classical fall/redemption theology, presented as 'truth'.

Love is the power that emerges from within creation, specifically from relationships, and is what is ultimate. But on what is this view based? Evidential practice? Where does this stream of the reflection fit with the logic of determining the nature of God?

Bishop writes that it is not an option whether one commits to the truth of basic Christian beliefs (which ones are these?). The same applies to the truth of perceptually basic beliefs. He also goes on to say that venturing *contrary* to the weight of one's total available evidence is epistemically wrong. One may venture *beyond*, with rationality and evidence, although one may not be right. This, he contends, is a moral argument, though I simply do not see in what way it is 'moral'.

Finally, Bishop claims that he is not an exclusivist because others are entitled to their committed stances. I am unconvinced. Bishop is tolerant, even respectful, of diversity, but without letting this influence transform his theological interpretations, which remain exclusivist. He portrays Christianity as one religious path among others, but his case in support of Christianity renders the Christian worldview as ultimate. Despite his vague evolutionary caveat, Bishop holds that there is a full and final revelation of the divine in Christ. What Bishop offers is a theology of world religions, not a pluralist, culturally and historically based theory of religion. When he writes that "God delights in the breadth of religious disagreement as essential to the process of continuing evolution in the understanding of his self-revelation

First Response   139

to humanity" (22), this reads as only another version of the 'anonymous Christian' theory. It may be a form of inclusivism, but even inclusivism is often no more than a mollified version of exclusivism, as we enfold other religions into our embrace and our theological frameworks. A different road would be to enter their worldview and try to understand it from the inside.

Response to Trakakis: Orthodox Christianity

General comments

I appreciate the nuanced distinctions provided in this general overview of Orthodox theology, and predominantly about God. My knowledge of the Orthodox tradition comes from being familiar with some of the work of Pseudo-Dionysius and John Zizioulas, and a great deal of the ecological work of the Ecumenical Patriarch Bartholomew. A second source is working for sixteen years at Saint Paul University (Ottawa, Canada) in theology with the Orthodox theologians of the Metropolitan Andrey Sheptytsky Institute of Eastern Christian Studies. A third manner in which I can grasp aspects of Orthodox Christianity is from much time spent in silent prayer and in contemplative monasteries. The emphasis on mystery, the unknowing and the profound apophatic orientation is one I deeply share.

However, the Orthodox world is overwhelmingly male, with very few women playing leadership roles, and where feminist (not feminine) analysis is imperceptible. The exclusive male language in Trakakis' text reflects this reality and is unacceptable outside of conservative theological contexts. Few Orthodox scholars dialogue with liberation theologians or address the social and ecological issues raised by such theologians. Most Orthodox theologians are not regularly engaged in ecumenical and even less in multi-religious contexts (except in rituals or liturgies, usually Roman Catholic and Orthodox). Thus, my 'work contexts' rarely overlap with Orthodox streams of Christianity. My comments must be understood in consideration of these provisos.

Remarks and questions

Trakakis opens the door to considerable nuances and precisions about Orthodox theology in this essay. I appreciate the carefulness with which he carves a path through scripture, tradition and the church before addressing the doctrines and language about God and the Trinity. He notes that Catholic, Orthodox and Protestant traditions have diverged on the basis of how "specific authorities and sources are understood and evaluated" (this volume: 89). This strikes me as more than theologically and epistemologically crucial. If one stands at this crossroad, as I do deliberately, one is much more cautious of certitudes, theological methods and especially of theological claims. One notes the breadth and depth of differences and is perplexed by the way in which certitudes around 'divine revelation' are

140 *Heather Eaton*

affirmed, seemingly oblivious to the existence of epistemological and theological diversity and discord.

There is a certain 'epistemological protection' in Orthodox Christianity(ies) that Trakakis explains well. He describes the complex dance among the authorities of scripture, tradition and the church, reiterating the ultimately unknowable nature of God. He notes that this 'protection' (not his own term) is not to be found amongst those who adhere to fundamentalist readings of biblical texts. While I would agree, there are many forms of this kind of 'protection', which prevents an in-depth scrutiny of epistemological methods. I consider many forms of Christianity to be close to Gnosticism, literalism, ideology, dogmatism, fundamentalism or "conceptual idolatry."

In a general way I appreciate, and am attracted to, the mystical dimension of the Orthodox tradition. Somehow the language renders God into a verb rather than a noun, an energy or dynamic rather than a stasis or 'entity'. The fluid and multiple metaphors and imagery employed in language about God resonate with my theological orientation, as an academic, and from personal experience. I am very much at home with the dialectic of 'God is . . .' and 'God is not . . .' and with the notion that the spiritual journey requires the whole person and the surpassing of reason.

The apophatic nature of Orthodox theologies is well described by Trakakis, from light to darkness, into silence, mystery and the *via negativa*. I agree with Trakakis' metaphor of a spiritual *journey* rather than any simplistic claim to revelatory knowledge accepted in faith. In my case, this journey has been a movement from more to less certitude with respect to the absolute claims made in Christian doctrine – especially in light of my increasing understanding of the histories of religions and the nature of religio-symbolic consciousness. Yet I concur with Trakakis that this journey "widens the space for the way of affirmation" (95), for more clear affirmations. For myself, I have much a greater certitude about living in a *divine milieu* (Teilhard de Chardin). Because of my journey into this "brilliant darkness of a hidden silence" (Pseudo-Dionysus), I am extremely hesitant to confirm most theological claims as ultimate.

It is here that I part company with Trakakis. The affirmations surrounding the Trinity, in spite of the nuanced and masterful discussion, are too certain for me. The historical and current (and seemingly endless) discussions of the essence, form, substance, interrelationship, freedom and divine nature of the Trinity are more than highly abstract and speculative. Further, from my perspective, these are all exceptionally flexible exercises of the human imagination. I do not think that we are imagining (as in *fabricating*) these aspects of how we experience the Divine presence in our lives. Rather, I think that we are imagining (i.e., employing images), speculating, desiring and even intuiting aspects of reality beyond our knowing and doing so in exceedingly symbolic – and thus not in transparent – language.

I am confident that we really do not know what we are talking about when we venture this far into speculating about how the Godhead interrelates.

First Response 141

I recognize that a vast amount of human psychic energy has been and continues to be spent on this topic, but what drives the pursuit is unclear. To what end is this quest?

I am much more attracted to the 'other end of the stick'. What are the human experiences that correspond to this imagery? How does the language of the Trinity, which is only a metaphor (symbol, image), function in human lives? How does it inspire and guide us? How do we verify, assess and correct our interpretations? How is it that not only are there very different interpretations, but they lead to distinct and even contradictory actions? How can the images of a loving, dynamic and plural-yet-singular Godhead result in constructive as well as despicable historical results? Thus, the rejoinder that Christian truths are stable but humans are frail, weak, fallen or corrupt is insufficient. Theology requires a more robust connection between interpretation and action. The separation between them is usually host to various presuppositions about objective truths and subjective understandings, or pure revelations and impure interpretations, both of which are epistemologically frail.

It seems that Trakakis, even with all the caveats and protections provided by the Orthodox traditions, maintains an implicit boundary around revelation and Christian doctrines that is untouched by these human frailties. It is the classic position of many theologies that there is a pure 'revelation' and that we work to grapple with it in our impurity and frailty.

Here the divisions between us are starker. From my view, humans write scripture as well as express their experience and ongoing understanding and interpretations of God. Christian scriptures concern the encounters with Jesus, written by a few individuals. We know very little about the historical base of these theologized texts. It is theology, not history. It is to be understood symbolically, not literally. Scriptures are filled with ambiguities, contradictions, ethical atrocities and deep insights. They are in the form of poetry, prose, imagery, symbols, metaphors and so on. When Trakakis says "there is no greater authority than the Bible" because it is the written revelation of God, thus making God the primary author of scripture, this is a belief, not a coherent argument. To make a claim based on belief is fine, although belief rests on existential dynamics. To be transparent here would be welcome. Otherwise, the belief masquerades as knowledge even though it is a personal opinion. I read it as a tautology.

Further, Trakakis' interpretation of scripture bypasses the complexities and contradictions found in the Bible, as well as its (usually morally) unacceptable passages. His view leads inevitably to a selective reading, with some texts having more 'revelatory content' than others. Trakakis also states that the church is a dialogue partner when scripture is unclear or in dispute. But my extensive experience with this manner of negotiating 'scripture' and 'church' on the topic of (Catholic) women's ordination has shown, without a shadow of a doubt, that this process has had little theological integrity throughout history or in the present. Both sides use the same biblical

142 *Heather Eaton*

passages, and each brings forth the phrases or pericopes that best support their stance. I find much the same with ecological issues. So I return to my view that we are dealing with imagination and interpretation, often with overt or covert biases. I would consider gender equity or the preferential option for the poor to be an overt bias; whereas misogyny is often covert and can occur when women are not noticeably absent.

Another claim with which I disagree is that "the pinnacle of God's creation is man [*sic*]" (100). We would like to think this is the case, but there is no evidence in support of it, except in our ideas about our self-proclaimed self-importance. We have decided that we are the pinnacle. This is based on different foundations: most complex creature, only moral creature, distinct from the rest of creation, not an animal, the only self-reflective creation, only one with rationality or reason, God came in human form, etc. Each of these arguments has been challenged by creation-based theologies, the evolutionary sciences, ethography (a more sophisticated form of animal studies) and multi-religious studies. This 'pinnacle of God's creation' position is almost always with 'man' as the best representative of humanity and humanity as the best representative of God's creativity or creation. I see it as the best example of human hubris.

Trakakis seeks to support this idea by conceiving of 'man' as "called to draw the whole created (dis)order into harmony with itself and into union with God, thus healing the divisions within the human person and the cosmos" (100). But *contra* Trakakis, this is anthropocentrism, not theocentrism. It is a form of human idolatry. Trakakis claims that this is a view with far-reaching ecological implications. I would agree, but only as an obstacle, as a further reason for rejecting this view.

Most (non-Orthodox) ecological theologians would reject such a theological position and would suggest that theologians need to become better acquainted with the evolutionary sciences in order to counter their inflated self-importance. Christian theology, in all its tributaries, is radically anthropocentric, and eco-theologians address this constantly. Few Orthodox theologians are involved consistently with ecological issues or eco-theology. I am aware that Zizioulas would share a similar position as that made by Trakakis, though Patriarch Bartholomew would not endorse such anthropocentric claims. I am also aware that these claims are embedded within the Orthodox and most classical Christian worldviews, which have interdependent rationalizations of the fall, distortions/corruptions, salvation and the future unity and restoration. I simply do not share the validity of the entire fall/redemption edifice as it has been developed in traditional Christianity. Rather, I regard it as fatally flawed.

Therefore, I do not share the belief in 'Adam's fall', nor do I accept the classical version of the Incarnation as the solution to the fall. I have a different starting point, one which would dovetail with the fall/redemption, except that I would phrase it as the human ambivalence with existence and our inability to live fully and with moral integrity. I therefore share the existential problem but not the formulation of the question nor the answer given to it. I observe that religions share some understanding that we need a rebirth to comprehend how to live or to navigate our way in life and in this world. Being lost, asleep, dead, confused or corrupt are versions of our sense of incompleteness and our deep existential uncertainties and angst. Being found, awake, alive, enlightened and redeemed are the responses.

The problem of immorality is genuine. The idea that humans need some form of 'salvation' seems to be shared across the world's religions. But how this salvation is conceptualized and enacted is quite distinct, and decisive. I do not take it as *prima facie* true that humans have fallen, are corrupt, are embedded in sin or even have a propensity for sin. This is one explanation for our existential condition. There are others.

I agree with Trakakis that our highest vocation is to become authentic persons, and we do so in relationships.

My last comment with regard to Trakakis' chapter is that the fundamental preoccupation of this chapter seems to be twofold: How do we image God? And how are we to think about God? My preoccupation is also twofold: How do we find God's presence and guidance in the activities and dynamics of the world, *this divine milieu*? And how are we to live and have life in abundance? The differences in the orienting preoccupations explain, to some extent, the agreements and disagreements.

Response to Rea: (Reformed) Protestantism

General comments

I very much appreciated the careful descriptions, style and structure of Michael Rea's Position Statement. I valued the meticulous manner in which Rea differentiated the meanings of the terms he used. I found most helpful the autobiographical approach of his paper, where Rea made clear distinctions between what he could claim to know and where he identified what he believed or accepted as true with or without evidence. Rea's worldview is interconnected, and the internal coherence is clear. I very much appreciated the nuances, although I do not share some of the presuppositions. The inclusive language was also well received.

Questions, clarifications and differences

What follows is a series of comments on different topics in Rea's paper. I am numbering them, not by way of importance but to distinguish themes.

(1) The discussion on faith and reason is very well done, with a particular focus on the relationship between evidence and faith and what would constitute a "serious epistemic malfunction". Rea recognizes that faith is sometimes rational and sometimes not, which I take to mean that it can be other-than-rational as opposed to irrational. In a similar vein, Rea differentiates public

144 Heather Eaton

and private evidence, which is crucial in speaking of the validity of accepting the claim a religious outlook may make upon a person's life.

(2) The argument that, if there is a God, God would likely reveal Godself by way of something like an incarnation, is not, in my view, probable or convincing. I am somewhat familiar with Swinburne's argument and the sophisticated use of formal logic to prove God's existence which is then used to make statements about what is reasonable or probable. Rea employs a similar approach, and yet the absolute emphasis on deductive reasoning seems flawed as a way to prove God, and God's freedom, goodness, omniscience, omnipotence, etc. This assumes that human reasoning, deductive reasoning in particular, corresponds to a genuine referent outside of the processes of human knowing or the workings of the mind. This is similar to the scientific method, with the exception that in science there are ways to assess and reassess our reasoning in conjunction with the object of that reasoning. In science, there is a reference point.

Theology, as Rea represents it, involves creating, through human reasoning, a boundary around doctrinal content. Yet this content is derived via human reasoning under the guise of a divine revelation that is untouched by human reason. This is a logical fallacy. The claim that this view is verified by scripture is also not convincing. Scripture too is a product of human reasoning, on the basis of experiences, ideas and images about God. Thus the whole argument is a classic tautology.

I do not doubt the reality of God (with caveats about the operative imagery), but my starting point is different from Rea's. There is a colossal amount of proof that humans invent, create, need or desire a divine presence. In my view, this strengthens the 'evidence' that there is a reality beyond human formulations. That we bend our will, our being and our lives to how we image this divine referent to be is also very obvious. Either our interior psychic processes easily dupe us, or we are intuiting something real; and neither stance is readily discernible or provable. I choose to 'believe' that we are discerning a divine reality. However, to proceed from here requires caution and the efforts of many disciplines and distinct premises that Rea alludes to elsewhere in his essay. Logic is insufficient.

Rea writes that, "at least some of the tenets of every worldview must be taken on faith" (this volume: 71). Does this mean that they are true? Or true to the adherents? I would rephrase Rea's point to say that it must be taken on faith that these tenets hold profound, even ultimate, descriptive or explanatory power for those who live within the relevant worldview. Of course, not all worldviews are equal in their breadth of data, horizon of concern, hermeneutics, explanatory power and ultimacy. In that case, what are we taking on faith?

According to Rea, the premise that the existence of God is reasonably probable leads logically to assigning a high probability to what Jesus is claimed to have said, to accepting a literal interpretation of Jesus' miracles and to accepting also Jesus' resurrection from the dead. This, in turn, is evidence that we too will rise from the dead in bodily form. While having a logical structure, Rea's case is not persuasive. It ignores the evidence that we live, think, navigate and postulate all aspects of our worldview within the realm of symbolic consciousness. This is a more complex and comprehensive form of human 'reasoning' that is inclusive of, but not grounded in, logic. Symbolic processes precede and encompass logic. So, while I very much appreciate the very careful step-by-step logic of Rea's approach, I do not find it satisfactory.

(3) The *sola scriptura* argument is the basis of many (but not all) Protestant traditions. The claim that scripture is *clear and sufficient* is a foundational claim. Yet the stance of *sola scriptura* has proven historically to be more than ambiguous, regardless if the interpretive body is a person (Protestant), the institutional bodies (Catholic, Orthodox) or that most abstruse term, 'the tradition'. Rea contends that we must use our best judgement in our interpretations. But then how do we deal with contradictory interpretations and consequences? Does this mean that the major differences in interpretation (especially those that have resulted in life or death, cultural genocide, Christian empire-building, misogyny, etc.) were not the *best judgements*? An alternative view is that humans interpret scripture according to the norms, biases, exigencies and demands of their era. This does not mean that scripture can be used to support *anything*, that it has unlimited interpretative possibilities, but that the limits of what it reveals are less apparent than the position of *sola scriptura* allows for. Also, historical evidence that scriptural interpretations are exceedingly variable is evident in every era.

What are these *settled judgements* about what scripture teaches? Gender, war, peace, non-violence, poverty, wealth, justice, morality, sexuality, leadership, politics, evolution, genetic manipulation, environmental issues, other religions . . . you name it, we have disagreement about what Christians claim scripture says we ought to do. If a rejoinder is made that appeals to human fallibility, error, bias or corruption . . . this is too easy. Also, disagreements are too pervasive. If another response is that these topics concern 'ethical' questions whose answers are to be derived from a fundamental orientation in scripture, then why is the latter not readily discernible? A more robust theory is required for understanding the interrelation between interpretations, actions and consequences.

Rea remarks that we need many tools of interpretation, and we need to use "our moral intuition", which could go against scripture. He states that we can use our moral intuition to help us recognize that "a divine author [of scripture] would not teach anything to the contrary" (would not affirm, e.g., gender inequality, slavery; 73). Is this how we evade the morally vague or reprehensible aspects of scripture or the morally dubious activities of Christians, churches and traditions? What then is *sola scriptura*?

This fine dance between revising one's understanding of scripture in light of intuitions or scientific beliefs, versus revising one's intuitions or scientific beliefs in light of scripture (73), is becoming almost ludicrous. Herein lies the

146   *Heather Eaton*

great problem with the package of *sola scriptura*, biblical inerrancy (in flexible or rigid forms), lack of transparency on the level of hermeneutics, and 2,000 years of ambiguous and contradictory cultural activities in the name of Christianity. I am reminded of Mieke Bal's comment that, "The Bible, of all books, is the most dangerous one, the one that has been endowed with the power to kill" (1989: 14).

(4) I find the section on the nature of God, especially on the nature of God's perfection, to be an erudite version of 'I believe what I imagine, or what I can deduce from logic'. I also find the discussion on the nature of the Trinity to be highly abstract and speculative. Again, the mode of deriving an understanding based on a logical progression, while exacting, is not sufficient to warrant a commitment to a worldview accepted as ultimate, or an existential or religious commitment. Further, I am always suspicious of those who claim to know a great deal about God.

(5) I do not share with Rea the various dualisms that inhabit his worldview: material/immaterial, mind/body, body/soul, perfection/corruption, natural/supernatural, etc. These are explanatory categories, modes of thinking and ways we use to differentiate aspects of our experiences or even distinctions within our intuitive grasp of the inscrutabilities within which we are embedded. There is no evidence, however, that these are existential ontologies. Rea suggests there is no counterevidence, but I find there is considerable such evidence within postmodern epistemologies, somatic theories, consciousness studies, theories of religion and symbolic processes, and worldview studies. I also do not share his belief in supernatural miracles.

(6) The section on the human condition was quite interesting. My questions arise from the fact that I would take a different starting point. For example, all religions share some form of belief, or intuition, that death is not final. The idea of resurrection is one manifestation of that belief. I am convinced that there is a basis to this 'intuition', but I am not certain of the accuracy of the manifestation (resurrection, reincarnation, returning to the Dao or Great Spirit, and so on). Because one believes something, that does not make it true.

Further, the facets of this explanation are based on non-evidentiary belief or faith (e.g., the body/soul division, an eschatology of eternal life). As Rea observes, it is a choice of beliefs based on suppositions and claims and supported by scriptural interpretations. I appreciate the transparency of the presuppositions of his worldview. Yet I find the substance rather thin. More cogent arguments in theology can, in my view, be developed from theories of religion and historical consciousness, as pointed out in my Position Statement. I wonder what Rea makes of these suggestions.

In addition, the historical consequences of the kind of Christian account of 'the human condition' given by Rea have not proven to be overall life-giving to the world. The notion of the corruption of the human condition coupled with an other-worldly, salvific-redemption theology have created the conditions for great damage to be done to the world. If we hold that "by their fruits you shall know them", then we might question the adequacy, dare I say accuracy, of such theologies.

That humans are to be held morally responsible is found across cultures, religions, humanist traditions and atheistic worldviews. That humans have an unusual capacity to damage themselves, others, their habitat and other animals is readily recognized. But from an evolutionary perspective (that I take seriously), the idea of a temporal fall, or even an ontological fall, is unintelligible. The belief that perfection might turn corrupt, needing redemption, simply does not cohere with what is known about the evolution of humanity as a species and the development of a religio-symbolic consciousness and a cultural-religious base in civilizations. So I ask: what is the existential question to which this account of the human condition, salvation and eternal life is an answer?

Religions, if conceived as 'languages', address our confusion, our ability to harm, our incompetence to navigate the breadth and depth of the world, and our inability to appreciate larger, transcendent dimensions of existence. Religions orient us to a sacred dimension in multiple ways. Religions are maps. Or better: they are complex languages, responses to the allure and demands of the Sacred/Holy, which are then codified conceptually in scriptures and rituals. I believe humans cannot live without religion. If we were to ask, 'Which language is true?' what would we say? I find this similar to asking, 'Which religion is true?' They are all languages or maps. I don't *believe* in a language. I function and navigate within one. When I come to know more than one, I realize that there are multiple languages. The same metaphor applies to religion.

Reference

Bal, M. 1989. "Introduction." *Anti-Covenant: Counter-Reading Women's Lives in the Hebrew Bible*, edited by M. Bal, 11–24. Sheffield: Almond Press.

8   Kevin Hart

Rather than respond point by point to the four other Position Statements, I shall comment on some themes that are common to all of them. In particular, I shall focus on the doctrine of God, especially the triune nature of God, and the status and roles of apophatic theology. First, though, I would like to make some preliminary points which will supply a context for my responses and which are in addition to the phenomenological approach to the divine that I outlined in my paper.

In the first place, I take the Nicene-Constantinopolitan Creed (381), along with the definition of Chalcedon (451), to establish the vanishing points of what it means to confess orthodox belief in the Christian God. That these texts call for interpretation and that diverse theologies, orthodox or not, can be in tune with them goes without saying. And it must be acknowledged that the Creed can even be amplified, as happened (illegally, to be sure, but with good theological reasons) with the addition of the *filioque* in the eleventh century. That said, the more one departs from the Creed and the Definition in one's philosophy of Christianity or one's theology, the less plausible it is to call that philosophy or theology 'Christian' in the traditional understanding of the word. One's philosophy or theology may have historical roots in Christianity, like Universalist Unitarians, creedless Christians, Oneness Pentecostals, various radical Protestant groups, and post-Christian communities that value Jesus of Nazareth as a moral teacher but not as divine. Yet these religious associations fall outside what I wish to defend. In the second place, I think that while phenomenology can describe the manifestation of the divine in Jesus of Nazareth and that it offers the best starting point for a systematic theology, such a theology must nonetheless use a metaphysics of one sort or another in developing a doctrine of God, even if the doctrine's metaphysical claims are ultimately called into question on apophatic grounds or grounds that exceed both kataphatic and apophatic theologies. In the third place, Christianity has a cognitive role to play in its presentations of God and the world; it seeks to explain how things are, not merely to ask and answer questions of meaning and value. Its vocabulary of grace and sin, fall and redemption, and so on is not merely normative; it aims to be descriptive. Yet it is not a final vocabulary, whether in its Augustinian,

First Response 149

Thomist, Lutheran, Calvinist or Barthian forms. A systematic theology does its best to see how the economy of salvation hangs together, but God in himself is not to be caught in any system.

With that said, I begin by drawing attention to the assumption, standard in orthodox Christianity, that God is a free Creator. Several things follow from this assumption. The first is that God does not need creation in order to become fully (or more fully) himself. He already enjoyed all possible perfections before the world came into being, and these perfections are unchanged by the act of creation. This view first achieves philosophical clarity with St Anselm's *Proslogion*, and thereafter it forms the basis of perfect being theology as developed to a high level by St Thomas Aquinas and by other theologians who follow him, whether closely or at a distance. I find perfect being theology the strongest contender to develop a doctrine of God, and while I acknowledge that it has redoubtable challenges, I think that it has fewer serious ones for Christian theology than its alternatives. For example, many analytic philosophers today reject the traditional view that God is simple and, as a consequence, see no reason to keep the divine attributes of eternality, immutability and impassivity.[1] Yet the God of many contemporary analytical philosophers is difficult to square with the deity of the Nicene-Constantinopolitan Creed and the definition of Chalcedon as the Church has interpreted them. For all the sophistication in talk of individuals and properties that seeks to disable the theory of divine simplicity, the finite super-being that is the result of this critique – a being who lives in time, who is subject to passion and who changes his mind – ends up seeming like a big guy in the sky, the God of the nursery more than the God of the Church.

Also, many readers of the Bible, including some of the philosophers just mentioned, observe that the eternal, immutable, impassive and maximally great deity of perfect being theology fails to square with the God depicted in Scripture and note that as Christians we are bound to Scripture rather than to philosophical theology, which is an interpretation of Scripture, one that draws deeply from Greek philosophy. Yet to someone committed to perfect being theology, at least with regard to the doctrine of God, this observation is not coercive. Christianity responds to Scripture, to be sure, but also to tradition and ecclesial authority. Besides, these philosophical readers of the Bible read Scripture somewhat naively, without taking sufficient note of the ways in which biblical writing works as apocalypse, epistle, gospel, historical narrative, law, poetry, visionary writing, and so on. The books of the Bible are narratives and poems, testimonies and visions, not drafts of papers that, at a pinch, could be reduced to propositions, their arguments formalized, and then sent to the *Journal of Analytic Theology*. Before engaging in the philosophy of religion, Christian philosophers need to learn how to read the Bible well. This does not mean mastering or even approving of the historical-critical method, which is open to all manner of criticisms, especially because its understanding of evidence excludes miracles *a priori*. But it does mean learning the biblical languages and learning how to read the

150 *Kevin Hart*

different genres of Scripture with rigour and respect, that is, with the help of biblical commentaries from the Fathers to writers of the present day. Part of that rigour and respect is in making due use of the principle of accommodation, as used since Origen.

In creating all that there is, God is not thereby constituted as other than the world. Instead, God is other than any play of sameness and otherness that operates within the world.[2] It is this understanding of the relation between God and the world that generates apophatic theologies (quests for God that deny predications associated with created being), which cannot be completely disassociated from kataphatic theologies (quests for God in the study of his self-revelation). God is "everywhere secret and everywhere out in the open," as St Augustine (2002: 74.9) says. We pass from the world to God not by denying the world as such but by a process of purification from sin and by following a path of unknowing that enables us to approach the radical otherness of God, which the tradition often designates as 'mystery'. We are commended to approach the divine mystery in reverent silence, although this silence usually comes only after many words have been spoken, some kataphatic and others apophatic; for the true approach to God is beyond both theologies. So says no less an authority than Pseudo-Dionysius the Areopagite: "Now we should not conclude that the negations are simply the opposites of the affirmations, but rather that the cause of all is considerably prior to this, beyond privations, beyond every denial, beyond every assertion" (1987: 136).

We are always encouraged by the Church to speak to God, but proponents of mystical theology invariably warn us that we shall encounter severe limits when speaking of God. Christian theology shuttles between two situations: while any child can always talk *to* God, great learning is required to talk *about* God, and no amount of learning can assure a theologian that he or she is talking properly or well about God. There is a reason for this. God, as Creator, is not just singular, he is *absolutely* singular, while you and I are *relatively* singular: unique yet relative to other things in the world (beings, animals, the species *homo sapiens*, the male and female genders). God is not relative to anything; his mode of being is fundamentally unlike that of anything else, and because no genus or species contains him, his being is strictly incomprehensible and unlimited. When I, along with many others, refer to God as 'he' it is not because God is imagined as male but because in the Lord's Prayer Jesus gives us the primal metaphor for God, 'Father', which indicates the sort of relationship we may hope to have with God.[3] The Creator of all that there is calls us to be in an intimate and loving relationship with him: it is an astonishing thing, and one that no Christian should ever forget or allow to become too familiar.

Because God does not relate to the world in the manner of other to the same, he does not simply transcend the world. More precisely, the divine transcendence does not have the basic characteristic of contrasting God with the world. Instead, God transcends the world while being completely free to

First Response 151

abide immanently within it. It is this transcendence that makes it appropriate for all created beings to feel awe before the deity and to figure divine holiness by way of a sense of radical otherness. One crucial aspect of this radical otherness is the triune nature of God. If we turn to the divine immanence, we may say that it makes it possible to speak of the incarnation of God in Jesus of Nazareth and to devise a theology of the sacraments.

* * *

John Bishop differs from many contemporary analytical philosophers of religion in that he rejects both perfect being theology and personal omniGod theism. In fact, although he does not speak in these terms, his proposal has roots in Schelling ('ground of Being'), discovered by way of Tillich, as well as in Hegel (a teleological view of God as love). It also has roots in Augustine (1991: VIII.12): "you do see a trinity if you see charity". And one might add that it is also in tune with the notion of development in doctrine proposed by Newman, although Bishop accepts that Christian doctrine is limited and fallible in places where Newman would not. For Bishop, God is not to be conceived as the Creator who precedes the world but as a deity that is the end or purpose of the world. This deity is not supernatural, depends on the natural world in order to become itself and is the full realization of love. Questions can be asked of the positive theory that Bishop proposes and of his criticisms of perfect being theology. I begin with the latter.

Perfect being theology is to be rejected, Bishop argues, because it turns on an incoherent idea: "*an existent* that is absolutely simple and necessary" (this volume: 6; emphasis in original). One might well put pressure on his choice of 'existent' here (and 'entity' and 'item' later), for perfect being theology, at least as proposed by Aquinas, turns not on a being like but above others with certain properties, but on an absolutely singular *actus essendi*: God is fully actualized in a pure act of being and has no potential at all. His being is not *ens commune* but *esse* (act of being); more precisely, it is *ipsum esse subsistens omnibus modis indeterminatum*, wholly undetermined pure subsistent act of being itself, or, if you wish, perfect being, which is simple.[4] Because God does not contrast with the world, *ens uncreatum* as distinct from *ens creatum*, there is no difficulty in him transcending time, which is created along with the cosmos, while also being free to enter its stream. That God is sometimes figured in the Bible as speaking, acting and changing his mind and not always as immutable, impassive and eternal is to do with the ways in which the deity is often represented in poetry and narrative. Often, not always: think for instance of Malachi 3:6 ("For I am the LORD, I change not"). Being related to God is a reality for us but not for God; when we ascribe acts and movements to God we are signifying changes in ourselves in relation to God, not in God himself.[5] If God were not simple he would be compound, but how could a deity who precedes Creation be compound? Every composite is posterior to its components, and God precedes

152 *Kevin Hart*

all *ens commune*.[6] Properly understood, God does not *have* properties such as mercy, supreme power, and so on; he *is* mercy, supreme power and all the rest. He is not a binding together of the abstract and the concrete, conceived as two heterogeneous ontological realms, but is a single act of being in which essence and existence are one. This unity guarantees that God is one with each attribute, and it follows that each attribute, being one with God, is one with every other attribute.[7]

Bishop is right to distance himself from the God affirmed by personal omniGod theists, for this deity is no more than Zeus by another name. And there is reason to allude to Meister Eckhart on the essential no-thing-ness of God, though for a slightly different reason than the Dominican ventured: an *act* of being has no thinghood at all. Yet Bishop is content with a deity who is remarkably thin by traditional standards, a *telos* that is realized in the world and that is the highest possible good. I am not clear how Bishop's God "*will* be" the ultimate cause of the world (my emphasis), especially since the world is already here. Nor is it evident to me what justifies Bishop's optimism that love (instead of complete and utter indifference, say) will triumph in a universe that is adequately explained by naturalism. I do not even see how love goes toward forming something that we could call 'God'.

Undoubtedly, for Bishop the preaching and resurrection of Jesus are together the strongest possible anticipation of this *telos*, although I must confess that I cannot credit his account of the resurrection of Jesus or square it with his rejection of immortality and eternal life. How, on naturalist grounds, does the love that Jesus embodied so fully cause his manifestations after his torture and execution? Is this love singular, or might others be just as loving? If it is singular, how can this singularity be explained on naturalist grounds? And if it is not singular, why would one not see manifestations of other deeply loving persons after their deaths: St Francis of Assisi or Mother Teresa of Calcutta, for example?

It seems that for Bishop, God will be "all in all" only with the realization of his Kingdom of love at the end of time. I am reminded of Pannenberg's eschatological ontology, in which being is determined retroactively from the future realization of the Kingdom.[8] It is hard to see how theodicy makes sense in such a theology. One will not find much of a theodicy in Bishop's theology, and I wonder what role there is for divine guidance through the answering of prayers. Is there a sufficient justification in his theology for prayer? And if not, can one really call this theology 'Christian', in a robust sense, for petitionary prayer and answers to it have a claim to being fundamental to the practice of the religion? I note also that Bishop rejects personal immortality, which I take to mean minimally the endless survival of a consciousness. Since he also rejects eternity, I suppose that he also denies eternal life, that is, being outside time (and hence endless succession) with God, so that one has, to the degree God grants, an intellectual vision of love. Yet can we rightly say that God *loves* us if he is willing to let those who love him remain dead? If I could have saved my father from death, I surely would

First Response 153

have done so because I loved him; and since God is infinitely more powerful than I am and is infinitely more loving than I am, it is not unreasonable to think that he will save my father from the finality of death. Lastly, can we reconcile Bishop's God with the God of the Nicene-Constantinopolitan Creed and the definition of Chalcedon? I find it hard to do so, and while I think that doctrine is always open to being developed, it looks to me as though Bishop's view of God pulls the meaning of 'Christian' somewhat out of shape.

One's doctrine of God comes from various sources. One of them is Scripture, and it is worthwhile to spend a few moments on this source, especially since Michael Rea raises it. Rea defends the Protestant notion of '*sola scriptura*' and in particular the views that Scripture is authoritative, clear and sufficient. Such views are indeed needed if a doctrine of God is to be drawn wholly from Scripture. Yet does the principle of '*sola scriptura*' make sense, even if one sets aside the Reformation formulation of the 'five *solæ*', in which the plural seems self-contradictory: how many 'only's' can one have? Christians have recourse to a great many scriptures, the Old Testament, the deutero-canonical Scriptures, the New Testament, as well as in modern times to the extra-canonical gospels Q and Thomas (to say nothing of the apocryphal gospels). There is no such thing as '*only* Scripture', for Scripture presumes canon, which presumes authority and ecclesial practices (and, in the early Church, the authority of the emperor), and it presumes theories and practices of translation and interpretation as well. R. P. C. Hanson (1988: xxi) puts the matter well: "The theologians of the Christian Church were slowly driven to a realization that the deepest questions which face Christianity cannot be answered in purely biblical language, because the questions are about the meaning of biblical language itself." The Reformed Bible to which Rea appeals in his essay involves a contestation of the canon established by the authority of the Church, and an appeal simply to '*sola scriptura*' hardly justifies the contestation. For what Luther and Calvin *count* as Scripture is a question at the heart of the Reformation, as is the basis of the *authority* of the Reformers to excise certain books from the Bible.

Let me pass from authority to clarity and sufficiency. I am not at all sure what Rea means when he says that Scripture is clear. Is the claim that it is clear in the original Hebrew, Aramaic and Koine Greek? Or that it is clear in certain translations but not others? Anyone who knows the biblical languages will readily point to all manner of grammatical ambiguities and textual uncertainties in Scripture which press on the formation of doctrine. There are also very difficult texts to interpret because of apparent contradictions between Scripture and doctrine (Genesis 1:2 and *creatio ex nihilo*, for instance) or Scripture and Scripture (Genesis 5:26, 1 Peter 3:20; Matthew 28:19, Acts 10:48, for example). There is also the problem of textual variants in codices that long precede the *textus receptus* of the Bible, which itself calls for correction according to many scholars. If Scripture is clear, why, I wonder, does biblical criticism generate a principle such as *lectio difficilior potior*?

154 *Kevin Hart*

If the New Testament claim that Jesus is the Christ is clear, why rearrange the books of the Hebrew Bible into the books of the Old Testament so that the Old Testament ends with Malachi, with its messianic promise, and not 2 Chronicles, with its vision of a restored Temple of Solomon? And anyone aware of ecclesial history will point to fierce disputes about the meaning of Scripture as it relates to the formation of doctrine: Proverbs 8:22, Amos 4:11, 12–13, Isaiah 53:8, many verses in John, and 1 Corinthians 15:28 are standard cruxes in the exegesis of the early Church.[9] I dare say that the framers of the Creed of Sirmium (357), or even those who composed the 'Dated Creed' (359), thought that the Scripture to which they appealed was quite clear. It must also be noted that Calvinists disagree with other Protestants, as well as with Catholics and Orthodox, about the meaning of many passages of Scripture as they relate to doctrine: the teaching of the Eucharist, for example.

Is Scripture sufficient for the formation of doctrine? I doubt it: authority and tradition are crucial when making doctrine. In making links between Scripture and doctrine, one should not underestimate the importance of liturgy, in particular: baptizing people in the name of the Father and the Son and the Holy Spirit (Matthew 28:19) was done long before there was a well-established doctrine of the Trinity, and the practice influenced the formation of the doctrine. One has to wait until the Nicene-Constantinopolitan Creed of 381 for a doctrinal formulation that is minimally clear, and for Aquinas' treatise on the Trinity in the *Summa theologiæ* 1a qq. 27–43 until clarity is gained about the difference between distinctness and distinction in the simple Godhead. Another example: orthodox Christian doctrine of God turns on the use of the word '*homoousios*', which is not biblical. The more one knows about the history of doctrine in the early Church, the less likely it is that one could plausibly say that Scripture is authoritative, clear or sufficient in the manner that Rea seems to have in mind. Nick Trakakis is largely right when he says, with appropriate emphasis, "*it is only in and through the Church that the Scriptures can be interpreted authoritatively*" (this volume: 90).[10] If we accept this, we also accept responsibility for learning about Christian theology and ecclesial history before engaging in the philosophy of religion; and that will require some changes in the practice of the philosophy of religion, especially in Protestant analytical philosophy, which tends to bypass history and literature and to move quickly, usually far too quickly, to argumentation, construction or speculation.

* * *

All four authors attend to the triune nature of God, and I shall say something about each person's remarks about the Trinity. Heather Eaton says that she doubts that "the Trinity is a functioning doctrine any more" (this volume: 32). "It is not alive in the religious imagination of most Christians I encounter," she says, "except as an insensible, at times rigid, belief" (32). We must move in very different circles, since I find that most Christians I meet regard the Trinity as the very ground of life. To hold the orthodox view need not be a sign of rigid thinking, though: orthodoxy is a moving, growing thing, and like all moving, growing things, it needs structures. Yet anecdotes about people one meets do not pass as arguments, and theology is not sociology. At the level of theological discussion, her dismissal of belief in the Trinity is a very odd statement, since talk about the triune nature of God has been intense since the mid-twentieth century: think of Barth and Pannenberg, Rahner and von Balthasar, among many others. We have come a long way from the liberal Protestant sidelining of the doctrine of the Trinity, associated with Kant, Schleiermacher and Ritschl. Yet at the level of parish life, especially in the Protestant churches, it is sadly true that many Christians shy away from the triune nature of God, thinking of 'Trinity' as shorthand for something like a troubling problem in advanced algebraic topology. As Rahner (1975: 10) observed some decades ago, most Christians in their daily spiritual lives are "mere monotheists" without due awareness of the triune nature of God. In the West, in particular, Christians tend to have underdeveloped theologies of the Holy Spirit, and one would not have to be a latter-day Cappadocian to discover that many church-goers today would not be able adequately to defend themselves against Arianism and, indeed, are sometimes Arians or Adoptionists or Modalists without being aware of it.

Eaton is no friend of orthodox Christian theology, finding its questions, at least those posed in a philosophical register, "somewhat dated"; and yet the style of criticism she adopts – based on the judgement that "humans invent Gods [*sic*]" – goes back to Xenophanes. What's important is not how old a question is but how well formed it is and how penetrating it is. Nonetheless, some of Eaton's views on the Trinity chime with others that have become quite common in recent Trinitarian theology. Thinking especially of the Holy Spirit, she says that the teaching should remind us that "nothing is determined" (34). Also, as she says, "the Trinity, as a whole, functions as an image of relationality, interdependence and community" (34). True enough, though I would adjust each remark. To the first I would add that God's being, which is absolutely singular, is mysterious, unable to be understood definitively by the human mind, and accordingly the doctrine of God is always open to being developed without thereby having to depart from orthodoxy and without ever making the being of God comprehensible. Talk of 'person' or 'relation' does not amount to a final vocabulary in Trinitarian theology, although we have not yet found a better one: Barth's proposal of Revealer, Revealedness and Revelation does not seem to have replaced the older terms even in his own church. And to the second point I would add a caution: one has to be very careful in speaking of the triune God in terms of community, as contemporary social Trinitarians do, for the divine persons are not taken to be individuals in relation with one another.

We might also think back to Richard of St Victor (2010: III.20): "If you pay attention to any one of the three persons, you will see that the other two concordantly love the third. If you look at the second person, you will likewise find that the rest are united in love of him with equal desire. If you bring the third person into consideration, then you will undoubtedly see the affection of the other two flowing together in him with equal concord." This puts the right emphasis on the meaning of God as love but at the risk of using language that suggests tri-theism. Aquinas, by contrast, stresses the simplicity of the divine nature when he speaks of the Trinity by way of real distinctions but at the risk of making God sound like a chilly metaphysical construction rather than love itself. (Only Aquinas' most superficial readers could think for long that he is cool in his discussion of God, however: often a calm remark, easily overlooked, such as *amor Dei est infundens et creans bonitatem in rebus*, opens onto a piercing vision of boundless love.[11]) Aquinas is not concerned to give a full, positive explanation of the Trinity but to show that at heart we cannot explain it. Eaton tells us that the doctrine of the Trinity "rarely illuminates something vital about life" (32). Yet to my mind that is precisely what it does: it says that the origin, end and meaning of life are nothing other than divine love.

Nick Trakakis gives an excellent short account of the Orthodox doctrine of the Trinity, and I have little to add to what he says so well. Besides, I am one of those Catholics who admire much in Orthodox theology and seek to learn from it. Only one flicker of concern is worth noting. "The divine persons," he says, "are 'consubstantial': each is God since all share the same essence or substance" (this volume: 97). He directs us immediately to a note, since a caveat is necessary: "This is not to say that God's unity or oneness is founded upon the consubstantiality of the three persons, so that God is one *because* the three persons share the same essence" (106n13; emphasis in original). What concerns me is the reason that Trakakis gives why this statement would be wrong. I would say it is wrong because God's essence and existence are one and because there is no sharing as between distinct individuals. He says it is wrong because it rubs against the doctrine of the monarchy of the Father, which teaches that God the Father is the source and cause of the Son and the Holy Spirit. The position gains prominence in the history of doctrine in part because of its role in meeting Arian arguments: Sts Athanasius and Basil of Caesaria are cases in point.[12]

One difficulty with this Orthodox teaching is that it suggests there was a time or an ontological state before there was a Son and a Holy Spirit. Yet the doctrine of the generation of the Son says that the generation is eternal, and the doctrine of the procession of the Holy Spirit says that the procession is eternal. If both the generation and the procession are eternal, it makes no sense to suggest that the Father is prior with respect to divinity to the Son and the Holy Spirit. I think the Catholic framing of the Trinitarian relations, as first elaborated in detail by Augustine in *De trinitate*, makes this clearer than the Orthodox account of the Trinity. In the Catholic teaching, the Holy Spirit proceeds from the Father and the Son, and so while the Father's primacy is retained, the structure of mutual love is presented as paramount. Needless to say, Trakakis is well aware of the differences between Catholic and Orthodox teaching on this point, and is finely aware too that some Orthodox theologians maintain the *filioque* (taken to mean 'through the Son', not 'and the Son') as a theologoumenon that illuminates the doctrine of the Nicene-Constantinopolitan Creed. There is no question of the primacy of the Father; it is embodied in the Creed, which they retain unchanged. To be sure, there is a *taxis* in God – Father, Son and Holy Spirit – but I would argue that this is not ontological but economic. It concerns the working out of our salvation, not the being of God in and of itself. For the Creed concerns the economic Trinity, not the immanent Trinity.

Michael Rea is less careful than Trakakis in articulating the doctrine of the Trinity: "To say that two things are consubstantial is to say that they share a common nature – that is, they are members of exactly the same kind" (Rea, this volume: 75). But there is no 'kind' at issue: the doctrine of the Trinity is monotheistic; it turns on God being absolutely singular, not belonging to any genus at all. Otherwise, one would be in a position to defend tri-theism. This is relevant to Rea's talk about the Trinitarian persons. He writes as though the Father, the Son and the Holy Spirit are three individuals sharing a single nature, much as St Gregory of Nyssa does in his letter to Ablabius, "On Not Three Gods". Rea concludes that, "The Father is *a* God, the Son is *a* God and the Holy Spirit is *a* God, but each is the same God as the others; so, since there are no other Gods, there is exactly one God" (77; my emphases). This conclusion may be drawn, he thinks, because the Father, Son and Holy Spirit are "genuinely distinct *compounds* [of the divine nature and a person-making property] and genuinely distinct *persons*" (77; emphases in original). There are two problems here. First, it needs to be made plain that the *ousia* of the Trinitarian persons does not precede the *hypostases* but that the two converge exactly, with no temporal gap intruding. (Aquinas' language of *actus essendi* makes this plainer than the Cappadocians were able to do with their ontology.) Without this safeguard, the door is left open to view the Trinitarian persons as being like human beings or for there to be a graded Trinity. Second, Rea uses the English word 'person' without any reference to the Greek '*prosopon*', which most certainly does not mean 'person' in the modern sense of the word; it is closer to 'mask', a situation that causes other problems, especially a temptation to modalism. Rea suggests that Father, Son and Holy Spirit are distinct individuals in relation, though the orthodox doctrine of the Trinity that comes to us from the Cappadocians insists that the relationships are prior to the persons and constitute the perichoretic life of the divine persons. In putting matters as he does, so differently from the way the tradition gives them, I do not think that Rea is developing doctrine so much as confusing the reality of the triune persons, as real distinctions, with applications of the doctrine of appropriation as formulated by St Hilary and refined by later Fathers. Good theological method requires us to keep the two things quite distinct.

158   *Kevin Hart*

The application of appropriation is also an issue in John Bishop's remarks on the Trinity. On the "God is love" theory that he proposes, "no one of the Persons exhausts the divine" (this volume: 16). Now the doctrine of appropriation tells us that, guided by Scripture, we appropriate certain names or qualities or acts to one or another of the divine persons. When we appropriate love to the Holy Spirit, it is not because the Holy Spirit exhausts all of divine love so that we are to think of the Father and Son being occupied with other things (power and wisdom, say) but because Scripture leads us to think of the Holy Spirit as being the divine person primarily associated with love in the economy of revelation. The theological reality is that the Father, the Son and the Holy Spirit are all equally loving (and all-powerful, all-merciful and all-wise, and so on). So there is no question of any one Trinitarian person exhausting the divine in the sense that the Son is "*an* aspect of reality" (my emphasis), thereby leaving other aspects of reality to be assigned to the Father and the Holy Spirit.

* * *

Few Christian theologies of any volume and sophistication are simply kataphatic; they are also apophatic. (Karl Barth's *Church Dogmatics* is one of the select few, thanks mainly to the creativity and flexibility of his thought in volumes two and four.) One might say that apophaticism is a way of ensuring that we mean *God* when we use the word 'God' and do not reduce God to an idol or a god. John Bishop is quite right, then, to criticize personal omniGod theism, which remains solely kataphatic, for leaving us with an idol instead of the deity of the Nicene-Constantinopolitan Creed. He is also right to reject what he calls a "stand-alone apophatic theology" (this volume: 11).[13] Such a thing would not leave us with any theology at all, since it would deny the very possibility of revelation. Kataphasis gives us the names of the Triune persons through Scripture but does not tell us about the divine being. Indeed, a purely kataphatic theology would run the terrible risk of making the divine being, *actus essendi*, appear like *ens commune*, confusing a verbal state with a nominal one. Apophaticism is needed in order to preserve the distinction between *esse* and *ens commune*, as we say in the West, or to maintain the distinction between God's essence and his energies, as they say in the East. Nor is it something derived from pagan thought. Nick Trakakis has reason to remind us that apophaticism is a current running through both Testaments. The apophatic names that Bishop lists ("atemporality, immutability, impassibility, necessity and simplicity" ([11]) serve to distinguish God from *ens commune*. In particular, it must be remembered that when Aquinas writes of the simple nature of God, he is not saying something positive about the divine being but dismissing the possibility of composition within God.

When we say with Maximus the Confessor or Pseudo-Dionysius the Areopagite that God is above or beyond being, we are saying that God is

First Response 159

radically other than the being of his Creation (and not that the divine being contrasts with it).[14] We approach the mystery of God's being by removing predicates associated with *ens commune* and that are therefore inappropriate to divine being; we do not thereby reach that divine being, but nor do we confuse God with an idol of our own construction.[15] It is because of the tendency that humans have, as Eaton puts it, to "invent Gods", and to do so in our own image, that orthodox theology takes extreme care in negating affirmative and negative predications of the divine being. But not all predications of the divine being are always negated: Aquinas, who is strongly committed to apophatic theology, nonetheless tells us unequivocally that God is form as well as act.[16] So Michael Rea is not quite right to tell us that his commitment to human concepts applying univocally to God is "strongly at odds" with apophatic theology. It depends on the apophatic theology at issue, and he does not tell us which one or ones he rejects: the apophaticism of Pseudo-Dionysius is very different in scope from that of Nicolas of Cusa, for instance, and both differ in that way from Aquinas'. Apophaticism allows us to move, intellectually at least, from the economic Trinity towards the immanent Trinity, but it does not guarantee that we shall arrive at the immanent Trinity, God as God is in himself. We may prepare ourselves for God, but we cannot reach God by our own efforts, even our own religious efforts. Indeed, apophatic theology is not to be regarded as the right path to God, for it also can give rise to a negative objectification of the deity, a thin abstraction from phenomena that is inconsistent with the deity of abounding love and that gives undue prominence to the power of the human intellect in approaching God. This is why we must say, as has been done earlier in this response, that God's being is beyond both kataphasis and apophasis.

* * *

As a coda to this response, I would like to add a word or two about a couple of related issues that come up in the chapters. The first is the issue of the relation between philosophy and theology, and the second is the development of doctrine. When I read the papers by Bishop and Rea I find myself in the company of Protestant analytical philosophers who are taking different tacks with respect to Christianity. Rea outlines a systematic theology based on Calvin and the peculiar inflection of Calvinism that comes from Reformed epistemology. Bishop, finding himself impressed by the success of naturalism, attempts to rethink Christianity so that it falls into line with its assumptions, trajectories and conclusions. What is common to them is that they tend to abstract Christianity from its historical, ecclesial and theological contexts in order to view it as a series of problems of the kind one deals with in analytical philosophy. I ask myself how their work would be different if they had been trained in reading the Bible and in theology as well as in analytical philosophy; and the answer comes back that the essays would

160   Kevin Hart

have ended up being more useful to Christianity in general and to Christian theology in particular than they are at the moment. For example, the tradition insists that the persons of the Trinity are in relation with one another but that the relations precede the persons. This teaching is far from self-evident, and yet is the sort of thing that analytical philosophers are expert at discussing and straightening out. But would one know the importance of the Cappadocian doctrine without studying the early Church? I do not think so, and most analytical philosophers are not learned in the history of doctrine. Their interest is in recent philosophical debates, not longstanding theological ones, which is understandable yet regrettable if the end point is the extension and illumination of Christian thought. I wonder for whom Bishop and Rea write and, outside the guild of analytical philosophy, who they think will profit from their speculations.

Of course, Christian theology feeds off peculiar positions and arguments; it looks to any piece of learning if it can augment or elucidate Christian teaching. It has been so since Origen's letter to Gregory the Wonderworker. And the Church takes as much time as it wishes in considering what is fruitful and what is unfruitful. Theology may have important things to learn from cosmology or string theory or postmodernism or gender criticism. Yet the development of Christian teaching and Christian understanding can take place only within a plane whose vanishing points have been set by the Creed and Definition. Not that the Nicene-Constantinopolitan Creed proposes everything that needs to be considered in theology. Far from it: one would never know that the Jesus of history did anything while alive if one restricted oneself to it. The Creed is not a systematic theology and still less a theological encyclopedia *in nuce*. My own work begins with Jesus' concrete preaching of the coming of the Kingdom, which is not explicitly evoked in the Creed, which is concerned solely with the Kingdom of Heaven at the end of time. One has to decide whether one's concern is development of doctrine or alternatives to doctrine: it seems to me that Trakakis and I are concerned with the former, that Rea would like to be, and that Bishop and Eaton are committed to the latter. I dare say that Rea thinks that he stands firmly within the tradition, but his formulation of the triune nature of God seems to me to be not quite orthodox in execution, if not intent. Bishop is actively seeking to find an intellectually credible alternative to the doctrine of God in orthodox Christianity, even while looking back towards some of its major creeds. Eaton, it seems to me, is content to find alternatives to orthodox Christianity and has no wish to stay within its intellectual and spiritual world.

Notes

1   See, for example, Plantinga (1980), where Plantinga rejects divine simplicity and figures God as temporal.
2   See, with regard to this position, Sokolowski's (1995) articulation of what he calls 'the Christian distinction'. Also see Tanner (2005: ch. 2), and Burrell's (2004) extensions of the Christian distinction.

3 In the Hebrew Bible, God is also figured as mother: see, in particular, Isaiah 42:14, 46:3–14, 49:14–15, 66:12–13 but also Numbers 11:12 and Deuteronomy 32:11–12. And when we figure God as a father it needs to be underlined that he is both like a father and unlike any father we might know.
4 See Aquinas, *Summa theologiæ* 1a, q. 11, art. 4 *responsio*.
5 See Aquinas, *Summa theologiæ* 1a, q. 13, art. 7 *responsio*.
6 See Aquinas, *Summa theologiæ* 1a, q. 3, art. 7.
7 I cannot engage in close discussion of the topic here. However, see Vallicella (2015).
8 See, for example, Pannenberg (1969: 64–67).
9 Also see Hilary of Poitiers, *De Trinitate*, 7.10.
10 The authority of the emperor, as already mentioned, also needs to be taken into account in resolving disputes in the early Church.
11 Aquinas, *Summa theologiæ* 1a, q. 20, art. 2 *responsio*.
12 See St Athanasius, *Orations Against the Arians*, 4.1, and St Basil of Caesarea, *Against Eunomius*, 1.25. For the Neo-Arian position, see Eunomius' "Confession of Faith," in *The Extant Works*, pp. 150–159.
13 I take it that Bishop is thinking of the post-Kantian position defended by Kaufman (1972). This radical apophasis is quite different from the apophasis variously endorsed by the Fathers.
14 See Maximus the Confessor, *Mystagogia*, Prooem, *PG* 91: 664b, and Pseudo-Dionysius, "The Celestial Hierarchy," *The Complete Works*, 2.3.
15 For an early example, see Basil of Caesarea, *Against Eunomius*, 1.10.
16 See Aquinas, *Summa theologiæ* 1a, q. 3, art. 2 *responsio*.

References

Augustine. 1991. *The Trinity*, translated by E. Hill. Brooklyn: New City Press.
Augustine. 2002. *Exposition of the Psalms, 73–98*, translated by M. Boulding. Hyde Park: New City Press.
Burrell, D. 2004. *Faith and Freedom: An Interfaith Perspective*. Oxford: Basil Blackwell.
Eunomius. 1987. "*Expositio fidei*: The Confession of Faith." In *The Extant Works*, translated by R. P. Vaggione, 150–159. Oxford: Clarendon Press.
Hanson, R. P. C. 1988. *The Search for the Christian Doctrine of God: The Arian Controversy 318–381*. Edinburgh: T & T Clark.
Kaufman, G. 1972. *God the Problem*. Cambridge: Harvard University Press.
Maximus Confessor. 1985. "The Church's Mystagogy." In *Selected Writings*, translated by G. C. Berthold, 181–225. Mahwah: Paulist Press.
Pannenberg, W. 1969. *Theology and the Kingdom of God*. Philadelphia: Westminster Press.
Plantinga, A. 1980. *Does God Have a Nature?* Milwaukee: Marquette University Press.
Pseudo-Dionysius. 1987. *The Complete Works*, translated by C. Luibheid. Mahwah: Paulist Press.
Rahner, K. 1975. *The Trinity*, translated by J. Donceel. London: Burns and Oates.
Richard of St Victor. 2010. "On the Trinity." In *Trinity and Creation: A Selection of Works of Hugh, Richard and Adam of St Victor*, edited by B. Taylor Coolman and D. M. Coulter, translated by C. P. Evans, 195–382. Turnhout, Belgium: Brepols.

162 *Kevin Hart*

Sokolowski, R. 1995. *The God of Faith and Reason: Foundations of Christian Theology*, 2nd ed. Notre Dame: Notre Dame University Press.

Tanner, K. 2005. *God and Creation in Christian Theology: Tyranny or Empowerment?* Minneapolis: Fortress Press.

Vallicella, W. F. 2015. "Divine Simplicity." In *The Stanford Encyclopedia of Philosophy*, Spring 2015 ed., edited by E. N. Zalta. https://plato.stanford.edu/archives/spr2015/entries/divine-simplicity/.

9   Michael C. Rea[‡]

On the December 3, 2012, episode of *The Daily Show*, Jon Stewart, in characteristic form, mercilessly mocked Bill O'Reilly for insisting on *The O'Reilly Factor* that Christianity is "not a religion; it's a philosophy". It is easy to sympathize with Stewart. On any ordinary understanding of the terms *religion* and *philosophy*, Christianity is obviously a religion and obviously not a (mere) philosophy. In the clip shown on *The Daily Show*, however, O'Reilly defends his remarkable claim with the following comment: "Christianity is a philosophy. You don't have to believe that Jesus is God in order to admire his view on life." Set aside the question of how, exactly, the second sentence is supposed to support the first. What I want to call attention to is the implied view about what it is to be Christian. O'Reilly seems to think that merely admiring Jesus' view on life is sufficient for properly bearing the label 'Christian'. Stewart, along with most of the rest of us, vehemently disagrees. But how does one adjudicate a dispute like this? O'Reilly's view is not idiosyncratic. Many people think that being a Christian is just a matter of 'following Christ' in some sense; and simply admiring Jesus' view on life seems to be one way of 'following Christ' without doing so religiously.

My own view is that the term 'Christian' is the English equivalent of a term of art which was invented to refer to all and only those who accept and practice the loosely defined body of doctrines, norms and values that are referred to collectively as 'the Christian faith'. There is much disagreement about precisely which doctrines, norms and values comprise the Christian faith, and it cannot be denied that the content of the Christian faith has to some extent evolved over time. Still, over the course of the past two millennia there has been substantial agreement among the official confessions and councils of the Catholic, Orthodox and Protestant churches as to what constitutes the core of the Christian faith and on what exactly it means to be a follower of Christ. In particular, since the fourth century CE, there has been substantial agreement across the East-West and Catholic-Protestant divides that the doctrinal boundaries of the Christian faith are captured at least in part by the content of the ecumenical creeds – most importantly, the Apostles' Creed and the Nicene Creed.

This longstanding agreement amongst the traditions is important because it is a salient determiner of the very *meaning* of the term 'Christian faith'.

164   *Michael C. Rea*

The Reformers were accused of abandoning the Christian faith, but the accusation could not stick because the Reformers manifestly accepted and practiced what had already been determined to be the core of that faith. The charge does stick to neo-Arians, on the other hand, because they manifestly do *not* accept what has (since the controversies of the fourth century) been determined to be the core of the Christian faith. The boundaries are loose, and there is vagueness to contend with. But they are not so loose as to vindicate (say) Bill O'Reilly's understanding of the term 'Christian'.

I say all of this by way of introducing an objection that applies equally to the Position Statements of both John Bishop and Heather Eaton. Given my understanding of the way in which the meaning of the terms 'Christianity' and 'Christian faith' are fixed, I do not see how those labels can appropriately be applied to either of their positions.

According to Bishop, God is not a supernatural being but is, rather, a part of the natural world. In particular, God is to be identified either with the love that unites the three divine persons – Father, Son and Holy Spirit – or with the "full cosmic meaning" of that love.[1] By the end of his essay, it becomes clear that God (either as a particular kind of love, or as the cosmic meaning of that love) is *emergent*. Far from being metaphysically or causally prior to the cosmos, God is dependent on and emergent from things within the cosmos.[2] Bishop does say that God is the creator of the universe; but, on his view, this means only that God is the final cause, the *telos*, of the universe. He denies that God is the *producer* of the universe. Thus, Bishop cannot (straightforwardly) affirm the opening lines of the Apostles' and Nicene Creeds. In the Nicene Creed, the opening lines run as follows: "We believe in one God, the Father almighty, maker of heaven and earth (ποιητὴν οὐρανοῦ καὶ γῆς), of all things visible and invisible." But, on Bishop's view, though God is the 'creator' in the extended sense mentioned previously, God is emphatically not the *maker* – not the ποιητής – of heaven or earth.

Moreover, Bishop says explicitly that he thinks there is a successful argument from evil against the existence of a personal 'omniGod' – a personal being with at least the attributes of omnipotence, omniscience and omnibenevolence. This is obviously a non-traditional claim. Moreover, if he is right, then he cannot sensibly affirm that Father, Son and Holy Spirit exemplify the omni-attributes. Nor, given his anti-supernaturalism, can he affirm that Father, Son or Holy Spirit are supernatural beings. Indeed, their very divinity is derivative, grounded somehow in their perichoretic love for one another. Given all of this, it is hard to imagine what basis Bishop might have for affirming that there have *always* been (non-supernatural) persons loving one another in the divine sort of way. Absent such an affirmation, however, it looks as if Bishop's view implies that there was a time in the evolution of the cosmos when there was no God.

As one might expect from what has been said thus far, Bishop also denies that God is a "personal agent". Thus, neither Father, Son nor Holy Spirit *is God*, since they are persons and God is not personal. Moreover, and quite

First Response 165

ironically, although "God is love" on Bishop's view, God *cannot love*, since only personal beings are capable of love.[3] Father, Son and Holy Spirit can love, of course; but, since they are, on this view, mere natural persons who lack the omni-attributes, one might be forgiven for wondering what grounds we might have for thinking that their love extends to anybody who has lived after the crucifixion of Jesus.

It should be obvious, then, that Bishop's theology is in tension with several of the most central claims affirmed in the Christian scriptures and the ecumenical Christian creeds. Interesting as his theology might be, I cannot see how the term 'Christian' can appropriately be applied to a view with such a manifestly uneasy relationship to some of the most important claims affirmed in all of the major branches of Christendom. I have already mentioned that I think this same basic concern applies to Heather Eaton's position; but before turning to her essay, let me first raise two further objections against Bishop's view.

The first is that it is very hard to imagine what, on his view, the divine persons might be, or what role they are supposed to play in his theology. Bishop says that his theology is naturalistic "just in the sense that it is *anti-supernaturalist*: it rejects the ontological realm separate from and prior to the natural universe that is required for personal omniGod theism" (14). He does not say what he means by "separate from" in this context. But it would be surprising, to say the least, if positing a realm of immaterial, non-spatiotemporally located spirits were consistent with his denial of an ontological realm separate from the natural universe. If he does not posit such a realm, however, then his naturalistic theology implies that Father, Son and Holy Spirit are spatiotemporally located material persons. Where, then, are they? When did (or do) they exist? *What* are they? Are they superbeings like the gods of Olympus, or like Q from *Star Trek*? Are they mammals like you and me? Or are they something else entirely? It is hard to imagine what the answers to these questions might be.

Just as it is hard to tell what the divine persons might be on Bishop's view, so too it is hard to know what to think about their theological significance. Speaking of their divinity, he says:

> [E]ach Person of the Trinity is God in a derivative sense, namely, that each equally has the property of being essential to the interpersonal perichoretic relationship that is God in the primary sense. So the divinity of Christ . . . is only derivatively the divinity of the person Jesus: what it is primarily is *the loving relationality* into which Jesus consistently and steadfastly enters.
>
> (16–17; emphasis in original)

But if the divinity of Christ (and of the Father and Holy Spirit) is primarily the loving relationality into which Jesus consistently and steadfastly enters, and if (as seems to be the case on Bishop's view) entering into that sort of

166   *Michael C. Rea*

loving relationality is sufficient for being divine in the relevantly derivative sense, then it would seem that *anyone* can be divine in the way that Jesus is divine, so long as they can enter into the right sort of loving relationality. Moreover, nothing that Bishop says suggests that ordinary mortals cannot enter into the right sort of loving relationality. Indeed, as we have already seen, Bishop is committed to saying that the divine persons themselves are natural beings who lack the omni-attributes, and so, for all we know, *they* are ordinary mortals. Given all of this, it is hard to see why we should think that Father, Son and Holy Spirit are worthy of worship (or even that any of them still exist). So it would appear that we have no grounds for thinking that their theological significance runs any deeper than that of (say) an admirable priest, which is odd, to say the least.

The second objection concerns Bishop's conception of divinity. I cannot see how to reconcile all the various claims he makes. For example, Bishop says (as we have already noted) that God is to be identified with the full cosmic meaning of the love that unites the divine persons. However, just a few lines earlier (in the passage quoted earlier), he speaks of the "perichoretic relationship that *is God in the primary sense*" (my emphasis). Elsewhere, he seems to say simply that God *is love*. Elsewhere still, he says that the divine is *"loving interpersonal relationships within the universe"* (15; my emphasis). But *love* is one thing; a particular *perichoretic relationship* is another thing; the (sum of?) loving interpersonal relationships throughout the universe is yet another thing; and the "full cosmic meaning" of any of these is something else entirely. So which is God?

It appears that Bishop's most considered view is that God is the "full cosmic meaning of the love that unites the divine persons"; but that seems to make God an *effect* of the various loving relationships that exist in the universe. The consequence of this is that God is a *created* being: the love of Father, Son and Holy Spirit, or the love of relevantly similar others, creates God. Ancient pagan religions, of course, allowed for created deities, but the idea of a created God is wholly foreign to the western monotheisms.

More importantly, though, it is hard to see how Bishop's God can possibly satisfy what Bishop himself takes to be the most salient features of the concept of God. Bishop says that the concept of God is the concept of a trustworthy, worship-worthy, obedience-worthy being. But what would it even mean to *trust* or *obey* the *full cosmic significance of the love that unites the divine persons*? How could one possibly worship such a thing? I cannot help but be reminded of Heidegger's complaint about the so-called god of philosophy: "Man can neither pray nor sacrifice to this god. Before [this god] man can neither fall to his knees in awe nor can he play music and dance" (Heidegger 2002: 72). So too, I would say, with the God of John Bishop.

One final comment about Bishop's Position Statement: despite the concerns raised here, I do not wish my comments to be taken as expressing opposition to just anything that might go under the label (from Bishop's title) of 'Naturalist Christian Theism'. As I have argued in detail elsewhere

(Rea 2002), the best characterization of naturalism (i.e., most stable and most faithful to the views of the most central figures in the naturalist tradition) identifies it with a disposition to treat the methods of science and those methods alone as basic sources of evidence. As even Quine acknowledges, there is no opposition *in principle* between naturalism thus construed and belief in God, human souls or other sorts of spirits and powers (Quine 1995: 252). To be sure, there is at present an obstacle *in practice*. Virtually nobody right now thinks that the methods of science justify belief in God, and virtually nobody right now thinks that the methods of science certify the reliability of any other source of evidence from which we might acquire justification for belief in God. But, having no reason to think that circumstances shall always be this way, I am reluctant to conclude that 'Naturalist Christian Theism' is, in principle, not viable.

Let us now move on to Eaton's essay. Even more so than with Bishop's position, I find it hard to imagine what would justify characterizing Eaton's view as a version of Christianity. Eaton herself expresses uncertainty about whether she accepts Christianity. She begins by locating herself at the "margins" of the Christian tradition. By the end of her chapter, one finds her declaring that "historically there is no such actuality as 'Christianity'" (this volume: 41). It is surely hard to have a Christian worldview if there is no such thing as Christianity!

More pertinently, however, she distances herself from just about every doctrine that one might sensibly take as definitive of Christianity. God is a mere human invention, she says. The doctrine of the Trinity is a mere symbol. The traditional story of creation, fall and redemption is offensive. The doctrine of the resurrection is unintelligible. Moreover, Eaton makes it clear that her view is *not* that these traditional Christian views are strictly false but nevertheless useful metaphors. On her view, the notions of truth and falsity do not even apply to religious claims; and, taken as mere symbols, traditional Christian claims about creation, fall, redemption, the Trinity and the resurrection are outmoded at best and offensively patriarchal and otherworldly at worst. Whatever merits or demerits one might otherwise associate with Eaton's 'theology' (if that is even an appropriate label), it can hardly be called a 'Christian philosophy of religion'.

That issue aside, my main critical concern with Eaton's essay has to do with tensions in her understanding of rationality and evidence. As early as the first paragraph of her chapter, Eaton declares that "[in religion?] there is no objective or truthful vantage point" (25). Later, she says that, with respect to religious belief, the "categories of 'true' and 'false' are inapplicable" (29). One consequence of these claims is that religious beliefs (and so, presumably, religious *doctrines*) do not have truth-values. That is, every religious belief and every religious doctrine is neither true nor false.

Remarkably, Eaton does not say why she holds the view that the categories of true and false do not apply to religious matters. She gives no indication that she thinks that all putative religious claims are *meaningless*. Perhaps,

168   *Michael C. Rea*

then, the idea is that what appear to be religious *claims* are, in reality, just expressions of religious *sentiment*. Attributing this view to her helps to make sense of her tendency to characterize her own theology in terms of claims to which she is "attracted" rather than in terms of what she believes in light of her overall evidence. Or perhaps, following George Lindbeck (1984), her idea is that religious doctrines are more a kind of 'grammar' for religious discourse – a set of rules about how certain religious terms are to be used – than tools for expressing propositions. Or perhaps the idea is something else entirely. In any case, the claim that truth and falsity are inapplicable to religious matters sits uneasily with what she identifies as her preferred approach to the assessment of religious claims.

Toward the beginning of her section on the nature of God, Eaton lays out her primary methodological values. She writes:

> I am not inclined towards speculative or highly abstract theology. I reject beliefs, concepts, doctrines or 'eternal truths' on the basis of tradition, authority, unverifiable revelations or non-evidentiary arguments. My primary considerations are thus evidential and reasonable, not magical, supernatural or esoteric. More so than morality, I seek a coherent framework able to address the origins, emergence, histories and presence of 'religions'. I desire an epistemologically comprehensive view, one that includes a cosmological horizon and is capable of including phenomenological and scientific evidence.
>
> (26–27)

Later, she rejects the doctrine of the resurrection of the dead as "speculative, consisting of beliefs without evidence of any kind" (37), and, later still, she says that "[b]elief in what is nonsensical, not reasonable or rational is often a sign of lunacy" (43). So, to put it mildly, Eaton values rationality and evidence.

The trouble, however, is that if religious beliefs and doctrines are neither true nor false, then it is hard to see what it could mean to say that *evidence* can be brought to bear on them. If they are meaningless, then we can no more have evidence for or against them than we could have evidence for or against the thesis that *'twas brillig and the slithy toves did gyre and gimble in the wabe*. Likewise if they function as a mere grammar for religious discourse. If they are expressions of religious sentiment, then we can no more have evidence for or against them than we could have evidence for or against a mere feeling of attraction or revulsion.[4] If they are none of the above, then I am at a loss to see how religious claims might be devoid of truth-value but nonetheless supported (or disconfirmed) by evidence.

This is not a trivial issue. Considerations about what views (or, better, symbols) are useful or outdated, attractive or offensive, politically fruitful or harmful loom large in Eaton's assessment of the traditional doctrines of Christianity and seem to play the driving role in the development of her own religious outlook. Indeed, one gets the strong impression that her own religious outlook does not consist in first-order religious views at all. After expressing uncertainty about her own acceptance of Christianity and, indeed, of "what acceptance means", she goes on to say:

> I have learned and do learn from the tradition and seek to expand my interpretive horizons with respect to the concerns and questions I have. But I do not feel compelled to stay inside the periphery, wherever that is. Further, I don't think notions to do with the 'acceptance' or 'rejection' of a particular religion are viable in a postmodern world swirling with images and amalgamations of worldviews.
>
> (42)

All of this fits quite nicely with her non-cognitivist stance on religious doctrine – indeed, it is exactly what she ought to be saying, given that stance. But it makes very little sense if one thinks (as she claims to) that one's *primary* considerations in the assessment of religious claims ought to be *evidential* and *reasonable*.[5] Likewise, her continued emphasis on the importance of evidence in the assessment of religious claims is hard to square with the fact that, though she speaks freely about what claims she finds attractive and offensive, she offers virtually no evidence in support of what she says about the existence and nature of God, about the Trinity, about Incarnation, and so on.

Indeed, one sometimes gets the sense that she is simply operating with a non-standard concept of evidence. For example, she dismisses the Christian doctrine of the resurrection of the dead as "consisting of beliefs without evidence of any kind" – and this despite the fact that, of all the doctrines promulgated by the Christian church, this is perhaps the only one that the Apostle Paul himself takes to stand or fall with the *evidence* (1 Corinthians 15:12–20). And, of course, many contemporary philosophers and theologians agree that it is a mistake to say that there is no evidence of any kind for the resurrection (see, for starters, Swinburne 2003 and Wright 2003). My point here does not depend on an assessment of the evidence as *good*. Rather, my claim is just that, *contra* Eaton, this of all claims in Christianity is the one about which it makes the most sense to say that Christians are enjoined – even by the apostles – to believe it on the basis of evidence.

I turn now to Kevin Hart's essay, in which he proposes a phenomenological theology from a Catholic philosophical theologian's perspective. As might be expected from a Reformed Protestant, I have a few non-trivial disagreements with the doctrines of the Roman Catholic Church (some of which I already mentioned in my own Position Statement). Surprisingly, however, few of these translate into clear disagreements with Hart. But we do have substantial methodological disagreements that lead me to reject the normative necessity and priority of the phenomenological approach as Hart outlines it. These are not doctrinal disagreements; nor are they disagreements that I wish to pursue as such in detail here. Rather, what I want to focus on is what seems to me to be the most important theological topic

170   Michael C. Rea

on which we are divided – namely, the question of whether God, or, more specifically, God the Father, 'appears' in experience.

Hart's chapter begins with the declaration that "Christian theology properly begins by considering the confession that Jesus is the Christ" (this volume: 48). He says that Christ is "the one who receives the revelation of God" and is also "the genitive of revelation" – the one from whom we receive the revelation of God (48). Following upon these claims, he concludes that "Christian theology therefore requires a phenomenology of the Christ before anything else" (48). Why a phenomenology of the Christ in particular and not, say, a phenomenology of the triune God? Because, as he says a couple of pages later in the section that is devoted to preliminary clarifications, the "self-revelation of God must be reckoned a special mode of manifestation, one that cannot be prompted by way of ἐποχή and reduction but that is *given only by the God who himself does not appear* (John 6:46)" (49; my emphasis).

The idea that God 'does not appear' evidently plays an important role in Hart's theology. It is at least part of the reason why Christian theology must begin with a phenomenology of the Christ – Christ is a phenomenon; God is not. It is also the reason why phenomenological theology must attend to "how Jesus himself does a peculiar form of phenomenology" (48).[6] Moreover, the idea is revisited and emphasized several times throughout the essay. Hart tells us that we do not have experience of God:

> We do not have experience of God as proposed by Schleiermacher ('feeling of absolute dependence') or a direct intuition of the deity as advocated by Hamann and Jacobi, or even the 'transcendental experience' of God affirmed by Rahner. We do not have any experience at all, except as intentional rapport with the noema given to us ('βασιλεία'). Nor do we have knowledge of God, as Hegel thinks can be achieved.
>
> (54)

Hart maintains that the quest to make God present in experience leads to vice, and that *Christianity* eschews this quest and denies that God 'gives himself directly':

> God may reveal himself to some extent in the elegance of a mathematical theorem. . . . Or, equally, the beauty of the theorem might attune one to the Christian revelation. . . . And one may read the works of the mystics to be buoyed up by those who have received special graces or the gift of passive contemplation and been led to a fuller life with God. Yet Christianity is finally not a matter of bringing God to the presence of human consciousness but rather of allowing oneself to come into the presence of God, the two modes of 'presence' being quite different, one a matter of presence to consciousness . . . and the other a matter of ἀγάπη. If taken alone, as a relentless hunger for proof or experience of God, the

First Response 171

quest to make God present leads to pride or conceptual idolatry, while trust that we are present to God is the very meaning of 'faith'. . . . In Christianity, then, God does not usually give himself directly but rather in and through the βασιλεία.

(54–55)

A little later, in talking about how a parable "calls forth apophasis" and "sets us on the path to approach God in the darkness of unknowing", Hart emphasizes the point yet again: "[this], I underline, presumes the acceptance that we cannot make God present to ourselves though we can take ourselves to be present to God" (55). And again further on he writes:

We do not have direct experience of the Father, only experience of living under his kingly and fatherly rule when we see it indicated by Jesus. We take ourselves to be present to him ('redeemed', as we say in church) and do not presume to make him present to us.

(61)

Why the repeated emphasis? The following sentences, located at the end of Hart's essay, seem to me to be the clear summary answer:[7]

The Father gives himself only in and through the βασιλεία; so if we inquire after the phenomenality of God we shall have to say that it consists in the revelation of the βασιλεία: a revealing and a re-veiling. Yet if the revelation is finally Christ himself, if the Church is right to say that Christ is not simply the vehicle of communicating God's revelation but is the content of that revelation as well . . . then we may say that Christ is the phenomenality of God. So the phenomenality of God, as Christianity understands things, is apparently divided, βασιλεία and Christ, though only *apparently* since the two are one.

(64; emphasis in original)

Thus, the idea that 'God does not appear' seems to lie at the very core of Hart's βασιλεία-oriented phenomenological theology.

The question I want to ask, however, is just this: Why should we think that in general God does not appear in experience, that we cannot make God present to us but can only be present to God, that God is not a phenomenon? Hart cites John 6:46, which is rendered in the NRSV translation as follows: "Not that anyone has seen the Father except the one who is from God; he has seen the Father." Obviously enough, this claim is *compatible* with the thesis that God does not appear in experience; but it does not straightforwardly *imply* that God does not appear in experience. In fact, it would be quite surprising if that verse were meant to imply that God does not appear in experience; for, after all, the gospel stories of Jesus' baptism and transfiguration have God appearing audibly, declaring that Jesus is God's beloved Son and that

172 *Michael C. Rea*

God is pleased with him (Matthew 3:13–17, 17:1–9). Moreover, Hart himself acknowledges that the baptism of Jesus is an exception to the general rule that God does not appear when he writes (immediately after saying that, in Christianity, God does not generally give himself directly in experience):

> There are exceptions to the general rule: the baptism of Jesus (Matthew 3:13–17) and Saul on the road to Damascus (Acts 9:1–31), for instance, and of course these have different statuses.
>
> (55)

The claim in John 6:46, however, admits no exceptions: *no one* has seen the Father. Thus, if (as Hart acknowledges) there *are* exceptions to the claim that God does not appear, then *seeing God* – which John 6:46 suggests *never* happens – cannot be identical to *having God appear in one's experience*.

Neither John 6:46 nor anything else in scripture seems to me to be plausibly interpreted as categorically ruling out the idea that God often and in various different ways appears in human experience. Neither – if this makes a difference – does it rule out the idea that God is often an object of *direct* experience.[8] In light of this, and in light of the fact that many Christians both presently and throughout history have thought that the presence of God is (often and for many people) made available in experience in prayer, in Christian liturgy, in nature and in a variety of other activities and contexts, the claim that *Christianity* understands 'the phenomenality of God' in the way that Hart does seems mistaken. More credible would be the slightly more modest thesis that Christianity *ought* to understand the phenomenality of God in the way that Hart does; but even that claim strikes me as implausible and would, in any case, require substantial argument to defend it.

Finally, I come to the essay by Trakakis. Ultimately, I think that there are more points of agreement between Trakakis and me than points of disagreement. Still, two points of disagreement seem particularly worth highlighting.

First: divine transcendence. In the section that deals with this topic – the section on divine mystery – Trakakis locates himself, and Orthodoxy generally, within the apophatic tradition of theology. As we have already seen, I do not locate myself within that tradition. Still, it is an interesting question to what extent and at just what point we disagree; for the conceptions of transcendence and of apophasis that he seems to endorse leave remarkable room for what I would think of as a robustly kataphatic approach to theology.

Trakakis opens the section by quoting Kallistos Ware, who says, paradoxically, that God is "beyond all words, beyond all understanding" (quoted from Ware 1995: 11). Speaking in his own voice, however, Trakakis offers what seems to be a much more modest view. Divine transcendence (he seems to say) implies that God is mysterious in just this sense:

T1 No definition of God is possible; God is incomprehensible in just the sense that we cannot achieve exhaustive understanding or "conceptual mastery" of God; and negative statements about God are "more ultimate or truer" than positive statements about God (94).

This is obviously a weaker conception of transcendence than the quotation from Ware would suggest. Moreover, as Trakakis explicitly acknowledges, his conception of mystery and apophasis is consistent with the idea that that we can truthfully speak in positive terms about God.

The real work in T1 is done by the second clause. The first clause – the claim that we human beings cannot fully grasp or exhaustively understand God – is so banal as to be virtually undeniable. We cannot *fully* grasp or *exhaustively* understand other human beings, dolphins, galaxies, earthworms, rocks or even our very selves. Who, then, would dare even to hope that we might fully grasp or exhaustively understand God? No, the real bite comes in the claim that negative statements are "more ultimate or truer" than positive statements about God.

But just how much bite is there in that claim? The answer depends on how we are to understand the phrase 'more ultimate or truer'. 'Ultimate' and 'true' mean different things. So one possibility is that Trakakis means to affirm a disjunction: that is, every negative claim about God is either more ultimate than every positive claim or truer than every positive claim. This might make sense if there were some reason to think that negative claims about God divide into two classes: those which are more ultimate, and those which are more true. But I think that there is no reason to think this. At any rate, I can't imagine any reason and Trakakis has offered none. So I think that it is more natural to interpret Trakakis as treating 'ultimate' and 'true' (somewhat oddly) as synonyms, either using both to mean 'more ultimate' or using both to mean 'more true'. I'll take each of these interpretations in turn.

Let's start with 'more ultimate'. On this interpretation, I think that it is natural to understand Trakakis to be saying that negative predications are *more fundamental* than positive predications, and to be treating 'more fundamental' as implying greater proximity to truth. But, on this interpretation, it is singularly implausible to say that negative predications are, one and all, 'more ultimate' than any positive predication. Presumably, the fundamentality of a *predication* is a function of the fundamentality of its *predicate*. But now consider the following statements, and the predicates therein:

1   God is conscious.
2   God is not an egg.
3   God is wise.
4   God is not unwise.
5   God is good.
6   God is neither grue nor prime nor a property.[9]

174   *Michael C. Rea*

Trakakis' view, thus interpreted, implies that *is conscious, is wise* and *is good* are less fundamental than *is not an egg, is not unwise* and *is neither grue nor prime nor a property*. But I am aware of no plausible conception of fundamentality that would support this judgement. On the most plausible conceptions, either some of the positive predicates here are more fundamental than any of the negative predicates or else all are equally fundamental (by virtue of failing to be fundamental at all).

What if, instead, we interpret Trakakis as understanding 'more ultimate' in terms of 'truer'? On this interpretation, Trakakis' claim is that negative statements about God are, one and all, closer to the truth than positive statements. But this too is untenable, as it conflicts with the following very plausible principle (where the expression '$\bar{F}$' stands for 'the complement of F'):

> (Equiv)   For any predicate F and object x, if Fx is logically equivalent to $\neg\bar{F}x$, it is no truer to say that Fx than to say that $\neg\bar{F}x$.

If Equiv is true, then it is no truer to say that God is not unwise than it is to say that God is wise; it is no truer to say that God is not unloving than it is to say that God is loving; and so on.

The second issue to raise in connection with Trakakis' essay concerns the doctrine of the Trinity. According to Trakakis, "God as Trinity consists in interpersonal and perichoretic communion" (97). Trakakis does not say what he means by this, but it is natural to take it as affirming a version of what is commonly referred to as *social trinitarianism*. As I understand it (Rea 2009), the core of social trinitarianism consists in the following three theses:

1   Father, Son and Holy Spirit are not numerically the same substance. Rather, the persons of the Trinity are consubstantial only in the sense that they share a common nature; and the sharing is to be understood straightforwardly on analogy with the way in which three human beings share a common nature.
2   Monotheism does not imply that there is exactly one divine substance. Rather, it implies at most only that all divine substances – all gods, in the ordinary sense of the term 'god' – stand in some particular relation R to one another, a relation other than being the same divine substance.
3   The persons of the Trinity stand to one another in the relation R that is required for monotheism to be true.

The different versions of social trinitarianism are, on this way of thinking about the view, individuated by differences in what they take relation R to be. The most popular choice is the part-whole relation: Father, Son and Holy Spirit are proper parts of the one God.

Trakakis seems to take R to be the relation of interpersonal and perichoretic communion. Note, however, that there are at least two ways of reading

Trakakis here. On one way of reading him, the claim is simply that Father, Son and Holy Spirit stand in that relation and, somehow by virtue of their standing in that relation, it is true that there is exactly one triune God. Alternatively, one might read him as saying that *God, qua* triune, *consists in* the relation of interpersonal and perichoretic communion among the persons. Such a view is not unprecedented; C. J. F. Williams, for example, identifies God with the love that holds between the persons (2002: 243). On neither reading, however, do we have a viable understanding of the Trinity. Just as standing in the relation of interpersonal and perichoretic communion would not make three human beings one man or woman, so too the divine persons' standing in that relation does not suffice to make it true that there is exactly one God. Nor, crucially, does it suffice to make them consubstantial, as the Nicene Creed requires.[10]

Trakakis also affirms John D. Zizioulas' 'being as communion' (henceforth, 'BAC') thesis: that *"to be* and *to be in relation* [are] identical" (Zizioulas 1985: 88). This is a rich and interesting thesis that has inspired a great deal of theological reflection. Here I wish only to register two brief concerns. First, as Thomas McCall (2010) has argued, BAC stands in tension with another traditional claim that Zizioulas affirms – what McCall, following others, refers to as the 'Sovereignty-Aseity Conviction' (henceforth, 'SAC'). SAC affirms the absolute priority of the Father. For Zizioulas, this means that God is radically free – so much so that existing in trinity is a matter of choice for the Father. Here the tension with BAC is obvious: if existing in trinity is a matter of choice, then it can't be that *to be is to be in communion*; for if BAC is true, it is absolutely impossible for the Father (or any other person) to exist outside of communion. Moreover, even if we back off from Zizioulas' strong interpretation of SAC, it seems that BAC will still lead to trouble. For the idea that the Father is at least *logically* prior to the other members of the Trinity seems well-entrenched in the tradition – for example, in the claim that the Son is *begotten* of the Father and that the Spirit *proceeds from* the Father. If BAC is true – if to be *is* to be in communion, such claims make no sense; for there cannot be even logical priority relations among the members of the Trinity.

In discussing the Position Statements of my interlocutors, I have focused much more on points of disagreement than upon points of agreement. This, of course, is due to the fact that my assignment was to provide a *critical* response rather than an *affirming* response. Nevertheless, I want to close by noting that there are many points of agreement among us – even between myself and those from whom my position seems most distant. Between some of us, moreover, I think that the points of agreement vastly overshadow the points of disagreement. This latter fact is unfortunately often overlooked when members of different lines of the Christian tradition interact with one another; but I hope that it will not be eclipsed in the present discussion, even as we engage one another in a more critical mode.

176 Michael C. Rea

Notes

‡ For very helpful comments on an earlier draft, I am grateful to Michael Berg-mann, Jeff Brower and Cristian Mihut.

1 I confess that I do not exactly know what this latter suggestion means. But I leave that aside for now; I shall return to it shortly.

2 Bishop acknowledges that this claim might sound scandalous, but he deflects the objection by claiming that "scandal of just this kind is entrenched in the Chris-tian tradition, in the endorsement of Mary's title as *theotokos* (God-bearer)" (this volume: 14). But, in fact, whatever scandal is involved in the application of the title '*theotokos*' to Mary is *not* of the same kind as that involved in saying that God is dependent on and emergent from the cosmos. The former is consis-tent with, whereas the latter contradicts, the traditional view that everything in the universe (Mary included) depends for its very existence on the triune God.

3 Note that I do *not* say "God cannot love, since mere relations cannot love". There is strong precedent in the Christian tradition for identifying the divine persons with subsistent relations, and this without denying that they love one another and all of creation. I am not sure that one can make sense of the idea that a loving person might be a relation, but neither would I wish simply to presup-pose its falsity.

4 *Objection:* non-cognitivists about morality engage in what looks like moral rea-soning and argument. So why not non-cognitivists about religion? *Reply:* insofar as they are non-cognitivists, it does not make sense to think of them as mar-shalling *evidence* in support of (the truth!) of the moral views they are seeking to defend. Moral arguments given by a non-cognitivist are best understood as attempts to induce epistemically non-rational changes in the moral preferences of their interlocutors by citing considerations that will appeal to their sentiments.

5 Indeed, if one thinks that religious sentences are not truth-apt, one should prob-ably say that *there are no religious claims*, since no religious sentence manages to express anything with a truth-value. However, since Eaton herself does not make a point of avoiding reference to 'religious claims', 'claims about God', etc., I shall follow suit and ignore this concern in the discussion that follows.

6 As already indicated, in the New Testament God is not regarded as a phenom-enon: the one Jesus calls 'Father' does not appear. What comes to the horizon of appearing is the kingly rule of the Father, what Jesus calls the βασιλεία . . . though even here one must be wary of calling it a 'manifestation' pure and simple. . . . The central issue is how Jesus makes 'God', that most abstract of abstract nouns, name a concrete reality in his parables, sayings and acts by telling us or showing us what the kingly rule of God looks like.

7 Of course, I don't mean to suggest that the answer isn't in some sense clear much earlier on.

8 As I see it, John 6:46 is more plausibly interpreted as saying that no one ever has *direct* experience of God than as saying that, in general, God does not appear in experience; but even this more plausible interpretation does not seem to me to be mandated by the text. What exactly 'seeing God' amounts to there and elsewhere in scripture seems to me to admit of a variety of interpretations.

9 Following Goodman (1983), let us say that something is grue if it is green and has been examined prior to a certain time (say, 2100 CE) or it is blue and has not been examined prior to 2100 CE.

10 See Rea (2009) and references therein for further discussion.

References

Goodman, N. 1983. *Fact, Fiction, and Forecast*, 4th ed. Harvard: Harvard University Press.

Heidegger, M. 2002. *Identity and Difference*, translated by J. Stambaugh. Chicago: University of Chicago Press.

Lindbeck, G. A. 1984. *The Nature of Doctrine: Religion and Theology in a Postliberal Age*. Philadelphia: Westminster John Knox Press.

McCall, T. H. 2010. *Which Trinity? Whose Monotheism?: Philosophical and Systematic Theologians on the Metaphysics of Trinitarian Theology*. Grand Rapids: Wm. B. Eerdmans Publishing.

Quine, W. V. 1995. "Naturalism: Or, Living within One's Means." *Dialectica* 49 (2–4): 251–263.

Rea, M. 2002. *World without Design: The Ontological Consequences of Naturalism*. Oxford: Clarendon Press.

Rea, M. 2009. "The Trinity." In *The Oxford Handbook of Philosophical Theology*, edited by T. P. Flint and M. C. Rea, 403–429. Oxford: Oxford University Press.

Swinburne, R. 2003. *The Resurrection of God Incarnate*. Oxford: Oxford University Press.

Ware, K. 1995. *The Orthodox Way*, rev. ed. Crestwood, NY: St Vladimir's Seminary Press.

Williams, C. J. F. 2002. "Neither Confounding the Persons nor Dividing the Substance." In *Reason and the Christian Religion: Essays in Honour of Richard Swinburne*, edited by A. G. Padgett, 227–243. Oxford: Clarendon Press.

Wright, N. T. 2003. *The Resurrection of the Son of God*. Minneapolis: Augsburg Fortress Publishers.

Zizioulas, J. D. 1985. *Being as Communion: Studies in Personhood and the Church*. Crestwood, NY: St Vladimir's Seminary Press.

10 N.N. Trakakis

I am deeply grateful to each of my interlocutors for presenting informative and stimulating accounts of Christianity. I was already acquainted with the work of three of these interlocutors (Kevin Hart, John Bishop, and Michael Rea), and indeed I have long regarded their contributions to philosophy of religion and philosophical theology as representing work of the highest calibre and as a model for my own efforts in these fields. Heather Eaton's writings were not as familiar to me, though I felt her provocative perspective provides a much-needed corrective and challenge to some of the biases and assumptions prevalent in contemporary philosophy of religion. That said, I enter into debate and dialogue with my four interlocutors with great pleasure but also in 'fear and trembling'.

I have been constrained in what follows to respond to only certain aspects of each Position Statement, and I have chosen to focus on some aspects I found to be particularly interesting and challenging though also disputable and contestable. This unavoidably creates a somewhat critical and negative tone, and this needs to be set in the context of (usually) broad agreement and indeed great appreciation for the ways in which my dialogue partners have committed themselves to the task of 'faith seeking understanding'.

Response to Hart: Catholic Christianity

One of the distinctive points but also one of the greatest difficulties about Christianity is that much – and perhaps even everything – seems to hang on certain claims of a historical nature. For example, it is traditionally believed by Christians that Jesus of Nazareth had a virginal birth, that he performed a number of miracles, that various divine titles (such as 'Son of God', 'Messiah', and 'Lord') were applied to him by his earliest followers or even by himself, that he was sinless throughout his life, and that he was crucified, died, and was resurrected from the dead. The reason these historical claims pose a great difficulty is fairly obvious. On the one hand, Christianity (of the traditional, creedal sort) stands or falls on the basis of these historical beliefs. As the apostle Paul put it, "if Christ has not been raised, then our proclamation has been in vain and your faith has been in vain" (1 Corinthians 15:14).

First Response 179

So central have these beliefs seemed to the church that they have become 'articles of faith'. The Apostles' Creed, for example, affirms of Jesus that "he was born of the Virgin Mary" and that "on the third day he rose again". Thus, these are beliefs that we, as Christians, are enjoined to affirm in faith. And yet, on the other hand, these are beliefs that are, by their very nature, open to historical investigation in a way that other Christian beliefs (for example, the belief that the Son is consubstantial with the Father) are not. To be more precise, the belief that Jesus rose from the dead is open to precisely the same kind of investigation that historians make of any other event (though some historians and philosophers deny this, and I will come back to this shortly). But if that is the case, then the belief that Jesus rose from the dead is open to all the vagaries, doubts, and interpretive and evidential problems confronting any historical statement. In fact, the situation is far worse than this. Given that the historical evidence in support of the belief that Jesus rose from the dead is highly controversial – that is, the historical evidence in this case, much more than in many other cases, is hotly disputed amongst reputable scholars – this alone suggests that a certain amount of tentativeness and skepticism is required, *no matter which conclusion one draws from the evidence*. On the one hand, then, faith and commitment are encouraged. But on the other hand, a degree of doubt and conjecture seems inescapable. This is not to present faith and doubt as mutually exclusive but only to highlight the unfortunate predicament that Christians (unlike many other religious believers) find themselves in, as they have to rest their faith (in the resurrection) on always shifting and shaking foundations (due to the provisional and often speculative character of historical evidence).

One of my concerns with Hart's phenomenological approach is that it does not countenance or come to grips with this difficulty. Hart concedes that "one needs the wealth of material supplied by modern historical criticism partly for purposes of clearing away pious constructions and partly to determine the realm of discursive possibilities for a rabbi of the first century" (this volume: 50). This is progress, at least in comparison with phenomenological works like Michel Henry's *Words of Christ* which float free from historical research into the life and teachings of Jesus. But Hart then goes on to say that such historical research

> is entirely unable to deal with the question of *Evidenz* required by faith. No amount of testimony about the resurrection of Jesus could ever satisfy a historical critic that it was a historical event, the crucial one for Christian faith. The historical critic, writing as a historian, limits phenomenality to the realm of the empirical.[1]

(51)

There are, to be sure, historians who conceive of their historiographical practice as limited in precisely this way, but are such self-imposed limitations valid? Insofar as Jesus' resurrection is something that happened in time and

180   N.N. Trakakis

space ("on the third day"), why can't its factuality be assessed according to such standard criteria as explanatory scope and power, internal consistency, simplicity, degree of being *ad hoc*, etc.? Perhaps the idea is that the historian, *qua* historian, cannot make any appeals to supernatural causes when accounting for an event; the historian is constrained to history, to explaining events purely in terms of natural causes, these being the kinds of causes publicly accessible by the methods of scientific research. This methodological constraint bears some similarities to the *epoché* in Husserlian phenomenology. Husserl invited philosophers to undertake an *epoché*, a 'suspension' or 'bracketing' of everything that remains transcendent to the stream of intentional consciousness, where this includes questions regarding the existence of the external world or the existence of God. I suspect that Hart is advocating something similar, but now transplanted to the field of historical research, so that the historian suspends judgement about supernatural causes or miraculous events. Given such a 'methodological agnosticism', it is inevitable that (as Hart says), "No amount of testimony about the resurrection of Jesus could ever satisfy a historical critic that it was a historical event" (51).

However, the *epoché* is just as unwarranted in historical research as it is in philosophy. There is no plausible reason why the philosopher, when practicing phenomenology, must always suspend belief in God or other supernatural entities (and, insofar as a phenomenologist is a theist or Christian, it is doubtful in any case that they can consistently suspend their religious beliefs in this way, as critics of the 'theological turn' in phenomenology have pointed out). The desire to sequester philosophy (whether it be in the form of phenomenology or not), and in particular to separate it from theology, strikes me as arbitrary and unjustified, particularly in the current climate of interdisciplinarity, where the concepts and methods of one field are often related in illuminating ways to those of other fields. Hart's own work stands as a marvellous testament to the benefits to be had by bringing together theology, philosophy, and literature in a conciliatory rather than combative way. As they say, "pigeonholes are for pigeons". For the historian, then, to adopt a strictly naturalist methodology is to make the same mistake as Husserl: imposing arbitrary boundaries rather than truly following the argument or evidence wherever it may lead.

This brings me to a more general difficulty I find with the use of phenomenology in theology. There is much to be said for Hart's broad conception of phenomenology "as a way of seeing" or "a conversion of the gaze" rather than the narrower or classical conception which takes it "as a particular philosophical position clarified and ramified by Husserl and his successors" (51). Also interesting and intriguing is Hart's view of Jesus as someone who himself does phenomenology in telling parables with the aim of getting his audience to see, in often strange and surprising ways, what it means to be in relationship with God. The problem, however, is this: Jesus was preaching to the converted – that is, to fellow Jews who, even if hypocritical in their religious life or not fully observant, nonetheless never thought to doubt the existence

First Response   181

of God or their commitment to Judaism. Our predicament, however, is vastly different, and this raises the question of the value of a phenomenological approach in philosophy and theology today. I see phenomenology (in Hart's broad sense) as an integral part of the arts, where the process of disclosure or manifestation is relatively immediate, affective, and non-discursive. Poets or painters, for example, may seek to get their audience to look at things in perhaps unfamiliar ways so as to disclose a previously hidden realm of meaning or truth. But it would be a travesty to the work of a poem or a painting to paraphrase or translate it in propositional terms so as to evaluate its validity or soundness, as you would for a piece of inductive or deductive reasoning.

This approach works quite successfully in the arts (and Hart's own poetry is a case in point), but in philosophy and theology such a method is very limited, especially today. I say "especially today" because of the widespread skepticism and unbelief found nowadays not only amongst scholars but also in people from all walks of life. This has been brought about, in part, by a newfound willingness to enter into honest and respectful dialogue with people of other faiths (or no faith at all) rather than demonizing and persecuting them, as was often done in the past (particularly by the church). Given, then, the pervasive diversity that exists with respect to religious beliefs and beliefs about the nature of ultimate reality, and given also our informed appreciation and awareness of this diversity (and hence our refusal to swiftly dismiss it as, for example, the effects of sinfulness), how can a phenomenological theology help to resolve and adjudicate the conflicting claims to religious truth? The phenomenological method can be deployed by anyone, regardless of the credibility of his or her beliefs. As the late Philip Quinn once objected to Alvin Plantinga's Reformed epistemology, "The difficulty is, of course, that this is a game any number can play. Followers of Muhammed, followers of Buddha, and even followers of the Reverend Moon can join in the fun" (Quinn 1985: 473). This was not an entirely fair criticism of Plantinga (since Plantinga was doing epistemology, not apologetics), and it may not be an entirely fair objection to direct against Hart's phenomenological theology. However, it does point to an important deficiency in seeking to ground theology in phenomenology – namely, that such a procedure cannot provide us with the tools we require to defend and substantiate our fundamental religious convictions. (This is not simply a problem about converting or convincing the other, but is also a problem about working out what to believe oneself or how to justify one's beliefs.)

Hart admits as much when he states: "Concretion does not supply *Evidenz* by itself; it only enables one to think God concretely and to venture into the presence of God by living one's life in the manner disclosed by the parables of the kingdom and by imitating Jesus" (54). He goes on to say that the arguments of natural theology may have some value, though they are no substitute for revelation and faith. But how does one decide between the competing (alleged) revelations found not only across the world religions but also within Christianity itself (as evidenced by the numerous churches and 'heresies' that have arisen in the history of Christianity)? As Hart notes, one

182 N. N. Trakakis

cannot arrogantly demand that God present himself to our consciousness. But one would hope, if not expect, that a loving God who desires that we enter into relationship with him would not obscure his presence to such an extent that reasonable and diligent seekers of him would find it almost impossible to sort through the morass of competing truth-claims that the various religions make so as to ascertain where the truth about ultimate reality actually lies. Unfortunately, it is this very predicament of 'divine hiddenness' that is our lot, and phenomenology is of little help in delivering us from it.

Response to Rea: (Reformed) Protestantism

Sola scriptura

Protestants and Orthodox, unlike Catholics and Orthodox, have quite divergent views on the relationship between Scripture and Church. Although I found Rea's explication of the *sola scriptura* doctrine to be very clear, I was still left with some questions which I hope he can address.

Firstly, Rea states that the *sola scriptura* view holds, in part, that Scripture is 'foundationally authoritative' in the sense that Scripture is "more authoritative than any other source of information or advice" (this volume: 71–72). I would assume that he would include the Church within the ambit of "any other source of information or advice". But in that case, why does he believe that Scripture is foundationally authoritative? Specifically, what justification could he provide in support of this belief, given that the pronouncements or testimony of the Church could not be relied upon as sources of justification (for if the Church could be relied upon in this respect, then it and not Scripture would be foundationally authoritative)? I would assume that, in the Protestant tradition, the justification for holding that Scripture is foundationally authoritative is to be located within Scripture itself, and Scripture is to be believed because it is the Word of God. But this doesn't seem much of a justification, as the question then arises: Why believe that Scripture is the Word of God? To reply that this is what Scripture itself teaches is, of course, not much of an answer. A better reply might be that Scripture bears certain marks or signs of its divine origins, though it would take some work to substantiate this (especially in light of evidence to the contrary, relating to such things as seeming inconsistencies and immoral practices or teachings). But these signs or marks of divine origins are always understood as such within a community of interpreters, the Church, and this brings me to my next point.

Rea states that the *sola scriptura* doctrine also includes the claim that Scripture is 'clear' and 'sufficient', where this means that "all doctrines and prescriptions necessary for salvation can easily be derived from scripture by persons concerned about the salvation of their souls *without the help of the Church or Church tradition*" (72; my emphasis). This seems to minimize, even undermine, the place of the Church in the interpretation of Scripture,

First Response 183

something that is difficult to square with the historical fact that it was the Church that established the New Testament canon in the first place. Doesn't this historical fact suggest that the Church is also a fundamental and authoritative source in theology? Indeed, Rea's own practice in his Position Statement in deferring at various points to the authority of Church creeds indicates that he himself does not rely solely on Scripture, or his own individual understanding of Scripture. I suggest that a more historically accurate and theologically illuminating account of the relationship between Church and Scripture is one that sees both existing in symbiotic relationship, mutually supporting and reinforcing one other. To be sure, ultimate authority in theology (as in all else) rests with God, not with Scripture or the Church, but given that the Church assembled the Scriptures and decided what is to be included and excluded, does it not follow that a decisive role in interpreting the Scriptures (and, more generally, in furthering the salvation of individuals) belongs to the Church? (Again, the history of the formation of Christian doctrine testifies to the intimate interconnections between Scripture and Church, where, in response to various controversies during the early centuries, the central christological and trinitarian doctrines were derived from Scripture *by the Church*.)

The Trinity

I have always been highly skeptical of attempts to resolve the paradoxes lying at the heart of the doctrines of the Trinity and the Incarnation in a way that seeks to remain within Christian orthodoxy while, at the same time, keeping within the bounds of 'classical' logic (consisting, at least, of the two-valued sentence calculus and first-order predicate calculus) and adhering to 'classical' principles such as the principle of non-contradiction, or Leibniz's law (i.e., the principle of the indiscernibility of identicals) – something that even Rea's model of the Trinity does not succeed in doing, given that it requires a departure from the classical or absolute account of identity enshrined in Leibniz's law. This suggests to me an intractable element of *mystery* in the doctrines of God as triune and God as incarnate that no amount of philosophical theorizing can remove (though this is not to say that no meaningful expression of these doctrines is possible).

There are, to be sure, many innovative and ingenious proposals for resolving the paradoxes, and the Aristotelian model developed by Rea (together with Jeffrey Brower) is just such a proposal. However, let's suppose for the sake of argument that this model succeeds in what it purports to do – namely, to provide a coherent and intelligible explanation, within the limits set by creedal formulas, as to how God can be a triunity. If Rea's model succeeded in this respect, then what mystery would remain in the doctrine of the Trinity? Perhaps some mystery would remain insofar as the model is limited or defective in certain respects, drawn as it is from an imperfect analogy with the constitution of material objects. The Church Fathers, of course, also employed multiple analogies in an attempt to get some grip on the Trinity.

184   N. N. Trakakis

But they always remained dissatisfied with these analogies, especially when they misleadingly suggest composition in the Godhead, or some lapse of time or notion of interval between the divine persons. And so, analogies were used with great caution and even in ways to deliberately highlight the paradoxical and mysterious nature of the Trinity. It is this apophatic character of trinitarian thought which was an integral part of patristic theology and yet is unfortunately lacking in Rea's approach.

But putting the matter of mystery to the side, it is questionable whether Rea's Aristotelian model succeeds on its own terms at removing the logical contradiction that seems to inhere in the doctrine of the Trinity. Here I will refer to an objection raised by William Lane Craig, who wrote that Rea's model:

> . . . does not tell us how seemingly mutually exclusive hylomorphic compounds can be numerically the same object. We are told that one object can be both a hand and a fist. All right. But how can one object be simultaneously a clenched fist and an open hand? How can a quantity of gold be at once a U.S. twenty-dollar coin and a Spanish doubloon? How can Socrates be at once seated Socrates, standing Socrates, and reclining Socrates? How can the Winged Victory and the David and the Venus de Milo be numerically the same object?
>
> (2005: 82–3)

Craig's point, I take it, is that the divine persons – much like the material compounds he lists – bear mutually exclusive intrinsic properties. For example, the Son alone bears the property 'begotten from the Father', and the Father alone has the property of 'unbegottenness'. Now, on Rea's model, the divine persons are analogous to material objects in being like hylomorphic structures, compounds of matter and form. A statue is typically composed of matter (say, marble) and bears a certain form (which makes it into a statue of, say, Aphrodite). One could then imagine the same material object (namely, the lump of marble) having two forms at the same time: a statue and a pillar. In this case, there is one material object but two hylomorphic compounds. Similarly, in the case of the Trinity, the same divine nature (the same 'matter', in an extended or analogous sense) has three forms: the Father, the Son and the Holy Spirit. As in the material case, there are here a commonly shared substance (the divine nature) and three hylomorphic compounds (the divine persons). But, as Craig observes, the analogy breaks down at this point, once it is borne in mind that: (i) the divine persons are mutually exclusive hylomorphic compounds (given that each person [necessarily] has a property that the other persons lack), while (ii) the statue and the pillar are not mutually exclusive hylomorphic compounds, for a single material object (such as a lump of marble) can clearly be both at once, occupying the same region of space and time. Therefore, it does not follow that, if a statue and a pillar can be counted as numerically the same (material) object, then for analogous reasons the divine persons can be counted as numerically the same (immaterial or divine) object. The mystery of the Trinity remains impenetrable.

The Incarnation

Similar difficulties beset attempts to 'explain away' the paradox of the Incarnation. In this case, Rea defers to the 'two-minds' christology of Thomas Morris, and (following Morris) he briefly explains, by appeal to depth psychology, how this christology does not succumb to Nestorianism (the view that Christ is composed of two separate persons, one human and the other divine). One worry raised by critics is that the relationship between the divine mind and the human mind on this model – where the conscious, earthly mind of Jesus is only a 'subsystem' within the subconscious, eternal mind of the Son – resembles the monophysite view that Christ's human attributes were submerged or subsumed by the divine nature, leaving no distinct and subsistent human nature. Eleonore Stump, in a review of Morris' *The Logic of God Incarnate*, gave voice to this criticism when pointing out that "if [as Morris holds] the only constituents of the human nature Christ takes on are those properties essential to human beings but not incompatible with any divine properties, then what I share with Christ as regards human nature seems rather meager" (1989: 220).

This brings me to an aspect of Morris' proposal that Rea did not mention but which is crucial in that it seeks to show how the doctrine of the Incarnation is not internally inconsistent. Morris makes the dubious assumption that 'limitation properties' – properties such as being limited in power or knowledge – are not properties essential to being human. With that assumption in place, it is perhaps easier (though by no means easy) to go on to show that there is no contradiction in affirming that Jesus is both fully human and fully divine. But as I have argued previously (Trakakis 1997), there is good reason to take limitation properties as being essential to what it is to be human, given that these are properties we are all born with (and in that sense they are common or universal human properties), and there is nothing we could ever do to be rid of them (if, by chance or some technological or miraculous intervention, humans became omnipotent and omniscient they would arguably cease being human and would have evolved into *superhumans*). This is to do no more than repeat Gregory of Nyssa's notion of the infinite distance or divide (*diastema*) between the Creator and the creation.

Response to Bishop: 'Naturalist' Christian theism

Classical theism

Bishop writes that the God of classical theism – a God who is said to be simple, immutable, and impassible – "does not fit the God who speaks and acts decisively in human history", and that such a deity "seems patently

186   N. N. Trakakis

religiously inadequate with respect to the lived Abrahamic faiths" (this volume: 6; emphasis in original). In saying this, however, it is important not to overlook the imperative, recognized well in the Abrahamic faiths, to guard against anthropomorphism and idolatry, an imperative which explains to some degree the classical conception of God as simple, immutable, and impassible. It does not *obviously* follow, then, that the God of classical theism is *religiously* inadequate, given that it is designed to meet a strongly felt desire to express the radical transcendence and incomprehensibility of God. (To be fair, I think Bishop recognizes this, and in his Position Statement he concedes that the core classical divine attributes can be thought of in apophatic terms, as delineating what God is not.)

Personal omniGod theism

I will restrict myself to two brief remarks here. First, in seeking to develop a non-personal conception of God, or at least one that is not idolatrously anthropomorphic, Bishop draws a distinction between the psychology of the believer and the believer's philosophy (or theoretical understanding), and then states: "Relating to God person-to-person is psychologically healthy and even unavoidable, but it does not follow that God is to be understood as 'a' person, however unique and supreme" (8). I did not find this overly helpful or clear. How could one rationally or justifiably relate to something x (e.g., the sea) in a personal way if x is not a person or a personal being and one knows this to be so? Of course, one could in such circumstances engage in pretence (e.g., behaving towards the sea *as if* it were endowed with intentional capacities), but would this be healthy and unavoidable?

Second, Bishop proceeds a little later to say that God should not be thought of as one being or item amongst others, for "God is not 'an item' *at all*, not 'a' being, not 'an' entity" (8; emphasis in original). But I don't see any insuperable difficulty in conceiving of God as *a being* (or an entity). It is sometimes suspected that to think of God as a being, or as one being amongst other beings, somehow reduces God to the status of a creature. But there is no warrant for this suspicion, at least if a careful analysis is given of what it means to call God 'a being' or 'the supreme being'.

The problem of evil

I am familiar with Bishop's version of the logical argument from evil, and also sympathetic to it. From the moment Bishop expressed the kernel of the argument to me (many years ago, as it happens), I have felt that there is something quite right about it even though I have not been entirely persuaded. And his recent defence of the argument in print (Bishop and Perszyk 2011), although characteristically rigorous and insightful, still leaves me unconvinced – despite the fact that I (as an 'anti-theodicist') should very much want to be convinced!

Allow me to express my reservation briefly as follows. The central claim of Bishop and Perszyk (hereafter 'B-K') is that "there are facts about evil that are logically inconsistent with the perfect goodness of an omnipotent and omniscient creator of the world, *at least relative to certain value commitments which a reasonable person may have*" (2011: 110; emphasis in original). In §2 of their paper, B-K seek to substantiate this claim. One important stage in this process involves the notion of 'divine concurrence': God (under 'personal omniGod theism') creates and sustains the causal and other conditions necessary for the occurrence of any evil (pp. 121–22). This gives expression to the idea that, "Given his omnipotence, God must be deeply involved in bringing all evils into existence" (p. 121). Another significant element in B-K's case is a certain kind of theological ethics that many theists would find congenial – this is an ethic that takes the notion of *right relationship* as central, so that the highest good consists in having the right sort of (loving) relationship with God and other creatures (p. 122). Finally, according to B-K, these two elements, the notion of divine concurrence and an ethics of right relationship, can be brought together to produce a plausible version of the logical argument from evil. How so? B-K hold that (i) divine concurrence and (ii) an ethics of right relationship are mutually incompatible, in the sense that a God who acts in the way described under (i) cannot also fulfill the conditions necessary for (ii). But why exactly (i) and (ii) are incompatible has, to my mind, been left unclear.

In their 2011 paper, B-K devote no more than one short paragraph (at the beginning of p. 122) in support of this alleged logical incompatibility. In his Position Statement, Bishop writes that "It is difficult to see how God could be in *perfect relationship with sufferers* even though he may have – to us unknown – good reasons for allowing their suffering and even though he ultimately compensates for and redeems their suffering" (this volume: 10; my emphasis). Given that the notion of 'God having a perfect relationship with humans' seems to carry great weight in Bishop's argument, perhaps he could elucidate it a little, and especially explain what precisely in this notion excludes or conflicts with the notion of God permitting humans to suffer horrific evil. The mere fact that God is causally involved in bringing human suffering about is not sufficient to show that any relationship that God has with humans is defective.

Doctrinal development

I heartily concur with Bishop's emphasis on "evolving theological understanding" given that "the revelation of God to humanity is essentially limited, fallible and developmental" (12, 4). The understanding that we have (whether individually or collectively as church) of the nature of divinity is something that should be allowed to deepen and develop, particularly in the light of new or unfamiliar ideas and theories that may in origin be non-Christian or even anti-Christian. This may require, as Bishop notes,

188   N. N. Trakakis

challenging established authorities and ways of thinking. His example of Joshua ch. 6 makes the point very well, given that the kind of ethics most people in western society today are inclined to accept would look upon the actions described in many parts of the Old Testament as barbaric and unfitting for any benevolent being, let alone God, to endorse.

The naturalist, euteleological conception of the divine

(i) God as creator

It seems somewhat odd to describe God as a 'creator' when he is neither a personal agent nor an efficient cause (in the Aristotelian sense of the producer or principle that is the primary source of some change). Of course, one is free to use words in non-standard or technical ways, but it has to be admitted that Bishop's understanding of divine creation not only diverges from the traditional theological view of *creatio ex nihilo*, but also from the ordinary or common meaning of what it is to create something.

One may also question whether a teleological explanation of the universe (that is, one given in terms of final causality) is possible without any appeal to intentionality, agency or efficient causality, but I am prepared to concede that this is at least intelligible.

(ii) The naturalist conception of the divine

It would be helpful to distinguish *methodological naturalism* from *ontological naturalism*. According to methodological naturalism, or at least a strong version of it, the best or only way to attain knowledge of the world is through the methods of science. According to ontological naturalism, the natural world and its inhabitants are all that exist, so that supernatural (or 'spooky') entities such as gods and ghosts are eliminated as non-existent. Bishop makes it plain that he is an ontological, not a methodological, naturalist. Although he doesn't make it clear what exactly naturalism, in this ontological sense, amounts to, I take it that his view is somewhat like David Armstrong's naturalist hypothesis "that nothing but Nature, the single, all-embracing spatio-temporal system, exists" (1978: 138).

As Bishop would be aware, ontological naturalism faces many challenges, even if one is not a theist. But when theism is added to the picture, then the problems are only exacerbated, for if nothing but the natural world exists, what room is left for God? Bishop also speaks of Jesus' resurrection and ascension, but it is far from clear how such miraculous events cohere with the naturalist outlook. Bishop states that, "On my naturalist understanding, the Resurrection is not effected by external supernatural agency but by the altogether more amazing *inherent* effect of absolute steadfastness in living lovingly" (19; emphasis in original). But how can a purely natural process or power, even the power of love, raise someone from the dead? (I suspect that Bishop is interpreting Jesus' resurrection not as a historical event but as a myth or metaphor expressing something like the transformation caused by Jesus in the lives of his followers.)

One could render theism and naturalism compatible by adopting a non-realist account of theism, where 'God', properly understood, is not a mind-independent or objective reality but is rather a human creation – whether it be in the form of a subjective projection, or a social construction, or a mythical embodiment of moral values (in which case the further assumption would have to be made that any such normativity can be accommodated within a naturalist framework). But as is clear from Bishop's response to the work of Lloyd Geering (New Zealand's leading theological non-realist), Bishop wishes to remain within the realist fold (see Bishop 2006). (In his Position Statement, also, Bishop states that his proposal "is not to identify the divine with an ethical ideal" [15].)

How, then, can God be accommodated within the spatio-temporal frame of naturalism? Bishop's answer consists in identifying the divine with loving, creaturely interpersonal interactions and relationships within the natural world. These relations are not (or not merely?) *manifestations* of the divine; rather, they are *instantiations* of the divine. That is to say, the divine just is the various instantiations of love, or loving relationship, found in the universe – which is to take the New Testament statement that 'God is Love' in a quite literal way.

The problem with this conception of divinity is clear, and Bishop gestures at it at certain points: the *aseity* or ontological independence of God is compromised, so that God (on Bishop's conception) becomes dependent for his existence on the created world, rather than (as is traditionally held) the created world being radically contingent and dependent upon God. (Similarly, Bishop has elsewhere spoken of the universe as "that which . . . gives birth to the Divine" and the existence of the Divine as "ultimately contingent"; Bishop 2007: 401.) Consider, for example, the question: If there were no physical world, would there be a God? Bishop must respond negatively, while no traditional theist would accept such an answer. But it is doubtful that a God whose existence is dependent on the natural world in this way would fit the 'God-role', as Bishop characterizes it, as that which is "*worthy of* the special kind of trust, worship and obedience that constitute the commitment of faith" (this volume: 7).

(iii) Afterlife

If (as Bishop thinks) the ultimate purpose of humanity is the kind of transformation in love and incarnation of the divine exemplified by Jesus, and if (as Bishop also holds) the universe is set up in such a way as to allow for, and even promote, the fulfillment of this purpose, then would it not be necessary to postulate (in the manner of John Hick) the continuation of the process of human transformation in an afterlife *given* the countless failed attempts to

190 N. N. *Trakakis*

attain this goal in this life? In rejecting the afterlife, as Bishop must (due to his commitment to naturalism), the goal of transformation for a very large swathe of the human population would amount to (to borrow Bishop's own words) "a fantastic pipe dream", though I'd be more prone to call it a 'cruel joke'.

Response to Eaton: Ecological Christianity

Truth

In her opening Preamble, Heather Eaton makes some highly controversial claims, but without elaborating or clarifying them. One such claim is that "there is no objective or truthful vantage point in the past or present" (this volume: 25). The other claim, drawn from the American writer and theologian Frederick Buechner, is that "all theology is autobiographical". How seriously are we to take such statements? For one thing, there are well-known problems of self-referential consistency. Is the claim that there is no objective truth itself an objective truth? Is the claim that all theology is autobiography itself something more or other than an autobiographical statement? If 'yes', then incoherence looms. If 'no', then it is not clear how the mere expression of Eaton's own attitudes or preferences (which is what these statements, in such a case, would amount to) can have any purchase on us. Moreover, Eaton's practice in her Position Statement (and, I would conjecture, in her scholarly work at large) does not cohere with these blanket denials of truth and objectivity, for it seems that various beliefs (about, e.g., the age of the universe, biological evolution, and the nature of religious belief) are being presented as true – that is, true in an objective, and not purely autobiographical or subjective, sense.

I wonder, also, how exactly Eaton understands the way in which the notion of 'truth' functions in religious discourse. At one revealing point, she notes in relation to the beliefs and doctrines of religion that "The categories of 'true' and 'false' are inapplicable. Religious symbols are active, alive or dynamic, or they are dying or dead" (29). But why are the categories of truth and falsity to be dispensed with when it comes to religious discourse? Indeed, if the concepts of truth and falsity were dispensed with in theology, would not the central ideas and doctrines of any theological system lose much of their dialectical and existential force? For example, would one commit their life to Christianity if one came to believe that Christianity is not true (or neither true nor false)? Perhaps, in Eaton's view, what is vital and necessary is not so much 'truth' in the traditional, correspondence sense but 'truth' in a pragmatic sense, where a theology is to be accepted insofar as it embodies a symbolic imagery that is "active, alive or dynamic" rather than one that is "dying or dead". But such an understanding of truth in theology would seem to engender only ironic detachment, not committed participation in religious life. Religious commitment requires the meta-belief that one's religious beliefs are factually or objectively true. Eaton herself states that "It seemed evident to me that we live in a *'divine milieu'* (Teilhard de Chardin). I cannot prove this, but I would stake my life on it" (30). But why stake your life on something that you do not take to be (objectively) true?

Certainty

Eaton seems quite certain that certainty in religion (or theology) is not possible. She states, for example, that "we cannot know the nature of God or have any certainty about the existence of a divine entity" (26). And a little later she writes: "I am not attracted to any claims about God that assume certainty, for several reasons. One, there is no certainty" (30). Such a categorical denial of certainty itself bespeaks of certainty, and once more a performative contradiction lurks here.

Nevertheless, I sympathize with the tenor of Eaton's critique of certainty: in our age of informed awareness of the rich diversity of worldviews (religious and otherwise), at least a degree of epistemic humility is appropriate, exercising a hermeneutic of suspicion not only towards the beliefs of others but also towards one's own cherished beliefs (and, similarly, adopting a hermeneutics of charity not only towards one's own religious community but also towards religious communities with which one disagrees). Dogmatism and triumphalism no longer have a place in religion and theology, and it is incumbent on Christian churches and leaders to instill in their faithful the value and virtue of doubt, critical inquiry and questioning rather than attempting to eradicate these as sinful or persecuting those who challenge church tradition (as the Vatican has done to Gebara). For as Heidegger once put it, "questioning is the piety of thought" (Heidegger 2008: 341).

The afterlife

I agree with Eaton that "we all need an intelligent conversation about the resurrection, the afterlife and eternity" (38). But I'm not sure her discussion of these topics genuinely furthers the debate, particularly in passages such as the following:

> I am offended by all the God-talk and Christian teachings that denigrate this world, that claim human origins and destiny are 'elsewhere' and presume a better and future life 'somewhere else' uniting humans and God. As such, the Christian tradition, overall, functions as an inoculation against 'this life' – to varying degrees.
>
> (30)

My own position, which I cannot detail or defend here, is that if there is no afterlife then human life has no objective value or purpose (and this, even if there is a God). The objection that Eaton raises is a common one, but rarely is much provided by way of explanation or justification. Here are some questions worth considering.

First, what is so great and wonderful about life here on Earth, given that it is over in the blink of an eye, all earthly pleasures and goods are transient and attached to some degree of pain or suffering, and the world is replete with illness, tragedy and evil? I do not mean to deny that earthly life is to be valued, cherished and enjoyed. But to overestimate the worth and goodness of this life is not simply naïve but also insensitive to the darkness, sorrow and cruelty of so much of human (and animal) existence. One of the great strengths of the religious traditions of the world, especially Christianity and Buddhism, is that they acknowledge this darkness and seek to offer a solution (a soteriology) in response. Eaton writes that "Christianity has a particular resistance to and denial of death. I think that this is because Christianity has developed an extreme opposition to, even refusal of, the conditions of life as given: vulnerability, finitude and mortality" (38). But, once again, what is so great about vulnerability when it includes an openness to horrific evil, or finitude when it makes possible devastating forms of ignorance and impotence, or mortality when it deprives us of those people who matter most to us? Eaton regards the 'refusal' of these conditions of life as 'sinful': "the primal sin is negating the non-negotiable existential circumstances of life" (39). Of course, no one in his or her right mind (whether Christian or not) would deny that the human condition consists in vulnerability, finitude and mortality. But I gather that Eaton's point is that the human condition, thus conceived, is not to be negated or refused but is to be affirmed and maybe even celebrated. But, to repeat, why should we accept this? I would rather, like Camus, *rebel* against our wretched predicament and seek to ameliorate it as far as possible. (Eaton claims that the negation of the inbuilt conditions of life produces "escapist spiritualities, otherworldly ideations. The result is a fall into domination – of land, animals and peoples" (39). But more needs to be said to make such claims credible. Why should escapism, let alone domination, be the *inevitable* result of the belief in an afterlife or the refusal of the conditions of life?)

Second, why is life here on Earth necessarily or intrinsically better than any other life we could imagine – including an afterlife of eternal felicity in the presence of God? Third, if we think of the afterlife as better and more valuable than earthly life, does this constitute a *denigration* of earthly life? It is perfectly possible to affirm earthly life as immensely valuable and good while also holding that there is another, even better (perhaps infinitely better) form of life awaiting us somewhere else. Finally, let's assume that there is no afterlife. Does it follow that life here on Earth can finally be accorded the value it deserves? Or does it rather follow that life now takes on the contours of radical contingency, absurdity and meaninglessness described so powerfully in existentialist literature? The answer is by no means obvious. (Eaton countenances the possibility that, in some circumstances, evil and injustice will triumph. But what she fails to notice is that for scores of people

First Response   193

[e.g., those killed in the Holocaust], the ultimate triumph of evil is no mere abstract possibility but the actual and unfortunate truth of the matter – *at least if no afterlife is granted them.*)

Later in her Position Statement, under the heading of 'The Resurrection of the Dead', Eaton states: "I cannot fathom an intelligible world where humans exist and reunite after death. It seems like magical, wishful thinking. It may be correct, but I am more than skeptical. It defies all other processes of the universe and the natural world" (37). It is not clear, however, what is *unintelligible* in the belief that human persons in some form survive their death. The mere fact that so many people in the past – in fact, the vast majority of the world's human population – have accepted this belief should indicate all on its own that there is nothing *obviously incoherent* in the belief in the afterlife. A possible reason why such beliefs nowadays present themselves (to many academics) as unintelligible or meaningless is the prevailing naturalism (or materialism) in the academy: if one believes that nothing but the natural world exists and that a human person is identical with their physical body or brain, then notions like 'God', 'miracles', and 'resurrection' are likely to strike one as incredible, superstitious, and perhaps even incoherent. But if one were already committed to a position of dualism (both material and spiritual entities exist) or even a position of idealism (reality is mind-like), then I would suspect that much of the contemporary skepticism and disbelief towards the afterlife would disappear. In other words, one's views on the resurrection and the afterlife are, in part at least, influenced by one's larger metaphysical commitments. I do not put this forward as a discovery on my part but only as a reminder and a call to greater circumspection.

When outlining her understanding of the afterlife, Eaton lists a number of possible explanations of a psychological and biological nature for the persistence of afterlife-beliefs. I assume that she is well aware of the 'genetic fallacy', and therefore in putting forward these explanations she is not attempting to disprove or disconfirm the existence of an afterlife. That would be a clumsy error. But then why does she so confidently reject the afterlife? I suspect, as indicated earlier, that a prior commitment to naturalism is doing much of the work here.

The divine

I found Eaton's idea of the 'divine milieu' intriguing, and I would like to know more. In light of her comments on this notion, I take it that God or the divine is, in her understanding, entirely immanent and hence does not exist beyond or independently of the (physical) world. But in that case would not 'pantheism' be a more accurate description of this position than Eaton's preferred self-description as a 'classical panentheist'? Panentheism (which literally means 'all is in God') is the view that God is *both* immanent within all creation *and* transcends the physical world. Perhaps *pantheism*

194   *N. N. Trakakis*

(literally, 'all is God') is a better way of representing what Eaton wishes to say about the divine. Pantheism may be thought of as the view that the world as a whole is identical with God; or, alternatively, that everything that exists constitutes a 'unity' and this all-inclusive unity is in some sense divine. This is the view of divinity one encounters in the Stoics and in Spinoza, and it gives expression to the immanence and embodiment of the divine that are also highlighted in Eaton's notion of the 'divine milieu'. It was not clear, however, whether Eaton wishes to take the crucial step of affirming, in line with pantheism, that nature and divinity are (in some significant sense) identical or one.

Note

1 Towards the end of his chapter, Hart states that, even if there were good evidence in support of Jesus' resurrection, that would not suffice to show that Jesus was God, or God incarnate: "Certainly there is no proof that can be offered of it [i.e., Jesus' resurrection], and even if it were established strongly by one means or another it would not compel us to regard Jesus Christ as God Incarnate. God could raise from the dead a holy man or an incarnate angel, as the Arians believed" (62). This is no doubt true, though the evidence in support of the resurrection is usually taken *in combination with other evidence* (e.g., evidence concerning Jesus' miracles and his self-understanding) as confirming Jesus' divinity.

References

Armstrong, D. M. 1978. *Universals and Scientific Realism, vol. 1: Nominalism and Realism*. Cambridge: Cambridge University Press.

Bishop, J. 2006. "Revisionary Theology: Realism and Non-Realism." In *A Religious Atheist? Critical Essays on the Work of Lloyd Geering*, edited by R. Pelly and P. Stuart, 99–110. Otago: Otago University Press.

Bishop, J. 2007. "How a Modest Fideism May Constrain Theistic Commitments: Exploring an Alternative to Classical Theism." *Philosophia* 35: 387–402.

Bishop, J. and K. Perszyk. 2011. "The Normatively Relativised Logical Argument from Evil." *International Journal for Philosophy of Religion* 70: 109–126.

Craig, W. L. 2005. "Does the Problem of Material Constitution Illuminate the Doctrine of the Trinity?" *Faith and Philosophy* 22: 77–86.

Heidegger, M. 2008. "The Question Concerning Technology." In *Basic Writings*, edited by D. Farrell Krell, rev. and expanded ed., 307–341. London: HarperCollins.

Quinn, P. L. 1985. "In Search of the Foundations of Theism." *Faith and Philosophy* 2: 469–486.

Stump, E. 1989. "Review of Thomas Morris: *The Logic of God Incarnate*." *Faith and Philosophy* 6: 218–223.

Trakakis, N. 1997. "The Absolutist Theory of Omnipotence." *Sophia: International Journal for Philosophical Theology* 36: 55–78.

Second Responses

11 John Bishop

Feeling chastened by Kevin Hart's saying in his First Response, of myself and Michael Rea, that he "wonder[s] for whom [we] write and, outside the guild of analytical philosophy, who [we] think will profit from [our] speculations" (160), I found myself reflecting on my intended audience. I have concluded that, at the deepest motivational level, I am writing for myself. That conclusion seems a little less egotistical when I add that I write for myself from the classical stance of *fides quaerens intellectum*. I take myself to have and to seek to live by Christian faith. That I have this faith (if indeed I do have it) I regard as God's gracious gift. It is a further gift that I desire to grow in understanding this faith – and yet further gifts follow if and when I advance in my understanding. This search for understanding is not an attempt to justify faith-commitment from some neutral starting point. It is itself a work of faith. I do not see myself, then, as spinning speculations for my own gratification or for the attention of others. Anselm sets the standard when, in the *Proslogion*, he seeks to understand that God exists in the context of prayer. We should infer, I think, that the desire to understand faith may hope for fulfillment only in the presence of the attitudes characteristic of prayer.[1]

The suggestion that Anselm's philosophizing in the context of prayer sets a precedent we Christian philosophers should follow does not imply that advancing in understanding is a merely private or subjective matter, however. It would be wrong to think that my Christian philosophizing – maybe, even, *any* of my praying – was 'just between me and God'.[2] Philosophizing, even in prayer, is apt for being overheard. I may be writing *au fond* for myself, but anyone may consider what I say. Indeed, in so far as I favour accepting a certain understanding of Christian faith, I am, as Sartre puts it, 'deciding for others'. Even if I hold back from endorsing my understanding as *the* correct interpretation, I am still endorsing it as *a* viable one. Since I thus implicitly announce to my fellow Christians that this is *an* interpretation they at least ought to allow, I am therefore accountable to others for my favoured understanding. I may not, therefore, be satisfied that I have made an intellectual advance until I am satisfied that I have met that accountability.

What are the standards implied by this accountability? Some are the objective – or, at least, widely intersubjective – standards of intellectual

198   *John Bishop*

rationality, governing logical consistency and inference, judgements of wider coherence, judgements of probability on a given body of evidence, and so on. Other standards govern *religious* adequacy, determining whether particular interpretations may be accepted as viable understandings of the content of faith. A grasp of these standards is possible only from within Christian commitment. Though these standards may be appreciated by some not so committed, the required 'insider' expertise is most securely found in those with long experience of living and thinking within the Christian 'form of life'.

In so far as they do belong to *fides quaerens intellectum*, then, my attempts at an alternative to the 'personal omniGod' conception of the principal object of Christian faith are properly subject to scrutiny by Christians with insider expertise. Judging by the responses of my colleagues in this current project, the euteleological conception of God I have been exploring seems unlikely to fare well by the shared standards of religious adequacy.[3]

Even those who concur in rejecting the personal omniGod conception express considerable doubt about my positive alternative. Kevin Hart identifies me as a "Protestant analytical philosopher" whose concern is not "the development of doctrine" but rather "alternatives to doctrine" (this volume: 160). Hart concludes that "Bishop is actively seeking to find an intellectually credible alternative to the doctrine of God in orthodox Christianity, even while looking back towards some of its major creeds" (160). The only thing I own in these descriptions is that I am an analytical philosopher. As an Anglican with Anglo-Catholic sympathies I do not identify myself as Protestant *as opposed to* Catholic. More importantly, my efforts are aimed at developing an alternative *to the personal omniGod conception of the divine prevailing amongst my fellow analytical philosophers*, and not at all at replacing "the doctrine of God in orthodox Christianity".

Hart agrees with me in rejecting what I call the personal omniGod as "the God of the nursery more than the God of the Church" (149) and, later, as "no more than Zeus by another name" (152). Hart also agrees, I think, that a faith-stance that understands God as 'the apotheosis of the controlling ego' (my phrase, not Hart's) is not apt for promoting believers' transformation from egotism to *agape*. While, of course, I welcome criticism of my substantive attempts at an alternative and admit that (as Hart observes) I lack a theologian's learning in the history of doctrine, I am discouraged by the construal Hart places on my intentions. I see myself as engaged in the serious business of philosopher-believers, whose philosophizing about the faith is not independent of their actual faith-commitment. For *fides quaerens intellectum*, then, what might otherwise seem to be speculative discussions about the divine need to be treated with pastoral seriousness and a proper sense of their essential limits. And perhaps an analytical philosopher who has been immersed in the faith for all his life can bring to the search for understanding something worthwhile in part because it does not proceed from an extensive scholarly knowledge of theology.

Hart may have mistaken my intentions through making a certain assumption about the 'naturalist' Christianity I defend. Hart says: "Bishop, finding himself impressed by the success of naturalism, attempts to rethink Christianity so that it falls into line with its assumptions, trajectories and conclusions" (159). Now, the naturalism whose success Hart has in mind is presumably *scientific* naturalism. But my 'naturalist' Christianity accepts the orthodox view that God transcends reality as intelligible through the empirical sciences. It is naturalist – or, perhaps better, anti-supernaturalist – in resisting the ontological dualism that locates God in a separate supernatural realm.[4] That resistance is something my position *shares* with classical theology as described by Hart: euteleology fully accepts that, as Hart says, "[i]n creating all that there is, *God is not thereby constituted as other than the world* . . . the divine transcendence does not have the basic characteristic of contrasting God with the world" (150; my emphasis).

On this point about God's otherness, then, Hart's classical theology and my euteleological naturalism agree. But Hart takes me to reject classical 'perfect being theology' because I doubt the coherence of the notion of an absolutely simple and necessary existent. Now, I do indeed reject the view that there is, or even could be, a unique entity amongst other entities (called 'God') that has simplicity and necessity *as positive properties*. But that is not the correct way to understand the classical claim that God is simple and necessary. The classical claim is apophatic: God lacks the contingency that characterizes existents and God lacks composition, in particular, the composition of essence and existence. 'He' is not an instance of any kind.

There may be considerable compatibilities, I believe, between the euteleological view and classical theology.[5] Hart, however, describes me as "content with a deity who is remarkably thin by traditional standards" (152) and opines that my position "pulls the meaning of 'Christian' somewhat out of shape" (153). So, what is the euteleological view, exactly? Hart characterizes it as claiming that "God is not to be conceived as the Creator who precedes the world but as a deity that is the end or purpose of the world [where] . . . [t]his deity is not supernatural, depends on the natural world in order to become itself and is the full realization of love" (151).

Now it is true that, in my Position Statement, I did identify God on the euteleological view with the universe's realized ultimate *telos*, the supreme good, revealed to us as love. My explorations of euteleology have since developed in joint work undertaken with Ken Perszyk and in continuing conversations with Thomas Harvey,[6] and I am now more cautious about this identification. Indeed, I want to sound a note of caution about *any* straightforward identification of the divine, including my own earlier identification of God with love as naturally realized in the world (see Bishop 2013). This caution stems from the traditional doctrine of divine incomprehensibility, which I take to mean not that God is unintelligible but that God can never be *fully* grasped in a completed intellectual act that satisfies the 'controlling' epistemic desire to 'know just what one is dealing with'.[7]

200   *John Bishop*

As Michael Rea observes, in my Position Statement I made several *different* identifications of the divine which Rea understandably finds hard to reconcile. Rea is correct to judge that my "most considered view" in that chapter is that "God is the 'full cosmic meaning of the love that unites the divine persons'" (this volume: 166). But what does that description mean? Rea suggests that it implies that God is a created being (as "an effect of the various loving relationships that exist in the universe" [166]). That is certainly not what I intend, but I agree that one cannot extract a clear and precise meaning from this description, though I hope it does convey something in the wider context of the account I gave of the euteleological view. But it is, surely, a bad look for an analytical philosopher to come up with something apparently so feebly imprecise when asked what he takes God to be. Or is it? Good analytical philosophers need to accept and work within the inherent limitations on analysis applicable to the concepts with which they are concerned. When it comes to analytical philosophy of religion, the doctrine of divine incomprehensibility implies that the desire for a completed analytical understanding of the divine cannot be satisfied.

I suggest, then, that it is a *virtue* of the euteleological view that it cannot sustain a settled identificatory description of just who or what the divine is. One should be suspicious, I think, of any claim to have succeeded in pinning God down with analytical clarity. It does not follow, however, that faith's desire for understanding should be extinguished. Nor does it follow that the skills of the analytical philosopher should be set aside in seeking such understanding. Indeed, these are just the skills that *fides quaerens intellectum* needs, as Hart acknowledges (while at the same time regretting the lack of theological education in the 'guild' of analytical philosophers that would enable our skills to be more effectively deployed).

But how may one honour the analytical virtues in advancing understanding of the Christian faith – and of its principal object – without aiming to provide straightforwardly clear and precise identifications of the divine? All I can say is that I hope to show how this is possible in my attempts to articulate the euteleological view. I think one can provide clear and precise enough statements of how reality is on the euteleological view, but those statements do not include stable or complete identifications of the divine as any kind of entity, property or aspect of reality. Nevertheless, from the whole set of statements that express what it would be for euteleology to obtain, an understanding of our talk about God does emerge. Of course, any success in such a project will be limited, and perhaps I am not making a very good job of it. I do hope, however, that others (especially fellow Christians) will at least recognize what I am aiming to do. So, let me now renew my statement of the euteleological position, making a virtue of the instability and incompleteness of the various identifications for God that emerge, even to the point of suggesting that these identifications participate in a perichoretic dynamic in which the limitations of each requires it to give way to the others.[8]

The place to start in articulating the euteleological view is with the claim that the universe (meaning *all* of Reality) is God's creation. On the euteleological view, the universe's being God's creation consists in its being *inherently* directed upon the supreme good as its *telos* and being such that its existence is explained by the fact that the supreme good is concretely realized within it.[9] Christianity holds that the supreme good has been revealed to us as love, where the ultimate point of reference for understanding what 'love' means is Christ's new commandment that we love one another as he has loved us. If we try to identify who or what God is on this view, we will not, as I say, succeed in settling on a single comprehensible identification. Nevertheless it is important to see what identifications, plural, may be made and to note the limitations of each.

First, God may be identified with the universe's efficient cause. The euteleological view does *not* repudiate the notion of the universe having an efficient cause – all it repudiates is taking that efficient cause to be of a type with the efficient causes found within the universe, in particular, with causes that are *producers* of their effects. Trakakis suggests that I am here playing fast and loose with the established notion of an efficient cause. But I protest that I am not. Trakakis himself says that the Aristotelian notion of an efficient cause is that of "the producer *or principle* that is the primary source of some change" (this volume: 188; my emphasis). This description, let it be noted, does not simply equate 'efficient cause of x' with 'producer of x': and very well and good, say I! At root an efficient cause is that to which the actuality of its effect can be attributed, that which explains why something actual is actual – and, while effects typically are changes, it is not obvious that they must be so, nor that they could be so in the unique case of the actuality of Reality as a whole. Euteleology explains the existence of all of Reality as due to the fact that all of Reality contains within it the realization of its *telos*, the supreme good. (Euteleology thus advances beyond Platonic axiarchism by holding that the universe exists not because it is good that it should exist but because the good is achieved within it.[10]) It is thus mistaken to say, as Rea does, that all that God's being creator means on the euteleological view is that God is the universe's final cause. God's being creator implies that the universe has an overall efficient cause, where what is meant by 'efficient cause' is that which explains the actuality of its effect. And the euteleological view does affirm that the universe has an efficient cause in this sense.

Rea nevertheless maintains that someone with the euteleological understanding of divine creation "cannot (straightforwardly) affirm" that "we believe in one God, the Father Almighty, maker of heaven and earth . . . of all things visible and invisible" (164), as the Nicene Creed proclaims (and Hart makes the same complaint). Well, I do affirm this creedal claim – in accordance with my confirmation promise – and euteleology provides a way to understand what it is that I affirm.[11] Rea implies, however, that the euteleological understanding of God as maker is not 'straightforward'. But Rea's 'standard' account of God as producer of *all* things can hardly be

202 *John Bishop*

straightforward either, as the traditional qualification 'creation *ex nihilo*' indicates. There are serious difficulties in making coherent the notion of a literal producer *ex nihilo* of all concrete reality, and in dispelling the suspicion that this idea results from an anthropomorphic projection from our own experience as agent-causes and must therefore fail to grasp the uniqueness of divine creation.[12] Even if these difficulties can in the end be overcome, the affirmation that God is thus maker of all that exists will require sophisticated understanding. My point, then, is that *no one* who sincerely affirms the Creed's opening claim may fairly suppose that what it means is *straightforwardly* comprehensible, however simple-heartedly they accept it as true.

On the euteleological view, the efficient cause of "all things, visible and invisible" is the fact that the universe realizes the supreme good which is its *telos*. That cause may seem too abstract and propositional to be identified with God, the Father Almighty. Perhaps, then, God is the *concrete correlate* of this fact, namely the universe itself – all reality unified in relation to its inherent *telos* and existing because this *telos* is realized. This is, I think, *an* apt identification for the euteleological view to make. Euteleology therefore counts as a form of panentheism, since indeed 'all is in God'. God transcends 'the all', however, since the whole of reality's existing because it realizes the good as its *telos* transcends any item, feature or aspect that makes it up.

A further apt euteleological identification is of God with the Supreme Good (that God is 'Goodness itself' is, of course, a standard claim in classical theism). That object is too abstract, however, for this identification to be complete (unless one turns to Platonism, which will not be an option for a 'naturalist' account that seeks to avoid the ontological dualism of supernatural and natural). The realizations, manifestations or incarnations of the supreme good are entirely concrete, however, and there must be such concrete manifestations for the universe to exist at all on the euteleological view, since its explanation for the universe's existence is that it *realizes* the supreme good. Identifying God with the manifestations of the supreme good, then, is a further apt identification – for two reasons: first, because these manifestations reveal the authentic actual character of the divine (identified as the Supreme Good), and, second, for the reason that it is only because there are such manifestations that the universe exists as it does. What we may call the 'First Person' identifications of God ('the Father') as Creator *ex nihilo*, as Reality *qua* directed upon the Supreme Good, and as the Supreme Good itself, thus require recognizing 'Second Person' identifications of God ('the Son') as concrete manifestations that reveal the character of the Supreme Good (as love), and are such that "without them was not anything made that was made". These Second Person identifications, however, do not exhaust the divine. Though Trakakis cites (from Bishop 2013) some of my earlier views to the contrary, euteleology as I sought to express it in my Position Statement does *not* maintain that "the divine just is the various instantiations of love, or loving relationship, found in the universe" (189).

Finally, there wouldn't be realizations of the Supreme Good, nor *a fortiori* any universe itself, unless Reality – the universe – had the capacity within it to *produce* such realizations. That suggests a 'Third Person' identification of God as 'the Spirit', 'breathing' in and through the natural creation in order to generate – through long evolution – realizations of the supreme good. This spiritual power includes all the forces of nature, but it is perfected in the power of realized love itself to produce more such realizations (though its operations transcend processes accessible to natural scientific understanding).[13] It is important to emphasize, however, that euteleology does *not* hold (in Hegelian fashion) that the Spirit itself evolves, achieving the fullness of divinity only at an ultimate end point.[14] Divinity itself is not emergent, though its particular manifestations ('Second Person' identifications of the divine) certainly are. On the euteleological view, Reality is such that there must be some such manifestations, though it is contingent what particular manifestations of the supreme good there actually are.

I have not pinned down who or what God is on the euteleological view. But complete analysis of the concept of God is not to be expected. What may be possible is an intellectual appreciation of what view of reality is involved in believing in God, and I believe that what I have said provides at least the bare bones of such an appreciation. But could this euteleological view prove viable? In what follows, I consider some further objections made by my colleagues.

I will preface my responses to further objections by considering how I stand with respect to perfect being theology, which Hart describes as "the strongest contender to develop a doctrine of God" (149). On my understanding, perfect being theology rests on the Anselmian formula that God is that than which a greater cannot be thought, where greatness is understood as greatness *qua* being. As such, this formula offers only *a theology of the God-role*, not of that which fills it. That is to say: it is a feature of the way the concept of God functions in the theist 'language game' that, whatever God is, 'He' must be such that nothing greater *qua* being is even conceivable. (This aspect of the God-role, of course, is related to the requirement that God be a proper object of worship, where worship is understood as requiring what Tillich calls 'ultimate concern'.) It remains open, however, what it is that *actually constitutes* 'perfect being'. And it is therefore intelligible to propose that it is the God of euteleology that constitutes that than which a greater cannot be thought – albeit with the proviso that no fully comprehensible 'pinning down' of the filler for the God-role is possible, so that none of the particular identifications of the divine that are apt on the euteleological view are to be accepted as complete specifications of what God is. But, then, as I have been emphasizing, on the euteleological view, as on *any* viable conception of the divine, an understanding of the God of faith can be achieved only in the absence of any such final specification. The perfection of perfect being outruns our efforts at perfectly grasping what constitutes it.

I reckon, then, that I *do* endorse perfect being theology and can do so while holding the euteleological view. Hart states that, for Aquinas, God

204   *John Bishop*

is *ipsum esse subsistens omnibus modis indeterminatum*, with '*esse*' referring to the *act* of being (where, of course, what is meant is not any agent's action but the *actualization* implied in every actuality, including the totality). This identification of God as 'the true life of all', while not 'Himself' being any kind of existing item, is certainly *an* apt identification. But it is not, I suggest, a complete identification, since it makes no mention of the point or purpose of being – and God's status as final cause also has to be acknowledged centre stage.[15]

Hart argues, however, that euteleology departs from perfect being theology in failing to accommodate the orthodox view that God is a free Creator who has no need of creation. What does God's freedom amount to, though, if – as Hart and I are agreed – it is not the free will of a supernatural personal agent? Hart does not say. And if, as Hart does say, God is "eternal, immutable, impassive [*sic*] and maximally great" (149),[16] how does God's freedom in creating align with these attributes?[17] The euteleological view does require a necessary relation between God and creation, and that may seem to compromise divine *aseity*, as Trakakis objects. But nothing that actually exists is necessary for God to be real: all that is essential to the reality of the divine is that there *be* a creation – and, furthermore, one that realizes the supreme good. That the supreme good is actually realized in *this* way, and *that*, and *the other*, is not necessary, however: the contingency of these actual realizations can then be seen as the expression of divine freedom, as the Spirit 'blowing as it wills'. Does God stand in need of creation? Euteleology's answer is: God stands in need, not of the creation as it actually is, but of *a* creation in which the supreme good is *somehow* realized. But it does not follow that God is in any sense 'a needy being'. And perhaps that answer is not very different from the answer a classical, 'perfect being', theologian would give.[18]

As a non-personal conception of divinity, euteleology faces the objection that it does not fit with the spirituality and practices of Christianity that presuppose interpersonal relationship between God and believers. Trakakis does not find "helpful or clear" the distinction – which I take to be of the first importance – between what is psychologically necessary for believers' relationships with God and what is apt for an adequate understanding of God's reality. Given our own status as persons, it may be fitting for us to relate to God as a person, and Scripture, prayer and liturgy abound in this way of relating to God. But – and this is a point Hart emphasizes – to read off from this a personal metaphysics of the divine is to be insensitive to the function and nature of inspired scriptural books, liturgy and prayers. *Contra* Trakakis, I suggest that it can be rational to relate to something one understands not to be a personal being as if it were so (for example, in our interaction with certain machines). As personal beings who come to know the divine character in the context of interpersonal love, it is fitting that we should relate to God in just those interpersonal ways. Indeed, our tradition teaches us that we are *children* of the Most High and God *wants us* to relate to him as such. When we relate to God as if God were a person,

Second Response 205

then, we are not engaging in invented make-believe (as Trakakis suggests my view might imply), but following the promptings of our highest natural capacities for relational interaction in accordance with the divine will. In making this point, of course, I am consciously using personal language in reference to God. This usage may be understood on the euteleological view as in classical theism, namely as language that attributes personal properties analogously and has real reference to what is inconceivably greater than any individual person.

Hart wonders what room there can be on the euteleological view for "divine guidance through the answering of prayers" (152). Hart himself, drawing on Aquinas, says that "being related to God is a reality for us but not for God; when we ascribe acts and movements to God we are signifying changes in ourselves in relation to God, not in God himself" (151). Consonant with that important claim, I understand prayer as our seeking to align ourselves with the unchanging divine will and the answering of prayer as our being transformed accordingly. That classical view is equally at home in euteleology.

But euteleology, it may be claimed, cannot accommodate Christian soteriology and eschatology. Hart has the impression that I think that "God will be 'all in all' only with the realization of his Kingdom of love at the end of time" (152), and he asks "what justifies Bishop's optimism that love . . . will triumph in a universe that is adequately explained by naturalism?" (152). Actually, I did not speak quite in those terms. My eschatology is austerely non-triumphalist, and cannot, I think, recognize anything more eschatological than the realization of the supreme good within the natural universe on just those occasions when it is indeed instantiated. Eschatology is anyway highly contested theologically, and the understanding of it that is available under euteleology is, I like to think, at least on the spectrum of admissible views that emphasize *realized* eschatology.

Salvation, for Christianity, essentially involves becoming secure in the hope of eternal life, effected and proclaimed in the death and Resurrection of the Christ. Does this soteriology need something more than euteleology can provide – namely, a supremely powerful personal agent good enough to guarantee salvation? Naturalist euteleology rejects any understanding of eternal life as personal immortality in a supernatural realm. But it need not deny Christian inheritance of eternal life (as Hart suspects me of doing). I agree that God saves us from being brought to nothing in the finality of death, but I do not believe he does so by granting endless continuing existence to our individual consciousness or personhood. It is the sting of death that is removed; death herself need not be feared and can be understood as an integral part of the goodness of the natural created order.[19]

Nevertheless, it is fair to ask how a naturalist theology can possibly accommodate the divine power that raised Jesus from the dead. Trakakis suggests that I may be interpreting the Resurrection "not as a historical event, but as a myth or metaphor expressing something like the transformation caused

206 *John Bishop*

by Jesus in the lives of his followers" (189). But, while there surely is metaphor involved in believing that the Christ is raised "to the right hand of the Father", the event described has to be real, otherwise our Christian faith is in vain, as St Paul says (1 Corinthians 15:14). The transformation of the disciples' lives *was caused by* the Resurrection and their recognition of its authenticity. The Resurrection is not, therefore, a community-constructed mythical symbol, as theological non-realists maintain. Neither, though, is the Resurrection a comprehensible historical event (in the strict sense of 'comprehensible'). It is no mere 'coming back' to life, no restoration of the *status quo ante*, but a transformation into a life absolutely beyond death that vindicates Jesus' true humanity as the Anointed One who perfects obedience to the divine will. For the first disciples the Resurrection was confirmed in a range of (differing) experiences of embodied interaction with the crucified and risen Jesus, but its reality is no less affirmed by later generations who proclaim the mystery that the Christ has died, the Christ is risen and the Christ will come again, necessarily without having had any such experiences. (The story of Jesus making himself known in the breaking of bread at Emmaus [Luke 24: 13–35] expresses a mode of experiencing the dead and risen Christ that has been accessible to all generations of Christians in the regular celebration of the Eucharist. And this experience can and should extend to wider experiences of the Christ – in others, both those whom we love and serve and those who love and serve us, and even in our natural environment and the wider cosmos. In the Spirit-filled era, experiences of interaction with a dead and risen Jesus-in-the-flesh would be *de trop*: it is a transformed, universally accessible, crucified and risen Christ whom we now recognize, over and over again.)

On the euteleological view, the power of God in the Resurrection can only be a power exercised *within* the one reality. Trakakis' question – "how can a purely natural process or power, even the power of love, raise someone from the dead?" (188) – carries the implicature that it is straightforward to suppose that a power that was *not* 'purely natural' could raise someone from the dead. But I doubt that Resurrection power is really any more intelligible under supernaturalist dualism than it is under a monist, euteleological, view. In either case, appeal must be made to a power that transcends *scientific* intelligibility – but, as explained earlier, a 'naturalist' theology is committed to this kind of transcendence, even though it regards talk of a separate supernatural realm as metaphorical. In response to my suggestion that Resurrection power emerges (somehow) from perfect obedience to the law of love, Hart asks whether others might be just as loving as Christ, so that one might "see manifestations of other deeply loving persons after their deaths: St Francis of Assisi or Mother Teresa of Calcutta, for example" (152). In my Position Statement, I affirmed the Christian tradition of *theosis*: I said that "[t]he pattern set by Christ has its purpose in its being potentially repeated by all humanity" (19). Francis and Teresa, then, have indeed followed the way Christ has shown and they share in Christ's death and Resurrection. And many Christians believe (I certainly do) that our forebears in faith provide resources for us who are now followers of the Way. Their keeping the law of love is not only an example and inspiration for us; from it, as well, there emerges grace for us to manifest the same obedience. I accept, though, that it is a mystery why the experiences of bodily resurrection that challenged and transformed the first disciples do not seem to have been repeated with Francis, or Teresa, or other saints. But I do not see why this mystery, which may reasonably be regarded as a mark of the unique perfecting of humanity in Jesus the Christ, should be regarded as more of a mystery under euteleological monism than it would be under supernaturalist dualism.

Finally, there is the question of how euteleology may deal with the problem of evil. Hart observes that "one will not find much of a theodicy in Bishop's theology" (152). Some philosophers – Trakakis (2013), for one – will see that as an advantage rather than a flaw. Evidently, euteleology neither needs nor permits any speculative account of God's reasons for including evil in the plan of creation, since it rejects the metaphysics of the supreme personal agent. Euteleology is thus free to hold that evil is pointless, a sheer absence of the fulfillment of the divine purposes – and this, of course, is a view it takes from classical theism. Nevertheless, the question does arise how such 'sheer absences' can belong within a reality directed upon the supreme good as its ultimate *telos* and existing only because that *telos* is realized within it. The euteleologist has to hold, I think, that the existence of evil is inherent in what is concretely required for the emergence of real instantiations of the supreme good. To some extent, the resources of traditional theodicies may help in elaborating how this may be so – though without any implication that causing or permitting evil for the sake of some higher good belongs to any actual *plan* for producing a created order that would have to be endorsed and implemented by an ultimately responsible supreme agent. For example, manifesting the supreme good may require morally free personal beings, yet such beings will be able to make, and may actually make, choices that frustrate or undermine manifestations of the good. Or, for another example, the supreme good may be realizable only in a natural causal order whose regular workings sometimes result in the suffering of sentient beings. For all we know, these flaws and limitations are inevitably inherent in further ways we cannot fathom in what it takes for there to concretely exist a reality great enough to realize the supreme good. As God (in effect) says to Job from the whirlwind, 'What would you know about the business of world-building?'[20]

Since, according to euteleology, *everything* that exists does so only because it belongs to an overall reality in which the supreme good is realized, this will be true also of the most horrendous sufferings and injustices. That commitment may seem offensively to diminish the significance of evil – and indeed such offence may be caused by the aesthetic analogy sometimes employed that compares evil with the discordant notes essential

208   *John Bishop*

to an overall harmony. Euteleology is not committed to any such analogy, however. On the contrary, the fact that evils belong to an overall reality that is inherently directed upon the supreme good underlines just how scandalously bad they are! By contrast with a non-theist worldview, euteleology affirms the sovereignty of the good (while at the same time, as indicated in the previous paragraph, allowing that its realization concretely implicates evil). It may be granted that, from an initially neutral standpoint, our experience of good and evil in the world provides no compelling evidence for euteleology's theist affirmation of the sovereignty of the good. From that neutral stance, one may reasonably prefer the view that reality as such is indifferent as to the good, or the Manichean view that reality constitutes a struggle between rather evenly matched forces of good and evil. But euteleology is, of course, an understanding of the divine that is based on faith in the authenticity of the Gospel revelation, which carries the good news of the ultimate sovereignty of the good. Such a faith can, I think, be rationally legitimate – though I accept that this contention may be defended only by rejecting a narrowly evidentialist account of what it is for practical commitment to an overall worldview to be reasonable (and that defence is, for now, another story).[21]

Eaton expresses skepticism about revelatory claims "that come from outside history and time" (137). There is no avoiding Christian reliance on revelation, however. If there is a decisive critique of revelation – either of its very coherence or of the reasonableness of ever accepting commitment to specific revealed truths – then a rational Christianity is untenable. As a naturalist – or anti-supernaturalist – I am as suspicious as Eaton is of revelation "from outside history and time". Revelation, to be consistent with euteleology's monist ontology, can only be revelation of reality's ultimate character *through processes that occur within reality itself*, and, in particular, within the world of those creatures who have developed the consciousness that can receive it. That is the kind of revelation that I think we have in Jesus the Christ.

Do I accept that there might also be, in other religious traditions including those that are non-theist, equally authentic and significant revelations of reality? Yes, I do. From the perspective of a faith that understands itself the euteleological way, however, any apparent revelation that is inconsistent with the stance that takes reality to be inherently directed upon the supreme good and existing only because it realizes the supreme good will have to be judged to be, in that respect, mistaken. Eaton accordingly accuses me of an inclusiveness that is "no more than a mollified version of exclusivism" (139) and of being in danger of making the condescending error of ascribing 'anonymous Christianity' to adherents of other religions that pass the test of coherence with my Christian euteleology. This is an important accusation, not to be taken lightly, and deserving of much further reflection. In that further reflection, I would hope to show that the alternative approach Eaton proposes – namely, "to enter [another's] worldview and try to understand it from the inside" (139) – is not really a "different road"

Second Response 209

from the one I find myself on where I accept my own historical situatedness and seek understanding from the perspective of the religious commitment that is mine. Understanding another's perspective from the inside does not require abandoning or even loosening one's own reasonable commitments, provided these do not entail that all alternative commitments are unreasonable (and here it is vital to allow that one can acknowledge the reasonableness of another's commitment to a worldview that one is oneself committed to regarding as false in some substantive way). Indeed, I suspect that any attempt to enter another's worldview as if one were not oneself committed will produce an understanding that does not go beyond merely objective descriptions of beliefs and practices. The 'inner soul' of a religious worldview is likely to disclose itself only to those who enter into it with their whole self, commitments and all.

Notes

1 I was taught that *a*doration, *c*onfession, *t*hanksgiving and *s*upplication were the 'acts' of prayer. That teaching suggests that the claim that philosophical understanding should be prayerful entails that it can be gained only when we place 'ultimate concern' (as Tillich puts it) in God alone, while cultivating thankfulness as a basic existential orientation and acknowledging our own limitations and shortcomings.

2 Some may hold that in prayer we may be completely open with God without regard to any wider accountability. I suspect that this view is mistaken and am inclined to hold that *in general* openness to God and accountability to others (the right others, and in the right ways) go together. Here, however, I am content to make the point only in relation to Anselm-style philosophizing: asking God, if it be his will, to enable one 'by God's light' to gain understanding of the meaning of one's faith through philosophical reflection, analysis and argumentation absolutely requires appropriate accountability to others.

3 I note that, at one point in her First Response, Heather Eaton reads me as *affirming* the personal omniGod conception, when, in fact, I am just articulating a view I oppose. She may thus be somewhat more friendly to my actual position than she appears.

4 Trakakis correctly describes me as an ontological naturalist, but I would qualify the statement of this position he quotes from David Armstrong "that nothing but Nature, the single, all-embracing spatio-temporal system, exists" (quoted in this volume: 188). This statement is intended only to apply to *concrete* reality – there are also abstracta. And physical concrete reality may be a 'multiverse', consisting not of a single but of a multiplicity of spatio-temporal systems arising from some fundamental physical 'ground'. Most importantly, though, I reject any inference from Armstrong's claim to the conclusion that, concretely, there is no reality but physical reality. There are metaphysically *emergent* things, properties and relations, and some of them are beyond empirical scientific understanding. Though everything concrete is *physically realized*, it is coherent to hold that the physical realizers exist *for the sake of* what they realize (rather than to hold that what is realized is 'nothing but' the physical realizers).

5 I note, in reply to Trakakis, that I did not *endorse* my comment that the God of classical theism "seems patently *religiously* inadequate" (this volume: 6; emphasis in original; emphasis in original). I meant only to report a view that leads many philosophers to reject classical theism, or, at least, 'develop' it in favour of personal

210   *John Bishop*

omniGod theism. I agree with Trakakis that classical theism is religiously motivated by "a strongly felt desire to express the radical transcendence and [the] incomprehensibility of God" (this volume: 186), and I believe that euteleology, too, can satisfy this desire. I am surprised, however, that Trakakis says, a little later, that he sees no "insuperable difficulty in conceiving of God as *a* being" (186), since identifying God as an entity of some kind seems to be precisely what must be avoided if God's radical transcendence is to be honoured.

6   Ken Perszyk and I, as fellow philosophers of religion, share the view that the prevailing personal omniGod conception distorts the theist traditions and have found our explorations of euteleology worth pursuing in the search for viable non-personal alternatives (see Bishop and Perszyk 2014). Perszyk does not share all my philosopher-believer motivations, however. Thomas Harvey does share these motivations, and he is a classical Thomist who rejects certain contemporary interpretations of Thomism that make it out to be in line with personal omniGod theism. Conversations with Harvey have motivated me to consider how my earlier accounts of the euteleological view may be modified or augmented to honour more of the key points of classical Christian theology.

7   Hart puts the point nicely when he says: "while any child can talk *to* God, great learning is required to talk *about* God, and no amount of learning can assure a theologian that he or she is talking properly or well about God" (this volume: 150; emphasis in original).

8   It is implicit in Trinitarianism, I think, that stable complete identifications of the divine cannot be had: to offer complete stable identifications of each of the three Persons would be to fall into tritheism. I am suggesting, then, that the perichoresis of the Trinitarian Persons is reflected in an *intellectual* perichoresis generated when we seek to understand, as far as we may, the Trinitarian mystery.

9   Trakakis concedes that it is "at least intelligible" (this volume: 188) that a teleological explanation may apply in the absence of any appeal to intentional agency. But my position is not that there is a teleological explanation of the universe (in the sense of *all* of reality) in the absence of *any* efficient causal explanation of the universe's actuality: the second clause of the present sentence provides just such an explanation.

10   John Leslie (1989) is a recent defender of an axiarchic understanding of the existence of the universe.

11   Heather Eaton reports that she does not follow my meaning when I say, in my Position Statement, that my baptismal promise to believe all the articles of the Christian faith could not have been a promise to find them true but only to 'accept' them. The belief/acceptance distinction is an analytical philosopher's technicality, no doubt – but I did explain acceptance as taking a proposition to be true in practical reasoning (whether or not one has the attitude that it is true). As I then suggested, the stance of *fides quaerens intellectum* is implicit in carrying out the promise to affirm the articles of the Creed: "This is the faith of the Church: this is my faith, and I seek a viable interpretation of it under which I may indeed find it true." Eaton interprets me as claiming certainty as to the revealed truth of the creeds: well, if there is certainty here, it is a kind of certainty that meets Eaton's proper concern for openness to changing and developing interpretations of what is accepted as revealed. And – as my naturalism should surely suggest? – I am far from "[placing] 'revelation' outside [historical] processes" (135), as Eaton charges. To the contrary, I hold that revelation is possible only within the constraints of lengthy moral and theological cultural evolution. On this theme, see King (2008).

12   The fundamental difficulty in the 'God as Producer of the Universe' picture lies in accommodating the reality of the Producer 'Himself'. Although one may start

Second Response 211

with the affirmation that God is the Creator of *all* things visible and invisible, one has to add *sotto voce* 'except Himself, of course'. God's reality thus gets 'super-added' to the reality of the universe and requires attributing to him special status in order to block the obviously threatening explanatory regress. Doubts then emerge, not only about the coherence of the special attributes that God has to have (such as necessity) but also about how to make sense of God's being in relationship with the creation, given his special ontological status (consider, for example, the puzzles over God's relation to time). And finally, of course, even if the coherence of God as immaterial personal agent-cause of all reality (save himself) is vindicated, there is the problem of how to reconcile his possessing perfect personal goodness given the existence of evil in the creation over which he has ultimate complete control.

13 In response to Eaton's important question about the notion of evolutionary development to which I here appeal, I confirm that it does indeed include the "emergent complexity, adaptation or the symbiotic processes in [biological] evolution" (136) though it goes beyond these and may indeed be, as Eaton says, "a process that is never complete, and is dynamic and never fully understood" (136). One aspect of evolution towards manifestations of the supreme good is a developing moral consciousness that rejects straightforward identification of the good with contingent individual or group human interests. Eaton says: "Christians identify God with their own interests. I see Bishop doing the same, even if I support his images and conclusions" (136). That is an unsettling charge – amounting to an accusation of idolatry – and I do not clearly understand Eaton's reasons for making it (a defence mechanism on my part, no doubt!). I have, indeed, gone on record as accepting a theological ethical egoism (Bishop 1985), and I continue to believe that *right relationship with* God is in my own truest ultimate interests, as it is for all creatures. But that is not at all the same as identifying God with interests of my own that compete with the interests of others: 'competitive' self-interest is a 'false ultimate'.

14 Hart identifies Hegelian roots for the euteleological view and takes me to hold that God "will be" the ultimate cause of the world. He understandably queries this claim, since, as he says, "the world is already here". I did not, however, mean to say that God's being Creator is something purely for the future. But I accept that what I said was potentially misleading. Here is what I said: "[I]n a suitably broad sense, the actuality of the universe will (on this [euteleological] proposal) have an efficient cause, because it will be explicable in terms of its actually realized ultimate and supremely good *telos*. Its *telos* will be its cause, its Omega will be its Alpha" (14). I was using the future tense here only to draw out the implications of the euteleological view, and not with any intended future reference. By 'its *telos* will be its cause' I meant only that '*it will follow that* its *telos* is its cause': as I have here been emphasizing, however, this is only one apt identification euteleology makes of the divine, and – like all the rest – it is necessarily not a complete one.

15 Such an acknowledgment is to be found in Aquinas. Indeed, Aquinas speaks of God as an end "which, just as it precedes in causing, so also does it precede in being" (*Summa Contra Gentiles*, III.18).

16 I think Hart means 'impassible', rather than 'impassive', which connotes that one does suffer, or, at least, may be suffering but without showing it.

17 Hart also says that God transcends time "while also being free to enter its stream" (151): what can this mean if it does not involve a reversion to understanding God as a supernatural personal agent?

18 There are, I think, further aspects of classical theology that euteleology may endorse, such as divine simplicity (God is not the result of any composition, in

212 *John Bishop*

particular the composition of essence and existence) and the related principle that God does not *have* his properties (such as his goodness), rather he *is* them.

19 I am thinking of St Francis' Canticle of the Sun, which, in an early twentieth-century version due to William Draper ("All Creatures of our God and King"), has a verse that runs as follows:

> And thou most kind and gentle Death,
> Waiting to hush our latest breath,
> O praise Him! Alleluia!
> Thou leadest home the child of God,
> And Christ our Lord the way hath trod.

20 See Job 38:4. The personification aptly conveys the point, which applies just as much on the non-personal divine metaphysics proposed by euteleology.
21 I defend a 'modest' fideism based on William James' "The Will to Believe" in Bishop (2007).

References

Bishop, J. 1985. "Theism, Morality and the 'Why Should I Be Moral?' Question." *International Journal for Philosophy of Religion* 17: 3–21.

Bishop, J. 2007. *Believing by Faith: An Essay in the Epistemology and Ethics of Religious Belief*. Oxford: Clarendon Press.

Bishop, J. 2013. "How a Modest Fideism May Constrain Concepts of God: A Christian Alternative to Classical Theism." In *Models of God and Alternative Ultimate Realities*, edited by J. Diller and A. Kasher, 525–542. Dordrecht: Springer. [Reprinted from *Philosophia* 35 (2007): 387–402.]

Bishop, J. and K. Perszyk. 2014. "Divine Action Beyond the Personal OmniGod." In *Oxford Studies in Philosophy of Religion*, edited by J. Kvanvig, vol. 5, 1–21. Oxford: Oxford University Press.

King, R. 2008. *Obstacles to Divine Revelation: God and the Reorientation of Human Reason*. London: Continuum.

Leslie, J. 1989. *Universes*. London: Routledge.

Trakakis, N. 2013. "Antitheodicy." In *The Blackwell Companion to the Problem of Evil*, edited by J. P. McBrayer and D. Howard-Snyder, 363–375. Chichester: Wiley-Blackwell.

12 Heather Eaton

Before responding to each paper there are a few remarks I will make in order to clarify some of the issues arising from my Position Statement.

The first concerns what I mean when claiming there is no such thing as 'Christianity': there are only historical forms of Christianities. The historical and contemporary varieties defy all description. Just the current forms resist classification. In addition to the customary differentiations among Catholics, Protestant(s), Evangelicals, Pentecostals, Southern Baptists, Mennonites, Mormons and others, it is evident that these groupings are unsatisfactory. The mere term 'Catholic' is itself a loose grouping of Roman Catholic and Eastern traditions (Greek, Ukrainian, Russian, etc.). The 'Christianity' of feminist Catholics, moreover, has little in common with that of Vatican clerics, to the point where Rosemary Radford Ruether considered theological communication between the two to be a form of interreligious dialogue (assuming there is dialogue, when in fact there is virtually none). Feminist Catholics in India are also not necessarily 'in communion' with North American feminist Catholics. However, this is still only one level of differentiation.

A second level is cultural. I have travelled extensively, and have been exposed to multiplicities of Christian communities in North America, Europe, Africa, India, China, Korea, and South and Latin America. Then there are the Korean communities in Texas, the Russian Orthodox in Toronto, and on and on. These groups can be further individuated according to whether they are monastic, contemplative, urban, rural, politically active or impervious to politics, open to modernity or not, or hospitable towards postmodernity or not. Some are dedicated to peace and nonviolence, while others, in parts of the United States, for example, encourage all good God-lovin' Christians to carry guns. These differentiations can be endlessly dissected into examinations of rituals, a vast array of beliefs, the interpretation and use of the Bible, central doctrines or dogmas, leadership, communal and personal religious practices, attitudes about sexuality, and interest in and knowledge of other religions. So much more can be mentioned here. The point is: what do we mean by 'Christianity' in the face of all this cultural diversity? Each 'tradition' assumes that it lies within the bounds of a truthful (or Truthful) version

214   *Heather Eaton*

of Christianity. Assuming they cannot all be 'true' in any simple manner, then, it is necessary to develop a sufficiently robust theory of the meaning of 'Christianity' (and I would add of 'religion') that can account for this expanse of diversity across time, cultures and communities.

A third level of diversity relates to the individual Christian. Religions, while not individualistic, are deeply personal. The issue of Christian diversity enlarges exponentially. No two people adhere to Christianity in the same way, with the same meanings, depth, knowledge, identity, understanding, affectivity, core beliefs, actions, etc. We have very little access to the inner realms of others and to the ways in which their 'religiosity' works. People can tell us what they believe, but that does not necessarily provide us with insights into 'how' their religious life infiltrates into and influences their being. Furthermore, some account must be taken of the extensive amount of research that has been undertaken on Christianity, and religion, and the human person (psychology, anthropology, sociology, cognitive sciences, etc.). Alongside this are the many spiritual traditions emphasizing Christianity as a path or way, a journey or pilgrimage with stages or passages and levels of integration, and as an art of living. Christianity is therefore related to living and being and is something dynamic and transformative. It is anything but uniform. Moreover, many religious believers feel they are certain: they are sure they possess the Truth, understood as absolute (which is easier to believe when one ignores differences). I would say that this notion of Truth is projected as existing outside of oneself in a firm or absolute and ahistorical form. This absolves many from uncertainty, or seeking knowledge of, and entering into, the murky realm of deep introspection about how the dynamics of culture, belief, action and personality interact and function. Thus, to answer a question about the Trinity is not straightforward. I have a view – we all hold views – but epistemologically they are views, assumptions, convictions, beliefs, ideas, images, etc. I take the more pertinent questions to be about *how* these ideas are powerful religiously, *how* they function, *how* we bestow meaning, *how* we address the diversity of meanings, and so on. A further and very important topic concerns the historical robustness of Christianity: the narrative and symbols are potent. One could say this is because they are or embody the Truth. However, all religions, including those that no longer exist, make the very same claims to truth.

I refuse to think that the only choices are truth or relativism, objective or subjective, fact or fiction. These are epistemologically weak alternatives and relate truth to content. This, in my view, is a failing of much contemporary Christian theology. Truth is far more complex, differentiated, layered and nuanced. Thus, if religions are as relevant as they seem, and their claims have truth-value, and if one is not to fall into the trap of relativism, then my conclusion is that religions must be akin to languages. Religions are languages about a depth and breadth of reality that can only be presented in highly symbolized forms. Each religion emerges from and speaks to certain experiences. Thus religious languages point to aspects of reality that

Second Response 215

can be experienced and expressed, but the expressions are not literal. They represent, make conscious, refer to, and make present via living symbols something that is real. To learn a language in a classroom is barely meaningful; it would be like learning musical notes without hearing the music. To learn the word 'car' without knowing what a car is is not meaningful. The same is true of religious doctrines. There are experiential references in religious language which supersede the articulation. Importantly, the notes alone cannot reveal the music. However, the experience and articulation function together. Music, of course, can be appreciated without learning the notes. The ability, however, to read, interpret and play according to a musical notation would provide for a more complete experience. Hence theology, without lived experience, might be described as 'notes without music'. To extend this analogy, if we entertain the question of which language is true and which false, the absurdity becomes clear. The same is true of religion.

In an attempt to grapple with this question of religious truth, I have studied the realm of religious imagination and symbolic consciousness. Christianity and all religions are symbolic languages in an inner dialectic between experiences, imaging, interpreting, articulating and communicating. But these 'symbolic languages' are not 'mere symbols'. They are the principal way in which we process images, thoughts, feelings, experiences, acumen, communication and meaning making: we interpret all aspects of life with, and within, symbols in self-amplifying loops of symbolic living. Furthermore, symbolic consciousness is the only way to make sense of all the levels of diversity mentioned earlier.

Having lived in several Christian communities, worked as a chaplain for many years prior to and during my doctoral studies, and taught theology and Christian spirituality for close to two decades, it is the differences amongst Christian communities that have made the greatest impression on me. The theological topic of most interest to me has become not *what* people believe as Christians but *how* they believe, *how* their religiosity functions and what impact it has on them and the world, in this way placing the emphasis on 'why' and 'how' questions. Influenced as I have been by extensive theological studies as well as contemplative Christian spiritualities, religious experiences, the preferential option for the poor, radical justice, feminism and multi-religious contexts, I have my own version of what constitutes 'true' Christianity. At the same time, however, I hold it to be intellectually necessary to be suspicious of certainty, given what I have learned and encountered. Oddly enough, and perhaps unintelligible in this conversation, these expansions of my horizon and knowledge – which have led to skepticism towards the universality and perpetuity of Christianity – have enlarged my religious worldview and increased my spiritual awareness. My sense of the oneness of reality and as well as of a Divine and intricately embedded presence has amplified. As this grows, so does my negative assessment of what passes for 'Christianity'.

Thus when I say there is no such thing as Christianity, only historical forms of Christianities, that the boundaries are not clear, that the truth-claims in themselves are not transparent, that multiplicity reigns and that certainty is arrogant, I am presupposing the above three levels of differentiation and diversity. Also, given this diversity, we might ask: What are the parameters of Christianity? Are the parameters fixed by beliefs, practices, interiority, biblical acumen, doctrinal knowledge, adherence to authorities, community involvement, faith, etc.? And who decides who is in, out, or on the margins? Based on what, precisely? Who's to say who is a Christian? What if it is a way of life that is the measure?

Given that I have no personal knowledge of any of my four dialogue partners, I do not know how they came to occupy the Christian positions they do, or if they have had to engage in battles to find their way. For me, as a feminist in the Catholic tradition, there are many battles. Although a mild feminist when I started my master of divinity degree, by the time I finished my doctorate I was quite radical. I came to learn a great deal about the mechanisms of patriarchy, the nature of beliefs, the relationship between beliefs and social control, about power, about the use of 'tradition' as a weapon, about authority, patriarchal scriptural interpretations, and much more. Hermeneutics and epistemology are the daily bread of feminist theologies. I do not know how many of my dialogue partners have exchanged views – in depth – with feminist Christians, but the questions I raise, and the skepticism I have, are quite customary among feminists. If one then adds an interest in the entire gamut of religions, plus an interest in the evolutionary sciences and distress about the Earth community, then perhaps my intense concern about interpretations, assumptions and biases will make more sense.

I say I am on the 'margins' because many theologians are not willing to engage in depth with – and take seriously the implications of – evolution. Many do not display genuine interest in, or awareness of, the multiplicity, diversity and transient nature of specific religions. Last, few, theologically at least, seem concerned with what is happening to the planet. Other than liberation theologians and ethicists, few contemporary theologians are dedicated to assessing the ambiguous impact of Christianities on the world. Many do not consider the ideological, perhaps even gnostic, nature of a considerable swath of Christian theology. I have, nonetheless, encountered a growing number of fellow-travellers who share my concerns and outlook, but they often travel in more multi-religious intellectual circles. On the other side, there are many Christians who feel certain about the 'content' of Christian revelation and the salvation modalities. The latter group often does not consider the former to be 'Christian'.

In addition, I am on the margins of Christianity as it is delivered in institutional and traditional churches. I do not share the Christian imperialism that permeates the liturgy, especially in North American contexts. I am more than saddened by the large swath of middle-class Christians who remain oblivious to the historical, contemporary and myriad versions of Christianity in the world today, as well as to other, equally potent, rich and highly developed religions. Academically, I find it disturbing and religiously distorting that most theology in North America is taught as if there were no other major world religions. Occasionally reference is made to 'non-Christian religions' – except that these are not 'non-Christian'; they are, rather, religions that are as developed and culturally powerful as Christianity, and some are considerably older. Even the innumerable disparities among Christians are not factored into whatever Christian tradition is under discussion. Finally, I find it appalling that there is so much theological focus on belief, dogma, doctrine, liturgy, biblical exegesis and 'the tradition' and considerably less interest in the impact Christianity has on the world. I find that dogmatism, triumphalism and fundamentalism have seeped far into Christian worldviews, theological methods and content. Therefore, it is more simple to say that I am on the margins of the hegemonic forms. This does not mean I am not deeply spiritually informed and oriented by 'the Christian tradition', or that it is not central to my worldview.

Response to Bishop: 'Naturalist' Christian theism

First, I would like to thank Professor Bishop for taking the time to enter into the spaces out of which I am trying to do theology. I admit that I may come across as a relativist, pragmatist or critical realist, or as utterly selective or subjective. However, I seek to be none of these. I am deeply influenced by the Christian tradition, its soteriology and its view of a unified and integrated reality. I firmly believe that realty, as we know it, is a *divine milieu*, and that human senses have developed to be receptive to the presence of the divine. I claim this to be true, though I have no proof that it is. The experiences out of which religions are born arise from and orient us to see, feel and align ourselves with this dimension of reality (ultimate, foundational). My own experiences attest to this. It all bogs down for me in the assumptions of certitude, the inflexibility of interpretations and the stance that Christian 'content' (beliefs, dogmas, etc.) are transparent. I do not share the assumption that religious language readily reveals its secrets. The hyper-rational and literalist formation of the Euro-western mind inhibits the attempt to seep into the depths of knowing. In theology, it seems, forms of literal meaning have overtaken metaphoric and symbolic meanings.

For example, I have no hesitation in saying that I believe in the resurrection. But that does not actually say much. What I believe is that 'resurrection' is a fundamental dynamic of the biosphere. Life overcomes or emerges from death, regularly. On another level, resurrection is a moral claim, that evil is not the final note of the symphony, nor is chaos, randomness, the will to power, or wealth and success. There are many levels to gleaning the meaning of 'resurrection' as embedded in reality. In spite of what we see occurring within human communities, including the colossal waste of life and the pervasiveness of immorality, these are not the fundamental orientation of life. Life does not thrive in these circumstances: there is no life abundant. This does not mean that after three days Jesus, in bodily form, rose from the dead, and that we too will rise from the dead and find ourselves in a bodily form forever. That makes no sense to me. Resurrection is a symbol about the fundamental alignment of all we can know and thus gives guidance as to how to live. It is a spiritual horizon and moral compass, an imperative even.

"What needs adding" to the outlook of my Position Statement, according to Bishop, "is the transcendent power of the love revealed and vindicated in Christ, for it is this which grounds Christian hope in the midst of life's struggles. Is it possible to understand the transcendence of the power of love without falling back into 'two worlds' supernaturalism? I dare to think that this is possible" (this volume: 127–128).

I cannot agree, or disagree, when it comes to the language of "love revealed and vindicated in Christ", as I don't know what this means. Is this a historical event, a soteriological event, or a notion that refers to, or invites, a fundamental change in history? Is this an analogy, a metaphor or a symbol? There are many variations on how to interpret these images. Further, what are the boundaries of such an expression? Is it the cosmos, the Earth community and/or humanity? How are interpretations substantiated? Such religious language does not reveal what kind of knowledge and experiences it is referencing. I can affirm that 'the Jesus story' symbolizes that there is a transcendent power to love and that more than compliance to the social order is possible, indeed required, for those who commit to this 'story'. Christians are also called to resist that which diminishes such life-giving activities and to be radically generous, whatever the cost. Hope does not concern the future, but the possibilities of the present that we do not see and hence do not believe are a potential. To commit to resurrection as a symbol about the truth of existence – meaning a dynamic that is active in all reality – changes profoundly what one lives for and how one lives, suffers, resists, hopes and dies. I do not regard this as 'post-Christian', though I am aware that it is not the mainstream. Furthermore, I have noticed similar ideas in other religions and spiritualities, which confirms for me that my view is not illusory (or an ideal about living forever) but is a perception. In short, I do not think life is given to us forever or for eternity, sad as that reality may be. The notion of 'resurrection', therefore, must mean something else if it is to have any claim to truth. I believe this is what Ivone Gebara is trying to get at, although she takes the notion of divine immanence further than I would.

Response to Hart: Catholic Christianity

It is evident from both of his papers that Kevin Hart's knowledge of classical theological traditions is stellar. His ability to quote and counter-quote is more than impressive. My background in classical theology is certainly less extensive. My interest in classical theological debates is also not overly high. Such formulations represent one 'form of theology' or theological method, but there are others. For example, much of contemporary theology has shifted dialogue partners from classical philosophies to social sciences.

The questions they are pursuing are distinct. Even the issue of if and how we 'invent and image God', as I have raised it and as has been raised repeatedly over time, is dealt with differently across different eras and contexts. Thus, I cannot accept the tone that 'this is how theology is' that I perceive from Hart's rejoinder.

In Hart's responses to me, he quotes readily from the classics of the tradition. In the discussion on the Trinity he states that since the mid-twentieth century the Trinity has been a significant topic for Barth, Pannenberg, Rahner and von Balthasar, among many others. This is certainly true. However, in one sense these figures were all in the same epistemology and theology class. Although I have studied each of them and appreciate Rahner the most, they do not reveal sufficiently a particular theory of epistemology, theories of religion, methods of interpretation, worldview assumptions and the ethical commitments that ensue. They also do not reveal the religious experiences upon which their theological claims are based. They come from and work within an era of Christian supremacy that seeks to engage with and incorporate the modern (rather than the postmodern) world. Even Rahner and his notion of 'anonymous Christians' could be considered to be intellectually (not habitually) outdated. These theologians are unaware of, and in some cases uninterested in, feminist challenges to theology. They all speak one language, as if there were no other languages. For them, what passes for theology is relatively uniform; otherwise it does not count as theology. Some consider this to be historical, but not contemporary, theology. It represents an era of theology, and a dogmatic theology at that, but it is not my era.

As an aside, I recently directed a doctoral dissertation on evangelical soteriology containing a vocabulary brimming with talk of premillennialism, dispensationalism and crucicentrism and which included much discussion of various interpretations of conversion. This vocabulary is only intelligible within certain Christian communities. The language and symbolism are not alive, and thus not meaningful, in many present-day Catholic settings in North America. Such language, however, is central and even definitive in many evangelical contexts. I am not saying that the questions lying behind the language are not meaningful or that the experiences to which the language refers are not significant: just the actual theological language. I am questioning the transparency of a particular theological vocabulary which passes for 'universal', ultimate, truthful, certain, etc. The only conclusion I can draw is that language is not transparent unless it is lived and symbolically alive, and even then the multiplicity of experiences and interpretations associated with it are difficult to discern. Much theological language is not transportable over time and place.

Hart writes: "Eaton is no friend of orthodox Christian theology, finding its questions, at least those posed in a philosophical register, 'somewhat dated'" (this volume: 155). I did indeed find the initial set of questions given to all of us posed in a manner that is historically dated. However, Hart is quite mistaken in saying that I am "no friend of orthodox Christian theology".

220　*Heather Eaton*

I am interested in contextual theologies, because theology is contextual. The languages are different and are not comprehensible outside of contextual boundaries. Those who claim orthodoxy are nearly always conservative traditionalists and usually male. That constitutes a context, not an orthodoxy. Even feminists have their orthodoxies.

A few years ago I organized a conference on ecumenical, global ecotheology held at the Orthodox Academy of Crete, convened with the assistance of Dr Alexandros Papaderos and others. Dozens of presenters from various countries and Christian traditions participated. This was an excellent example of the diversity of Christianity, likened as it may be to the diversity of languages across the world. At one point I was seated beside a renowned theologian from South Africa who belonged to a conservative-leaning branch of the Christian Reformed Church, listening to a Greek Orthodox theologian from Athens discussing the Trinity. The South African turned to me and said, "I have no idea what he is talking about." I was able to understand the speaker, however, as I come from a (Roman Catholic) tradition that has closer ties to Eastern Orthodoxy than does the South African Dutch Reformed tradition. Yet, if I were to discuss the topic of the Trinity, I would venture in a quite different direction from the Orthodox presenter. These discussions and dialogues cannot function properly without adequate appreciation of context, language and what is meaningful to whom and why. Theological language is highly symbolic and not self-evident. Hart's comments, although quite learned, are also not transparent. They come from and speak to a linguistic club, where those in the club share the same 'PIN' number. But there are always other clubs.

With respect to my comments about the Trinity, I had mentioned that the Trinity is not operative as a living symbol in the religious imagination of many whom I meet. I find this to be quite true. Yet, I am not dismissing the Trinity, as Hart suggests. I am saying that the religious symbol of the Trinity is enormously important to a Christian worldview – not as a belief but as a living, dynamic symbol. However, for most people it is a static belief. Hart states that "most Christians I meet regard the Trinity as the very ground of life" (155). But how could one know this? What does this even mean? How is the belief in the Trinity intertwined into these people's lives?

Throughout his response Hart makes multiple references to God and the Trinity, at one point saying that the term 'person' is inadequate, while elsewhere referring to the Trinity as three 'persons'. Therein lies the conundrum of religious language: it reveals and simultaneously does not reveal to what it is referring. These are the limits of language, and religious language is a very delicate business. And yet, the power of religious language to shape worldviews, personal actions and social orientations must be taken seriously. We must go to great lengths to be clear, and when I say that classical theology is dated what I mean is that such theology is no longer clear to many. Finally, language shapes the world. For example, masculine language for God has been used in most domains of classical theology, past and present. Yet, as

Mary Daly aptly observed, "if God is male, then the male is God". That too is a problem.

Response to Trakakis: Orthodox Christianity

In elaboration and defence of my appeal to Buechner's statement that "all theology is autobiographical" (this volume: 25), I note that theology is not an empirical science. It is rarely verifiable, as compared to cell biology, for example. Doing theology is somewhat akin to interpreting literature, but with a great deal more at stake, in two ways. One, it is individuals (i.e., persons) doing theology, with many aspects of their identity structure and life choices entangled in their views. Two, any theology is as comprehensive as a worldview, and we commit to these worldviews. Yet theologians interpret and adhere to different parts of the Christian worldview and to different degrees. Indeed, the complexities of religious experience and the impact these have on individual lives are quite limitless. In light of these facts, how can theology be anything but autobiographical?

Turning to the matter of 'objective truth', obviously solar systems exist, as does the Bible. The existence of our solar system is verifiable. The Bible is a book of religious teachings and spiritual insights. Both are true, but of course not the same kind of truth. The Bible contains truth, or truths, and yet must be interpreted. In addition, is everything in the Bible equally true? Does the Book of Numbers embody or express the same kind of truth as wisdom literature? The Bible is powerful – that much is true. I am reminded of Mieke Bal's comment: "The Bible, of all books, is the most dangerous one, the one that has been endowed with the power to kill" (1989: 14). To claim biblical truth means that one can indicate *what* exactly is 'true' in the Bible. The challenge is also to discuss *why* and *how* the Bible is truthful. Truth, interpretation and introspection intersect and cannot be separated from one another. There is very little agreement among Christians about the Bible's veracity. I engage with feminists and liberationists who view the Bible as prophetic, thematic of liberation, insightful and revelatory (with many qualifications), and I am sure this would not be enough to be in the Christian club of this group.

From another truth angle, the evidence in support of evolution seems objective and factual. It is truthful about the processes and dynamics of the Earth, and yet it can be readily dismissed on the basis of certain biblical or Christian ideological commitments. This is what Stephen Jay Gould called the 'non-overlapping magisterium'. Do we accept this view of 'truth', retreating into positions that we have different truths, different modalities of truth or different worldviews?

Truth in religious discourse is difficult to elucidate. There is no doubt that people find meaning in Christianity, but often it is not the same meaning. From the early church to the present there has never been much agreement about such things as the meaning of the scriptures or tradition, or about what constitutes the ideal Christian life. One must also take into account the Inquisition, slavery, patriarchy, colonial conquests and other such cultural expressions of Christianity. We could call these aberrations, but intellectually this is a dubious approach. What does Trakakis make of all this interpretative sprawl and the cultural consequences of 'Christianity'?

In my view, then, truth does not relate in any simplistic way to biblical content or theological doctrine, or to the meaning drawn, but to the process of meaning making. But that also is not sufficiently clear. Bias, agenda, personal interests, cultural events, levels of inquiry and biblical and religious knowledge all come into play in this process. There are also queries about what kind of 'truth' is derived from what kinds of passages in the Bible – historical, ethical, metaphysical, theological, etc. And that is just the Bible.

Religions are true, in the same manner that music and languages are true. This does not simply mean that they exist. Rather, the point is that they are saying and doing something from the most profound realms of human existence, where experience, intuition, symbolism and ultimate concern intersect. Religions emerge from deep experiential places and demand articulation. They are communal languages. They inspire, and if integrated into our lives, make demands upon us. They live and die. Theology, especially of the systematic or philosophical kind, deals with the articulation level, which is always highly symbolic. Discourse at this level must be meaningful and alive in the religious imagination in order to have 'truth' power. Nonetheless, such discourse often seems disconnected from its experiential source, because most often it is understood or accepted as an autonomous realm of knowledge.

For example, I do not pray to Zeus or Hera, and I imagine few today do. Similarly, the rituals of Zoroastrianism are not intelligible to me, yet these were (and are) true for the practitioners of this religion. I could study this religion, even in depth, but *never* experience and thus *never* understand their form of religiosity. What is true is that the enterprise of religion refers: it points to, illuminates, inspires, evokes, educates the imagination. Religious language refers more than it describes.

Furthermore, religions come and go. But what abides, from my viewpoint, is the religious or spiritual dimension (dynamic, orientation, invocation) of humankind and the Earth community. Is this objectively true? I'm not sure, but the evidence I have accumulated to date suggests so. As I see it, the more one learns about the many religions of the world, past and present, and the more one discovers about evolution and cosmic processes, the more certain I am of the 'divine milieu' and its revelatory dynamic. By the same token, the less certain I am of the eternal or universal quality of any specific articulation.

So wherein lies my certainty? Trakakis writes of my rejection of certainty: "Such a categorical denial of certainty itself bespeaks of certainty, and once more a performative contradiction lurks here" (191). The analogy of religions as languages is again appropriate in this context. If religions are languages, then to ask which language is true is absurd. How can one have,

Second Response 223

or not have, certainty about a language? I can only understand and navigate the world within it (to varying degrees), or not. In addition, my quest for a solid foundation to 'truth' has taken me down multi-religious paths, scientific inquiries, extensive forays into interiority (including the domains of experience, consciousness and imagination at work in religious contexts) and research into the cultural impacts of Christianity, as mentioned earlier. Certainty is easy when the horizon is very limited. It is dogmatic formulations, of the Trinity for example, that I cannot embrace wholeheartedly. But if the Trinity refers to the presence of the divine, as experienced, in the ways I explained in my Position Statement, then all is well. Doctrines are highly sophisticated attempts to give expression to such experiences. The experience is where certainty lies, not the expression.

I am convinced that people have religious experiences, in various forms. In the same way that poetry attempts to open spaces that are otherwise closed, religious expressions, albeit highly symbolic, seek to open spaces for people to see, hear and feel levels of reality that are not immediately apparent. If the circumstances align, and one 'sees', then this takes on the dimensions of truth and reality. Such experiences are revelatory in that one sees what others do or could see. They are personal but not individualistic. In this way they are revelatory and universal. We feel compelled to give expression to these experiences in words like the following: "God is my rock, saviour, lover . . . God is like a potter, a mother eagle . . .". Another religion, an alternate version of Christianity or simply another person will employ their own vocabulary. Put simplistically, what can be considered 'true' here? These expressions are fluid, contextually contained and often personal and historically contingent. The experiences, while differentiated, are foundational. There is little doubt that experiences we call 'religious' occur, but not to everyone, and yet there are infinite possibilities.

Religious experiences can be particular, as one sees the divine presence in this child, or that tree; or they can be vast, such that the universe is saturated with beauty, that the thrust of life is towards abundance, that forgiveness is possible, that justice is a possibility and worth the struggle. Mircea Eliade uses the term 'hierophany' – meaning a revelation of the sacred – to describe these experiences. Eliade (1961: 12) writes that "for those who have a religious experience all nature is capable of revealing itself as cosmic sacrality. The cosmos in its entirety can become a hierophany . . . the sacred is equivalent to a power, and, in the last analysis, to reality. The sacred is saturated with being." In like fashion, North American Indigenous traditions teach that every leaf and tree reveals the Mystery of the Great Spirit. I 'see' this.

I remain convinced that many people have religious experiences and do not identify them as such and are often overwhelmed and disoriented by them. I am equally convinced that many 'true' believers who can quote scripture and tradition by heart have not had religious experiences. However, in order to attain some level of spiritual maturity, it is vital that something from this 'sacrality' be experienced, taught, articulated and affirmed.

224   Heather Eaton

What in all this counts as 'objectively' true, as something upon which I would be prepared to stake my life? Although I do not think it can be proven to be objectively true (which in itself does not render it subjective or relative), I hold as *true* that the universe is saturated with Divine presence. I take this as objectively, universally true. I am not inventing or fantasizing it; I am discovering or discerning it. It is a revelation. It is true for all who can 'see' it as such. It is a shared insight, once experienced. It must, however, be experienced – and then it can be recognized as 'objectively' true. Learning the catechism or memorizing the scriptures will not substitute for (though they may affirm) these experiences.

I will avoid questions to do with Jesus for the moment, although of course 'the Jesus story' is central to Christianity and also to me – but again as a living religious symbol. Symbols indeed are the highest form of religious consciousness, surpassing other forms of human knowing. To describe my view as one where, say, the Trinity is "a mere symbol" (to quote Michael Rea, this volume: 167) is to fail to appreciate the significance, vitality, richness and complexity of symbols.

From a theological stance, I take the onus upon and within myself to claim that there are religious experiences which are real, ultimate and truthful. I do not make appeal to the authority of church fathers, the Bible (although they recount a plethora of religious experiences) or tradition, even though I could. I would not find such a methodology intellectually honest. These aspects of Christianity as a religious tradition describe, explain and affirm such experiences. Even so, the interpretative moment lies within myself, and I consent and conform to this truth. Yet I am not alone. Pseudo-Dionysius, Eliade, Blondel, Otto, Teilhard de Chardin, Hildegaard von Bingen, Eckhart, Thomas Berry, Rosemary Radford Ruether, Ivone Gebara and many others could be cited as fellow travellers. We may all be wrong. It is a gamble of truth, but it is one I am willing to make with my life. Is there a performative contradiction in this, as Trakakis thinks? Perhaps.

The key difference is wherein lies the authority of interpretation. I refuse to place the authority of truth in dogmatic statements, historical documents, religious texts or 'mere beliefs'. For example, I do not believe that Mary was a virgin in any literal sense; this would be to invoke a magical or miraculous realm, which I find unpersuasive. Further, there were many virgin-mother goddesses in Mesopotamian cultures of that time. A virgin-mother was an operative symbol in many cultures, one that has been carried over into the present. What it meant, how it functioned, and the dialectic between the symbol, religious consciousness or imagination and cultural practices are impossible to assess. It was, and perhaps still is, a multi-faceted symbol.

Many people I encounter think of Mary as literally a virgin. Contemporary theologians and especially the Catholic tradition continue to support and seek to substantiate this view of Mary rather than challenging it. As a result, Mariology cascades into endless ideologies about and demands on women, women's bodies, sexuality and motherhood.

The urgent problem that needs to be addressed, in my view, is that religious experiences are not foundational within contemporary Christian theology. The content has become objectified, or is discussed primarily in terms of belief, or becomes a matter of faith if you are unable to 'believe'. Doctrines and teachings are not perceived as symbols emerging from and speaking to depth experiences. Theology is often a stagnant language, becoming information that one is required to accept on faith. Such a framework for understanding Christianity or religion has become dominant and is often adhered to in rigid, fundamentalist ways.

Trakakis asks, "why stake your life on something that you do not take to be (objectively) true?" (191). But much of our life is built on hope. Is what I hope in objectively true? Not always. I stake my life on the premise that moral judgements and ethics are matters of human responsibility and must be struggled for and made visible in their absence. I consider the beauty of creation and the Earth community to be modes of divine presence and that ecological ruin is sinful. I stake my life on this, against how the vast majority (including Christians) understand the dialectic of nature and sacrality. What is objectively true here? I would stake my life on the view that justice – in spite of its overwhelming deficiencies in practice – is not merely a better pragmatic option. Justice is a means to revealing the dignity of life, even if in potential and not obvious form. My positions, however, are not 'provable'; they are interpretations and constitute my religious commitments. According to Trakakis, "religious commitment requires the meta-belief that one's religious beliefs are factually or objectively true" (190). This is an absolute and normative – but also utterly undefended – claim.

'Objective truth' is a problematic category. Beauty, also in the eye of the beholder, is a powerful force. That beauty is part of the human array of experiences is objectively true. But what we each experience to be beautiful is radically different. Experiences of beauty cannot be commanded or enforced. They are individually experienced, or not. What is objectively true here? If religions are understood as languages, then that religious languages exist is factual or objectively true. But that is as far as the concept of factuality or objective truth will go in this context. Beyond this we enter myriad modalities of interpretation.

In light of my earlier statement that "we cannot know the nature of God, or have any certainty about the existence of a divine entity" (26), Trakakis goes on to say: "Eaton seems quite certain that certainty in religion (or theology) is not possible" (191). I did not put these together in this manner. My view is that certainties lie on a spectrum from relatively easy to extremely difficult. As one moves towards claims of certainty about the nature of God, the meaning of 'truth' becomes increasingly complex and multi-layered. People who claim certainty about the nature of God (assuming they derive this from some proof) are . . . unique. Trakakis seems to have certainty of some kinds. I suggest this is the certainty of one's beliefs, held up

226 *Heather Eaton*

by a tradition, communities and a life dedicated to learning about and living within these parameters.

Trakakis also states that dogmatism and triumphalism no longer have a place in religion and theology. The intent no doubt is that they should not have a place. Yet in practice they are omnipresent. Is theology what we prescribe or what we describe? If we start with what is lived, then it gets messy immediately. If we start with how it 'should be', then immediately we have issues of authority, interpretation, relationship to the tradition(s), etc.

Turning, now, to the subject of the afterlife, Trakakis writes: "My own position, which I cannot detail or defend here, is that if there is no afterlife, then human life has no objective value or purpose (and this, even if there is a God)" (191). From there he proceeds to critique my position. Yet I would not connect these ideas: no afterlife, thus human life has no objective value. Trakakis goes on to ask,

> What is so great and wonderful about life here on Earth, given that it is over in the blink of an eye, all earthly pleasures and goods are transient and attached to some degree of pain or suffering, and the world is replete with illness, tragedy and evil? I do not mean to deny that earthly life is to be valued, cherished and enjoyed. But to overestimate the worth and goodness of this life is not simply naïve but also insensitive to the darkness, sorrow and cruelty of so much of human (and animal) existence.
>
> (192)

I see this as an interpretation, influenced by the author's own experiences and beliefs regarding goodness and suffering, vulnerability and death. Trakakis holds that a solution of sorts is provided in Christianity and Buddhism in terms of the postulation of an afterlife. I do not share his judgements about human life, and that is not because I am naïve or insensitive to darkness, sorrow and cruelty, as seems implied in this quotation. Quite the opposite, in fact, and that is precisely why the afterlife is less appealing to me. Back to the labyrinth of interpretations.

Trakakis later writes: "I would rather, like Camus, *rebel* against our wretched predicament and seek to ameliorate it as far as possible" (192; emphasis in original). The amelioration is sought in an afterlife. By contrast, I seek amelioration in this life, because this as far as we know is all that has been given us. Anything else is sheer speculation. Trakakis further asks, "why is life here on Earth necessarily or intrinsically better than any other life we could imagine?" (192). I ask in turn: why are we imagining another life when we know very little about this one? We have not properly attended to the present life; there is much in this life that we disregard and ignore, and thus we do not value it. We could of course imagine alternative realities, but why should we? Do we do so because we cannot accept the possibility that we have been given life for a fraction of time, and that is all? Perhaps gratitude is the appropriate spiritual response. This does not entail gratitude for a wretched life but rather means that we have a shared responsibility that all life be abundant, not wretched. Perhaps God's creation is woven throughout with fragility, vulnerability and death so as to ensure sensitivity, gratitude, creativity, attentiveness, carefulness, responsibility and heightened awareness. We may not like this, but perhaps this is the gift that has been granted us.

The fact that we can imagine alternatives should not be confused with factual evidence. On the other hand, our imagination can be employed as a vehicle for the interpretation of existence – in this respect, fact and fiction often blend. Maybe there is more to life, maybe not. I do not know, and I am not prone to staking my life on something so tenuous. Furthermore, while I agree that belief in the afterlife does not necessarily lead to the denigration of this life, I think the evidence is compelling that it has in fact done just that.

Trakakis states that most people share the belief that human persons in some form survive their death. I think it would be more accurate to suggest that it is not necessarily the human 'person' that survives but more that life itself does not end with death. These are quite distinct. I consider the latter to be true but the former pure speculation. As I mentioned previously, we want to see ourselves as infinite and of ultimate value because we deny the conditions of life as we experience them: we refuse to accept that we could be transient. Also, just because most people believe something is not proof of anything except that they believe it. Countless examples confirm this.

Trakakis writes of beliefs in the afterlife:

> A possible reason why such beliefs nowadays present themselves (to many academics) as unintelligible or meaningless is the prevailing naturalism (or materialism) in the academy: if one believes that nothing but the natural world exists, and that a human person is identical with their physical body or brain, then notions like 'God', 'miracles' and 'resurrection' are likely to strike one as incredible, superstitious and perhaps even incoherent. But if one were already committed to a position of dualism (both material and spiritual entities exist) or even a position of idealism (reality is mind-like), then I would suspect that much of the contemporary skepticism and disbelief towards the afterlife would disappear. (193)

I think there are more than these choices. I don't know if there is a decline in belief in the afterlife. And if so, I am not sure this quotation reveals the reason why. Furthermore, dualistic positions are declining in academic discourses. Regardless, belief in the afterlife is a *belief*, one that is built into the salvation scaffold of Christianity. It may be fine to be committed to such a belief and its accompanying worldview, as long as it is acknowledged as a belief, conviction and commitment. What is involved here, in other words, is an interpretation that consists in judgements about suffering, evil, vulnerability and the significance of the human person in the grand scheme of things. But other interpretations are also possible, even if they are not

228 *Heather Eaton*

palatable in relation to the 'tradition', which usually only means in sync with one's own presuppositions.

Trakakis wonders whether I have succumbed to the genetic fallacy when offering explanations for the continued endurance of afterlife-beliefs. He concedes that I am "not attempting to disprove or disconfirm the existence of an afterlife. That would be a clumsy error" (193). He goes on to ask: "But then why does she so confidently reject the afterlife? I suspect . . . that a prior commitment to naturalism is doing much of the work here" (193). I don't reject the afterlife. I don't believe in it either. I have no idea if there is an afterlife, and I regard those who believe in it as though it were the 'Truth' and organize their lives around it as if it were a certainty are fooling themselves. I think none of us knows. I reject beliefs masquerading as truths, and I desire greater honesty from Christians and especially theologians. They ought to at least admit that the belief in an afterlife is nothing more than a belief, or something analogous to an idea, hypothesis or ideal. The hegemonic Christian salvation scaffold that includes an afterlife for each person is, in my view, a house built on sand. Each aspect can be reinterpreted, but such attempts are only occurring at the margins. Further, contemporary Christian theology is doing a poor job of portraying that there are intimations of larger spiritual forces at work in the universe and that 'we' may not be the centre of the story.

Finally, my views are not reducible to naturalism or materialism. I explained throughout my Position Statement that I am a panentheist. I am fully aware of the difference between pantheism and panentheism. I am simply more cautious than others about claiming to know what is beyond a temporal existential knowing.

Response to Rea: (Reformed) Protestantism

It seems from Rea's Position Statement and First Response that he takes there to be far more homogeneity within Christianity than I do, and also that his understanding of Christianity is much more centred on doctrine than is mine. Also, I sense that there is an underlying assumption that the positions expressed are 'how it is'. Thus these presuppositions operating throughout become the gauge of Christian legitimacy.

Quoting from my Position Statement, Rea writes: "By the end of her chapter, one finds her declaring that 'historically there is no such actuality as "Christianity"'. It is surely hard to have a Christian worldview if there is no such thing as Christianity!" (this volume: 167). But he omits to note that I immediately went on to say that "there are countless forms, interpretations, contradictions and inconsistencies" within Christianity. Clearly, the point being made was that, in the light of diverse historical, contemporary and cross-cultural forms of Christianity, it is more accurate to speak of 'Christianities' (or Christian worldviews) in the plural rather than 'Christianity' in the singular. If there were only one Christian worldview, how could we account

Second Response 229

for the radical diversity that actually exists amongst Christians? Also, how could Rea, or anyone for that matter, confidently assume that they possess the sole 'correct' Christian perspective? I would like to pose a challenge and to probe how the constellations of certainties work within Christian circles.

Rea, as I mentioned, seems to think that there is considerably greater uniformity within Christianity than actually seems to be the case. Also, Rea makes doctrine, or consistency with traditional creedal formulas, the benchmark for judging who is to count as a (genuine) Christian. I would say, however, that most Christians in the pews (and I speak as someone who has spent over thirty-five years in pews as both parishioner and pastor) and many students (and here I speak from my twenty years' experience in teaching theology) do not know the doctrines in any depth. Would Rea therefore say that all these people are not Christian?

Rea speaks of "the way in which the meaning of the terms 'Christianity' and 'Christian faith' are fixed" (164). There is, however, less consistency than he claims, there being far-ranging interpretations of what he calls the central and 'fixed' meaning of Christianity and the Christian faith.

Later Rea summarizes my position as follows:

> God is a mere human invention. . . . The doctrine of the Trinity is a mere symbol. The traditional story of creation, fall and redemption is offensive. The doctrine of the resurrection is unintelligible. Moreover, Eaton makes it clear that her view is *not* that these traditional Christian views are strictly false but nevertheless useful metaphors. On her view, the notions of truth and falsity do not even apply to religious claims; and, taken as mere symbols, traditional Christian claims about creation, fall, redemption, the Trinity and the resurrection are outmoded at best and offensively patriarchal and otherworldly at worst.
>
> (167; emphasis in original)

Much of this is simply incorrect. On my view, God is *not* an invention. What humans invent are images of God. The derogatory use of the phrase "mere symbol" bespeaks a lack of familiarity with the meaning and use of symbols, the nature of symbolic consciousness and, more broadly, research into the complexities of how the human mind forms representations of experiences, communicating them through symbolic language. The languages of the various religions are indeed the most profound and complex kinds of symbolism we have.

Regarding the doctrine of the resurrection, I do reject simplistic or literal interpretations of it, though it must be borne in mind that this is a doctrine that has received many interpretations through history and continues to do so today.

As to the question of truth, I return to the analogy that religions are akin to languages. On this view, the categories of truth and falsity do not apply in any conventional or straightforward manner to religious beliefs, as the

230   Heather Eaton

content of these beliefs is not literal. If, like Rea, we reject or minimize the use of metaphor and symbols in philosophy of religion, then how are religious truths to be expressed? My quarrel with much philosophical theology is this lack of transparency about issues to do with religious language and the nature, meaning and epistemology of doctrinal statements. Further, if religious truths are so readily obvious, and the meaning transparent, then why is there such extensive disagreement? If Christian truths are so clear for all to see, then why has Christianity given birth to the Inquisition, the Lord's Resistance Army, just war theories as well as pacifist traditions, Catholics for free choice as well as anti-abortion leagues, and so on. How does Rea deal with these inconsistencies within the Christian community? No doubt, he adopts a position on each or many of these matters, as do I, but my point is that Rea as well as those within the Christian fold who take positions contrary to his make appeal to the same scriptures and tradition. I too have a gauge of what Christianity means, but I am acutely aware it is an interpretation.

I appreciate Rea's queries concerning my use and understanding of the notion of 'evidence'. I think this is an accurate assessment – that is, I use the term in different ways. I am not a rationalist only, and certainly not a materialist, and I am not interested in some levels of speculation. For example, I have colleagues who speculate on multiple universes and engage in theological reflection with this in mind. This is something that holds no interest to me. I am deeply concerned about our planet and what is happening to our 'divine milieu'. I regard the Christianity I have adopted as something that has been shaped and driven by religious experiences brought forth by the natural environment, as well as something formed through encounters with people carrying immense vulnerabilities at L'Arche and later Covenant House. I have regularly come face-to-face with imperialism, dogmatism and fundamentalism in the Christian community, and this too has likely influenced my views. I do think facts, values, interpretations and ideals are blended, so no doubt I am not consistent with what I mean by 'evidence'. I will pay closer attention to that.

I remain committed to a religious life, but I resist the tight boundaries Christians often place around their tradition, arrogating for themselves the right to judge who is in and who is out on the basis of what I see as arbitrary beliefs. I find Christian theological conflicts, ideological territories and supremacy and ignorance with regard to other world religions quite tiresome now. I find Christian theology to be internally preoccupied, and this is why I say I am on the margins. Still, why does one have to be a Christian in an exclusive sense? Why cannot someone learn from Christianity, Indigenous traditions and others? Several theologians (Kwok Piu Lan, for example) consider themselves hybrids, learning from and identifying with various religious traditions at once. Why must one be either in or out, Christian or not? Such either/or thinking is invalid.

References

Bal, M. (ed.). 1989. *Anti-Covenant: Counter-Reading Women's Lives in the Hebrew Bible*. Sheffield: Almond Press.

Eliade, M. 1961. *The Sacred and the Profane: The Nature of Religion*, translated by W. R. Trask. New York: Harper & Row.

13 Kevin Hart

I thank my four respondents for the time and interest they have taken in reading my Position Statement, which was originally entitled 'Phenomenology of the Christ: A Very Brief Sketch', but was given the editorial title 'Catholic Christianity'. Of course, the editorial title elides some things and adds others. I doubt that any Catholic theologian could give, in the compass of a short essay, much of an idea of what the Church teaches about the faith. Not even if I had hewed simply to Aquinas could I have done so; close attention to even one question posed by the editors that took into account even a little of the *Summa theologiæ*, let alone requisite reference to his exposition of Boethius' *De hebdomadibus*, which is so important for his understanding of God, would exceed the bounds of even a long essay, and reference to the various Thomist schools would turn an essay into a book. What is elided in the editorial title is the particular project of which the essay is 'a very brief sketch', namely the attempt to develop a phenomenology of the Christ. My work in this area draws from phenomenology at large and is informed by my contemporaries, especially Jean-Yves Lacoste, Jean-Luc Marion and Robert Sokolowski, although it strikes out in a new direction, one informed, I trust, by Scripture and conditioned by the magisterium of the Church.

* * *

Catholicism and Orthodoxy are the closest of the Christian communions; we share a common history for the first thousand years of church life, and our doctrines are, for the most part, either the same or similar, or the differences are not difficult to grasp in outline. The main doctrinal issue that separates us is our varying interpretations of the triune nature of God, but there are also cultural and methodological matters to keep in mind. Orthodoxy has maintained a very considerable reserve with respect to the rights of modern scholarship of Scripture and doctrine that the Catholic Church has significantly reduced since *Divino afflante spiritu* (1943).

Oddly, though, it is not the understanding of the Trinity with which Trakakis and I disagree, but about the scope, status and strength of modern skepticism with respect to the central claims of Christianity. It is not what

Second Response 233

one would expect from someone in the Orthodox communion. In particular, what disturbs Trakakis is that I place weight on "certain claims of a historical nature", all to do with Jesus of Nazareth, and in particular Trakakis is bothered by "the belief that Jesus rose from the dead" on the ground that this teaching "is open to precisely the same kind of investigation that historians make of any other event" and consequently this belief "is open to all the vagaries, doubts and interpretive and evidential problems confronting any historical statement". Worse, given those doubts, interpretations and problems, "a certain tentativeness and skepticism is required" (this volume: 179).

As I read these precautions, all of which are very familiar to me and, I suppose, all Christian theologians, I wonder first if not "a certain tentativeness and skepticism is required" for a great many events reputed to have occurred in the ancient world, and if historians can do very well in overcoming a skeptic determined not to yield ground. What hard evidence do we have that Koroibos won the first stadion race at the Olympic Games? Yet most of us readily follow the principle of credulity and do not doubt Koroibos' victory. The case is somewhat different with the resurrection, needless to say, yet is it reasonable to expect historical documentation of a kind that a modern person would find satisfying for a highly unusual event witnessed by uneducated men and women in the backwaters of the Roman Empire? I also wonder how Trakakis deals with the skeptical questions he puts to me, for they apply just as much to anyone in the Orthodox communion, which is not known for either tentativeness or skepticism in its promulgation of doctrine. Rather, its spirituality draws its character and its strength from being suffused in the divine mystery. Trakakis wants some sort of certitude about core Christian beliefs, and he is not alone. His fellow Orthodox analytic philosopher Richard Swinburne also eschews historical criticism and maintains by way of Bayes' theorem that it is about 0.97 probable that Jesus was raised from the dead (see Swinburne 2003). But the approach is at best shared by very few. Indeed, while many analytic philosophers of religion write often about God, hardly any ever write about Jesus.

Trakakis asks why the historicity of the resurrection of Jesus cannot be "assessed according to such standard criteria as explanatory scope and power, internal consistency, simplicity, degree of being *ad hoc*, etc." (180). Now historical critics of the Gospels do all these things, and in doing so they make the methodological assumption that the Gospels are just like any other ancient text. In some ways they are, and historical criticism has been able to tell us a great deal about the composition and transmission of the Gospels: the Q hypothesis, for example, is able to answer many questions about Matthew and Luke. It is a hypothesis – no one has a document in hand called 'Q' – and is therefore open to revision in the light of further research. Historical critics also make assumptions by virtue of their trade, and one assumption is troubling for Christians. It is this: no one can be raised from the dead and return to life in this world. When reading any literature of the past, even that which purports to be historical (according to our modern

234   *Kevin Hart*

understanding of the word), one must simply assume what we all know to be true: once someone is dead he or she does not return to life on earth. It is precisely this assumption that is vigorously contested by the Gospels, and it is contested in the mode of testimony.

Historians, like lawyers, must often rely on testimony; and, as is well known, they probe testimony wherever possible by putting it to the question. (Even so, testimony plays several significant epistemic roles, as philosophers are well aware these days.[1]) Is there room to question the testimony about the resurrection of Jesus? To be sure, there is. It is not wholly consistent across the Gospels and Paul's letters, for one thing, although what historians can tell us about the dates of composition of the Gospels hardly inclines us to think that we should expect first-hand testimonies from diverse places to cohere. We are talking about Gospel testimonies most likely given in Aramaic and then written in Koine Greek decades after Jesus had been executed. These are testimonies that are not to be measured by the canons of modern history but were already embedded in faith-commitments of various sorts and that were meant to shore up faith as it had been received from earlier generations and by liturgical practices. Belief in the resurrection of Jesus is early, common and general; it easily passes the Vincentian test of orthodoxy, and that is what Christians look to. Exactly what 'resurrection' means, however, is open to competing interpretations: the raising of the physical body, the raising of the 'flesh' (*Leib*: the subjective body), and so on.

The historian's commitment that all ancient texts, no matter what, must be subject to the same assumptions about human life and its relations with the divine is, Trakakis says, similar to Husserl's ἐποχή, and that claim is mistaken. When Husserl speaks of ἐποχή he has in mind suspending the thesis of the natural world, and it is that thesis that historical critics decline to suspend in any way or to any extent. They are committed to the world as pre-given and have no motivation, as historians, to bracket the very cast of mind that enables them to do their job. Husserl would call them 'naïve' not because their researches are not valuable but because they have an uncritical relation to the empiricism on which they depend for their insights. Myself, I have little interest in following Husserl in his quest for absolute consciousness as a firm ground for history and the other sciences, social as well as natural; but I shall leave any explanation of my sense of phenomenology until later in this response. Suffice it to say now that, once again, Trakakis is mistaken when he says that the ἐποχή "is just as unwarranted in historical research as it is in philosophy" (180). Not all philosophers practice ἐποχή with transcendental reduction in mind, but many of them suspend common sense when doing philosophy. One takes a step away from explanatory and normative frameworks and looks at them sideways, as it were, in order to pose and consider philosophical questions. The philosopher writing a skeptical essay on cause and effect, nonetheless, does not caution her friend who smokes to disregard the warning 'Smoking causes cancer' when they are at the checkout of the supermarket. Nor does she demand from the

Second Response 235

management a narrow account of the evidence he or she has for advancing the statement or the steps in reasoning taken to reach it. Instead, she goes home, brackets a commonsense understanding of cause and effect, and continues to write her essay.

My approach to Christian theology requires me to begin as close to the synoptic Jesus as possible, and that means that I place emphasis on his parables. For Trakakis, this is a big problem. He tells us that Jesus "was preaching to the converted" since the Jews of his day already believed in God and followed Torah to a greater or lesser extent (180). It is certainly true that Jesus offers no arguments for the existence of God, and to expect him to have done so would be anachronistic. Also, it is a good thing that he did not venture any arguments of that sort: none of them, considered just by themselves, has anything like the coercive power that philosophers these days would like to find. What Jesus did was far more compelling. He spoke with authority to the people who knew the word 'God' and made the person it refers to concretely thinkable. (The note of authority is distinctly heard, for example, in John 3:3–5 and John 6:26–27.) God is not an abstraction, inherited from one's forefathers and foremothers, but a loving Father who is at once like one's own father yet at the same time utterly unlike any human father. Jesus was not engaging in apologetics; he was seeking for those he met in the villages and on the roads of the Holy Land to be in an intimate relationship with the one he called 'Father'. I am not engaged in apologetics, either; but if I were I would not go door to door with the ontological argument or the teleological argument, or with a volume by Swinburne under my arm so I could argue, tooth and nail, that the resurrection of Jesus very probably happened.

Rather, I would want people to read the testimonies about Jesus with all due care and to come to see, in the context of prayer, that it is indeed possible to live in a relationship with the one he called 'Father', a relationship that can be sustained and nourished by the sacraments of the Church. In the context of that relationship, other things can be of use to bolster it: natural theology offers *prima facie* evidence for God's existence, which is not to be sneezed at (even Hume was very strongly tempted by it), and some of the proofs have merit, when they are regarded as pointers and not as theorems (see Hume 1948: 94). The theological virtues, Aquinas says, are faith, hope and charity. It should be noted that knowledge is not one of them; and yet Aquinas goes on to point out that the gifts of the Holy Spirit entwine themselves in and around those virtues, strengthening them and supplementing them: knowledge, understanding, counsel and wisdom are of particular interest to the philosopher, since, Aquinas says, they direct the intellect (see Aquinas, *Summa theologiæ*, Ia-IIæ q. 68). But one receives them only once one has committed oneself to Christ. *Crede ut intelligas*, as Augustine says.

Trakakis ends with another issue coming to the fore, namely that phenomenology cannot help in delivering us from "divine hiddenness" and, in particular, from "the morass of competing truth-claims that the various

236   *Kevin Hart*

religions make" (182). To these complaints I can say just two things. In the first place, the hiddenness of the Father is stated in the New Testament (John 6:46), and no philosophical or theological method can make him visible. The Father has sent the Son, who is the image of the Father, so believers hold; and it is phenomenology's task to describe, as concretely as possible, the meaning of this image. To my mind, Jesus suspends 'world' in telling his parables in order to lead us back to a prior claim that his Father has on us, which Jesus illuminates by calling it the βασιλεία. This leads to the second issue. Does phenomenology have something to contribute to comparative theology? I think it does: it can tell us quite a lot about the βασιλεία in the analogues of it envisaged by people of other faiths. Jesus tells us that we are to love God and to help to bring on the βασιλεία and that these two things are fundamentally one. For those brought up in the Christian faith that is quite enough; and for those who practice other faiths they are to bring on the βασιλεία by their own lights and, in that activity, they will be living lives that are pleasing to God. In the Catholic faith God is not divided from the truth, and to seek God is to seek the truth.

Finally, let me say a word in response to Trakakis' general reflections on phenomenology. He is happy enough to acknowledge the value of phenomenology in the arts, although his reasons for valuing it there strike me as unsatisfactory. He confuses ἐποχή and reduction with what Viktor Shklovsky calls 'de-familiarizing'. Now de-familiarizing is an important function of poetic language – think of poems by Boris Pasternak and Tomas Tranströmer, for instance – but it remains in the natural attitude, whereas ἐποχή and reduction seek to lead one to adopt a transcendental attitude and to explicate the full intentional rapport that one has with phenomena. Besides, when Husserl speaks of phenomenology leading to description, he has in mind philosophical descriptions – of ontological structures, structures of consciousness, structures of meaning – and not literary ones. Things are quite different with the divine, for there, in my view, one is concerned with counter-intentionality: I do not seek to constitute God but instead I am constituted in his gaze, I am turned from world to Kingdom. Classical phenomenology, then, needs to be modified before it can serve many of the most important interests of Christian theology.

Trakakis is also doubtful about the value of phenomenology in philosophy, saying that "such a method is very limited, especially today" (181). It is hard to know what to say in response to this extraordinary remark. Are we to understand Trakakis to deny the achievements of Husserl and Heidegger, Ingarden and Stein, Scheler and Fink, Merleau-Ponty and Sartre, Lévinas and Derrida, Marion and Lacoste, to name only the most important representatives of the tradition in modern philosophy? If we include their predecessors from Kant to Kierkegaard in a wholesale excision of phenomenology from the canon we eliminate a vast library of modern philosophy. It is also worth considering that some of the strongest analytic philosophers alive today are attending to Kant and Hegel, to the latter's *Phenomenology* no less, in articulating their positions.[2] It would be a good thing for this practice to continue and to include later philosophers in the phenomenological tradition.

To eliminate the representatives of the phenomenological tradition as being only, at best, of limited value in modern philosophy, including the philosophy of religion, would commit one to a parochial vision of the discipline. But perhaps Trakakis' point is more modest. Perhaps he is asking us to trust instead analytic philosophy of religion in a bid to address unbelief in the contemporary world. If so, I must say that I have very little faith in that project. I cannot conceive of anyone turning to God after reading a paper in the analytic philosophy of religion. All that person has to do is read a later paper in the field and find that the arguments of the first paper have been roundly criticized, usually with no reference to Jesus and no awareness of theology, let alone spirituality. One might, with enough determination and enough patience to read essays by people who, as often as not, write English as though it were produced by a computer program, come to a position that survives criticism a bit better than other positions. Equally likely, one might succumb to the peculiar form of nihilism prevalent in analytic philosophy: the analytic world lays claim to having high standards of clarity and rigour, yet it is populated by people who cannot be persuaded by arguments that exhibit those very standards to a high degree.[3] Everyone has his or her niche in the profession, and these hidey-holes seem to be insulated quite successfully against the incursions of clarity and rigour when presented from another vantage point.

As regards resolving "the conflicting claims to religious truth" (181), it would be very interesting to hear from Trakakis where this has actually been done in analytic philosophy of religion or even where it is at all likely to occur. Where is it shown, in a convincing manner, that any given religious faith is the true one, even on a single point of doctrine? Where is there given a satisfying account of the theology of religions that spells out how to reconcile the truth-claims of one's own faith with the truth-claims of other faiths? Analytic philosophy of religion attends, almost single-mindedly, to arguments for a position or seeks to justify a position already in play; that is, the focus is on issues of soundness and validity. Few premises, if any, are so weak that they cannot be contested, and such contestation occurs these days at a giddy rate. It is a method that, as Trakakis says with respect to phenomenology, "can be deployed by anyone, regardless of the credibility of his or her beliefs" (181). One finds agnostics, atheists, evangelicals, Calvinists, Catholics, Mormons, Orthodox and doubtless many others all using the methods of analytic philosophy to shore up their pre-philosophical beliefs, all huffing and puffing about having very high standards of clarity and rigour, and all arguing against one another with, it seems, no way of telling (outside the canons of prestige in appointments and publishers) who has the upper hand.

Both major schools of modern philosophy attend to defending and justifying beliefs: the one is concerned with placing intentions, arguments and

238 *Kevin Hart*

so forth in the logical space of reasons, while the other does the same thing in the transcendental space of experience. Both run the risk of becoming culturally irrelevant: phenomenology because of its tendency to engage in phenomenological theory rather than phenomenology as such, and analytic philosophy because all too often it seeks to bolster naïve pre-philosophical religious beliefs with formalized arguments and, anyway, is confined to academic journals that only insiders know of, let alone read.

* * *

Michael Rea objects to my claim that God the Father does not appear in human experience, and he cites as counterevidence the Gospel stories of Jesus' baptism and transfiguration where God the Father is audible. Let us consider just the story of the baptism. Matthew tells us that Jesus "saw the Spirit of God descending like a dove, and alighting on him" (Matthew 3:16, RSV) and hears a voice saying, "This is my beloved Son, with whom I am well pleased" (Matthew 3:17, RSV). I do not doubt that John baptized Jesus: the event is highly inconvenient for early believers, for whom Jesus was held on theological grounds to be without sin and therefore in no need of baptism, and this makes it more than likely to have been a historical event. Yet Rea writes as though the Gospel of Matthew is first-person direct reporting of an actual empirical event in all its aspects. Our best estimate is that the Gospel of Matthew was written some fifty to eighty years after the death of Jesus; and of course that makes it almost impossible that it could have been written by anyone who knew Jesus. It is testimony of a community's belief that Jesus is the Messiah, specifically that he started his public ministry with God's blessing, which is shaped by familiar symbols available to the community. The dove is well known as a symbol in Canaanite and Phoenician religions, and quite naturally the symbol was taken up in the writing of the Tanakh and was available to the early Christian community.

Yet for Rea it seems that we are to conceive that one day someone looked over the river Jordan, saw a dove descend onto Jesus' head or shoulder, and then heard a voice from the heavens. Perhaps if this person had been fortunate enough to have a tape recorder he or she could have recorded the voice that came from the heavens. I presume that Rea thinks that the voice was in Hebrew, or perhaps he thinks it might have been in Aramaic, since that was the language Jesus would have spoken most often. Yet let us assume that God the Father would have spoken in good classical Hebrew on such a day. If Rea actually believes something like this, it is not unreasonable to ask him if someone listening attentively could have discerned the Father's accent: I wonder if it was more like that of the people of Ephraim or more like that of those of Gilead? The questions are of course ridiculous, if charming, but they are direct consequences of the pre-critical literalism of Rea's reading of Scripture.

In my paper I cite Paul's experience on the road to Damascus, but that is an experience of the risen Christ, and I have no problem in treating that as a phenomenon. The claim in contention is whether the Father appears in human experience. John 6:46 is the Scriptural authority here, and Rea takes it to mean that no one directly sees the Father but that people might very well have the Father appear in their experience. He gives as support that many Christians over history "have thought" that they have experienced God in prayer, liturgy, nature and other situations. Indeed, that is so: there is interesting testimony from St Teresa of Ávila (1957: 188) that she saw Christ (but not with the eyes of the body or the eyes of the soul), and Simone Weil (1959: 35) testifies that Christ took possession of her when reading George Herbert's lyric "Love" (III). As indicated, however, I do not wish to deny that Christ can be and has been experienced by people. The claim is whether God the Father appears in people's experience. Now Karl Rahner (1983) speaks of transcendental experience of the Holy Spirit, but he does not suggest that it is thematic or emotive or anything of the sort; and in any case his sophisticated theological view is a long way from Rea's pre-critical religious convictions. Rea's case is an elementary one, that people, even perhaps a good many people, "have thought" they have experienced God the Father in one or another way. It is an extremely weak argument. Could they have been mistaken? It might have been Christ, the Holy Spirit, the Virgin Mary, an angel, a blessed spirit, a devil in disguise, or even an effect of an anti-depressant in a severe Midwestern winter. And it could have been wish fulfillment, hysteria, pious self-deceit or any one of a number of things. There are, after all, people who "have thought" they have seen flying saucers and have been abducted by aliens; but we tend to treat such claims with a pinch or two of salt.

In my view one cannot perceive God the Father with one's senses; one can imagine him and can anticipate being with him in eternity, one can form an intentional relationship in prayer with God the Father and one can try to think of him. Yet in all these regions of being one's faith is that God has constituted one to be present to him; and that does not amount to an experience.

* * *

It is a pleasure to turn to John Bishop's reflections on my paper. I agree entirely that the βασιλεία is "the extension into the creation (even, ultimately, into all of it) of the *perichoresis* of the Holy Trinity" (118). Indeed, I would say that the βασιλεία is, on the one hand, what remains for us of the original blessing of creation – that God will be with us in our earthly lives – and, on the other hand, our hope of being eternally with the triune God. Part of that hope, as Bishop underscores, is that the entire universe (or, if you wish, pluriverse) may one day be suffused with trinitarian love. We may hope that all shall be saved. On earth there are analogues to the βασιλεία in the world religions, and Karl Barth was right to speak in the *Church Dogmatics* (IV: 3, §69) of "secular parables of the Kingdom"; and if God is to be "all in all", then it is to be hoped that all life is to be gathered in the βασιλεία.

240   *Kevin Hart*

One danger of focusing on the βασιλεία is that it has been and always can be detached from a liturgical and prayerful relation with God and fitted into one or another program in the theology of history. If that happens, the βασιλεία becomes no more than an ethical-political realm, as Bishop clearly recognizes. We need to retain a revelation "of the nature of the good" that is linked to "historically specific experiences mediated through living traditions" (this volume: 119). When that link is cut we can see a deflation of the notion of the divine reign; it happens in German philosophy and theology over the period from Kant to Ritschl, and we can see its collapse in the World War I. Take Fichte, for example. In his *Staatslehre* (1820) he holds that the freedom of all people in Christ is as much a political as a moral situation; it renders all men equal in terms of freedom to act and freedom not to act, although not all people have the same value when it comes to manifesting the divine (see Fichte 1820: 516). Fichte has no qualms about thinking of the Kingdom as earthly and historical, as what binds human beings together in determinate, shared action. It is a Kingdom of reason. If learned men in Germany – doubtless philosophers in particular, who may or may not believe in Christ – are the bearers of the Kingdom, all men and women may participate in it, which is the visible activity of social beings and the invisible activity of the Holy Spirit who has, for all intents and purposes, replaced Christ on earth. Not that the Kingdom includes all human beings, however, for there is a counter-Kingdom of evil that is almost everywhere apparent, especially, for Fichte, in the political aggressions of England and France.

The βασιλεία is always in danger of being reduced in the manner of Fichte, or in another way, and that is why I insist that it be linked to the worship of God in and through Jesus. Without the relationship with God, our work for the βασιλεία is unmoored; and without our endeavours to bring on the βασιλεία, our worship of God risks becoming merely formal. A phenomenology of the Christ is twofold in principle. It seeks to look hard at the Christ in his *mise-en-scène*, insofar as it is possible, and to see how he teaches, how he engages with people and how he regards his heavenly Father. Also, and perhaps more importantly, it seeks to see how Jesus himself practices a mode of phenomenology. He does not, for the most part, exemplify the path inwards that one associates with Plotinus and Augustine, early on, and that becomes drawn into phenomenology in a powerful manner with Husserl and many of his followers.[4] Reduction can be a step back from the world so that we can see how a phenomenon is given to us, or it can be a step back to an anterior point that allows us to see the world from a special vantage point. Husserl combines these two senses of stepping back and invites us to retreat to absolute consciousness from where we can see that, after proper methodological moves have been made, we constitute the world of sense around us. To my mind, Jesus invites us to step back to an anterior point so that we can see how God wishes us to live. The reduction he practices is to step back from world to Kingdom, and it mostly happens by way of him telling a parable. It is very seldom that this reduction is needed just the once: most believers need to be led back time and time again; the reduction is usually partial, and the world – αἰών, κόσμος, *mundum, orbis terrarum, imperium mundi,* and so on – holds us in thrall, as Eugen Fink rightly saw. But the βασιλεία is not merely a concept or an idea; it is a complex way of life in which one takes God as King, an unusual King in that he truly acts as a loving Father. In the world one might well try to constitute God as having sense, yet in the βασιλεία, insofar as we fully enter it, God constitutes us as meaningful to him. We stand under the gaze of God and under the gaze of those with whom we live and can serve.

So Bishop is entirely correct to note that for me the phenomenology of the Christ is only the base of a theology. It can give the Christian as secure a ground as is available to us because God, for us, is the Father of Jesus, God-for-us and God-with-us, not a bit of metaphysical construction. Yet there are things that we can say about God, and to do so is metaphysics. The issue in contention is not whether or not one can or should do metaphysics but which questions in metaphysics are appropriate to pose when considering the God who Jesus reveals to us. In brief, without a robust understanding of God, grounded in what Jesus says of his Father and reflectively considered so that it is finally grasped that Jesus is both the genitive and dative of revelation, "the ideals of the Kingdom will be no more than a pipe dream" (119).

* * *

Heather Eaton begins by noting that I refer to God with the masculine pronoun and observes that this "reveals a male bias" and then wildly leaps to the conclusion that I use this pronoun because I belong to a context of "male-dominated and conservative" Christianity (this volume: 130). In response, I simply note that in the paper under consideration I am hewing close to what Jesus says in Scripture, and it is uncontroversial that Jesus refers to God as his Father. Among many verses one might well cite the following: εἶπεν δὲ αὐτοῖς Ὅταν προσεύχησθε λέγετε Πάτερ ἡμῶν (Luke 11:2). At other places in Scripture God is figured in female terms: Hosea 11:3–4, Deuteronomy 32:18, Isaiah 66:13, for instance. But these are not in play in Jesus' references to God as his Father. Now if one passes from Jesus' relationship with his Father to considering God as absolutely singular (with the triune relations being real distinctions), there is no marking of gender whatsoever. There are no grounds, then, for the characterization of my religious context. Besides, the word 'conservative' is far too imprecise a word to use when describing a complex religious tradition. In the Catholic Church one might be conservative with respect to doctrine, ecclesial governance, liturgical music, the choice of rite or rites one prefers for the Mass, questions of social justice, and so on; and one might be liberal or centrist with regards to all those things. Chances are that most Catholics are conservative in some areas, liberal in others and centrist in yet others.

242 *Kevin Hart*

Eaton, it seems, would like to know the autobiographical roots of my religious convictions, and she sees these as central to an understanding of my ideas. Oscar Wilde (2006: 3) observed that "The highest as the lowest form of criticism is a mode of autobiography," and he had reason for thinking that. Yet I was asked to write an academic paper, not a spiritual autobiography, and had I been asked to write the latter I would not have agreed to do so. Francis Bacon's prescription *de nobis ipsis silemus*, adopted by Kant, is a bit too severe for my liking, but scholarly publication is not the place for personal revelations, which quickly become self-indulgent. Besides, there is quite enough for Eaton to ponder, if she wishes to do so, in my paper. I'm not sure how well she has read the paper, however. All too often she makes unwarranted assumptions about my views, and her scattering of very broad questions makes it difficult to respond to anything in detail. I have perhaps addressed some of her concerns in responding to the other readers of my essay.

So let me simply put aside, as basic misunderstandings of my position, some peculiar remarks that Eaton makes. She claims that my opening observation ("Christian theology properly begins by considering the confession that Jesus is the Christ") is an *a priori* statement. But it is plainly nothing of the kind. An *a priori* statement is completely independent of all experience, such as 'All children have biological parents', and my statement is not of that sort. My opening remark is a methodological statement, as should be quite clear from the context that derives from it. How should Christian theology begin? Well, history provides us with a wide range of possibilities, and I note several of them in my opening paragraph. It strikes me as surprising that Christian theology so often begins by pondering something other than the claim that Jesus of Nazareth is the Christ and talks of God as though for Christians he could be other than the Father of the Jewish rabbi, Jesus of Nazareth. My opening sentence, then, is methodological and normative. I think it is desirable to root Christian theology in a consideration of what it means to say that Jesus is the Christ.

Another odd feature of Eaton's response is her imputation to me of the claim that what I say in my opening sentence, a later remark that Christian theology's starting-point is the relationship with the God of Jesus, and the view that the central moment of the Christian faith is the resurrection of Jesus are "absolutely binding" on Christian believers. Now the word 'binding' occurs just twice in my chapter. The first is: "In phenomenology we are dealing genetically with Christianity, uncovering its sediments, and recognizing that while its claims are absolutely binding on believers they are not thereby necessarily universal" (60). And the second is: "The theses of the Nicene Creed are binding on mainstream Christians, but being brought to the anterior claim to serve God in and through the βασιλεία is primary in the faith" (64). Plainly my opening statement, and the claim that follows from it, cannot be binding on anyone: they are my statements and are neither creedal nor do they derive from the magisterium.

In the two sentences I have cited, however, things are different. The first is considerably more liberal than Eaton supposes. All Christians, of whatever sort, bind themselves to certain beliefs that distinguish them from Muslims, Hindus, Buddhists and persons of yet other faiths. They do not do so conditionally, if they are sincere in their faith, but unconditionally; for Christianity is about love, and conditioned love is no love at all. The second sentence distinguishes, as perhaps Eaton would wish, mainstream Christians from others, and says that the Nicene Creed is binding for those mainstream Christians. First of all, the sentence does not say that the creedal statements are to be interpreted in a particular way. Like all theologians, I have views about how given statements should be interpreted; but people at Mass are asked to repeat the Symbol, not a predetermined interpretation of the Symbol. What people actually understand by the resurrection from the dead varies a great deal, from bodily resurrection, to resurrection of the flesh (*Leib*), to spiritual resurrection, and so on. Second, the sentence says nothing about those Christians who belong to creedless congregations. Clearly, they cannot be bound to the formulations of the Nicene Creed. The second sentence also urges that what is most profound in Christianity is not a collection of theses to which one subscribes, with a greater or lesser understanding, but rather living a life that is pleasing to God: not a life that merely follows middle-class moral norms but one that is answerable to what Jesus called the βασιλεία.

I could continue in this manner, but I think I have made my point. Besides, Eaton and I agree on several things, and perhaps they are more important than the disagreements; and it is distinctly possible that when Eaton sees that she has leapt to unwarranted conclusions there may be fewer of these than she imagined at first.

Notes

1 For philosophical interest in epistemic issues to do with testimony, see, for instance, Coady (1992). It is not without interest that Coady is himself a practicing Catholic.
2 See, for instance, McDowell (2009) and Brandom (2000). To be sure, both McDowell and Brandom read Hegel through lenses ground by earlier analytic philosophers.
3 For a searing response to this situation from an insider, at least as regards the state of philosophy at the University of Cambridge, see Geuss (2014: 232).
4 Husserl (1977: 157) quotes Augustine with approval: "'Noli foras ire,' says Augustine, 'in te redi, in interiore homine habitat veritas.'"

References

Barth, K. 1961. *Church Dogmatics*, vol. 4, Part Three, First Half, edited by G. W. Bromiley and T. F. Torrance, translated by G. W. Bromiley. Edinburgh: T & T Clark.

Brandom, R. 2000. *Articulating Reasons: An Introduction to Inferentialism*. Cambridge, MA: Harvard University Press.

Coady, C. A. J. 1992. *Testimony: A Philosophical Study*. Oxford: Clarendon Press.

Fichte, J. G. 1820. *Die Staatslehre*. Berlin: G. Reimer.

Geuss, R. 2014. *A World without Why*. Princeton: Princeton University Press.

Hume, D. 1948. *Dialogues Concerning Natural Religion*, edited by H. D. Aiken. New York: Hafner Press.

Husserl, E. 1977. *Cartesian Meditations: An Introduction to Phenomenology*, translated by D. Cairns. The Hague: Martinus Nijhoff.

McDowell, J. 2009. *Having the World in View: Essays on Kant, Hegel, and Sellars*. Cambridge, MA: Harvard University Press.

Rahner, R. 1983. "Experience of the Holy Spirit." In *Theological Investigations*, XI: *God and Revelation*, translated by E. Quinn, 189–210. New York: Crossroad.

Swinburne, R. 2003. *The Resurrection of God Incarnate*. Oxford: Oxford University Press.

Teresa of Ávila. 1957. *The Life of Saint Teresa of Ávila by Herself*, translated by J. M. Cohen. London: Penguin.

Weil, S. 1959. "Spiritual Autobiography." In *Waiting on God*, translated by E. Craufurd, 28–49. London: Fontana Books.

Wilde, O. 2006. *The Picture of Dorian Gray*, edited by R. Mighall. London: Penguin.

14 Michael C. Rea

My interlocutors have raised a variety of interesting objections in their critiques of my Position Statement, and I am particularly grateful for the spirit of constructive and charitable engagement manifest in the contributions by Bishop, Eaton and Trakakis. The most substantive objections, and the ones to which it seems most productive to reply, pertain to my account of the Trinity and to my remarks on the authority, clarity and sufficiency of Scripture. Accordingly, these are the topics on which I shall mainly focus. I shall conclude, however, with some brief remarks about the enterprise of 'analytic theology', against which Hart's essay raises a few passing objections.

The Trinity

Speaking in very general terms, Bishop, Hart and Trakakis together raise three main objections to my account of the Trinity: (i) it is not faithful to the tradition either in its formulation of the doctrine of the Trinity or in what it implies about the unity of the divine persons; (ii) the 'material constitution' analogy and the doctrine of relative identity to which I appeal are problematic in various ways; and (iii) the account is not appropriately apophatic. Eaton observes that the account is "highly abstract and speculative"; but I do not disagree with her on this score, nor do I see the observation as an objection. Consequently I'll focus on the criticisms offered by Bishop, Hart and Trakakis.

Bishop observes (correctly) that, although the Nicene Creed of 381 affirms the consubstantiality of the Son with the Father, it does not explicitly affirm the consubstantiality of the Spirit with the Father. From this he concludes that it seems "safer in setting out what is essential to Trinitarianism simply to affirm the equal divinity of the Persons and leave it at that" (123). But this conclusion is problematic twice over. First, although the creed that issued from the First Council of Constantinople does not explicitly affirm the consubstantiality of the Spirit with the Father, the accompanying "Letter of the Bishops Gathered in Constantinople" does affirm this. Second, given my understanding of consubstantiality, affirming the equal divinity of the divine persons is *equivalent* to affirming their consubstantiality. The reason

246 *Michael C. Rea*

is simple: to say that they are equally divine is nothing other than to say that they have the same nature – they are exactly the same kind of thing. But to say *that* is just to say that they are consubstantial.

According to both Bishop and Hart, however, my understanding of consubstantiality is problematic, as is my employment of that notion in explicating the unity of the divine persons. Again: I say that two things are consubstantial if, and only if, they share the same nature or, in other words, are exactly the same kind of thing. This implies that two human beings – Peter and Paul, say – are consubstantial, just as the divine persons are. According to Bishop, this consequence is laughable, and witnesses both to the "ineptness" of my "reduction" of the relationship between the persons to consubstantiality and to the "oddity" of my formulation of the doctrine of the Trinity. But these are puzzling complaints given that Bishop *also* wants to criticize my view (incorrectly) for not being faithful to the Nicene Creed. For 'consubstantial' is just the English cognate of the Latin translation of ὁμοούσιος, which is the Greek word used in the Nicene Creed for expressing the relationship between the Father and the Son. That term, of course, means *of the same* οὐσία; and, notably, the very same term is used in the Greek text of the Symbol of Chalcedon (451) to express *both* the relationship between the Father and the Son and the relationship between the Son and *us* (human beings). But, obviously, the Son can be consubstantial with human beings as a group only if human beings are consubstantial with one another. Perhaps Bishop would want to follow his objection where it leads and say that this just shows the Symbol of Chalcedon to be laughable and inept as well. For my part, I'd rather not say this. Instead, I think that the terminology of the Symbol of Chalcedon together with a general understanding of the basic contours of the Trinitarian debates of the fourth century lends strong support to the characterization of consubstantiality offered in my Position Statement.[1] As I see it, the best understanding (in English) of what it means to say that one thing is of the same οὐσία as another is to say that the things in question share a common nature, or are things *of the same kind* – real, Aristotelian kinds, of course; not merely nominal kinds.

Hart accuses me of carelessness in my characterization of consubstantiality and says:

> There is no 'kind' at issue: the doctrine of the Trinity is monotheistic; it turns on God being absolutely singular, not belonging to any genus at all. Otherwise one would be in a position to defend tri-theism.
>
> (157)

He then goes on to say that I "write as though the Father, the Son and the Holy Spirit are three individuals sharing a single nature, much as St Gregory of Nyssa does in his letter to Ablabius" (157). Taking these remarks together, it seems as if Hart thinks that Nyssen and I are making a common mistake: we both are saying that the unity of the divine persons is no more or less than that of the unity that holds between *mundane physically separated* individuals of the same kind – for example, Peter and Paul. Hart is correct that this mistake naturally leads to tri-theism. But Nyssen does not make this mistake (indeed, he objects to the idea). The claim that he does make the mistake results from an all-too-common and now generally discredited misreading of the letter to Ablabius. Nor do I make the mistake. For, like Nyssen, I do not claim that the unity of the divine persons resides *merely* in their belonging to the same kind. Their belonging to the same kind is *part* of what it is for them to be one God; but the rest of the explanation comes from the fact that belonging to the same kind is equivalent to sharing a common nature, or essence, together with a particular metaphysical story about what nature-sharing comes to in the case of the divine persons. Furthermore, I have argued in some detail elsewhere that this understanding of the unity of the divine persons, taken together with the material constitution analogy that supports it, is faithful to and, indeed, suggested by the trinitarian writings of Gregory of Nyssa, Gregory of Nazianzus and St Augustine (cf. Rea 2009). For those who doubt my account's faithfulness to tradition, perhaps the best way to proceed is to examine that argument and identify where they think it goes wrong.[2]

In regard to the material constitution analogy itself, Bishop and Trakakis have both raised concerns. Bishop says that accepting my analogy would "surely" result in an "unacceptably modalist" account of the Trinity (124). Trakakis says that my view "requires a departure from the classical or absolute account of identity enshrined in Leibniz's Law" (183). These claims are simply mistaken, and I have addressed them explicitly and in detail in some of my other work on the Trinity (see Rea 2003, 2009).

Trakakis also raises an objection first lodged against my view by William Lane Craig (2005). The objection, in short, is that the statue/lump analogy fails because, whereas (say) coinciding pillars and statues are not "mutually exclusive hylomorphic compounds", the Father, Son and Holy Spirit would be. So, on Craig's view (as I understand it), if we were to stick with statue analogies, Father, Son and Holy Spirit would be more akin to the *David* and the *Winged Victory* than to a statue and a pillar that constitute one another. The former pair, unlike the latter, cannot possibly be numerically the same object. Likewise, then, Father, Son and Holy Spirit cannot possibly be numerically the same object.

The trouble with this objection, however, is that Craig offers no defence of the claim that the *David/Winged Victory* analogy more aptly expresses the relation between the divine persons than does the statue/pillar analogy. (Trakakis offers no defence of this claim either.) In the passage that Trakakis quotes, Craig says that my view "does not tell us how seemingly mutually exclusive hylomorphic compounds can be numerically the same object". This is true; it wasn't supposed to do that, because, as I see it, the divine persons aren't *seemingly mutually exclusive* hylomorphic compounds. Craig goes on: "We are told that one object can be both a hand and a fist. All right. But how

248   *Michael C. Rea*

can one object be simultaneously a clenched fist and an open hand?" Answer: it can't, and I never said that it could. Trakakis says that, "Craig's point . . . is that the divine persons . . . bear mutually exclusive intrinsic properties. For example, the Son alone bears the property 'begotten from the Father', and the Father alone has the property of 'unbegottenness'" (184). But Trakakis says nothing to show that these properties are mutually exclusive *in the relevant sense*. To be sure, no one *thing* can have both properties. But my model does not imply that these properties are properties of one thing. (Keep in mind that being *one thing*, on my view, is not the same as being *one material object* or *one God*.) The Father and the Son are, after all, distinct things on my view, despite being one God. What one would need to show in order to make the objection stick is that there are mutually exclusive properties p and q such that, on my account, the 'matter' for each of the divine persons – that is, the divine nature – has both p and q. In the *David/Winged Victory* case we have (at least) two such properties: for example, the *David*'s matter has the property *being shaped like a wingless man*, and the *Winged Victory* has the property *being shaped like a winged goddess*. These are incompatible properties; thus we can readily infer that the *David* and the *Winged Victory* do not share the same matter in common and so are not one material object. But so far neither Craig nor Trakakis has identified such a property in the case of the divine persons.

Finally, Trakakis objects that my model is not appropriately apophatic. He asks rhetorically what mystery would remain in the doctrine of the Trinity if my model were to succeed in providing a coherent and intelligible explanation of the doctrine. He also notes that the Church Fathers used analogies only with great caution and were always dissatisfied with the analogies they offered in their own explanations of trinitarian doctrine. He concludes by saying, "it is this apophatic character of trinitarian thought which was an integral part of patristic theology and yet is unfortunately lacking in Rea's approach" (184).

Apophaticism comes in degrees. Even among theologians who wish to make a lot of room for divine mystery, there is disagreement about the extent to which we can manage to talk and theorize about God. Trakakis is probably correct that my own approach is less apophatic than the approach taken by the Cappadocians (although, unlike Trakakis, I would not be so sanguine about making such comparisons. It is often hard to tell where on the kataphatic/apophatic spectrum a theologian *really* falls). But even so, I see no reason to think that this difference between me and the Cappadocians is an "unfortunate" one. I agree that there *would* be an unfortunate difference if I accorded no place for divine mystery; but, *contra* Trakakis, it is simply not true that I accord no place for divine mystery (in the doctrine of the Trinity, or elsewhere). My model shows how distinct divine persons might nevertheless count as one God; but it still leaves *lots* of questions about the ontology of the Godhead wholly untouched. Moreover, and more importantly, the *mystery* of the Trinity is hardly exhausted by the puzzle of how three divine persons could be one God. In contemporary systematic

Second Response 249

theology, this puzzle is, for the most part, a mere sideshow; the interesting theological mysteries of God's triune life reside elsewhere – in the nature of the perichoretic communion amongst the persons, in the cry of dereliction from the cross, in the set of facts expressed by Rahner's Rule, and so on. My account of the Trinity at best solves a puzzle that for many serves as an obstacle to belief. It leaves the more interesting mysteries wholly untouched and still within the realm of the mysterious.

Scripture

All four of my interlocutors objected to my brief remarks on Scripture. In my Position Statement, I said that I think Scripture is foundationally authoritative (i.e., more authoritative than any other source of information or advice) in matters of faith and practice. I also affirmed that it is *clear* and *sufficient* in (just) the following sense: all doctrines and prescriptions necessary for salvation can be easily derived from Scripture by persons concerned about the salvation of their souls without the help of the Church or Church tradition. These affirmations together constituted my gloss on what it is to affirm the *sola scriptura* doctrine. My interlocutors found all of these claims objectionable. In replying, I'll talk first about the clarity and sufficiency of Scripture, and then about the authority of Scripture.

Hart's main objections against the clarity and sufficiency doctrines can, it seems to me, be dealt with simply by re-emphasizing the fact that these doctrines claim nothing more than that doctrines and prescriptions *necessary for salvation* can be easily derived from Scripture without the help of the Church or Tradition. For example, he says that "[a]nyone who knows the biblical languages will readily point to all manner of grammatical ambiguities and textual uncertainties in Scripture which press on the formation of doctrine" (153). True; but this fact counts against the clarity doctrine only if the relevant ambiguities and uncertainties obscure the doctrines and prescriptions *necessary for salvation*. It is hardly obvious that they do. Hart asks why, if Scripture is clear, historical biblical critics would find it useful to employ the principle of *lectio difficilior potior*; and he asks why, if the New Testament claim that Jesus is the Christ is clear, the Church found it necessary to rearrange the books of the Hebrew Bible when forming the Christian Old Testament. Finally, he states that it "must be noted" that the Reformers themselves disagree with one another on matters of scriptural interpretation, often as it relates to the formation of doctrine. But these questions and observations are apropos in the present context only on the assumption that the clarity and sufficiency doctrines imply that all biblical texts are easy to understand, that all Christian doctrines are easily derivable from Scripture, and, indeed, that basic doctrines like the claim that Jesus is the Christ are easily derivable not just from the Old Testament and New Testament taken together but from the Old Testament texts *alone*,[3] independently of the New Testament and without the reordering introduced in the formation of the

250   *Michael C. Rea*

Old Testament canon. But in fact none of these claims are implied by the clarity and sufficiency doctrines as I have glossed them.[4]

In a similar vein, Eaton asks how we are to "deal with" contradictory interpretations of Scripture, the idea presumably being that, if Scripture is clear, it should not admit of contradictory interpretations. Again, the clarity doctrine as I have glossed it does not imply that *everything* in the Bible is clear; so the mere fact that people disagree about how to interpret it isn't evidence against its clarity in the sense under discussion here. But Eaton might just as easily have asked how we are to deal with contradictory interpretations of Scripture *on matters that (many) Christians do take to be salvifically essential*. Bishop points to the doctrine of the Trinity as one such case; but if you don't like that example, he could easily have pointed to others. The derivability of that doctrine from Scripture is notoriously controversial. But if Scripture is clear, and if belief in the doctrine of the Trinity (or your favourite alternative doctrine) is indeed necessary for salvation, how could learned people reasonably *disagree* – as they seem to – about whether it is derivable from Scripture?

This is a difficult question, and the best I can do here is simply to gesture in the direction of what I take to be the proper reply. Consider an analogy: I think that it is plain to the naked eye that there is a desk, a computer, some chairs and books and a human being in my office. One doesn't need help from instruments or philosophers, nor does one need testimony from a higher authority, in order to discover that these things are in the room. Even children, once they have the relevant concepts, can see that the room contains these things. But, of course, many people disagree. Many metaphysicians will deny that my office contains chairs, books, and so on; many will therefore deny that it is *plain to the naked eye* that it contains these things. Put a dozen metaphysicians in a room together and you may get a dozen conflicting reports about what the room contains and about which of its contents are plain to the naked eye. Even so, it seems perfectly reasonable for me to say (without apology or qualification) that it is plain to the naked eye that there is a desk, a computer, and so on in the room. The reason is that this claim is – so I believe – a consequence of various reasonably held background assumptions. *Given* those background assumptions, I can reasonably affirm that the presence of the desk, chairs, and so on is plainly visible even to children; and I can explain the fact that learned people deny the existence or plain visibility of the desk, chairs, and so on by citing their disagreement with my background assumptions. So likewise with the claim that all doctrines necessary for salvation are plainly visible (so to speak) in Scripture. This claim is a consequence of various controversial background assumptions about the nature and authorship of the scriptural texts, about how to interpret those texts, and so on. Given the right background assumptions, it is perfectly reasonable to affirm that (e.g.) all doctrines necessary for salvation are easily derivable from Scripture; and one can explain disagreements about particular cases either by appeal to different assumptions about what is necessary for salvation or by appeal to different assumptions about the nature, authorship and proper interpretation of Scripture.

In closing this section, let me now comment briefly on the objections raised against my views on the authority of Scripture. Several of my interlocutors pointed out that the Church has an important (and authoritative) role to play in canon formation. They also pointed out that interpretations of Scripture that are wholly disconnected from Church tradition are thereby suspect and that I myself seem to defer to the authority of tradition in my interpretation of certain texts. Trakakis even goes so far as to ask the following rhetorical question: "[G]iven that the Church assembled the Scriptures and decided what is to be included and excluded, does it not follow that a decisive role in interpreting the Scriptures . . . belongs to the Church?" (183).

By way of response, I simply note that I never denied (and Protestants in general need not deny) that Church tradition, ecumenical creeds and confessions and even select creeds and confessions produced during and after the Reformation are in some sense authoritative with regard to what counts as Scripture, how Scripture is to be interpreted or what doctrines are or are not consistent with Christian belief and practice. My claims were far more limited. I said that one does not *need* the help of the Church in order to discover in Scripture the doctrines or prescriptions necessary for salvation; and I said that nothing is *as* authoritative as Scripture on matters of faith and practice. As it happens, I also deny that "a decisive role in interpreting the Scriptures . . . belongs to the Church"; and, *contra* Trakakis, I see no reason to think that the claim just quoted logically follows from the fact that the Church established the canon. But my views on this score are fully consistent with the belief that the ecumenical creeds and confessions, the pronouncements of Church leaders and so on count as authorities in matters of doctrine and interpretation to which we are well-advised to defer. For to say (simply) that they are authoritative is not the same as saying that their pronouncements are indefeasible; nor is it the same as saying that their pronouncements automatically trump our own best judgements when there is conflict between the two.

Analytic theology

Finally, I turn to the topic of 'analytic theology'. Here I shall be engaging just a few remarks made by Kevin Hart.

Analytic theology differs from other forms of theology primarily in its methodology: its ambitions, its style, its conversation partners, and so on. It is, roughly, theology done with the ambitions characteristic of analytic philosophy in a style that conforms to the prescriptions that are distinctive of analytic philosophical discourse; and it is theology that is informed by the same evolving body of literature that the analytic philosophers are themselves trying to engage.

In my introduction to *Analytic Theology: New Essays in the Philosophy of Theology* (Crisp and Rea 2011), I said that, roughly speaking, analytic

252 *Michael C. Rea*

philosophy is an approach to philosophical topics characterized by a certain rhetorical style, a set of common ambitions, an evolving technical vocabulary and a tendency to pursue one's projects in conversation with a particular evolving body of literature. I identified two ambitions as characteristic of analytic philosophy: (i) to identify the scope and limits of our powers to obtain knowledge of the world, and (ii) to provide such true explanatory theories as we can for non-scientific phenomena. I characterized the rhetorical style by saying that paradigmatic instances of it conform (more or less) to the following five prescriptions:

- Write as if philosophical positions and conclusions can be adequately formulated in sentences that can be formalized and logically manipulated.
- Prioritize precision, clarity and logical coherence.
- Avoid substantive (non-decorative) use of metaphor and other tropes whose semantic content outstrips their propositional content.
- Work as much as possible with well-understood primitive concepts and concepts that can be analyzed in terms of those.
- Treat conceptual analysis (insofar as it is possible) as a source of evidence.

I focused on these five prescriptions because, unlike other prescriptions in accord with which analytic philosophers tend to write, these five are prescriptions that those working outside the tradition of analytic philosophy typically *aim* to violate, often for principled reasons. I then went on to consider a variety of more or less common objections against analytic theology: most notably, that it is ahistorical; that it is overly optimistic about the possibility of expressing theological facts by way of simple, precise, logically manipulable sentences; that it is not sufficiently apophatic; that it is not appropriately conducive to the cultivation of wisdom, virtue and the love of God; and that it is potentially idolatrous. The objections considered there are in many cases intimately related to one another. They also overlap substantially with objections raised – generally indirectly or in passing – by Kevin Hart (and, to some extent, Bishop, Eaton and Trakakis as well) against my Position Statement in this volume.

Readers will surely have noticed several passing 'objections' and occasional bits of barbed rhetoric sprinkled throughout Hart's First Response that were directed not so much at my first-order views but rather at me personally or at analytic philosophy and theology in general. Below are a few such remarks:

1 "[T]he God of many contemporary analytical philosophers . . . ends up seeming like a big guy in the sky, the God of the nursery more than the God of the Church" (149).

2   "The books of the Bible are narratives and poems, testimonies and visions, not drafts of papers that, at a pinch, could be reduced to propositions, their arguments formalized, and then sent to the *Journal of Analytic Theology*. Before engaging in the philosophy of religion, Christian philosophers need to learn how to read the Bible well" (149).

3   "*Anyone who knows the biblical languages* will readily point to all manner of grammatical ambiguities and textual uncertainties in Scripture which press on the formation of doctrine. . . . *And anyone aware of ecclesial history* will point to fierce disputes about the meaning of Scripture as it relates to the formation of doctrine. . . . *The more one knows about the history of doctrine* in the early Church, *the less likely it is that one could plausibly say* that Scripture is authoritative, clear or sufficient in the manner that Rea seems to have in mind" (153, 154; my emphases).

4   "What is common to [the essays by Bishop and Rea] is that they tend to abstract Christianity from its historical, ecclesial and theological contexts in order to view it as a series of problems of the kind one deals with in analytical philosophy. I ask myself how their work would be different if they had been trained in reading the Bible and in theology as well as in analytical philosophy; and the answer comes back that the essays would have ended up being more useful to Christianity in general and to Christian theology in particular than they are at the moment. . . . I wonder for whom Bishop and Rea write and, outside the guild of analytical philosophy, who they think will profit from their speculations" (159–160).

Embedded in and suggested by these remarks is a mixture of substantive objection and summary dismissal. So far as I can tell, the substantive objections are simply a subset of those that I mentioned a few paragraphs ago: that analytic theology is ahistorical, potentially idolatrous, not "useful" (at least in the sense of cultivating wisdom and virtue), and so on. Apart from those objections, the upshot of the remainder is a summary dismissal of me (and, to an extent, Bishop) as a credible practitioner of theology and a dismissal of analytic theology generally as a worthwhile enterprise. Analytic theology is dismissed as often producing a childish concept of God; analytic *theologians* are dismissed as generally incompetent readers of the Bible who have a tendency to do theology in a way that involves a naïve, slapdash and ham-fisted attempt to reduce the richness of the Bible to a series of propositions and arguments; it is insinuated that the papers published in the *Journal of Analytic Theology* – of which I am a Senior Editor – are paradigmatic of this naïve, slapdash and ham-fisted approach; and I myself am dismissed (along with Bishop, to an extent) as someone who lacks proper training in biblical studies, biblical languages, ecclesial history and historical and dogmatic theology, and who, as a result, ends up saying things that would not be said by anybody who *has* the relevant training and which are not generally useful to anyone outside the guild of analytic philosophy.

254 *Michael C. Rea*

Happily, I detect in these remarks no untoward insinuations about my upbringing or table manners.

I will not respond here to the content of Hart's summary dismissals of me and of analytic theology more generally. Readers who are familiar with my work and with the field of analytic theology can judge for themselves whether those remarks have any merit. But I do think that it is important to note something about their nature and function. Notably, they are not defended with evidence. Hart does not even suggest that he is prevented by space considerations from defending them with evidence. They are, instead, handed down from on high as pronouncements from someone *inside* the guild upon the credibility of someone *outside* the guild who has dared to encroach on sacred turf. As such, they function as obstacles to further interdisciplinary dialogue; and to that extent, they are detrimental to a goal that Hart and I both seem otherwise to agree would be well worth furthering: namely, the goal of encouraging analytic philosophers to learn from and engage the work of biblical scholars and historical and systematic theologians as they pursue their research on theological topics.[5] It is also detrimental to another goal that, it seems to me, a great many philosophers and theologians have lately come to think is well worthwhile – namely, that of building bridges between the so-called 'analytic' and 'Continental' traditions in philosophy and philosophical theology and putting an end to the sorry history of mockery and dismissal (from both sides of the divide) that helped to keep the two traditions isolated throughout most of the twentieth century.

In contrast to the summary dismissals, the substantive objections embedded in or implied by Hart's remarks do deserve a serious hearing and a careful response. For example, I do not think that analytic theology is idolatrous (as Hart's first objection suggests that it is); but the idolatry objection in its various different forms is a serious, interesting objection that cannot simply be dismissed out of hand. So likewise with the complaints that analytic theology is *objectionably* ahistorical, or that analytic theologians read Scripture not just *differently* from the way in which (say) historical biblical critics read it but *incorrectly*. (Those engaged in so-called 'theological interpretation of Scripture' also read the Bible differently from the way in which it is read by historical biblical critics; but the status of that difference is the subject of an interesting and ongoing debate.[6]) Precisely because they are substantive objections, however, they cannot sensibly be asserted without argument. There are deep methodological issues here and important conversations to be had about them. To simply assert the objections without argument (and then to follow them with summary dismissals) impedes those conversations and, indeed, helps to create an environment in which the targets of those objections do not even begin to take them seriously. One of my main goals in trying to think through and articulate these objections myself in the introduction to the *Analytic Theology* volume and in other work has been to stimulate interdisciplinary dialogue on them by presenting them in a way that (so I hoped) would resonate with both theologians and analytic philosophers. It would surely be a welcome development in the field to find theologians of Hart's stature and calibre doing likewise.

Obviously I cannot actually engage these substantive objections in the space allotted to me here. But, in closing, I do want to note that those raising the objections need to reckon with the fact that much recent work in analytic theology *is* more historically sensitive, more conversant with biblical studies and systematic theology and (in general) more genuinely interdisciplinary than Hart's objections would ever lead one to expect. To be sure, some papers and books achieve these goals better than others; and, to be sure, plenty of theologians (and philosophers) will continue to think – for substantive, interesting reasons – that analytic theology will *always* be susceptible to objections of this sort precisely because its methodology is fundamentally flawed. But the time is now gone when analytic theologians can sensibly be dismissed out of hand *as a class* with the claim that their work is ahistorical, theologically uninformed or insensitive to relevant developments in biblical studies. The field of analytic theology is rapidly changing, and objections that applied (at least at the level of stereotype) as recently as a decade ago are now obsolete.[7]

Notes

1 Cf. Anatolios (2011), Ayres (2004) and Rea (2009).
2 Hart also chides me for not referencing the Greek term *'prosopon'* in my discussion of the divine persons. Thus:

> Rea uses the English word 'person' without any reference to the Greek "*prosopon*", which most certainly does not mean 'person' in the modern sense of the word; it is closer to 'mask', a situation that causes other problems, especially a temptation to modalism.
>
> (157)

To be sure, there is a substantial literature on the relationship between the terms *'prosopon'* and 'person', and on the significance of that relationship for trinitarian concerns. (A good start into this discussion is Turcescu 2005.) The question here, though, is whether those differences *make a difference* to anything I said in my Position Statement. I think that they do not, and Hart offers no evidence that they do. Hart seems to think that the mere failure to *mention* the term *'prosopon'* in my discussion (perhaps simply in order to demonstrate facility with Greek?) is problematic; but I think that he is wrong on that score. Here we have just one among many methodological disagreements.

3 Note that I talk about the Old Testament *texts* whereas Hart, in raising his objection, uses the term 'Hebrew Bible'. Why the difference? In short, the term 'Hebrew Bible' is problematic as a 'neutral' term for the texts shared in common by the Christian Old Testament and the Jewish Bible. James Sanders (1972) sums up the problem nicely:

> Another problem [arising around the middle of the twentieth century] was what Christians should call the first of their double-testament Bible. Most wanted to drop the sub-title, Old Testament, out of respect for the continuing existence and variety of Judaism. . . . Some Christians began to say 'Hebrew Bible' instead of Old Testament, but this is clearly inaccurate and

256 *Michael C. Rea*

> inappropriate since 'Hebrew Bible', or *Biblia Hebraica*, is a time-honored term for the Jewish tri-partite Bible, the Tanak, and not for the Old Testament (besides there being a few Aramaic portions in it). The unfortunate designation persists even in sophisticated circles despite the fact that the Christian First Testament and the Hebrew Bible are significantly different from one another in shape and even contents. Another suggestion, my own in fact, was to refer to it as the First Christian Testament, but some object to this because it apparently suggests that Jews should have a Second Testament as well. . . . In Jewish institutions it is called simply 'Bible' to distinguish it from Talmud and Responsa.
>
> (pp. 7–8)

In light of all of this, it seems in the present context better just to speak of the texts comprising the Old Testament, since those are clearly what Hart has in mind.

4 Nor is my understanding of these doctrines idiosyncratic. On this, see for example Bavinck (2003: 477, 488) and Berkhof (1992: 167–168), both cited in my Position Statement, as well as Turretin (1992: 134–147).

5 I also think that theologians have much to learn from analytic philosophers; but, unlike the point that analytic philosophers have much to learn from theologians, I do not think that this is a point of agreement between Hart and myself.

6 Cf. Fowl (2008, 2009).

7 I am grateful to Michael Bergmann for helpful comments on an earlier draft of this response.

References

Anatolios, K. 2011. *Retrieving Nicaea: The Development and Meaning of Trinitarian Doctrine*. Grand Rapids: Baker Academic.

Ayres, L. 2004. *Nicaea and Its Legacy: An Approach to Fourth-Century Trinitarian Theology*. Oxford: Oxford University Press.

Bavinck, H. 2003. *Reformed Dogmatics, vol. 1: Prolegomena*. Grand Rapids: Baker Academic.

Berkhof, L. 1992. *Systematic Theology*. Grand Rapids: Wm. B. Eerdmans Publishing.

Craig, W. L. 2005. "Does the Problem of Material Constitution Illuminate the Doctrine of the Trinity?" *Faith and Philosophy* 22: 77–86.

Crisp, O. D. and M. C. Rea. 2011. *Analytic Theology: New Essays in the Philosophy of Theology*. Oxford: Oxford University Press.

Fowl, S. E. 2008. *Engaging Scripture: A Model for Theological Interpretation*. Eugene: Wipf & Stock.

Fowl, S. E. 2009. *Theological Interpretation of Scripture*. Eugene: Wipf & Stock.

Rea, M. C. 2003. "Relative Identity and the Doctrine of the Trinity." *Philosophia Christi* 5: 431–445.

Rea, M. C. 2009. "The Trinity." In *The Oxford Handbook of Philosophical Theology*, edited by T. P. Flint and M. C. Rea, 403–429. Oxford: Oxford University Press.

Sanders, J. A. 1972. *Torah and Canon*. Philadelphia: Fortress Press.

Turcescu, L. 2005. *Gregory of Nyssa and the Concept of Divine Persons*. Oxford: Oxford University Press.

Turretin, F. 1992. *Institutes of Elenctic Theology, vol. 1: First through Tenth Topics*, edited by J. T. Dennison, Jr., translated by G. Musgrave Giger. Phillipsburg: P & R Publishing.

15 N. N. Trakakis

Response to Rea: (Reformed) Protestantism

Rea isolates two possible points of disagreement with my Position Statement, the first of which centres on divine transcendence, and in particular on the nature and function of apophatic discourse in theology. He takes the most contentious aspect of my views on divine transcendence to consist in the claim that "negative statements about God are 'more ultimate or truer' than positive statements about God" (this volume: 173). Call this my 'Priority Thesis', given that priority of some sort is accorded to apophatic statements over kataphatic ones.

The difficulty here is to explicate the phrase 'more ultimate or truer'. Rea suggests that 'ultimate' and 'true' in this context could be understood as synonyms, where both terms mean either one of the following two things. On one reading, the emphasis is placed on 'more ultimate', so that "negative predications are *more fundamental* than positive predications" (173; emphasis in original), where 'more fundamental' implies greater proximity to truth. On a second reading, it is the notion of 'truer' that is emphasized, so that "negative statements about God are, one and all, closer to the truth than positive statements" (174).

But I do not see any important difference between these two readings, for both readings interpret the claim to ultimacy in terms of truth. More specifically, both readings suggested by Rea interpret the claim (made in my Position Statement) that "what we deny about God is more ultimate or truer than what we affirm about him" (Trakakis, this volume: 94) as meaning that apophatic statements about God are *closer to the truth* about God than are kataphatic statements about God. Thus, Rea's distinction between the 'ultimacy' interpretation and the 'truth' interpretation seems to be a distinction without a difference.

In any case, let us consider the objections Rea raises against the Priority Thesis. Rea objects to the first reading of the Priority Thesis, given in terms of ultimacy or fundamentality, on the grounds that some positive statements about God seem to be more fundamental than some negative statements about God. Rea points out that when we affirm positive predicates of

258 N.N. Trakakis

God such as that he *is conscious*, *is wise* and *is good*, we seem to be saying something more fundamental about God, or the nature of God, than when we make negative predications of God such as that he *is not an egg*, *is not unwise* and *is neither grue nor prime nor a property*.

Assuming that ultimacy and fundamentality are to be cashed out in terms of proximity to truth, as Rea himself suggests, then no sensible objection could be raised against Rea on this point. However, this only betrays a certain woodenness or narrowness in Rea's interpretation of the Priority Thesis. To be sure, in my Position Statement I stated this thesis in a fairly brief and ambiguous way, thus perhaps provoking the kind of response Rea has made. But note, to begin with, that the Priority Thesis or something close to it is standard fare in traditional (Nicene) Christianity; it is not something supported only by wild mystics but can be located within the *consensus patrum*, that which the theologians and teachers of the Christian faith have consistently professed, in both western and eastern streams of Christianity. Indeed, I would go further to say that a version of the Priority Thesis is a recurring theme not only in Christian teaching but in the vast majority of the world religions. The idea, put succinctly, is that 'ultimate reality' (however this is conceptualized within the diverse religious traditions) exceeds the range of our human categories of thought in such a way that silence and negation must take precedence over speech and affirmation. This, I think it is safe to say, is an almost universal religious response to the wonder and mystery of ultimate or divine reality. Philosophers, in the West at least, have often been reluctant to endorse such religious responses, perhaps fearing a slide into irrationalism and obscurantism. But such fears are not well founded.

Once the Priority Thesis is seen in this light as a way of signalling and safeguarding the mystery that lies at the heart of the divine reality, Rea's objection no longer appears relevant or forceful. Rea, to repeat, argues that the affirmative predications made of God that he *is conscious*, *is wise* and *is good* are more 'fundamental' than the negative predications that God *is not an egg*, *is not unwise* and *is neither grue nor prime nor a property*.

But the goal of the Priority Thesis is not to place *all* affirmative language below apophatic discourse. Rather, the thesis only seeks to deny that affirmations can hold the highest or most fundamental place in our language about God. The thesis, in other words, envisages a dialectical movement where any affirmation, no matter how exalted or reasonable it may seem, is always transcended by the negation of that affirmation. Such negations, however, do not necessarily imply that the affirmation in question is false in some straightforward sense. Rather, the ascent from affirmation to negation 'transcends' or 'raises up' the affirmation in the manner of a Hegelian *Aufheben* ('sublation') so that it can be seen in a new and more penetrating light, one that exposes its flaws or limitations. A similar idea was expressed in the well-known principle of the Fourth Lateran Council (1215) that any similarity or analogy between God and the world is preceded by an even greater dissimilarity or disanalogy. What this implies is that what we say about God (in kataphasis) will always be woefully inadequate – even to the point of appearing 'false' – in light of the infinite distance and difference of God. The negations of apophatic theology are thus aimed at highlighting and preserving the metaphysical and epistemic divide between Creator and creation.

This, in turn, indicates where Rea goes wrong in his response to the second reading of the Priority Thesis, stated directly now in terms of proximity to truth. This version of the Priority Thesis holds that all negative statements about God are alethically superior to any positive statements about God. Rea objects that this flouts the intuitively plausible principle he calls 'EQUIV', from which principle it follows that it cannot be truer to say that, for example, God is not unwise than it is to say that God is wise. But, as already mentioned, the Priority Thesis does not set out to place *all* positive statements about God below negative statements.

A second possible point of disagreement identified by Rea concerns the Trinity. In my Position Statement I briefly developed the trinitarian conception of God in terms of such categories as 'communion' and 'relationality': "God as Trinity consists in interpersonal and perichoretic communion," I stated (97).

Rea rightly presses for clarification on the relation of 'interpersonal and perichoretic communion' that is said to hold between the Father, Son and Holy Spirit. One way of construing this relation, Rea says, is by way of the claim that "Father, Son and Holy Spirit stand in that relation and, somehow by virtue of their standing in that relation, it is true that there is exactly one triune God" (175). But this, as Rea quickly points out, is open to the charge that the divine unity cannot be founded upon such flimsy grounds, for 'interpersonal and perichoretic communion' would not suffice to make three human persons one man (or woman), let alone securing the unity of three divine persons as one God.

However, I never sought to make 'interpersonal and perichoretic communion' the basis or justification for divine unity. I simply wished to emphasize this as the kind of relation in which the divine persons stand and then to draw some consequences for our understanding of being (both divine being and human being). Be that as it may, there is a possible and promising response to the objection raised by Rea, although I am not sure I entirely agree with it.

Gregory of Nyssa, in his short treatise *To Ablabius: On Not Three Gods* (Engl. trans. in Hardy and Richardson 1954: 256–267), states that the word 'Godhead' (*theotes, theoteta*) relates to the dimension of operation or activity, not to that of nature or essence. He goes on to say that since the activities of the Father, Son and Holy Spirit are the same, the power which gave rise to them is the same (or is one) – and, as a consequence, the (divine) nature in which that power is inherent must also be one. Perhaps this could be expressed by saying that there is one nature because there is one power, and there is one power because there is one activity.

Gregory then considers an objection, like that made by Rea, that we know of plenty of cases where there is a common operation or activity, although

260   N. N. Trakakis

distinct individuals are involved. For example, we speak of 'orators' to signify a plurality of people who share the same or a single operation. So, why could we not say that the word 'Godhead' likewise signifies a plurality of beings who share the same or a single operation?

Gregory replies that there is a relevant difference between the human case and the divine case. In the human case, different persons undertake the same task, but they do not directly participate in the action of others (and so we can differentiate the action of each while they are engaged in the same task). By contrast, in the divine case, each person participates in the action of the other persons – and the kind of participation involved is signalled by the term *perichoresis* (interpenetration, coinherence), although it was John of Damascus and not Gregory of Nyssa who introduced this notion into trinitarian theology. The idea is that the divine persons mutually interpenetrate one another in such a way that there results a unity of action or operation in God, and hence the nature that originates that action must also be one. In this fashion, perichoretic communion secures the essential unity of the divine persons.

Nonetheless, I have some reservations. Gregory's account may show that the unity of action (among the three divine persons) proves or presupposes the unity of the divine nature. But the dependence relation remains unclear. In particular, it is an open question as to whether the unity of the nature is founded upon the unity of action (or, alternatively put, that God is one because the three persons act as one). For it seems that Gregory's account is entirely consistent with the converse view that the unity of action is founded upon the unity of nature, or that the three persons act as one because God is one (or is one in essence). Despite this problem in Gregory's account, he does at least indicate how one may respond to the kind of objection made by Rea.[1]

Rea also raises questions about John Zizioulas' 'being as communion' thesis, which I sought to explicate and endorse. This thesis, abbreviated as 'BAC', holds that the nature of being ultimately consists in communion and relationality. Rea points to two difficulties, the first of which concerns the compatibility between BAC and Zizioulas' 'sovereignty-aseity conviction', which takes God the Father to have a priority or sovereignty that is so absolute and radical that it would allow him, if he so chooses, to exist outside of any relation with the Son and the Spirit. But the sovereignty-aseity conviction is no conviction of mine, and it is not a necessary part of BAC.[2]

The second difficulty, however, seems more intrinsic to BAC. Rea notes that "the idea that the Father is at least *logically* prior to the other members of the Trinity seems well-entrenched in the tradition – for example, in the claim that the Son is *begotten* of the Father and that the Spirit *proceeds from* the Father" (175; emphases in original). However, "if BAC is true – if to be *is* to be in communion, such claims make no sense; for there cannot be even logical priority relations among the members of the Trinity." (175; emphasis in original)

Second Response   261

In response, the logical priority of the Father does not imply that the Father could possibly exist without, or in isolation from, the Son and the Spirit. The Father, alone among the divine persons, is unbegotten, uncaused and without source. Nevertheless, the being or nature of the Father is intrinsically relational: the Father exists always and necessarily as the eternal source of the Son and Spirit. The priority (logical, or perhaps metaphysical) of the Father, therefore, can only mean that the Father is the source (ἀρχή) and cause (αἰτία) of the Son and Holy Spirit, and thus the source and cause of the Trinity as a whole.[3]

Response to Bishop: 'Naturalist' Christian theism

Matters of epistemology

Bishop points to a well-known conundrum in the distinction often made in Orthodox theology between the essence of God and the energies of God:

> It seems to me contradictory to say both that God is "unknowable and unapproachable in essence" and also that 'the energies' by which God is known and approached "are . . . God *himself* in his action and revelation to the world".
>
> (this volume: 115; emphasis in original)

I discuss this problem in detail in Trakakis (2013), and I will only provide a summary here.

I was alerted to what I came to see as the essence of the problem by a comment from another (honorary) New Zealander, the renowned modal logician G. E. Hughes. In a paper examining the paradoxes arising from the doctrine of the Incarnation, Hughes wrote:

> The language of religion, and not only of the Christian religion, is full of what might be called non-standard assertions of identity. Professor Ninian Smart taught me this, and I think it is of the greatest importance.
>
> (1962: 210)

This, I think, is exactly right, and it provides a clue as to how to approach the problem identified by Bishop. As Frege (1966) noticed, true identity statements can often be uninformative or tautologous (e.g., 7 = 7), but identity statements can sometimes provide new information or extend our knowledge (e.g., *water* = H_2O). The problem – which has come to be known as 'Frege's Puzzle' – is that both sets of statements seem to be saying the same thing (namely, that a particular object is identical with itself), and yet the latter (which have the form $a = b$) are informative while the former (which have the form $a = a$) are not. So what is it about the cognitive or semantic content of these statements that accounts for this peculiar fact?

262 *N. N. Trakakis*

Frege's own answer is given by way of the distinction between 'sense' (*Sinn*) and 'reference' (*Bedeutung*). The *reference* of a linguistic expression (such as a proper name or description) is the object it designates or picks out. According to Frege, linguistic expressions do not only denote or refer to objects but also express a *sense*, and it is the sense that gives the expression cognitive significance. Consider, to borrow Frege's example, the expressions 'the morning star' and 'the evening star'. These are identical in reference – the object to which they both refer is the same (namely, the planet Venus). However, the sense expressed by each expression is distinct and different. It is not entirely clear what Frege had in mind by 'the sense' of a linguistic sign or expression. Although he left the term undefined, he seems to have meant something along the lines of 'a mode of presentation' or 'a way of conceiving'. In other words, the very same object – say, the planet Venus – can be presented to us in various forms or guises, or it can be thought about and conceptualized in diverse ways. A sense, therefore, is something that encompasses the mode of presentation or conception of an object.

The sense–reference distinction has had a major impact in the philosophy of language, and I think it can also be of use in the philosophy of religion, particularly in elucidating the essence–energies distinction. Following Frege, we could say that the expressions 'divine essence' and 'divine energies' have the same reference (namely, God himself), but differ in sense. Further following Frege, we could say that the distinct senses of each of the names that are associated with the divine energies (such as 'goodness' and 'wisdom') represent ways of perceiving and conceiving God. The divine energies, on this view, are how we perceive God's action and presence in the world. We do not perceive God's essence, but we can experience and come to know God's energies, and these we conceptualize by means of various names or 'energies', such as goodness, wisdom, power, and the like.

This may help resolve Bishop's worries about contradiction. If we make this move, however, are we not committed to viewing the distinction between the essence and the energies as merely a conceptual one, one not having any foothold in the divine reality itself – just as the distinction we make between the evening star and the morning star is merely one that exists on a nominal or conceptual level, not in physical reality?

This is a difficult problem and one that is exacerbated by the ambiguity in Frege's notion of 'sense'. Frege wished to avoid any suggestion that meanings are purely mental or psychological, and so he placed 'senses' in a kind of metaphysical 'third realm' (*das dritte Reich*), where they are distinguished from mere 'ideas' – that is, from the private ideas or feelings people associate with linguistic expressions (Frege 1966: 60; 1977: 17). It is 'sense', on Frege's view, that accounts for the shareability of language: we understand and can communicate with each other because we recognize the (same) 'sense' and not merely the reference of the names we employ. Frege therefore concluded that 'senses' must possess an objective, or at least an intersubjective, reality.

This Fregean understanding of sense may help us to see that the essence–energies distinction is not a purely conceptual one, with no basis in reality. Frege holds, as already mentioned, that the mode of perception or presentation is not entirely arbitrary, idiosyncratic or private, and this is because senses must be shareable and hence objective (or intersubjective) for meaningful communication to even be possible. Similarly, the various senses of the names that are associated with the divine energies (e.g., holiness, beauty) are not simply projection or delusion. In conceiving of God in these ways we are not imposing upon God attributes or qualities that do not really exist in him. Rather, our talk of divine energies, like Fregean 'senses', represents a way of thinking about the divinity that is literally and objectively true.

The distinction between *ousia* and *energeia* is certainly not conceived as an ontological distinction – that is to say, as a partition or division within the very nature or being of God. By the same token, the energies and names of God are not intended as merely nominal in nature, ones that are only created or imposed by our understanding. The Fregean way out is to say that the energies are modes of presentation that reflect not a division in the divinity but a way of perceiving God – one that is not simply a product of the human mind but accurately represents who God is.[4]

Matters of ontology

Bishop takes issue with the conception of divine personhood in Zizioulas' trinitarian theology, which seeks to remove some of the unduly anthropomorphic imagery that often accrues to talk of the Father, Son and Holy Spirit as 'persons'. Zizioulas does so by employing a non-individualistic and relational understanding of what it is to be a person. But Bishop asks: "isn't it precisely *that* conception of a person [i.e., a person as an individual centre of consciousness and agent] that we need for the conception of God as dynamic *interpersonal* relationship?" (116; emphases in original) He goes on to suggest that it is the modern, Lockean conception of a person that may be required in order to see how the relationality of the divine persons consists in perfect interpersonal love. Although he does not explicate the Lockean view, I assume it is the idea of a person as an agent who acts by means of thought and will, and is capable of bearing moral responsibility for his or her actions. Bishop further suggests that the relata in the Trinity must be persons in this Lockean sense if the goal of human life is to be taken as participation in trinitarian love or as seeking to mirror the personhood had by the divine persons.

These are difficult and significant matters. But I have come to see that what they call for is not so much a reclamation of the Lockean conception of personhood as a renewed appreciation for the ways in which eastern (particularly Hindu and Buddhist) philosophy delimit or even refuse the notion of personhood when thinking about the divine or ultimate reality. This has often been regarded as a sore point between western and eastern relations,

264 N. N. Trakakis

with the Abrahamic traditions conceptualizing ultimate reality as personal or a personal deity (e.g., as Yahweh, the Trinity, Allah), while eastern traditions regularly express what is ultimate in non-personal or transpersonal terms (e.g., as Brahman, Nirvana, the Dao).

But recent work in comparative philosophy and theology has done much to show how seemingly incompatible views about personhood across western and eastern religious traditions can be reconciled, and also how eastern ideas regarding personhood can be employed to challenge long-standing western prejudices and positions. Important and pioneering work in this regard has been carried out by Richard De Smet and Sara Grant, who sought to seriously engage Christian theology and spirituality with the 'non-dual' Hindu tradition of Advaita Vedanta (on De Smet, see Malkovsky 1999, 2000; also see Grant 2002). On the face of it, nothing could be further from the personalistic and dualistic Christian perspective than the monistic and idealistic metaphysics of the Advaita Vedanta school. De Smet, for example, has noted that communicating an understanding of the Absolute as personal was one of the main obstacles he faced "constantly" in his dialogue with Hindus, who would often dismiss the God of Christianity as not a true Absolute. However, De Smet soon realized that terms such as 'person' and 'personal' were shunned by Hindu thinkers when referring to Brahman only because these attributions were taken to imply a 'limited, anthropomorphic individual'. For this reason, the Advaitins would rather think of Brahman as 'non-personal' and indeed as transcending such oppositions as the personal and impersonal, or subject and object (see Malkovsky 1999: 415, n74). However, this need not rule out a personal or relational conception of ultimate reality but may instead force us to reevaluate our understanding of personhood and relationality. Consider, for example, the following analysis of personality proffered by De Smet (1968), where the context is what it means to know or experience God:

> Is it possible that God should be, like a lifeless thing, investigable to man at will? Should we not say that the intimacy, the mystery, which characterise even the human person, are surely to be found in Him in the most eminent degree? How could God be within the reach of any sort of conquest when even the personality of a child remains hidden and inaccessible to our grasp unless he freely reveals himself to those he loves. No knowledge from outside can substitute for self-communication. A free being can retain his own secret even though he be subjected to the worst torture. Love alone, which is a free surrender, can unfold that secret. But God cannot be anything but the very Fulness of Consciousness, Freedom and Love. No one, therefore, can enter into His mystery, unless He first freely reveals and surrenders Himself to him.
>
> (p. 366)[5]

Personhood for De Smet does not consist in being a finite or limited individual, but in having a kind of interiority and alterity such that knowledge of a person is possible only on the basis of relationship, or through a process of loving surrender and free self-communication. Is not this conception of personhood, where the emphasis is placed on free and loving communion, more in keeping with the patristic understanding of divine personhood than the forensic Lockean view that highlights individual agency and responsibility?

Further, if we take seriously the radically relational view of reality developed in the Advaita tradition (but also in various idealist streams of western metaphysics, including that of F. H. Bradley and other British idealists), where the world is conceived as a complex web of interconnections and relations, then the modern notion of 'person' as an individual agent and centre of consciousness comes under much pressure. Take, for example, Bradley's view that all relations are 'internal', so that everything is related (e.g., temporally or spatially) to everything else, and the nature and identity of each thing depends upon its relation to all else. In such a relational world, what room is there for things or entities that are ontologically distinct, independent and self-sufficient? If the deepest level of reality consists in holistic connectivity, then personal existence must be a matter of relation and interaction rather than individual agency and responsibility. Indeed, the Absolute, construed as what is ultimately real, simply consists of this one, vast and intricately interconnected whole, which can be described as neither 'personal' nor 'impersonal'. Rather, the entire dichotomy between the personal and the impersonal is overcome. And this prompts the further question: Is the category of 'personality' finally dispensable from our ontology, from our account of the ultimate foundations of reality?

In short, if we travel eastwards as far as the Byzantine Empire, we may transform our understanding of personhood along more relational and less individualistic lines than is customary in the West. And if we dare to journey further east, towards India and beyond, we may countenance a foreign but inviting world where 'personality' is altogether abolished.

Response to Eaton: Ecological Christianity

I will confine myself to two aspects of Eaton's reply to my Position Statement.

Orthodoxy and (post)modernity

I agree with Eaton that Orthodox theologians tend to be dismissive and insufficiently aware of and engaged with feminist theology, as well as many other modern movements in theology (Eaton mentions liberation theology). This represents, in my view, Orthodoxy's unfortunate 'Babylonian captivity' – the dominance of the medieval (usually Greek) patristic tradition on contemporary Orthodox theology, allied with a refusal to sympathetically engage with, and be challenged and enriched by, modern and postmodern currents of thought. The key figures (or culprits) in this case have been the Russian émigré thinkers, Georges Florovsky (1893–1979) and Vladimir Lossky (1903–1959), and the ensuing 1960s generation of Greek theologians, led by Christos Yannaras (b. 1935) and John Zizioulas (b. 1931). In seeking to 'return to the Fathers' and achieve a 'neo-patristic synthesis', these theologians admirably reclaimed many significant aspects of Orthodox thought and practice that had been overlooked or rejected for some time, including the understanding of the church as a eucharistic community, the centrality of apophatic theology, the notion of deification (*theosis*) as the destiny of humanity, the rediscovery of Byzantine iconography, and a renewed interest in monasticism. However, in seeking to 'de-westernize' Orthodoxy, a polemical and hostile relationship with western thought has emerged in the writings of many of these theologians, with the result that opportunities for identifying points of similarity, if not also prospects for re-envisioning the theology and practice of the Orthodox Church, are sadly foregone.

But not all is lost. A new movement (yet to be fully recognized in the Anglophone world) has arisen in Greece, calling for an Orthodox Reformation that would bring about a more authentic and informed renewal of the Orthodox Church. The leading voice in this movement has been Professor Pantelis Kalaitzidis, director of the Academy for Theological Studies at Volos, in central Greece. According to Kalaitzidis and a growing group of younger Orthodox theologians, the earlier 'neo-patristic' movement was an utter failure in achieving renewal. The turn to the Fathers has, instead, only mythologized patristic theology and created an unhealthy anti-westernism that has rendered the Orthodox Church insulated and conservative to such a degree that it is now impotent against the challenges posed by the modern world. Kalaitzidis (2009) nicely summarizes the matter as follows:

> The famous 'return to the Fathers' principle has often been understood in such a way as actually to encourage a retreat into a fundamentalist interpretation of tradition, in that it has often contributed to the denigration of everything to do with the West, and especially Western modernity. . . . Indeed, Fr Florovsky's famous 'return to the Fathers' has been understood and interpreted . . . in such a way, at once scholarly and defensive, as ultimately to entrench the belief in always looking to the past, *to* the Fathers, rather than looking *with* the Fathers towards the future. . . . Not only this, but it has left Orthodox theology tongue-tied and at a loss before the challenges of the modern, contemporary world.
>
> (p. 154, emphases in original)

To correct this, the new movement is developing a range of proposals aimed at renewing the life of the Orthodox Church so that it can better meet the challenges it faces at the dawn of the third millennium. The most urgent of these challenges is coming to terms with the modern world, particularly its secular and pluralistic character. As Kalaitzidis (2009) states, "The Orthodox Church and its theology can no longer ignore modernity and act as if it were living in traditional or pre-modern societies" (p. 160). There are valuable lessons that the Orthodox Church stands to gain from a creative dialogue with the modern (and also postmodern) world, such as: recognizing the harm in a nationalistic understanding of Christianity; active participation of the laity in worship; espousing the values of democracy and human rights; rehabilitating the value of the body, physicality and sexuality; engaging more closely with the theories and discoveries of science; and (as Eaton stresses) rethinking the role of women in the church.[6] Simply idolizing the past and demonizing the West will no longer do. The younger generation of Greek theologians has therefore been demanding a radical reformation from within, a new synthesis that will not only look to the patristic witness of the past but also to the best from the postmodern secular world. This synthesis of East and West may involve the development within Orthodoxy of a 'post-patristic theology', a theology that goes beyond the patristic tradition in a way not attempted previously but without abandoning the spirit of the patristic era. This is a call for a new theology and a new church, one that is self-critical and open to the future. But if the call is not heeded, the consequences may well be disastrous: "If the Orthodox Church insists on renouncing all change and reform, often in the name of preserving its unity and stability, then that church may one day come crashing to the ground" (Kalaitzidis 2009: 164).

The language of theology

In Eaton's view, the concepts and images we develop to describe God – for example, as a Trinity of persons in loving communion with one another – are not technical or theoretical attempts to disclose the nature of the divine reality, but are rather "exceptionally flexible exercises of the human imagination" (140). She is careful to qualify this by adding that this is not meant to reduce the trinitarian model of God to a human fabrication or invention, but is only meant to highlight the way in which our language about God is a product of "imagining (i.e., employing images), speculating, desiring and even intuiting aspects of reality beyond our knowing and doing so in exceedingly symbolic – and thus not in transparent – language" (140).

In saying this, however, does Eaton mean to endorse the view that theological discourse is irredeemably symbolic or metaphorical, without having any factual or propositional content? A symbol or metaphor cannot be true or false; it can only be judged according to criteria such as usefulness (e.g., in helping one to turn to God and repent), aesthetic power, level of insightfulness and sublimity, etc. A proposition or statement, by contrast, seeks to represent the way the world is and so can be judged as true or false depending on whether it succeeds in representing reality accurately. Eaton seems to hold that, in the religious sphere at least, there are no truths but only non-cognitive expressions of religious experience couched in images, metaphors and symbols. As she put it in her Position Statement: "The categories of 'true' and 'false' are inapplicable. Religious symbols are active, alive or dynamic, or they are dying or dead" (29).

268   *N. N. Trakakis*

This brings Eaton's account of religious language quite close to so-called 'non-realist' views, such as those of D. Z. Phillips and other Wittgensteinians, who see religion as constituting a 'form of life' that is expressed in a variety of distinctive 'language games' that cannot be assimilated to, or modelled on, the fact-stating and evidence-based language games of the sciences. Unlike Eaton, however, these Wittgensteinians do countenance a notion of 'truth' in religion, though they would add that religious language games have a unique 'grammar' (their own set of rules) and their own criteria of truth, rationality and intelligibility which may or may not be shared by other language games.

Eaton's outright rejection of truth and falsehood (in religious discourse) is therefore likely to strike even Wittgensteinians as an implausible move to make, but it also conflicts with Eaton's own professed views in her Position Statement. There she emphasized that to think of our language about God as the work of human imagination "does not negate or reduce the validity of the activity, or suggest there is no divine referent outside of human imaginings" (26). She also identified herself as "a classical panentheist – the divine is present and beyond, at least beyond our knowing. Thus, for myself, divinity is both a perception and an act of the imagination" (31). But if there is something divine to be perceived, so that it is not merely the result of human invention or projection, then there is *a truth of the matter* as to whether the divine (or some form of divinity) exists. In other words, Eaton herself accepts as true the existence of divinity (which she conceptualizes in terms of the 'divine milieu'), but this is incompatible with her repudiation of truth in religion.

Also, one might wonder why our use and understanding of religious language should be reconstructed along the lines suggested by Eaton, where the categories of truth and falsity are displaced by symbols and metaphors. In my First Response to Eaton, I pointed out that such reconstruction would undermine religious commitment. A further unpalatable consequence (although I think there are many others) consists in the loss of the vital 'critical' dimension of adjudicating between different religious perspectives (and between religious perspectives and non-religious or naturalistic worldviews) according to standards of (objective) truth, justification and evidence (hence the charge of 'fideism' sometimes levelled against the Wittgensteinian school).

Response to Hart: Catholic Christianity

A question of great importance raised by Hart's First Response relates not so much to the conception or model of God we propose but to the method we use to arrive at such a conception or model. This 'problem of method' may be put as follows: How do we arrive at a religiously adequate idea of God or ultimate reality? What methods are there for arriving at an idea of God, and which of these is to be preferred? Hart opts for the method of 'perfect being theology', but there are significant limitations and problems with such a method. Here I can only point, somewhat sketchily, to several of these difficulties. (I do not mean to suggest that none of these difficulties can be surmounted, but only that perfect being theology is more problematic than may initially seem to be the case.)

To begin with, is the methodology of perfect being theology sufficient on its own, or must it be supplemented and even corrected by other methods? More biblically inclined theologians, for example, may wish to prioritize the Scriptures as a resource for developing the doctrine of God (although, as Hart notes, the clarity and sufficiency of Scripture can be questioned). Others might opt for the method of explanatory postulation, where our conception of God is derived from our attempt to explain the existence and nature of the cosmos. On this method, we attribute to God only those properties that are required to explain, for example, why there is a universe at all, or why there occur various religiously significant events such as miracles and mystical experiences.[7] These methods may be deficient and incomplete in certain respects, but they may be indispensable in filling lacunae or correcting excesses arising from the method of perfect being theology.

A second problem with perfect being theology is the widespread disagreement as to what counts as a 'perfection' or a 'perfect being'. This is why perfect being theology has yielded divergent results or divergent conceptions of God. Intuitions about what counts as a perfection or a 'great-making property' may vary: Is the property of being powerful a great-making property, or is it value-neutral? Are Thomists right to think of timelessness, immutability and impassibility as great-making properties, or are process and open theists correct in thinking of the capacity to be fully involved in and affected by temporal processes as a form of excellence that ought to be attributed to God? For Anselm, omniscience is a perfection; but for the Middle Platonist, Alcinous, it is not worthy of God to know about certain things, such as diseases and individuals. Even more problematically, the very notion of a 'perfection' or a 'great-making property' stands in need of clarification and analysis. What exactly is a perfection or a great-making property? There is disagreement about this, too. For some (e.g., Hoffman and Rosenkrantz 2002) great-making is a function of worship-worthiness and moral admirability, but for others (e.g., Morris 1987) great-making is a function of intrinsic goodness, or metaphysical status or stature.

Thirdly, perfect being theology faces the 'uniqueness problem': Is there *only one* perfect being? Or, if we adopt Thomas Morris' notion of God as a being with the greatest possible array of compossible great-making properties, how can we be sure that there is a *unique* greatest possible array of compossible great-making properties? For all we know, there may be *several* equally good sets of compossible great-making properties than which a greater set is not possible. (Even if there is a unique set of maximal perfections, can we be sure that these perfections are not exemplified by *more than one being*?)

Fourthly, perfect being theology gives rise to various 'coherence problems'. As is indicated by the infamous paradox of the stone, maximal perfection might entail individual properties (in this case, omnipotence) that are self-contradictory. Alternatively, it has often been argued that two or more properties (e.g., perfect goodness and perfect power) entailed by maximal perfection are logically incompatible with each other, and so the set of divine perfections is not mutually consistent.

I will mention two further difficulties faced by perfect being theology. There is the matter of its compatibility with revealed theology. Can the absolutely perfect God of Anselmian theism be identified with the God revealed in the Judeo-Christian Scriptures? This is, of course, a long-standing problem, but it takes much ingenious hermeneutics to render the all-too-human deity of the Old Testament compatible with the metaphysically exalted God of Anselm. This brings me to a final difficulty, the charge of *anthropomorphism*. It might be argued that not only the God of the Bible but even the Anselmian God seems to be created in man's image. The perfect being method involves the ascription to God of various great-making properties had by humans, such as knowledge, intelligence and power. On the perfect being model, however, God has these positive qualities to an absolute or infinite degree, unlike our finite and fragile possession of them. The gulf therefore between Creator and creature is only one of degree, not an absolute one. But this qualitative similarity between the divine and the human implies that God is very much like a human being, that he is 'one of us', one inhabitant of the universe amongst others, albeit one that is invisible and happens to be (in David Burrell's words) "the biggest thing around".

Hart holds that the price of rejecting divine simplicity is a conception of God as a "finite super-being", a God who resembles "a big guy in the sky, the God of the nursery more than the God of the Church" (149). But how is this problem of 'conceptual idolatry' overcome in perfect being theology, where the Creator again takes on the proportions of a creature, even if magnified to an infinite and perfected degree?

Is the answer to be found in Hart's deferral to simplicity? Simplicity, of course, registers a radical difference between God and creatures. But even this difference, no matter how radical, is set within a context of many points of similarity (or 'analogy'). Hart himself indicates this when employing the analogy of a human father to argue in defence of the afterlife: "If I could have saved my father from death, I surely would have done so because I loved him; and since God is infinitely more powerful than I am and is infinitely more loving than I am, it is not unreasonable to think that he will save my father from the finality of death" (152–153). But if such analogies or correspondences between the human and the divine hold, then in what sense can God be said to be "*absolutely* singular" (to borrow Hart's term)? The difficulty here, as I indicated in my response to Bishop earlier, is that western ideas of God are often developed in ways that do not amount to a 'true Absolute', that which alone is '*ultimate*'.

Second Response   271

This brings me to Hart's concluding dichotomy between *the development of doctrine* and *alternatives to doctrine*. Despite, in some sense, 'representing' the Orthodox Christian perspective in this exchange, my preference is to overcome such divisions between orthodoxy and heterodoxy (or, even more invidiously, orthodoxy and heresy). I have been suggesting, for example, that ideas about ultimate reality as they are to be found in eastern religions (especially the Advaita Vedanta school of Hinduism) may profitably be appropriated by Christians so as to enrich – and even challenge and overturn – received or traditional views concerning the nature of God or ultimate reality. A common reaction from Christian theologians is to say that those who decide to depart from Church doctrine in this manner can no longer be considered 'Christian', or at least 'orthodox Christians' (let alone big-O 'Orthodox Christians'!). But now we move from philosophy and theology to politics, and in particular to the politics of identity. In such contexts, I like to defer to Michel Foucault, someone acutely aware of the political implications of names and classifications:

> Do not ask who I am and do not ask me to remain the same: leave it to our bureaucrats and our police to see that our papers are in order. At least spare us their morality when we write.
>
> (2002: 19)

Notes

1 Rea also adverts to an alternative understanding of the relation of 'interpersonal and perichoretic communion', according to which "God, *qua* triune, *consists in* the relation of interpersonal and perichoretic communion among the persons" (175; emphasis in original). Rea rejects this conception of the Trinity but does not say why. As I indicated in note 14 of my Position Statement (106), I do not mean to reduce the divine persons to nothing but communal relation, although I do wish to elucidate the character of divine being by way of the category of relationality.
2 McCall's (2010: 207–209) proposal for rendering BAC compatible with the sovereignty-aseity conviction or 'SAC', which involves making certain alterations to SAC, seems promising to me.
3 This, I believe, also addresses Hart's concern that the Orthodox teaching on the monarchy of the Father "suggests there was a time or an ontological state before there was a Son and a Holy Spirit" (156).
4 In §3 of Trakakis (2013), I seek to elucidate the essence–energies distinction by comparing it not only to Frege's sense–reference distinction but also to Kant's distinction between noumena and phenomena.
   I might add that the Orthodox view (as represented by, among others, the Cappadocians) is unambiguously that the essence of God is *completely* (not partially) unknowable and unapproachable. I am not convinced that this is a "hopeless" view, particularly when understood in the context of the essence–energies distinction and the attempt to preserve the primacy of apophaticism in theology. This, however, need not mean that mystical knowledge of God rules out propositional or conceptual knowledge of God. One may more profitably picture the relationship between the propositional and the mystical in terms of a Hegelian (or even

Wittgensteinian) 'ascent', moving beyond one mode of knowledge (or, better, stage of the spiritual life) towards another and higher one, without thereby simply negating the earlier but rather taking it up and transforming it. Natural theology therefore retains its relevance without presuming to be the only or the ideal way to God.

5 De Smet goes on to say that, "God, of course, can gain nothing by self-surrender to us. The Fulness cannot be improved and supreme Love is supremely disinterested. But we have everything to gain" (p. 367). This repeats the familiar Thomistic doctrine of the lack of real relations in God, which entails that the relations between God and the world are 'one-way' relations, so that it is not within the ability of any creature to make a difference to God. I remain ambivalent about this doctrine; in any case, it is not a necessary feature of De Smet's conception of personhood.

6 Two excellent recent Orthodox studies on the role of women in the church are Kalaitzidis and Dondos (2004) and Liveris (2005).

7 The central notion in this method is 'ultimacy', not 'perfection', and although Hart enlists Aquinas as a proponent of perfect being theology, it is perhaps more accurate to see Aquinas as advocating a number of methods, including the method of explanatory postulation.

References

De Smet, R. 1968. "The Nature of Christian Philosophy." In *World Perspectives in Philosophy, Religion and Culture: Essays Presented to Professor Dhirendra Moran Datta*, edited by R. J. Singh, 362–368. Patna: Bharati Bhawan.

Foucault, M. 2002. *The Archaeology of Knowledge*, translated by A. M. Sheridan-Smith. London: Routledge.

Frege, G. 1966. "On Sense and Reference." In *Translations from the Philosophical Writings of Gottlob Frege*, edited by P. Geach and M. Black, translated by M. Black, 56–78. Oxford: Basil Blackwell.

Frege, G. 1977. *Logical Investigations*, edited by P. T. Geach, translated by P. T. Geach and R. H. Stoothoff. Oxford: Basil Blackwell.

Grant, S. 2002. *Toward an Alternative Theology: Confessions of a Non-Dualist Christian*. Notre Dame: University of Notre Dame Press.

Hardy, E. R. and C. C. Richardson (eds.). 1954. *Christology of the Later Fathers*, vol. 3. London: SCM Press.

Hoffman, J. and G. S. Rosenkrantz. 2002. *The Divine Attributes*. Oxford: Blackwell.

Hughes, G. E. 1962. "Mr. Martin on the Incarnation: A Reply to Mr. Plantinga and Mr. Rowe." *Australasian Journal of Philosophy* 40: 208–211.

Kalaitzidis, P. 2009. "Challenges of Renewal and Reformation Facing the Orthodox Church." *Ecumenical Review* 61: 136–164.

Kalaitzidis, P. and N. Dondos (eds.). 2004. *Gender and Religion: The Role of Women in the Church* (published in Greek). Athens: Indiktos.

Liveris, L. B. 2005. *Ancient Taboos and Gender Prejudice: Challenges for Orthodox Women and the Church*. Aldershot: Ashgate.

Malkovsky, B. 1999. "Advaita Vedanta and Christian Faith." *Journal of Ecumenical Studies* 36: 397–422.

Malkovsky, B. 2000. "The Life and Work of Richard V. De Smet, S. J." In *New Perspectives on Advaita Vedanta: Essays in Commemoration of Professor Richard De Smet, S. J.*, edited by B. Malkovsky, 1–17. Leiden: E. J. Brill.

McCall, T. H. 2010. *Which Trinity? Whose Monotheism?: Philosophical and Systematic Theologians on the Metaphysics of Trinitarian Theology.* Grand Rapids: Wm. B. Eerdmans Publishing.

Morris, T. V. 1987. "Perfect Being Theology." *Noûs* 21: 19–30.

Trakakis, N.N. 2013. "The Sense and Reference of the Essence and Energies." In *Divine Essence and Divine Energies: Ecumenical Reflections on the Presence of God in Eastern Orthodoxy*, edited by C. Athanasopoulos and C. Schneider, 210–231. Cambridge: James Clarke & Company.

Index

academia: challenges to moral and spiritual development 85
Advaita Vedanta 264, 265, 271
Aetius 94, 128n3
afterlife: ecological perspective 33, 35–6, 38–9, 191–3, 226–8; naturalist rejection of 189–90; Protestant view 77, 80
Alcinous 269
Alexandrian exegetical method 90
analogical predication 116
analytical philosophy: and philosophy of religion 154, 159–60, 188, 197, 200, 237–8
analytic theology 251–5
Analytic Theology (Crisp and Rea) 251–2, 254
ananthropic theism 127
Anselm 149, 269
Anselmian theism 270
anthropocentrism 30, 39, 126–7, 142
anthropomorphism 270
Antiochene exegetical method 90
apophatic (negative) theology 11, 94–5, 105n5–6, 115, 140, 158–9, 172–4, 257–9
Apostles' Creed 64, 163, 179
Aquinas, St Thomas: analogical predication 116; on efficient causes 23n7; five ways 96; on Jesus 51; and perfect being theology 149, 151, 272n7; on simple nature of God 156, 158; on theological virtues 235; on the Trinity 154, 156, 157, 159, 203–4, 205, 211n15
Arianism 51, 96–7, 98, 102, 155, 156
Aristotle 76, 98, 99
Arius 98
Armstrong, David 209n4

Assumption of the Blessed Virgin Mary 123
Athanasian Creed 11
Athanasian ontological revolution 117
Athanasius 98, 104, 107n20, 108n26, 108n30, 156
atonement 36–7, 82, 126
Augustine 61, 94, 101, 105n4, 115, 151, 247
awe 44
axarchism 210
axial age 42

Bachelard, Gaston 29, 43
Bacon, Francis 242
Bal, Mieke 146
baptismal promise 4, 135, 210n11
Barth, Karl 49, 155, 158, 219, 239
Bartholomew I: Ecumenical Patriarch 95, 142
basilaic reduction 56, 58
Basil of Caesarea 156
being as communion 98–9, 116, 175, 260
Belgic Confession 73
belief: content 5–6; 'in' God 4, 7; justifiability of 5; 'that' 4; *see also* faith
Berry, Thomas 224
Bible: exegesis 90, 154; historical criticism 233; New Testament 37–8, 49, 81, 83, 90; Old Testament 154, 188, 249–50, 255–6n3; Orthodox view of 90; veracity of 221
body/soul dualism 41, 146
Bradley, F. H. 265
Brower, Jeffery 183
Buddhism 192
Buechner, Frederick 190
Burrell, David 8

Index   275

Cabasilas, Nicholas 93
Calvinism 154, 159
Canticle of the Sun (St Francis) 212n19
Cappadocian Fathers 93, 94, 97, 98, 107n17, 128n3, 157
Catholic Christianity *see* phenomenological theology
certainty 30, 35, 133, 139–40, 191, 217, 222–3, 225–6
Chalcedonian Definition/Creed 102, 103, 125, 148, 149, 153, 160
Chittister, Joan 31
Christian commitment: justifiability of 20–3
Christian ethical ideal: accessibility of 17–18, 138
Christian faith: meaning of 163–4, 229
Christian imperialism 35, 216–17, 230
Christian life: rhythm of 58, 62, 63–4
Christianity: as aggressive religion 35, 137; central dialectic 63–4; dismissal of world as ground of life 62; historical forms and cultural diversity 213–14, 228–9; historical robustness 214; impact on the world 216, 217; meaning of 163–4, 229, 230; parameters of 160, 216, 229, 271; philosophical critique, openness to 5; as a philosophy 163; and science 135; skepticism re central claims 232–4; two worlds interpretation 126
Christian philosophers: elusiveness of 'position' 3; professional challenges 85
Christians: contradictory practices 137; distinguishing beliefs 242–3; diversity 214; spectrum of beliefs 131
Christian theology: diversity within 131; internal preoccupation of 230; metaphor and narrative 61, 63; phenomenology of the Christ 48; traditional understanding 148
Christology: Orthodox Christianity 101–4, 117
Chrysostom, John 90
Church Dogmatics (Barth) 158
classical panentheism 31, 193, 268
classical theism 209–10n5; divinity, conception of 6, 11, 185–6
classical theology 199
communion: persons in 98–9, 107n16
conceptual idolatry 94
concretion 53, 54
contemplative prayer 58, 60

contextual theologies 220
cosmology: Orthodox Christianity 99–101
Council of Chalcedon 102–3
Craig, William Lane 247–8
creatio ex nihilo 99–100, 117, 125, 127, 153, 188, 202

Dawkins, Richard 68, 120
de Chardin, Teilhard 30, 33, 127, 140, 224
De Smet, Richard 264, 272n5
divine hiddenness 182, 235–6
divine incomprehensibility 199
divine milieu 30, 31, 39, 43, 127, 193–4, 217
divine purpose: anthropocentric view 30, 39, 126
divine simplicity 149, 151, 270
divine transcendence 55, 150–1, 172–4, 257–9
divine wrath 87n19
divinity: argument from evil 9–10, 164; classical theistic conception 6; ecological perspective 29–31, 127; evolving understanding of 12–13, 136, 187–8, 211n13; personal omniGod theistic account 6–7; phenomenological theology approach 59–62, 150–3; philosophical theories, importance of 12–13; Protestant perspective 73–7, 123–4, 146; tradition-mediated positive conceptions 12; understanding nature of 6–11; *see also* euteleological conception of the divine; God
Divino afflante spiritu (Papal Encyclical) 232
doctrine: development of/alternatives to 160, 271
dogmatism 191, 217, 226
dualism 40, 41, 78, 135, 138, 146, 193

Earth: as sacred 43
Eckhart, Meister 152, 224
ecological Christianity: afterlife 33, 35–6, 38–9, 191–3, 226–8; atonement 36–7; defence of views 41–3; divinity 29–31; ethics, politics and everyday life 45; and fall/ redemption theology 138, 142–3; the Incarnation 35–6; New Testament account of Jesus 37–8; resurrection of the dead 37; symbolic consciousness

276 *Index*

27–9; theory of religion 26, 27–31, 43; the Trinity 32–4
ecological crisis: religious responses to 42–3
ecumenical creeds 163
ecumenicalism 64
efficient causality 14, 23n7, 201
enstatic phenomenology 59
epectasy 58, 63
epistemology: Orthodox Christianity 92–6, 115, 140, 261–3; of revelation 4–5, 135–6
epoché 49, 51, 52, 53, 56, 64, 180, 234, 236
eschatology 52, 58, 84, 104, 146, 205
essence/energies distinction 93, 104, 115, 261–3, 271–2n4
ethical knowledge 118–19
ethical theory-building 83–4
Eunomius 51, 94, 128n3
euteleological conception of divinity 13–14, 188–9; accessibility of ethical ideals 18; aim of 113–14; creatio ex nihilo 117, 127, 188, 201–2; ethics 17–18; God as realized telos 14–15, 152, 199; Incarnation 16–17; as non-personal conception 204–5; power of love 18–19, 200; supreme good, nature of 15, 202; transformation through love 19–20, 166, 200
Evagrius of Pontus 94, 104
evangelical theology 60
evidence: and reason 167–9, 230
evil, problem of 9–10, 108n27, 164, 186–7, 207–8
exchange formula 103–4, 117
exclusivism 138–9, 208

faith: evidential ambiguity 120, 121; evidentialist policy 121–2; and morality 83–4; and philosophy 85; and politics 84–5; and reason 43–4, 68–71, 120–2, 143–4
the Fall 79–80, 101, 107–8n26
fall/redemption theology: evolutionary perspective 138, 142–3, 147
Father: God as 52–4, 55–6, 57, 118, 150, 161n3, 235
feminist theologies 216, 265
Fichte, J. G. 50, 240
fideism 96, 115, 268
fides quaerens intellectum/faith seeking understanding 11, 127, 197–8, 200, 210n11

filioque controversy 32, 106n13, 123, 148, 157
First Council of Constantinople 245
First Council of Nicaea 55, 62, 97, 114
First Nation peoples: spiritual genocide 135
Florovsky, Georges 265
Foucault, Michel 271
Fourth Ecumenical Council, Chalcedon 102–3
Francis of Assisi 206–7
Frege's Puzzle 261–2
fundamentalism 43, 217

Gebara, Ivone 39, 127, 191, 218, 224
Gilkey, Langdon 31
Gnosticism 32, 133, 140
God: appearance in human experience 170–2, 176n8, 238–9; as Being Itself 8–9; concretion of 53, 54, 55, 57, 176n6; as creator 99–101, 117, 137, 149, 164, 188, 201–2, 210–11n12; as emergent 164; as Father 52–4, 55–6, 57, 118, 150, 161n3, 235; as female 241; as goodness 202–3; as the Ground of Being 9; as love 16, 138, 156, 158, 164–5, 199–200; as male 130, 137, 150, 220–1; as mother 161n3; as mystery 92–6, 115, 140, 172–4; omni-properties 137–8; as a person 8, 77, 86n11, 204–5, 263; phenomenality of 64; *see also* Trinity
God-imagery 133, 136
God-language 27, 28, 30, 31, 127
God-role 9, 203
God's presence: allowing oneself to come into 55, 134; quest to bring on 55, 170–1
Gould, Stephen Jay 221
Grant, Sara 264
Gregory of Nazianzus 90, 91, 103, 105n7, 117, 247
Gregory of Nyssa 62, 94–5, 99, 108n36, 157, 185, 246–7, 259–60

Hanson, R. P. C. 153
Harvey, Thomas 199, 210n6
Hebrew Bible 249, 255–6n3
Hegel, G. W. F. 48, 49, 54, 151, 236–7
Heidegger, M. 49, 166, 191
Hellenism: Christianization of 98
Henry, Michel 59, 179
Heschel, Abraham 44
Hick, John 189

Hinduism 101, 264
hope 225
Hughes, G. E. 251
human condition 80–3, 146–7, 192
human freedom 78, 124, 125
human nature: ecological perspective
    40–1; Protestant view 77–80, 124–5
human rights 136
Husserl, E. 49, 51, 52, 59, 60, 61, 180,
    234, 240
hypostasis/underlying substance 98,
    98–9, 106n15
hypostatic union: doctrine of 103, 117

idealism 193
imago dei doctrine 77
Incarnation: ecological perspective 33,
    35–6; naturalist view 16–17, 117;
    Orthodox understanding 101–2;
    Protestant view 80–3, 125–6, 185
inclusivism 22–3, 139, 208
Inquisition 135, 230
intelligent design theories 31
Isaac of Nineveh 108n30
Islam 101

James, William 120, 121
Jesus: baptism of 55, 172, 238; basilaic
    reduction 56, 58; as the Christ
    48, 64, 132, 170; as datum of
    revelation 48, 55, 132–3; function
    in the Trinity 33; as historical figure
    33, 37, 50–1, 132, 178–9, 233–4;
    as phenomenality of God 64; in
    phenomenological theology 50–1,
    52–3, 170; resurrection 19, 38, 62–3,
    205–6, 233–4; self-revelation of God
    in 49–50, 55, 132; symbolic power
    38; 'two minds' view 81–2, 125–6,
    185; see also Christology
Journal of Analytic Theology 253
Judaism 48; Shema 106n12
justice 225
just-war theory 136, 230

Kalaitzidis, Pantelis 266
Kant, I. 48, 59, 236
kataphatic (positive) theology 11,
    12–13, 95, 115, 158
kenosis 58, 63
Kingdom of God/basileia: for all
    faiths 236; attempts to bring on
    61–2; and basilaic reduction 56,
    58; challenge to political and social

structures 62–3, 118, 119; ethical
    characterization 118–19, 240; nature
    of 52–3, 57, 64, 118, 239, 240–1;
    and parable of father and two sons
    53–4, 58, 60–1

L'Arche communities 30, 46n3, 230
Leben-Jesu-Forschung 51
Leibniz's law 183, 247
liberation theologies 35–6, 138, 216
Lindbeck, George 168
Logic of God Incarnate,
    The (Morris) 185
Lord's Resistance Army 230
Lossky, Vladimir 91, 95–6, 106n9, 265
Lotos sutra 60
love: transcendent power 128, 218

McCall, Thomas 175
Mahayana Buddhism 108n29
man: as pinnacle of God's creation
    100, 142
Manicheanism 99
Mariology 224
Marion, J.-L. 66, 67
matter: key metaphysical role 128n6
Maximus the Confessor 100, 104,
    107n21, 107n24, 107n26, 108n30
Meier, J. P. 64n1
mind/body dualism 40, 41, 146
miracles 37
modalism 97
monarchy of the Father doctrine 106
Monophysitism 102–3, 108n31
morality: and ethical-theory building
    83–4
Morris, Thomas 81, 184, 269
Muhammad (Prophet) 101–2
Mulgan, Tim 127
mysogyny 135, 142
mystery: God as 92–6, 115, 140, 174
mystical theology 150
mysticism 105–6n9

natural attitude 56, 57
naturalism 167, 193, 199
naturalist Christian theism: alternatives
    to personal omniGod theism 11–13;
    on apophaticism 11; on classical
    theism 6, 185–6; contestability of
    truth-claims 4; epistemology of
    revelation 4–5; on God as a person
    8, 164–5; on God as being itself 8–9;
    on God-role 9; justifiability of belief

278 *Index*

5–6, 20–3; on personal omniGod theism 6–8, 9–11, 186; philosopher's position 3–6; on problem of evil 9–10, 164, 186–7, 207–8; viability of 166, 167; *see also* euteleological conception of the divine

natural theology: value of 12–13, 96, 115

negative theology *see* apophatic (negative) theology

Neo-Arians 164

Nestorius 103

Newman, John 151

New Testament 37–8, 49, 81, 83, 90

Nicaea I 55

Nicene Creed: Christological theses 51, 62; on constantiability 123, 175, 245, 246; content 64, 160, 163, 164; *filioque* controversy 32, 106n13, 123, 148, 157; interpretation and modification 148, 153; nature of 160, 242, 243; Trinity 154, 157

Nicolas of Cusa 159

non-intentional phenomenology 59

objective truth 221–5

omniproperties of God 137–8

ontological naturalism 209n4

ontology: Orthodox view 96–9, 115–16, 263; personhood 98–9, 106n15, 107n17, 263–5

O'Reilly, Bill 163, 164

Origen 55, 150, 160

original guilt 79, 86n19

original sin 79–80, 125; *see also* the Fall

Orthodox Christianity: apophatic character 94–5, 105n5–6, 115, 140, 172–4, 257–9; Babylonian captivity 265; and Catholicism 232; Christology and soteriology 101–4, 117; Church, role of 92; cosmology and anthropology 99–101; creator, God as 99–101; 'Eastern' qualifier 105n1; and eco-theology 142; epistemology 92–6, 115, 140, 261–3; the Fall, view of 101, 102, 107–8n26; history 89; mystery, God as 92–6, 140, 172–4; neo-patrist movement 265–6; ontology 96–9, 115–16, 263; reformation movement 266–7; relationship with western thought 266; Scripture, approach to 90, 141–2; Tradition, conception of 90–2,

105n2, 259–61; Trinity doctrine 96–9, 140–1, 156–7, 174–5

Orthodox Way, The (Ware) 89

Palamas, Gregory 93

panentheism 31, 193, 202, 228, 268

Pannenberg, W. 152, 155, 219

pantheism 6, 9, 193–4

Papaderos, Alexandros 220

Papanikolaou, Aristotle 95–6

parables: double structure of revelation 55–6; on father and his two sons 53–4, 58, 60–1, 134; Good Samaritan 57; Jesus's performance of epoché 53, 63; as pre-thetic experience of God's kingly rule 61

participation in God/metousia theou 101

patristic theology 91

Peirce, C. S. 44

penal substitution 82, 126

perfect being theology 74–5, 149, 151–2, 199, 203–4, 268–70, 272n7

perichoresis 11, 174, 175, 210, 259, 260

personal omniGod theism: and argument from evil 9–10; divinity, conception of 6–7; and God-role 9–10; as inconsistent with Trinitarianism 10–11; rejection of 127, 152, 158, 210n6; religious critique of 7–8

personhood 98–9, 106n15, 107n17, 263–5

person/prosopon 98

Perszyk, Ken 199, 210n6

phenomenality: nature and scope 48–50

phenomenological theology: basilaic reduction 56, 58; 'Jesus', meaning of 50–2; model of divinity 59–62; nature and scope of phenomenality 48–50; resurrection of Jesus 62–3; *see also* Kingdom of God/basileia

phenomenology: classical phenomenology 51, 59; in philosophy 236–8; use in theology 180–1, 235–6; as way of seeing 51–2, 180

phenomenology of the Christ 48, 170, 232, 241

Phillips, D. Z. 268

philosophical inquiry 114

philosophy as profession: and faith 85, 128

philosophy of religion: and analytical philosophy 154, 159–60, 188, 197,

200, 237–8, 251–5; Wittgensteinian method 95, 128n2
Plantinga, Alvin 181
Plato 99
Plotinus 99
pluralism 138
politics: and faith 45, 84–5
prayer: characteristics attitudes of 197, 209n1; contemplative prayer 58, 60; philosophizing in context of 197, 209n2
Proslogion (Anselm) 149, 197
Protestantism (Reformed): attributes of God 73–7, 123–4, 146; humanity and the human condition 77–83, 146–7; on Incarnation 80–3, 125–6, 185; life and practice 83–5; sola scriptura 71–3, 122–3, 145–6, 153–4, 182–3, 249–51; on triunity 75–7, 146, 157, 183–5
Pseudo-Dionysius 31, 99, 105n6, 105n7, 140, 150, 159, 224
purpose of existence 78–9

Quinn, Philip 181

Rahner, Karl 54, 155, 219, 239
rationality 43–4
reason: and evidence 167–9, 230; and faith 43–4, 68–71, 120–2, 143–4; and revelation 54–5
Reformed Bible 153–4
Reformed epistemology 96, 181
Reinarch, A. 61
relativism 22–3
religion: and science 167; theory of 26, 27–31, 43
religions: as maps or languages 147, 215, 222–3, 229–30; theology of 59–60
religious consciousness 27–8
religious discourse: and notion of 'truth' 90–1, 167–8, 214, 221–6, 267–8
religious diversity: accordance with divine will 22–3
religious experiences 70–1, 86n7, 214–15, 223–4, 225
religious languages 137, 214–15, 220–1, 222, 229
religious symbols: power of 28, 267
resurrection: of the body 39–40, 124–5; of the dead 37, 193; evidence for 169, 179–80, 194n1; idea of 146; of

Jesus 19, 38, 62–3, 205–6, 233–4; symbolic meaning of 217–18
revelation: epistemology of 4–5, 135–6; euteleological view 208; and reason 54–5; self-revelation of God in Jesus Christ 49–50, 55
Richard of St Victor 155–6
Ruether, Rosemary Radford 213, 224

Sabellianism 97
sacramental life 57–8
sacred, the: lure of 29–30
St Anselm 149
salvation 9, 35–6, 205; and afterlife 38–9; need for 143; original sin and 79–80, 125
salvific-redemption theology 18, 119, 146–7
Saul/Paul 55, 56, 172, 238
Schelling, Friedrich von 49, 151
Schweitzer, Albert 51
science: and religious belief 167
scientific knowledge 5
scripture: divine authorship 72, 73, 122, 128n1; orthodox perspective 90, 105n2, 114, 128n1, 141–2; Protestant perspective 71–3, 122–3, 145–6, 153–4, 182–3, 249–51; reading with rigour and respect 149–50
self, the: Christian theology's view 61
sense-reference distinction 262
Shema 106n12
sin: universality of 80
social trinitarianism 15, 155, 174
Socrates 84
sola scriptura 71–3, 122–3, 145–6, 153–4, 182–3, 249–51
soteriology: Orthodox Christianity 101–4, 117
soul/psyche 107n23
sovereignty-aseity conviction 175, 260
Spätphilosophie (Schelling) 49
spirit/pneuma 100
spiritual journey 45, 95, 140
Stewart, Jon 163
substance/ousia 98
Summa theologiae (Aquinas) 154
supernaturalism 56–7, 127, 164, 165
Swinburne, Richard 71, 144, 233
Symbol of Chalcedon 246
symbolic consciousness 27–9, 215, 229

Targum Jonathan to the Prophets 53, 60
Teresa 206–7

280   *Index*

Teresa of Ávila 239
theocentrism 100, 142
theological epistemology 4
theological language 130, 219–20
theology: as autobiographical 25, 190, 221; contemporary theology 218–19; sources for 71–3
theosis/deification 96, 104, 108n36
Thomism 210n6
Tillich, Paul 4, 9, 151
Tradition: Orthodox conception of 90–2
Trinity: Catholic teaching 156–7; consubstantiality 75–6, 97, 102, 123–4, 156–7, 174, 245–7; ecological perspective 32–4, 154–5, 156; *filioque* controversy 32, 106n13, 123, 148, 157; as functioning doctrine 32, 154–5, 220; generation of the Son 156; monarchy of the Father doctrine 106n13, 156; Orthodox doctrine 96–9, 115–16, 140–1, 156–7, 174–5, 259–61; perichoretic communion 11, 174, 175, 210n8, 259, 271n1; and personal omniGod theism 10–11; persons as modes of existence or relations 97–9, 116, 156; procession of the Holy Spirit 156; Protestant perspective 75–7, 157, 183–5, 245–9; 'proved' by scripture 123; 'social' interpretation 15, 155, 174
tritheism 97, 156

triumphalism 191, 217, 226
truth: objective truth 221–5; in religious discourse 90–1, 167–8, 214, 221–6
truth-claims: and certainty 30; contestability of 4–5
Turner, Denys 95

Vanier, Jean 30
Victorines 60
virgin-mother symbol 224
von Bingen, Hildegaard 224

Ware, Kallistos 89, 91–2, 92–3, 100, 106n10, 172
'war on terror' 136
Weber, Otto 56
Weil, Simone 239
Wilde, Oscar 242
Williams, C. J. F. 175
Wittgensteinian method 95, 128n2
women: ecclesial authority/ordination 73, 132, 139, 141–2
wonder 44
Words of Christ (Henry) 179
worldviews: entering and understanding from inside 208–9

Yannaras, Christos 266

Zizioulas, John 97–9, 104, 115–16, 142, 175, 260, 263, 266